SUPER-SQUAD

Other Tactics/Intel. Manuals from Posterity Press:

North Korea's Hidden Assets
Guardian Joe: How Less Force Helps the Warrior
Sinoland: The Subversion of Freedom's Bastion
Afrique: A Warning for America
Strategic Rifleman: Key to More Moral Warfare
Gung Ho: The Corps' Most Progressive Tradition
Global Warrior: Averting WWIII
Expeditionary Eagles: Outmaneuvering the Taliban
Homeland Siege: Tactics for Police and Military
Tequila Junction: 4th-Generation Counterinsurgency
Dragon Days: Time for "Unconventional" Tactics
Terrorist Trail: Backtracking the Foreign Fighter
Militant Tricks: Battlefield Ruses of the Islamic Militant
Tactics of the Crescent Moon: Militant Muslim Combat Methods
The Tiger's Way: A U.S. Private's Best Chance for Survival
Phantom Soldier: The Enemy's Answer to U.S. Firepower
One More Bridge to Cross: Lowering the Cost of War
The Last Hundred Yards: The NCO's Contribution to Warfare

SUPER-SQUAD

THE NOW MISSING COMPONENT

ILLUSTRATED EDITION

H. JOHN POOLE

FOREWORD BY

GEN. ANTHONY C. ZINNI USMC (RET.)

POSTERITY

PRESS®

Published by Posterity Press
P.O. Box 5360, Emerald Isle, NC 28594
(www.posteritypress.org)

Cataloging-in-Publication Data
Poole, H. John, 1943-

Super-Squad

Includes bibliography and index.

1. Infantry drill and tactics.
2. Military art and science.
3. Military history.

I. Title. ISBN: 978-0-9818659-6-6 2020 355'.42
Library of Congress Control Number: 2019905695

Edited by Dr. Mary Beth Poole

First printing, United States of America, January 2020

For all those U.S. military personnel lucky enough to have been part of a good infantry squad.

Cover art © by Col. Donald L. Dickson USMC (Ret.)
an actual veteran of the Guadalcanal Campaign in WWII

From 12-14 September 1942, there was heavy fighting at "Bloody Ridge" between an attacking Japanese brigade of 3000 men and roughly 830 U.S. Marines from 1st Raider Battalion commanded by Col. Merritt "Red Mike" Edson. This battalion (and its various reinforcements) had been asked to block the main avenue of advance into the Henderson Field perimeter. The task would soon turn into a series of "life of death" struggles between tiny adversarial groups. Squad cohesion and Edson's emphasis on light-infantry tactics would largely gain the victory for the close-knit Leatherneck outfit.

Disclaimer: This book repeatedly refers to the junior enlisted infantrymen who fought (and often died) during America's most recent major conflicts. Nothing planned or directed by their superiors can in any way detract from their heroic personal performance on the field of honor.

CONTENTS

ILLUSTRATIONS

Maps:

Figures:

Tables

Foreword

Mention the term "Super Squad" to a veteran Marine and what comes to mind is the long held competition that was conducted each year among the nine best squads in the Corps, each representing the nine infantry regiments. Each regiment held internal competitions to determine its best squad, then the three divisions and the brigade in Hawaii further trained the squads for a competition held at The Basic School (where new Second Lieutenants were schooled and trained) in Quantico, Virginia. A parade at Marine Barracks at 8th & I Street in Washington DC was held to announce the one through nine standings of the squads with the top three receiving gold, silver, and bronze medals. I trained the three squads from the Second Marine Division for two years. We won a gold and two silvers in that time. This came about after a short stint as the Commanding General's aide and the refusal of the general to allow me to command my eighth company.

I had been blessed to that point to command two infantry platoons and a Basic School platoon, three rifle companies (one in Vietnam), a Headquarters and Services company, a guard company, an infantry training company, and a bulk fuel company. I did a tour as an infantry advisor to the Vietnamese Marine Corps. I also spent two years teaching scouting and patrolling and counterinsurgency at the Basic School. Despite trying to get another rifle company, the general felt other captains needed that experience more than I did. He told me to report to the division G-3, Colonel Al Gray, a future Commandant of the Marine Corps, for assignment. When I reported to Colonel Gray, he asked me what I wanted to do. I told him I thought a job in the training section was probably where I could best fit. He said what would you want to do if you could create your own job. I said that I felt that the division needed a school or center that provided training in advanced infantry skills. He told me to take a week and come up with a plan to develop that center.

The result was the Second Marine Division Infantry Training Center. We trained companies, platoons, and squads in advanced infantry skills, special operations (in those days the definition of special operations dealt with operating in extreme conditions such as jungle, mountain, desert, and cold weather environments), and also trained the "Super Squads." As the head of this center and based on my previous experiences, I was able to get a good sense of our small-unit capabilities.

John Poole has written a tremendously valuable set of works that provides insights into the threats we face and how best to counter them. This book, *Super Squad,* hits on what kind of small-unit development we need to succeed on today's battlefield. It also describes how we did it better in the past and how administrative and bureaucratic decisions and processes have hindered our ability to create the kind of super small-unit capabilities he describes. What works against our ability to develop the Super Squad that Poole describes? In the Marine Corps, we bleed off some of very best infantry NCOs for the drill field, recruiting duty, Marine Security Guard requirements, Marine Barracks duty, and other specialized assignments. These are career enhancing more so than infantry assignments. Our promotion system moves Marines up and out too fast to gain unit cohesion to the level required by Poole's concepts. We do not have the manning levels to maintain the appropriate unit size and grade experience in team and squad leader positions. When we are required to take cuts, we strip out our small units and justify it by some cooked up studies that place more importance on technology than on unit structure and cohesion. We have put a great deal of reliance on Special Operations units and capabilities in recent years. These units have developed into elite and formidable organizations that have proven to be highly effective. They are unmatched in winning strategic firefights with high value importance. However, we have not invested anywhere near the same commitment in our small-unit infantry capabilities that will be required to win battles. The era of cannon fodder, semi-trained small units on a large battlefield is long past. We should have learned our lesson on our recent reliance on "Shock and Awe" and how it failed to supplant competent small units in Afghanistan and Iraq. Those of us who fought against North Vietnamese Army (NVA) and main line Viet Cong units have burned into our souls the importance of small-unit competence and cohesion over technological superiority.

We need to heed the lessons John Poole has drawn from history and experience. His unmatched knowledge of, and insights into, our war fighting requirements provide a road map for developing the kinds of small-unit capabilities for the future battlefields we will [be] thrown upon.

GEN. ANTHONY C. ZINNI USMC (RET.)
FORMER HEAD OF CENTCOM

PREFACE

This is not just another fun history of squad tactics to either read or not read, as the military buyer sees fit. It is the detailed solution to a chronic problem within the U.S. Armed Forces that has so far cost this country thousands of lives and all the extended ground conflicts since World War II (WWII). Unlike the other major infantry organizations in the world, those in America have not been allowed to adopt the evolutionary changes to small-unit tactics. That's because projecting maximum money-making firepower requires four things for safety: (1) mostly linear formations; (2) few forward deployed small units; (3) every squad member doing precisely as told; and (4) no frontline initiative.

The term "super-squad" is most often associated with a yearly competition between all U.S. Marine Corps (USMC) rifle squads. Each unit's tactical proficiency is mostly determined through its ability to mimic the age-old maneuvers in the manuals. Yet, the Staff Noncommissioned Officer (SNCO) in charge of the final Super-Squad Competition on Okinawa in 1992 was still able to tell which group had the best internal "chemistry."[1] Such a bond is not easy to describe to those who haven't personally experienced it. Somewhere between eternal optimism and group dedication, its most common indicator is a happy banter between all unit members.

In 1992, the 13-man contingent from 3rd Marine Regiment in Hawaii considered their parent unit leaders to be "good," competition judges "good," and every other contestant "good." Anyone overhearing such talk couldn't help but consider its source highly competent at their job. One former Super-Squad member describes the relationship as "family."[2]

Yet, squad chemistry seems now a thing of the past. After separate working parties, administrative audits, flu inoculations, human-relations classes, and any number of other "headquarters requirements," modern-day junior infantrymen no longer spend

Figure P.1: As Hard as It Gets on Iwo
(Source: "Closing In: Marines in the Seizure of Iwo Jima," by J.H. Alexander, Marines in WWII Commemorative Series, HQMC, 1994, drawing by Charles H. Waterhouse, p. 22.)

enough time together to develop this close a connection.[3] The loss of something this vital to mission accomplishment might have quite an effect on the next big war.

In fact, this extra "umph" that some Marine squads used to develop may be largely responsible for the Corps' success against a tactically superior foe late in WWII. Iwo Jima, in particular, was so well defended that no number of Leathernecks should have been able to occupy the place. (See Figure P.1.) After the five-week-long battle, Admiral Chester Nimitz may have been referring to this intangible squad quality when he declared: "Uncommon valor was a common virtue."[4]

A Marine squad of that era was well portrayed in the 1950 movie—"Sands of Iwo Jima." Near the beginning, Sgt. Stryker tells new squad members they must learn to "move like one man and think and like one man."[5] Instead of always doing the same thing, he meant they must regularly compensate for each other's inadequacies. In that way, the whole can become more powerful than a sum of its parts. Another former super-squad member explains this part of unit chemistry as knowing what everyone else is thinking and likely to do.[6] At this point, much of each member's motivation would come from "not wanting to let the others down."[7] This must be part of the "bond between brothers" that has come—over the years—to characterize the Corps itself. Its formal name is cohesion.

Exactly why a dozen or so enlisted personnel have been able to capture such a prestigious place in Marine Corps history has long baffled many commissioned infantrymen. Most have never been the member of a Fleet infantry squad, so its battlefield potential largely escapes them. So does the positive effect a squad's semi-autonomous status might have on the war's overall outcome.

> [A] small unit, a squad or even a fireteam, that is properly trained in modern, post-machinegun techniques can be just as effective as a much larger unit, while offering the enemy fewer targets. The German Army, which excelled in drawing lessons from its combat experiences, found as early as World War I [WWI] that the only difference between a squad attacking a machinegun [MG] position and a company doing so was in the number of casualties suffered. Not surprisingly, by 1918 the *Stosstrupp,* a squad-sized unit, was the basic German tactical building block. In contrast, in most Marine infantry units today, the squad is regarded as merely a subset of the platoon, seldom trained for independent action. The result, in combat, is likely to be a lot of dead Marines, Marines whose deaths could have been avoided if tasks were assigned to smaller units.[8]
>
> — W.S. Lind *(One More Bridge to Cross* Foreword)
> author of *Maneuver Warfare Handbook*

In a Christian society where human life is carefully protected in the military (though not everywhere else), infantrymen tend to be too little trained, too little trusted, and too little utilized. That's what this book hopes to alter. Everyone hates the loss of life in war, but when the war is only half-heartedly waged, every casualty from its onset may be in vain. The reason the Pentagon hasn't enjoyed a decisive victory in any extended ground conflict since WWII is too much emphasis on equipment, and not enough on the human element. Mao went so far as to say, "It is people, not things, that are decisive in war."[9] He was not alone in this assessment.

Wars may be fought with weapons, but they are won by men.
It is the spirit of men . . . that gains the victory.[10]
— Gen. George S. Patton, Jr.

Most U.S. military leaders now consider such a claim too dated to still be valid. They believe every officially published procedure to be the constantly refined product of the latest information. Should any further research be necessary, they expect an esoteric word game involving additional variables. But, there are no new variables. Even in this age of runaway technology, ground conflicts are still fought about the same way as they always have. This is because America's traditional foes have made a virtual art form out of countering technology. To now make U.S. warfighting unnecessarily complicated may be just another way to ignore its chronic inadequacy.

Not until government issues (GIs) can take down the next enemy bunker with more than just a stand-off rocket, should their leaders waste any more time on philosophy. Ground conflicts are won with basic infantry skills, and any number of well-respected U.S. military leaders have said so over the years. In reality, all the little sub-categories of each "basic" are more precisely responsible. But in the mind of a rapidly promoted American infantry officer, such categories don't exist. This is because Western culture more widely appreciates the opinion of senior leaders (the big picture) than frontline riflemen (the little picture).

What the "big-picture" Pentagon planners have been slow to realize is that "bottom-up" Eastern societies routinely fight at a smaller scale than their Western counterparts. Their battlefield momentum is established through a succession of tiny engagements instead of one overwhelming "push." Meeting such a piecemeal challenge takes American infantry squads with enough tactical proficiency to safely operate alone. But, because being deployed out in front of their parent unit's offensive or defensive formation would mask the formation's firepower, U.S. squads only rarely develop this much ability.

Such skill takes at least some "bottom-up" training (that which the troops themselves design). The U.S. military has never allowed that much decentralization of control over its troops' preparation and utilization. To complicate matters, training this "unconventionally" requires no additional funding. Any time money or control are to be sacrificed in a top-down capitalistic society, there will be considerable resistance. Yet, that's the only way to consistently win at war in the Eastern World.

Once those young American "grunts" have become properly versed in the evolutionary advances to offensive and defensive small-unit maneuver, they must be trusted, listened to, and then allowed some initiative. For a highly stratified military bureaucracy, this makes the more "promotion-oriented" leaders nervous. They don't like being blamed for mistakes of subordinates, though such mistakes in peacetime are much less likely to be repeated in active combat.

More bad news is never popular. There are pro-life issues more important than America's under-use of tactical surprise. But what has resulted within the U.S. infantry—with regard to battlefield capabilities—is more serious than any voter, officer candidate, or enlisted conscript would find acceptable.

Accurately to summarize this situation will require a series of rather disturbing (but fully supportable) statements. The arms manufacturers and control proponents have now made America's ground combat battalions so inept at small-unit maneuver that they couldn't follow an advanced-warfighting strategy if they wanted to. Such a battalion would be unable to conduct the 3rd Generation of Warfare (3GW) [bypassing a foe's security screen to get at his command and logistics apparatus]. Instead, it would be stuck with the less effective (but highly lucrative) 2nd Generation of Warfare (2GW) [killing as many enemy soldiers as possible.]

But, such an assessment will take many chapters to sufficiently prove to longtime infantrymen and commandos, much less the average citizen. And such a morally deficient "way of doing things" can only be corrected by allowing as much semi-autonomous-squad activity within the U.S. military as in the big Eastern armies. This will take something Washington has never relished—copying former foes by decentralized control over at least some military operations and training.

For the sake of precision, this book will only cover squad structure and armament modifications up to the 1980's. If some change hadn't been warranted through the extensive experience of WWI, WWII, Korea, and Vietnam, then it won't be necessary now. By 1973, all advanced forms of combat had been practiced, to include 4th Generation Warfare (4GW) [concurrent effort in martial, psychological/religious, economic, and political arenas.] However, the progress of fully 3GW-capable armies (those from the East) will be most useful.

Many new surveillance and targeting devices have since been developed, but with little effect on infantry tactics. The Pentagon's huge edge in technology did no good in Vietnam, and the subsequent flood of money-making gadgets has failed to contain the tiny loosely controlled elements of the current opposition. In effect, the mechanics (basics) of all levels of ground combat have remained the same since the machinegun appeared in 1914. This is largely the reason Asian Communists have continued to base their wartime strategies on the premise that all modern-day devices can be countered by frontline initiative.

> [I]n . . . regular warfare, . . . [armed struggle] is fully capable of . . . getting the better of a modern . . . U.S. Army. . . . This is a development of the . . . military art . . . which is to rely chiefly on [the] man, . . . to defeat an enemy with up-to-date weapons and equipment.[11]
>
> — Gen. Vo Nguyen Giap
> *The Military Art of People's War*

America's recent war record should adequately reflect how effective U.S. technology has been. The latest drone with thermal imaging still cannot spot a properly clothed enemy soldier in heavily vegetated terrain.

Before tackling this detailed a study, the reader may want to learn of its eventual contribution to national defense from the Epilogue. Some of its conclusions will be as unexpected as they are helpful to future combat. All ranks should benefit. In a military culture that approaches every problem from the top down, there may be bottom-echelon reasons why wars are hard to win. Fully to explore this possibility, one must try to think at a smaller scale than is customary for a person of their pay grade. For peak interest, imagine being a boot infantry private about to continually risk being killed (or the worried parent).

LT.COL. H. JOHN POOLE USMC (RET.)
FORMER FLEET MARINE FORCE GY.SGT. &
ILLINOIS BUREAU OF INVESTIGATION AGENT

Acknowledgments

A renown Catholic saint—Edith Stein—once said something to the effect that anyone who searches for truth will be placing themselves into God's presence, whether they want to be there or not. All Abrahamic faiths claim that fully comprehensive wisdom is something God reserves strictly for himself. That's why the professional U.S. soldier must never stop looking for the most moral way of performing the mission.

Part One

History of the Infantry Squad

"To be a successful soldier, you must know history."
— Gen. George S. Patton, Jr.

(Source: Attributed to Gen. George S. Patton.)

1 Recent Abandonment of Functional Heritage

- How has U.S. infantry squad make-up recently changed?
- What prompted such a repudiation of previous success?

A USMC squad leader has only three subordinates to direct.

(Source: "Army/Marine Clipart," U.S. Air University (www.au.af.mil/au/awc/awcgate/cliparmy.htm), image designator "1-07a.tif.")

Fateful Announcement of 2018

Ever since 1944, the U.S. Marine rifle squad has consisted of 13 men—three "four-man" fireteams and a squad leader. Most frontline veterans of that Pacific War claim it was low-ranking riflemen—and not the generals—who fought their way back to Tokyo.

But, since the mid-1980's, this victorious grouping of actual combatants has been under attack—with a reduction in cost as the normal reason. Even Gen. Alfred M. Gray, the most insightful Marine commandant of the modern age, may have at one point tried to emulate the U.S. Army's two-fire-team format to save money.[1] And just recently, that "triple combo" of squad subordinates, to which hundreds of thousands of young Marines have owed their success in combat for over 75 years, has once again been subjected to change. Someone came up with the bright idea of lowering the number of people in its main component—the fireteam.

Only where blood and sand mix, do such decisions make much difference. But, should the Corps go off to another big war, its rank and file could greatly suffer from this seemingly minor change to the infantry structure. Where those modern-day gladiators don't do well, neither will their parent-unit, their overall organization, or their home country. Those are the facts of life where the rubber meets the road.

The Unfortunate Details of This Mistake in Judgement

After 25 years of incrementally centralizing control over all infantry training and operations, Headquarters Marine Corps (HQMC) may have decided in 2018 to "disempower" its lowest infantry echelons. The new squad's composition would be ostensibly based on the "technological necessities" of modern combat. But in the process of adding two new personnel, staff planners had made an egregious error. To compensate for the increase in manpower, they had advised the commandant to end the life-saving tradition of the two-man buddy team. (See Figure 1.1.) All the while, he had—through command protocols—been well insulated from the collective wisdom of his junior enlisted, and obligated to obey his Commander in Chief's Pentagon representatives.

> Gen. Neller concluded that each rifle squad needed two additional billets—an assistant squad leader and a squad systems operator focused on technology. . . .
>
> . . . Not only did he add those new billets, he decided to reduce the squad's size to twelve by eliminating one Marine for each of its four fire teams.[2]
>
> — *Wall Street Journal,* 1 July 2018

Even if this fireteam were being temporarily cadred as a peacetime draw-down, how the average rifle squad trains and

Figure 1.1: Two-Man Buddy Team Has Been Backbone of Squad
(Source: "Ten Minute Break," by Sameul B. Alexander, U.S. Army Center of Military History, posters, illustration designator "w_1_9_68.jpg.")

operates would still change.[3] Squad-sized patrols would no longer have enough "buddy teams" to provide all-around security (it takes four).

Of course, some new weaponry would appear with the new arrangement. Most members would carry a rifle that may be fired on full automatic—the M27. Within each fireteam, one person would instead have a stand-alone M320 grenade launcher. And, somewhere in the squad would be a designated marksman with the accurized version of M27—the M38.[4] But, no increase in firepower is going to make up for the tactical restriction of fewer overall elements. Instead of six sub-units with which to fire or maneuver, the squad leader will now have only three.

The Misinterpreted Precedent

The Marine component of SOCOM (Special Operations Command) is now comprised of "Raider" battalions, in honor of the legendary Marine Raiders of WWII. The "Gyrene" Raiders' forefather—Lt.Col. Evans Fordyce Carlson—became the first American military commander to adopt a three-fire-team squad.

Each of those teams contained three men—in line with the organizational structure of Mao's 8th Route Army. In total, Carlson's infantry squads then contained 10 men—with the tenth being the squad leader himself. On his "end run" around the Japanese positions on Guadalcanal, here's how those men were equipped:

> Each Marine rifle squad was divided into [three] fireteams of three men [each], one with an M1 rifle, one with a Thompson submachine gun, and the third carrying a . . . (BAR). Added to this mix was a liberal dose of shotguns and .45-caliber pistols.[5]
>
> — "Carlson's Long Patrol," *Warfare Hist. Network*

This three-fireteam format was quite a precedent in its day. In the book *Edson's Raiders,* Col. Joseph Alexander confirms that all other Leatherneck squads of the period were still unitary in nature—each consisting of eight or nine men with no intermediate control.[6] In other words, the squad leader personally directed all squad members.[7] This nine-man structure would have made possible two equally sized increments.

But, Carlson's 2nd Battalion was not the only initial Raider outfit. The commander of 1st Raider Battalion—"Red Mike" Edson—had focused more on light-infantry than guerrilla tactics and initially retained the unitary eight-or-nine-man format. Yet, his squad contained two Browning Automatic Rifle (BAR) men instead of one, and a sniper. And, for whatever reason, Edson was soon to change his mind on how best to utilize that many people—likely dividing them in half.

But things were about to change. Having studied Chinese in Peking in 1937 and then watching Carlson's training,[8] Edson's Executive Officer—Maj. Samuel B. Griffith II—recognized the tactical potential of separate squad elements. (On Griffith's advice, Edson would later champion the four-man fireteam, each with a pair of buddy teams.[9])

Griffith did not share Edson's initial dislike for Carlson's unorthodox Asian methods. He had tried "to learn more of his (the latter officer's) unique organizational and training ideas."[10] Among them may have been how tiny Raider elements could mount a successful campaign with little, or no, guidance from above. As had Carlson, Edson probably allowed those fireteams to go off on their own from time to time. (See Figure 1.2.)

Upon assuming command of 1st Raider Battalion, Griffith switched over to Carlson's three-team squad, with three-men per team. At first, he called those teams "fire groups" (something briefly

Figure 1.2: Raider Fireteams Were Often Sent Out Alone

(Source: "Patrol in the Jungle," by Roger Blum U.S. Army Center of Military History, artphoto archives, illustration designator "jungle.jpg,") tried during the Banana Wars [11]). But, these teams had different weaponry billets than in 2nd Battalion. Instead of a Thompson submachinegunner in each fireteam, Griffith had substituted an assistant BAR man with his own rifle.

Then, in 1944, with Edson's blessing, the Corps finally adopted "four-man" fireteam with its own BAR.[12] But, gone would be the days of tiny elements "working together" without much supervision. The whole idea of semi-autonomous small units would fly too severely in the face of headquarters control.

The Bairoko Incident

At 0100 hours on 18 July 1943, all 700 men of 4th Raider Battalion [Maoist in orientation like Carlson's 2nd] debarked their destroyer-transports at Enogai Harbor on the western end of New

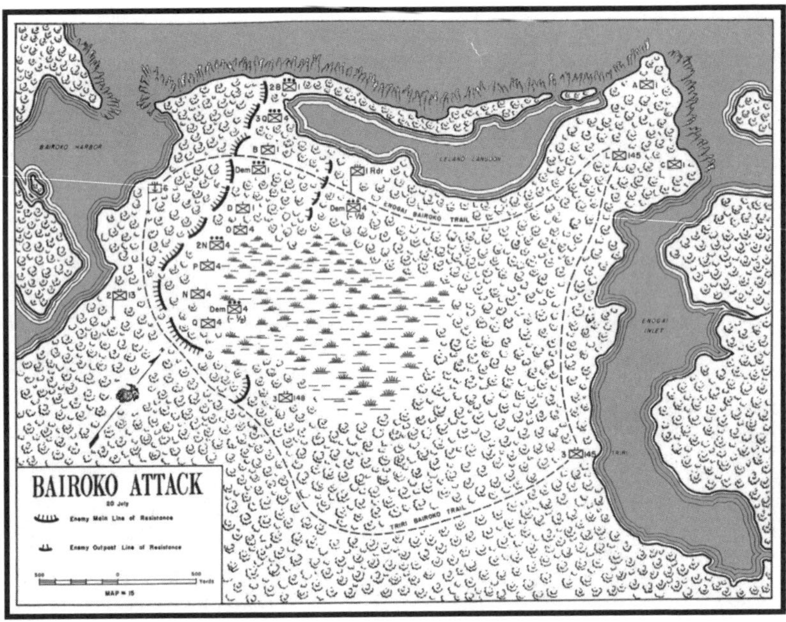

Map 1.1: Bunker Belts Facing 4th Raider Battalion at Bairoko
(Source: "Marines in the Central Solomons," by Maj. John N. Rentz, USMC Historical Monograph, HQMC, 1952, map 13,)

Georgia. Along with the rest of 1st Raider Regiment, they were to capture Bairoko Harbor on the far side of Dragons Peninsula the next day. Unfortunately, Baikoro's Nipponese garrison had been preparing for a land invasion.

After a difficult approach march and skipped air attack, the Raiders finally made contact with the Bairoko defenders about 1000 hours on the morning of 19 July.[13] (See Map 1.1.) For a whole day they fought, with 4th Raider Battalion on the left and 1st Raider Battalion on the right. In their path was a sophisticated matrix of defensive strongpoints.[14]

Some Raider units tried to skirt around the left end of the Japanese defenses, while others attacked at the right end. That's a "U.S.-doctrine-violating" double-envelopment, but standard operating procedure for Mao's Army. (See Figure 1.3.) However, the successive bunker belts could not be outflanked.

Against each, the Raiders would have to launch separate fireteam attacks against all forward emplacements at the same time (to limit the amount of cover fire they could provide each other). Then, within each separate bunker assault, half of each team (two buddies) probably went left through the microterrain while the other half (the other buddy pair) went right. In that way, they could play off each other's movements—each advancing after objective occupants had been distracted.

This series of maneuvers (and its lack of headquarters' control) should not be lost to history, because the 4th Battalion's direct descendent would use this same kind of "buddy team cooperation" to seize the toughest part of Okinawa's Shuri Line a year later. That makes it a viable alternative to America's standard steamroller approach to enemy strongholds.

With no airstrikes, artillery, heavy mortars, flame throwers, or much pre-practiced technique at Bairoko, the (self-coordinating) Raider fireteams had done something very exceptional. They had gotten three-fourths of the way through a defensive array that is to this day the state of the nonelectronic art. In a world where there's not always enough preparatory fire available, such a method still has tremendous utility.

A Repeat Success at Half Moon on Okinawa's Shuri Line

Though Carlson's 2nd Raider Battalion had been unceremoni-

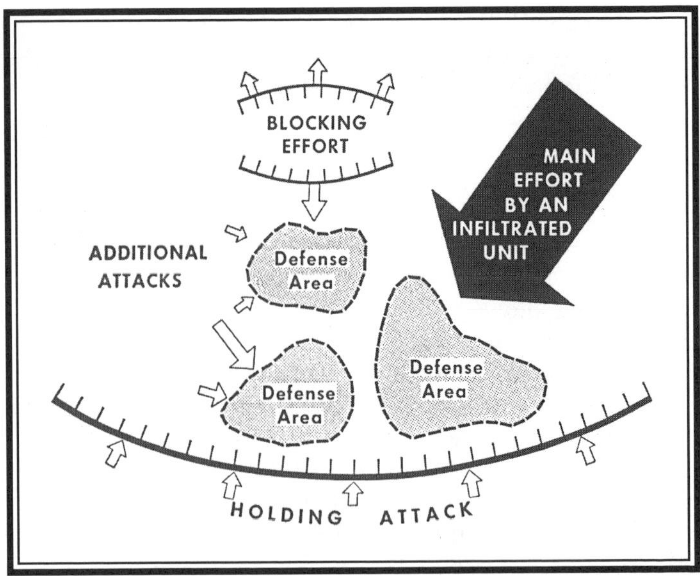

Figure 1.3: The "One-Point, Two-Sides" Chinese Attack
(Source: "Handbook on the Chinese Communist Army," DA Pamphlet 30-51 [1960], p. 24.)

ously disbanded in early 1943, the 4th Battalion (also Maoist in format) under Lt.Col. James "Jimmy" Roosevelt II was left intact to become 2nd Battalion, 4th Marines (2/4). That battalion was about to break the deadlock at the north end of Okinawa's virtually impregnable Shuri Line. (See Map 1.2.)

The top end of the Shuri Line was probably the most difficult defensive formation the U.S. Marines had so far faced in WWII. During the 10-day period leading up to the capture of Sugar Loaf Hill, the 6th Marine Division had lost 2,662 killed or wounded and 1,289 combat fatigue cases among young men who could have withstood almost anything.[15]

There are no detailed descriptions of that renewed "piecemeal" battle for the forward face of Half Moon (Crescent Hill)—within the untaken portion of the Sugar Loaf Complex—around 18 May 1945. (Look again more closely at Map 1.2.) But, any infantry veteran of an East Asian war can well imagine it. The machinegun bunkers along those steep slopes had been mutually supporting. Each was being protected by the crisscrossing fire of those next to but just

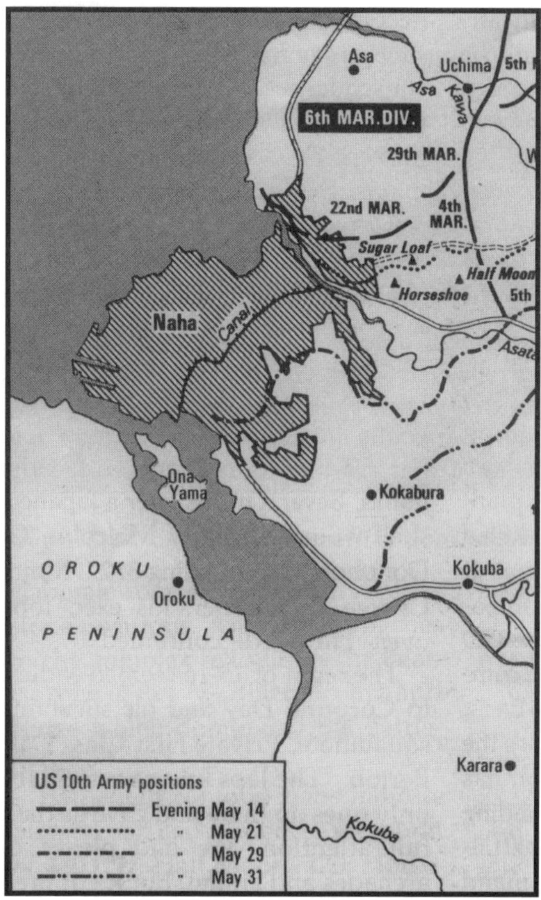

Map 1.2: Just Before 2/4's Attack on Half Moon Hill in May 1945
(Source: "The Final Campaign: Marines in the Victory on Okinawa," by Col. Joseph H. Alexander, Marines in WWII Commemorative Series, HQMC, 1996, p. 38.)

beyond it. Thus, 2/4 (as a former Maoist Raider battalion) would have deployed a ragged line of fireteams, each trying—through the microterrain—to double-envelop the bunker in its lane.

While the most forward enemy positions would have had the priority for attack, they could not have been seized without some pressure on those just behind them on either side. So, some buddy teams must have provided impromptu assistance—in the form of enemy machinegun suppression—to other-squad counterparts in adjacent lanes.[16]

No frontline commander could have controlled such a complicated interaction, nor would have preliminary practice done much good. This was a fight to the death that would necessarily depend on collective effort, individual initiative, and the surprise that only "microterrain crawling" can provide. It would have to develop on its own. Only important was the continuing cooperation between adjacent buddy teams of any squad. While a few pre-established double-envelopment procedures may have helped, the overall maneuver required no structure other than roughly parallel lanes and approximate alignment. (See Figures 1.4 through 1.6.) Staying roughly on line did not have to be coordinated from above, because young Marines of that era knew not to get too far ahead of each other.

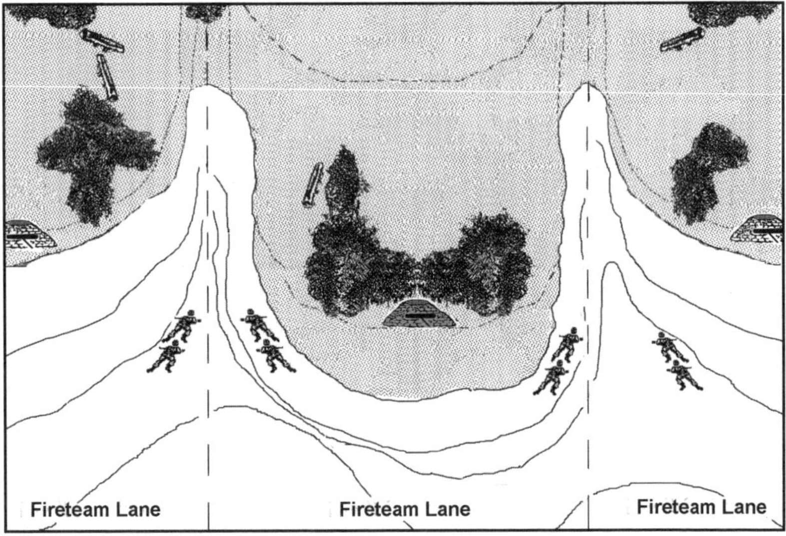

Figure 1.4: Fireteams Subdivide to Double-Envelop Their Bunkers

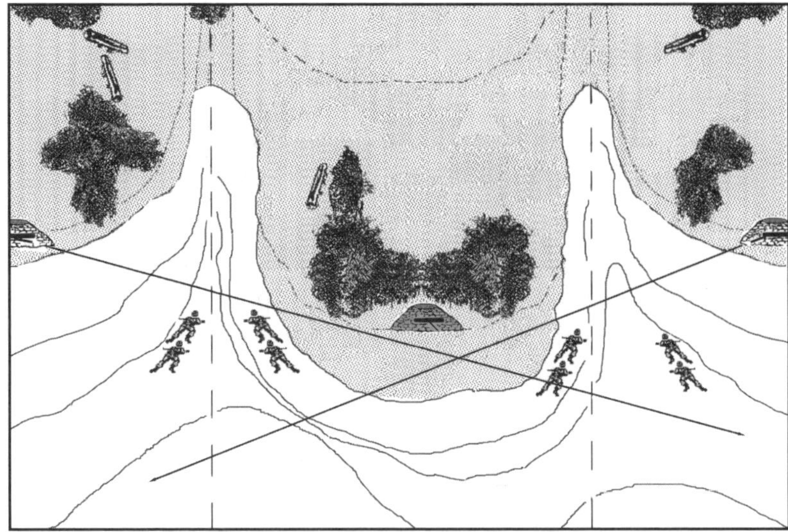

Figure 1.5: Rearward Bunkers Fire Across Front of U.S. Objective

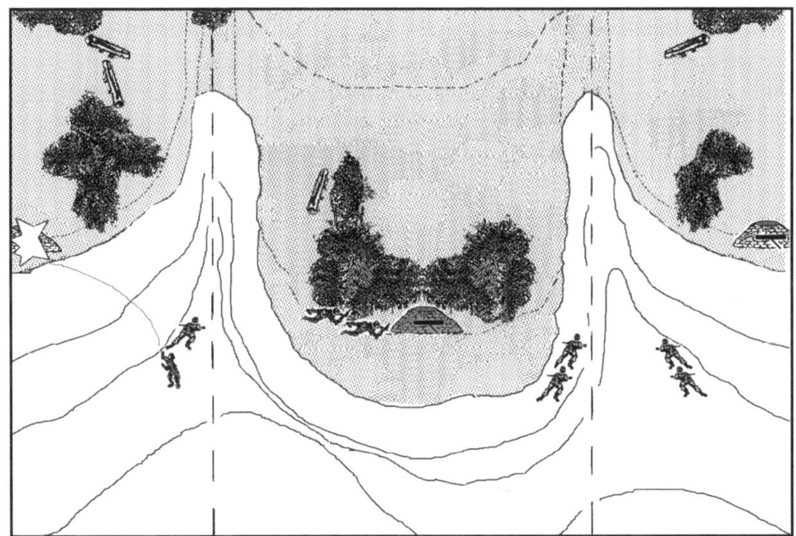

Figure 1.6: Adjacent-Lane Team Suppresses Crisscrossing Fire

Figure 1.7: All Had Depended on Two-Man "Buddy Teams"
(Source: "Two Soldiers on Night Patrol," by Harold von Schmidt, U.S. Army Ctr. of Mil. Hist., posters, from url: https://history.army.mil/art/Posters/WWII/WW2.htm.)

Not Enough of This Hard-Won Insight Has Survived

The closest modern parallel to this Bairoko effort is "fire and movement with grenades added"—a decidedly "hasty" type of attack. Yet, its forerunner had involved "recon pull," "infiltration," and some "swarming." Because a few pre-practiced moves had also been likely, the overall process could be considered a quick "deliberate attack" (one involving some reconnaissance and rehearsal.) Yet, no procedural formula (or its preliminary practice) could have done justice to that many situational variables. Its various parts had to concurrently emerge through mutual effort, individual initiative, and microterrain appreciation. This is why this nontraditional method was able—with "common sense and cooperation"—to improve upon "headquarters planning and supervision."

Such a concept may now deserve more recognition in the ongoing evolution of infantry tactics than it has so far received in the Western World. 2/4 had once again proven that the Bairoko kind of assault required no supporting arms whatsoever to defeat a state-of-the-art defense. It would not have been possible without two-man buddy teams. (See Figure 1.7.)

The Current Situation Within All U.S. Infantry Outfits

For whatever reason, the American Army has always preferred the denominator of two. Its infantry platoon continues to be split in half, with each section comprised of two nine-man squads. Because each squad then sports two equally sized fireteams, the many advantages of Carlson's three-team arrangement have been largely lost.

Only those who have extensively experimented with squad tactics realize how much more powerful the "triple combo" can be. Instead of the largely predictable "bounding overwatch" of a two-element attack, the squad leader has the use of an extra element. It can distract defenders, or just "beef-up" the base-of-fire (BOF) or maneuver elements. While the size of the USMC squad has increased, its leader still has only three direct subordinates to manage.

The double-envelopment (via perimeter trench) of a fortified position may violate U.S. doctrine, but a two-team maneuver element allows for a series of lifesaving feints while sharing the same route. One team can move forward while the other draws the defenders' fire; and then they can occasionally switch roles. In this way, all enemy eyes need not be riveted on the advancing group of fully mortal GIs.

Of course, the three fireteam setup is not only useful on offense. While the parent unit is in a defensive posture, the third team can man two more perimeter positions or frontal outposts. That, in turn, creates better coverage of any defense zone.

During a squad-sized patrol, the three-team format allows one full team to stay with the squad leader as a ready reaction force while the other two perform the security function. In fact, only with a third four-man fireteam will enough buddy teams be available for all-around protection of that patrol. Any one-man point, flank, or rear security element would have too little survivability in combat.

With three fireteams, the Marine squad leader has more tactical options than his Army counterpart. But, the extent to which he can exercise those options will depend on his number of buddy teams. Four men per fireteam allows for not only more buddy teams, but also for every rifleman to have someone to watch his back.

Thus, the USMC's traditional advantage in flexibility will be largely lost through its recent switch to three-man teams.

The Reds' Ongoing Use of a Three-Man Team

The three-element pattern still exists within every echelon of all Asian Communist armies.[17] Not only do their squads have three fireteams, but each team contains three men. (See Figure 1.8.) The Asians' reason for the three-man fireteam appears to be based more on expected attrition than mission flexibility. But that tiny trio can only be assigned one mission at a time.

The lower size of the Asian squad may have been thought to facilitate its "auto-pilot" capabilities—all teams working together instead of being always managed. Because of the "bottom-up" culture (and problem-solving heritage) of all Oriental societies, up to nine men might not have needed much direction from their leader during a chance contact. This would have given him more time to request the help of supporting arms, coordinate with other squads, or confer with headquarters.

As late as 1984, all Chinese Communist People's Liberation Army (PLA) infantry platoons consisted of three squads with 12 men each. As those squads had "deputy squad leaders," one can assume three fireteams of three men apiece (a veteran and two conscripts).[18] The veteran would have been considered a fighter, and not a leader. (See Table 1.1.) According to the Defense Information Agency's (DIA's) Table of Equipment, the eleventh man in each squad carried a light machinegun (LMG).[19] That makes a grand total of 12, counting the squad leader.

This automatic weapon within the Chinese squad should come as no surprise, because the Japanese, Soviets, and Germans had all married their infantry squads to a fully capable machinegun by the onset of WWII.[20] On defense, each squad could then operate its own strongpoint (with all riflemen protecting the LMG). On offense, it could establish a much-closer (and thus more accurate) BOF during any assault.

Less Tactical Proficiency Not the Only Problem

The new Marine rifle squad won't be able to conduct all-around security while on patrol (with only three buddy teams instead of the required four). Nor will it have a ready reaction force to deal with contingency situations. But those may not be the only side-effects of the new unit structure.

Figure 1.8: The 1955-Vintage Chinese Soldier
(Source: GlobalSecurity.org, s.v. "PLA Uniforms and Insignia," image designator "uniform-1955.jpg.")

Years in Service	Monthly PositionPay	Basic	(US $ Equivalent)
1	Conscript	7 yuan	($3.42)
2	Fighter	8 yuan	($3.51)
3	Deputy Squad Leader	9 yuan	($4.40)
4	Squad Leader	11 yuan	($5.38)
4 +	Deputy Platoon Leader	Increased by 5 yuan ($2.45) each year after 4 years in service	

Table 1.1: Enlisted Echelons Within the PLA Platoon
(Source: "Handbook on the Chinese PLA," DDB-2680-32-84, DIA, November 1984, p. 16.)

Since the disturbing casualty totals of WWII, there has been an on-and-off, yet still persistent, effort by the Department of Defense (DoD) to minimize the number of U.S. infantry personnel stationed in an active war zone. Many at the Pentagon apparently think that enough firepower will eventually eliminate the need for any boots on the ground whatsoever. But military historians scoff at such a suggestion. No extended ground conflict has ever been won without physically occupying the site. Still, this illogical trend in U.S. defense planning continues, at the expense of more than one lost war.

Almost certainly, the U.S. Army has experienced similar problems with this same issue, but those details must be left to an Army historian. This study will only address what the USMC has learned.

Previous Setbacks

Before this latest change to squad make-up, there were two events that severely damaged the Corps' infantry capabilities: (1) the discontinuance of "squad (or platoon) bays" in the late 1980's; and (2) the disempowerment of each rifle company's top enlisted leaders around 1973.[21]

When all platoon personnel lived side-by-side in the same huge room with their platoon sergeant in an adjoining cubicle, the SNCO (staff noncommissioned officer) Corps had little trouble staying apprised of all troop needs, opinions, and insights. Then, the two-man-room did away with all that upward communication, as well as much of the cohesion upon which every good infantry outfit depends.

Prior to 1973, each company's First Sergeant had handled any disciplinary problems. Then, when administrative control was shifted to battalion and all nonjudicial punishment suspended, unit morale was not the only thing to suffer.

Every Leatherneck's "minor-error history" had previously been expunged from his administrative file every time he moved on to a new command. Of late, only those with near perfect records have been able to reenlist. Unfortunately, most have also been careful not to attempt (or say) anything the least bit controversial. While a personal mistake generally arises out of a temporary lapse in judgment, it also indicates above-average initiative. Troop initiative can be quite valuable on an active battlefield. And, any mistake corrected at the subunit level in peacetime will not generally be repeated in wartime.

Before 1973, the Company Gunny Sergeant also took care of all enlisted training, to include that which was tactical in nature.[22] Then, he became nothing more than a "bean counter"—one who keeps track of all unit resupply. Regardless of his personal level of combat experience (often through many years of overseas deployment), he was no longer allowed near any maneuver-oriented instruction. Instead, recent college graduates would be given control over all enlisted training—as long as they were careful to comply with all HQMC directives.

The Importance of Squad Tactics to Parent Unit Success

Imperial Germany's development of semi-autonomous infantry squads in 1917 nearly allowed it to win WWI. Those tiny Stormtrooper contingents had little trouble penetrating any number of Doughboy lines in succession, but eventually ran out of ammunition.[23] Because each carried its own LMG,[24] their defensive strongpoints also did a good job of mowing down Allied attackers. Yet, with so many newly arrived Americans, their resupply system may not have been overly taxed.

Subsequent history is replete with similar reports of lone squad prowess. In WWII, independently operating Russian squads kept the German juggernaut from reaching the Volga River in Stalingrad.[25] Then in 1994, tiny loosely controlled Chechen groups needed only a "swarming" maneuver to completely destroy the first Russian mechanized column to enter Grozny.[26]

Before the onset of bulky headsets and electronically aimed rifles, no more than a dozen or so people could sneak up on an alert defender. That's what it took for a large-unit commander to generate full surprise over his opposition. With very little ordnance, he could attack into or defend against a much larger opponent without any advance notice. As a result, traditional squad dynamics—how squad members are able to getting things done together—has a place in modern combat.

While those internal dynamics remain useful, they must still be applied to the ongoing evolution of small-unit tactics. That evolution may not be readily apparent in all countries. One would expect to see a gradual improvement in the structure, armament, and utility of the rifle squad over the years in every major army. But where bureaucratic pressures have been at work, some of those armies may not have experienced much change to the way their infantry fights since early in WWI.

The Apparent Problem in America

Surprise and firepower just happen to be interchangeable in combat.[27] In other words, the first can accomplish as much as the second. But, in a society that tries to win overseas conflicts and make money at the same time, the maximum usage of high-tech ordnance takes precedence over small-unit maneuver. Big task forces make an occasional feint, but companies and below are only asked to gain fire superiority over whoever gets in their way. In the process, they incur enemy bullets they might have dodged, and then unnecessary losses.

America's underfunded Eastern adversaries haven't made this mistake. Their small units have been specifically designed to generate surprise. This can be done in any number of ways. The most obvious being one type of explosion that mimics another. Such deceptions would be the stock in trade of any modern-day super-squad from anywhere in the world.

2 The Evolutionary Changes to Squad Combat in WWI

- In which way was an infantry assault improved in WWI?
- How could that much surprise be generated noisily?

U.S. rifle squads were allowed no machinegun in WWI.

(Source: "Rock of the Marne," DA Poster 21-42, Wikimedia Commons, from *url: https://commons.wikimedia.org/wiki/File:The_Rock_of_the_Marne._DA_Poster_21-42.jpg.*)

Prelude to the First World War

Prior to the "War to End All Wars," U.S. troops occasionally attacked in total silence—with no shooting before, or during, their final assault. Such was the case at Yorktown in the Revolutionary War,[1] San Jacinto in the Texan War for Independence,[2] and Rappahannock Station during the Civil War.[3] Closing with the enemy this quietly had proven highly effective because all defenders were caught by complete surprise. But, as preparatory bombardment became more available, non-supported (silent) objective seizures became rare.

Then Came WWI

The Gatling Gun had been present since the later part of the American Civil War. Yet, not until the battlefield debut of its successor—the machinegun—in Europe, did any infantry outfit change how it maneuvered. The "Great War" would generate every lesson there was to learn about contemporary combat, but not all countries would be able to assimilate those lessons. American units would mostly bring home what they could ascertain from watching the French Army.

The Battle of Verdun in 1914 was the generally accepted wake-up call for how all-out war had changed infantry tactics. However, the ultimate instigator did not become readily apparent until the Second Battle of Champaign (at the Argonne) in 1915. There, 27 French divisions attacked six that were German for 40 days. Following a massive French bombardment, 144,000 French troops became casualties as opposed to 85,000 Germans—with very little territory being gained by the Allies. Hun "dugouts" and their resident machineguns had made the difference.[4] And then, after the four-month-long Battle of the Somme in 1916, the handwriting was definitely "on the wall." Here, over a million troops from both sides had become casualties—mostly from trying to assault each other's defensive positions.

> From the 1st of July until the 18th of November in 1916, a massive joint operation between British and French forces . . . occurred in the Somme area in northern France. . . . The British spearheaded the offensive and faced a German defense developed for many months. . . . Despite a seven day bombardment before the 1st July attack, the British did not achieve [the] success the military leadership of General Haig [had] anticipated, having sent 100,000 men to capture the German trenches. . . . [A]nd for 141 days the British advance captured only three square mile[s] of territory.
>
> Collectively, the opposing sides saw over a million casualties [mostly by whoever openly rushed enemy machineguns] . . . . But what stuck [in] the psyche of the British were the 57,470 casualties suffered on first day of Battle of the Somme, [of] which 19,240 . . . were killed. That made it the bloodiest day in British military history.[5]
>
> — *World Atlas*

Which Adversary Took Corrective Action?

The ongoing slaughter then prompted the side with the most bottom-up culture to drastically alter its tactics in 1917. German soldiers had been advisers to the Imperial Japanese Army (IJA) since 1886 and watched the Boers' infiltrate British lines in South Africa around 1900.[6] That's probably how they came up with the amazingly powerful "Stormtrooper squad" assault technique during the latter part of WWI. After shifting a precision artillery bombardment slightly forward, any German infantry squad in the Spring Offensives of 1918 could then secretly enter an Allied position, however strong. Its members did so by detonating a bangalore, tossing concussion grenades, and then bayoneting anyone in the way. By not firing their small arms during the actual assault, they could simulate a continuation of the first stage of the barrage. That, in turn, kept all defenders' heads down.

On defense, any German squad in this same 1918 Offensive could establish a defense matrix strongpoint that could be later abandoned at its own discretion.[7] (See Figure 2.1.) And thus came to pass what are still considered to be "post-machinegun infantry tactics." They are most easily characterized by "tiny ambushes in series" on defense, and a "short-range infiltration" through crawling on offense.[8] Unfortunately, only U.S. foes have regularly used them since 1918.

While several of America's European allies had attempted to match both Stormtrooper feats during WWI, their top-down and highly stratified military cultures would not allow them to do so.[9] Because a "soft" matrix of mutually supporting strongpoints requires some decentralization of control, those allies would be forever dependent on the old-fashioned linear defense. And instead of totally surprising defenders, their attack squads would be forced to rely on their parent unit's firepower to keep defenders' heads down. To this day, these are the main differences between how Eastern and Western forces fight.

The Great War Had Produced an Elastic Defense in Depth

At first in the War to End All Wars, the Huns had protected their riflemen with trenches and machinegunners with deep dugouts. Before long, they noticed too many riflemen succumbing to

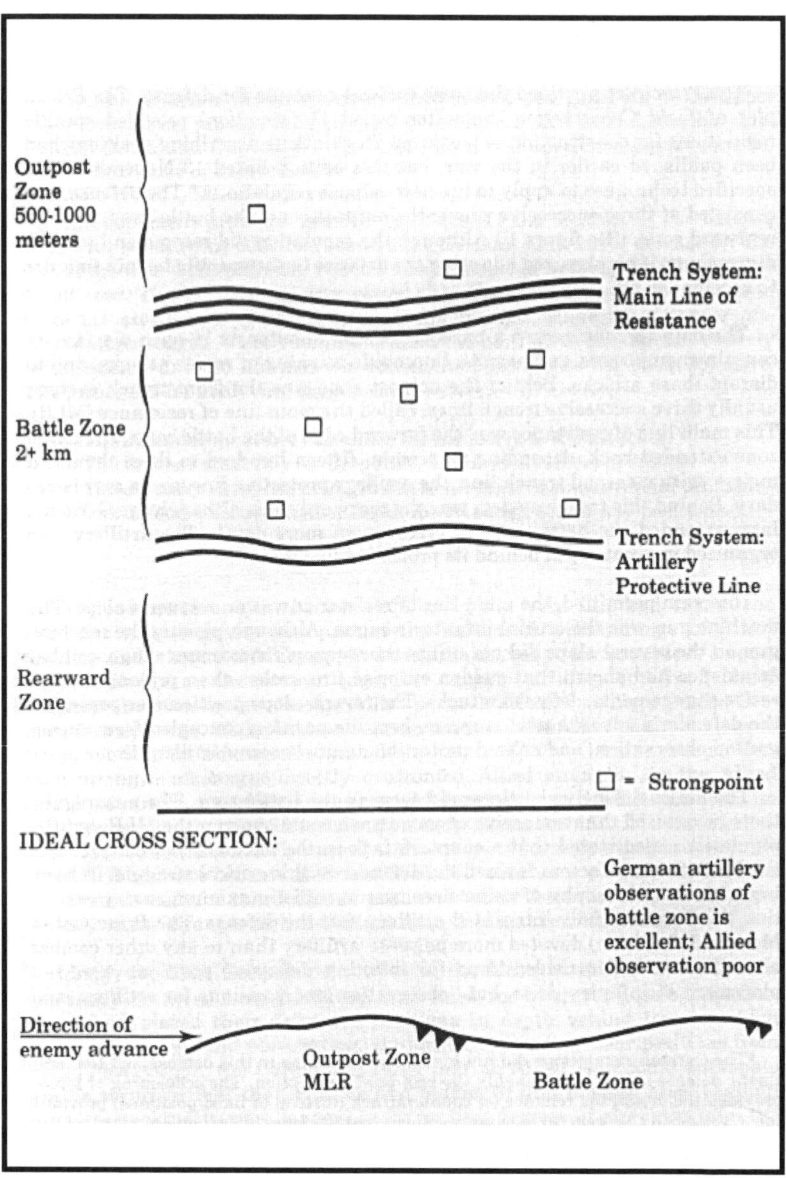

Figure 2.1: WWI Hun Improvement to Continuous Line of Holes
(Source: "The Changes in German Tactical Doctrine during the First World War," U.S. Army Combat Studies Inst., Leavenworth Paper No. 4 (1981), p. 14.)

bombardment,[10] and machinegunners to capture. During the Allies' pre-assault barrage, both were better off just scattering into nearby shell holes. From there, they could deliver unexpected fire into the advancing waves of Doughboys, Limies, and Frenchies. As each shell hole would accommodate roughly a squad, the role of the riflemen became that of protecting a crew-served weapon.[11] From a hastily fortified pit and with all other shell hole occupants providing covering fire,[12] the machinegunner and his all-important gun could then more easily shift location.

Soon, all German squads were being encouraged to move slightly forward, sideways, or backward as the situation dictated.[13] This loose a grouping of tiny forts could, in effect, bend without breaking. By April 1917, what had started out to be a randomly chosen series of shell holes then turned into a formidable array of carefully situated bunkers.[14] (Look again at Figure 2.1.) In effect, the Huns had begun the logical transition from a linear defense in depth to a seemingly random (but terrain-consistent) matrix of semi-independent strongpoints.[15]

Then, the Germans realized that on a reverse slope, such a strongpoint array would be out of sight of Allied gunners.[16] If additionally camouflaged, it could also elude aerial observation.[17] And when staggered, each tiny bastion could be protected by the interlocking machinegun fire from those on either side behind it. This barrier of hot lead would not only make each bastion harder to assault, but also easier to reinforce, resupply, or abandon. Even behind the Main Line of Resistance (MLR), each squad fort would provide its own 360° security. Its occupants would try to hold out until relieved by counterattack.

Only after the war was it realized that a strongpoint matrix is just as durable when forward-echelon personnel pre-establish fall-back positions. A gradually receding defensive belt would need no overall coordinator, as long as the NCO in charge of each fort made the decision to pull back in time.[18]

German Squad Structure in WWI

By March of 1917, the German infantry squad consisted of a seven-man maneuver element and four-man BOF element armed with an MG08/15 machinegun.[19] Though bipod mounted, water cooled, and an adaptation of the famous Maxim Gun, the MGO8/15 only weighed about 40 pounds. It thus qualified as an LMG. (Its sister—the MG08—was tripod mounted and a full 150 pounds.) The muffled chatter of a refurbished MGO8/15 is disturbing to hear when one considers how many unsuspecting Allied soldiers it could have mown down. This magnificent gun fired around 450-500 rounds per minute.[20]

Those two components of a German squad would on occasion exchange roles to "leapfrog" each other in combat.[21] So doing helped them to bypass an enemy strongpoint while moving forward under decentralized control, in what was later to be known as (long-range) "infiltration tactics."

Before long, the squads of all German Assault Battalions were carrying "reduced-charge grenades." So, by the Spring Offensives of 1918, most were able to conduct their own Stormtrooper-like assault against a heavily fortified Allied line.[22]

How the French Infantry Was Organized for the Great War

Early in WWI, the French infantry company consisted of four sections (instead of platoons), with four squads apiece. Each squad contained one corporal and 11 to 14 riflemen.

Then, in 1916, those squads became more specialized: (1) one squad of eight men with hand grenadiers; (2) one squad of seven men with two automatic riflemen plus their assistants; and (3) two squads of 12-13 "vaulters" each. Those vaulters were mostly riflemen with a few rifle grenadiers thrown in for support. By 1917, two of those same French squads had their own automatic rifleman, and all four had rifle grenadiers.

Then, in October 1918, the section was divided into three combat groups (instead of squads), each with two teams of six men. The automatic rifle team had one gunner and four assistants, while the grenadier team had grenade throwers, one rifle grenadier, and his helper.[23] All three French groups were exactly the same, which means they could have easily switched roles.

At some point near the end of the war, there was experimentation by the French with squads containing a "Shock Element" and a "Fire Element"—what the USMC may have later tried to emulate as a precursor to fireteams. The squad leader led the former, while the assistant squad leader was in charge of the latter. This Fire Element was tasked with providing suppressive fire for the Shock Element trying to outflank the enemy).[24]

The Fire Element was probably carrying a problematic *Fusil-mitrailleur Modele 1915 CSRG* light machine rifle (better known as the *Chauchat*). This weapon in no way qualified as an LMG.[25] And, the two French squad elements were not fireteams, in the modern sense of the term. There is no indication of their performing an "alternating fire and movement" or "bounding overwatch."

The British Army Infantry Structure of The Period

The British Army squad-sized "section" of WWI may have contained as few as eight men.[26] Each platoon had four such sections. One carried a heavy Lewis Gun along with its bulky ammunition. The second specialized in grenades, a third in rifle grenades, and the fourth contained ordinary riflemen.[27] In other words, that platoon had been organized to conduct its own attack, but none of the subordinate elements were supposed to switch roles or operate independently.

Doughboy Breakdown

Upon entering WWI, the deployed U.S. forces were tempted to copy the infantry structure of the French Army—namely, four specialized squad-sized sections within every platoon. However General Pershing instead chose to give heavier armaments to his equally endowed eight-man squads. This would, in turn, lead to the "half-platoon" (or section) as the basic combat unit of the U.S. Army.[28] Thus, each Army squad was not expected to do any internal maneuvering (cover the advance of any component with the fire of another). It was instead to move around the battlefield as a single entity.[29]

Then, for the rest of the war, the U.S. Army fielded an eight-man rifle squad (seven privates and one corporal), with two squads comprising each half-platoon.[30] The trend was for each squad to contain at least one automatic rifleman, one good grenade thrower, and one rifle grenadier.[31] But, an LMG was never part of its organic weap-

Figure 2.2: U.S. Marine Infantrymen at Belleau Wood
(Source: Public-domain painting by Georges Scott [1873-1943], illustration for French magazine, from https://commons.wikimedia.org/wiki/File:Scott_Belleau_Wood.jpg.)

onry. The BAR saw only limited service in Europe as a replacement for the French-made *Chauchat* and M1909 *Benét–Mercié* machine rifles that U.S. forces had initially been issued.[32]

When the Doughboys first arrived in France, they didn't have a good fragmentation grenade of their own. So, they ended up using either the British Mills Bomb or French F1. Soon, the American MK1 and MK2 appeared on the scene looking and behaving much like the F1.[33]

Meanwhile, the U.S. Marines had sent a slightly larger (but still unitary) nine-man squad into the fray. Such structure would give its leader two equally powerful teams with which to bound forward. But, to what extent he took advantage of such an asset is not really known. At first, most of those Marine squads probably lacked their own machine rifle.[34] The the first big American Expeditionary Force (AEF) operation of WWI was the Marines' seizure of Belleau Wood. (See Figure 2.2.)

Grenade Use During WWI

On the battlefields of Europe, grenades were initially seen as a way to break the stalemate of trench warfare. Since grenade employment focused on trench clearing, early "grenade team" composition and techniques were similar for both sides. The British fielded a "bombing reserve" composed of nine soldiers. Led by a non-commissioned officer (NCO), it sometimes included two grenade throwers, two grenade carriers, two bayonet men, and two soldiers in reserve. Another type of Allied "bombing squad" was composed of two teams of four and a squad leader.

French *escouades de grenadiers* (grenade thrower sections) would be copied by U.S. forces upon their arrival in 1917. They included two grenadiers, two assistant grenadiers, two grenade carriers, and one reserve soldier—all led by a corporal.

The Germans initially had six to eight man hand grenade teams, and then a nine-man *handgranatengruppe* (hand grenade squad), similar to the Allied formations. Regularly operating within hand grenade range of the enemy (20 to 45 yards), all members of these various units carried pistols and knives, as well as rifles and bayonets.[35]

At some point in the war, the distinction was made between offensive and defensive grenades—with the former designed to produce little or no shrapnel to keep users in the assault safe. While the Germans possessed such a "concussion" grenade as early as 1915 with the M15 *stielhandgranate*,[36] the late-arriving Americans were forced to improvise the cardboard MKIII.[37] That's because the British and French had been using only fragmentation grenades—the Mills Bomb and F1, respectively.[38] Yet, this makeshift U.S. concussion grenade was never used to simulate a mortar impact. In other words, none of the Allies attempted the tactically advanced assaults of the Germans.

Overall Effect of the Structural Differences

At the end of the War to End All Wars, the British and American squads were smaller than the others, making them easier for a single person to control. At the time, this made perfect sense. The infantry squad gains much of its power, after all, from all members being able to think and act like one man.

However, the leader of the German squad had only the respective heads of two subordinate elements to direct. So, he could control a slightly larger unit. And only the two-part German squad seemed able to "cover by fire" its own forward motion. That both parts—though unequal in size—had roughly the same firepower, may have helped in this regard.

Also, of note, the French Army had experimented with a squad consisting of three equal parts, each with a senior member. Three sub-units could also be easily controlled by a lone squad leader. That all were structured and armed in the same way meant they would have no trouble alternating roles. This finally made possible a seemingly random "fire and movement" exercise against light enemy resistance. The U.S. Marines were to take this idea back to America and briefly try it during the Banana Wars of the 1920's and 30's in the Caribbean region.[39]

The Effect of Ordnance Variations

Most of the rifle squads of the AEF had entered WWI carrying only the M1903 Springfield rifle.[40] (See Figure 2.3.) At some point, they were issued a single—poorly performing—machine rifle of foreign manufacture. But, only the German squad had an organic LMG—making it capable of operating semi-autonomously. It could perform two vital functions on its own: (1) suppress heavy enemy fire during an assault; and (2) establish a defensive strongpoint. The former came in particularly handy if a tiny, unseen bunker aperture were unexpectedly encountered during an assault. Only by filling this aperture with automatic-weapon fire can such a bunker normally be approached.

And, of course, only the German squad had the proper grenades for conducting a Stormtrooper-like assault. It may have left its LMG slightly behind while performing the final "non-shooting" part of the secretive penetration. From there, that gun could have more easily

Figure 2.3: M1903 Rifle Was Only U.S. Squad Weapon in 1917
(Source: "Our Boys in the Trenches," by unknown artist, U.S. Army Ctr. of Mil. Hist., posters, from this url: https://history.army.mil/art/Posters/WWI/WWI.htm.)

suppressed opposition automatic weapon fire from a flank. Such fire would prove disastrous to Japanese units attempting to follow their assault squads through breaches in the wire in the next big war.

Only One Participating Army Was Practicing 3GW

In conjunction with Stormtrooper tactics, the WWI Germans had come up with some very useful parameters for Maneuver Warfare (MW)—a variant of 3GW. In the coming years, both innovations would become widely known throughout the world, but only fully practiced by a few Eastern armies. In fact, Maoist Mobile Warfare and MW would end up sharing many of the same operational guidelines.[41]

Today, 3GW and MW are still largely synonymous. In MW, one side routinely avoids the enemy's forward bastions to more easily get at his soft underbelly. In the process, it looks for: (1) surfaces and gaps; and (2) centers of gravity. Then it applies: (1) focus of main effort; (2) speed and surprise; (3) "recon pull;" (4) mission-type orders; and (5) commander's intent.[42]

If 2GW (killing as many enemy soldiers as possible) were as helpful to modern warfare as 3GW, the Marine Corps would not have switched its doctrine to MW around 1990. Unfortunately for the Corps, a full 3GW capacity has proven elusive. In a country that demands full military compliance with all civilian directives, it had failed to decentralize enough control over the training and operations of its lowest infantry echelons to successfully conduct 3GW.

Squad Structure and Warfare Style Must Be Connected

Fully practicing 3GW would logically require semi-autonomous squads—those with enough ordnance and tactical skill to perform the long-range infiltration of enemy bastions without any help from supporting arms or their parent unit. Only the German squad of late WWI had been designed for such a role. Its composition of 12 men is significant. So is the fact that its maneuver element was roughly twice the size of the BOF element. Thereby possible were three equal parts.

A Much More Shocking Revelation from the Great War

At the end of a conflict in which literally millions of soldiers had been slain by machinegun fire, only one infantry force was practicing what later came to be known as "post-machinegun tactics." The German Army, alone, was using the equivalent of tiny ambushes in series for its defensive alignments, and a crawling "short-range-infiltration-like" tip for offensive thrusts. Those MLR matrices had contained "firesacks" between the squad strongpoints that looked to Western forces like "gaps," and its Western line breaches had been initiated by a surprise-oriented (though not always quiet) approach.

The Hun Army's more "bottom-up" culture than its Western opponents certainly contributed to the differences in how it would fight. But, so did the strict control over everything that happened on the battlefield by Allied army headquarters. Their public affairs departments must have worked very hard to keep all military members (and the voting public) convinced of Western infantry superiority. After the war, the money-making push for new technology within America would further reinforce this myth, though professional soldiers have long realized that equipment alone cannot win a war.

Before long, what should have become the Pentagon's future norm—post-machinegun tactics—instead came to be known as that to which less affluent adversaries resort for "Unconventional Warfare (UW)."[43] One cannot help but suspect an intentional play on words to sufficiently disguise—and thereby circumvent—a perfectly legitimate alternative to the bureaucracy-bolstering *status quo*. Such a thing could easily happen where political (and fiscal) considerations were allowed to override those that were strictly martial in nature. The very word "unconventional" implies disregard for established norms. In actuality, all aspects of UW are well-accepted components of 3GW.

By discouraging ambushes on defense and more stealth in the attack, the U.S. War Department and its successor has implicitly striven to do all fighting within clear view of the enemy. Against a foe armed with machineguns, this can result in unnecessary casualties or a questionable outcome.

To support such a wartime strategy, the Pentagon has frequently insinuated that only courageous and skilled opponents will risk meeting the best troops in the world at high-noon in the middle of the street. The end result has been a steady diet of 2GW, whereas a little 3GW might have achieved a victory. 3GW is considered a refinement to 2GW, because it bypasses the enemy's troop concentrations to more easily get at his centers of gravity. By destroying materiel instead of people, it more adequately meets the needs of modern warfare. Ground troops are easily replaced in war, so winning—with the least loss of life—requires quickly going after the centers of communications and logistics.

Another Way of Looking at Post-Machinegun Tactics

Ambushing on defense and crawling in the attack are ways to develop more surprise. The U.S. military manuals have acknowledged surprise as an alternate source of combat power for years. In other words, surprise and firepower are truly interchangeable in war.[44] Those manuals even contain a few company-sized attacks involving a little surprise. But the U.S. military does not fight that way on foreign soil. It tries instead to apply overwhelming firepower to anything in its way. So, the arms manufactures may take exception to the profits lost through surprise-oriented maneuvers. Nor would their advertising (and lobbying) take into account any tactical considerations.

Should the Axis forces of WWII also prove to be more UW capable than their Western counterparts, it would not reflect well on any Free-World military that had continued to insist on complete control over all small-unit operations and training. Yes, the Allies finally did win this conflagration as well (with the help of Zukov and his Eastern Russians). But at what additional cost in lives was it accomplished? And how will squad structure and ordnance further change within WWII's main contestant armies?

3 How Squads of the World _ Then Operated in WWII

- How did WWII squads deal with enemy machinegun fire?
- Why did Eastern and Western units counter it differently?

U.S. rifle squads of WWII lacked their own machinegun.

(Source: "Machine Gun Crew in Training," by Olin Dows, U.S. Army Ctr. of Mil. Hist., at the following url: https://history.army.mil/art/dows/DOWS.htm.)

The Machinegun's Role During the Second World War

By the time WWII rolled around, almost everything on the battlefield had something to do with machineguns. One side had increased its level of pre-assault bombardment to try to silence them. The other had allowed more crawling before and during the final assault to try to limit their effect. But, the machinegun continued to take a tremendous toll on the participants of any ground attack. At the Battle of Stalingrad, two Soviet machinegunners managed to stop an entire battalion of advancing German infantrymen. Before the bloodletting had ended, scores of highly skilled Nazi assault troops lay dead. And, even more remarkably, those two Russian machinegunners would live to tell the tale.[1] Thus, the lessons of 1917 and 1918 had made little difference in how the average ground offensive was waged.

The Machine Gun on Defense

During WWII, the Germans were still deploying squad-sized machinegun nests in echelon.[2] But now, those nests were often grouped into platoon, company, and even battalion arrays.[3] Each step in the progression was surrounded by barbed wire and mines. (See Figure 3.1.) And those squad-sized defensive building blocks could be located on a forward or reverse slope.[4] Unlike their WWI predecessors, each contained a zigzag piece of trench. (Look again at Figure 3.1.) This decidedly linear indentation at their center made them difficult to spot from the air—to distinguish from all the communication trenches around them. And their specific location could be easily shifted. To the basic strongpoint design of "two up and one back," the German commanders of WWII could add covered dugouts, fake minefields, breaks in the existing mine belts, gates in the wire, and communication trenches (to allow reinforcement or withdrawal).

Meanwhile, aerial photographs of the Japanese defensive alignments in WWII contain no consistent pattern. They do however reveal partial circles within a patchwork of trenchline.[5] While most of this trenchline may have been for aerial deception or ground communication, the partial circles were probably from barriers around squad- or platoon-sized strongpoints.

By the onset of WWII, the Russians had also replaced their old linear defense with one of the strongpoint variety. Again their bastions were arrayed in "V" formation. For each Russian battalion array, a partially manned dummy position was added between the strongpoints at the top of the "V" to conceal a firesack. Other dummies were added on either side of the "V" bottom to hide the strongpoint's exact location.[6] Each company-sized component had real and fake positions in the same configuration.[7] (See Figure 3.2.) That their platoon-sized elements were themselves comprised of squad strongpoints is evident from the Soviet tactics manual for the period.[8]

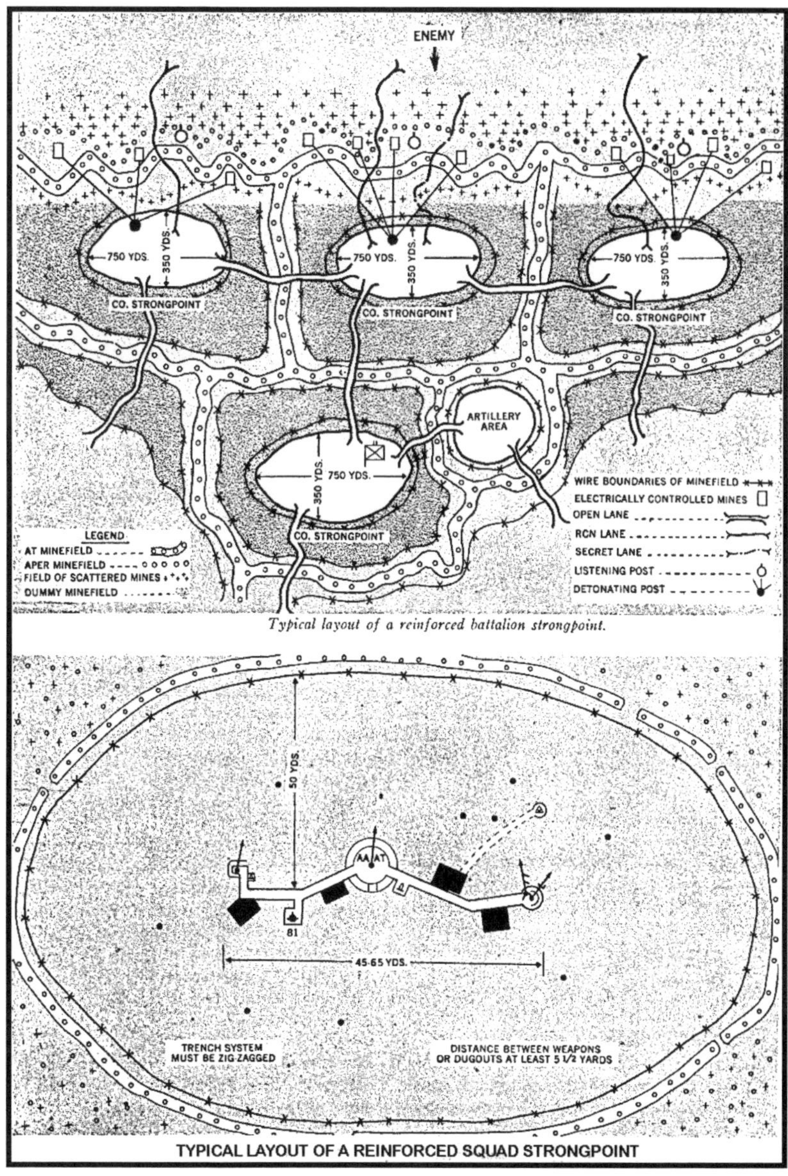

Typical layout of a reinforced battalion strongpoint.

TYPICAL LAYOUT OF A REINFORCED SQUAD STRONGPOINT

Figure 3.1: WWII Germans Improve Squad Strongpoint Matrix

(Source: "Handbook on German Military Forces," TM-E 30-451 (1945), p. 230.)

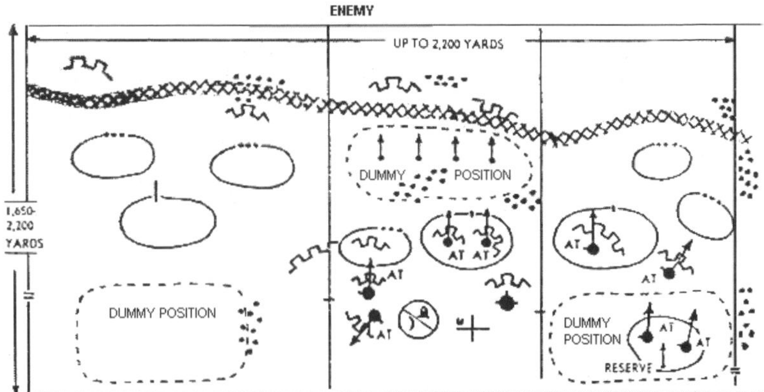

Figure 3.2: WWII Russians Add Fake Positions to Same Model
(Source: "Handbook for U.S.S.R. Military Forces," TM 30-340 (1945), p. V-47.)

All the while, the British, French, and American armies were still using the same linear defense formations from WWI, and only rarely in depth. Within this occasional succession of Allied lines were squad sectors with their approaches covered by machinegun fire from other sectors. But, those sectors failed to provide the self-sufficient (360° protected) strongpoint of an in-depth defense matrix. As such, they were relatively easy to penetrate.

The Machinegun on Offense

During WWII, the machinegun was also given a preeminent role in the attack. For one side, it traveled near the front of any approach march to an enemy objective, and then accompanied the final assault group. For the other side, it moved along well back in the march column and then conducted a standoff BOF during the final assault. Which side was which will require a closer look at the frontline participants.

The German Squad of WWII

Right before WWII, German troops had fought in the Spanish Civil War until 1938,[9] and while invading Poland in 1939. Their parent organization had come to believe that only a surprise-oriented offense was truly effective in war.[10]

Unlike the armed forces of most Western nations, the German Army considered the machinegun to be the backbone of infantry tactics. As a result, each WWII German squad was built around a machinegun.[11] Because the Germans also believed the infantry to be the queen of all arms,[12] they depended on those machingun-toting squads to do much of the fighting.

The German rifle company of WWII consisted of three platoons, with three squads apiece. Each squad (or *Gruppe)* contained a squad leader, deputy squad leader, LMG gunner, LMG assistant gunner, LMG ammunition carrier, and four to nine riflemen. Normally only 10 men in size, it was composed of two sections: (1) an LMG or BOF section; and (2) a rifle or maneuver section. In other words, it could conduct its own offensive.[13] However, German propaganda (and Allied intelligence) preferred to claim it no longer attacked alone as in the Spring Offensives of 1918 [14]—when it was the tip of every large-unit thrust into Allied lines.[15]

While on patrol or an approach march, the German squad's machinegunner and at least one assistant walked near the front of a single column.[16] Should this column make a chance contact requiring hasty attack, the LMG personnel formed a skirmish line with half of the maneuver section on either side. Those three elements then alternately moved forward in response to the squad leader's whistle.[17] Or, any number of riflemen could take turns advancing at the direction of the squad leader.[18] Rushing individuals would roll to one side after flopping down on the ground to disguise their final location. Smoke and concussion grenades were then tossed during the final assault. If that hasty attack failed, the squad leader had the authority to withdraw his unit.[19]

All members of the German squad had been trained as close combat fighters.[20] The assistant squad leader walked at the end of the squad column, led the maneuver section, and also controlled the expenditure of grenades.[21] Unlike the Russian rank and file of this era,[22] all German troops didn't know how to fight tanks. But, neither could they run from them. They were instead expected to direct all small-arms fire at the tanks' apertures and protective infantrymen.[23] Of course, some German soldiers had been specifically trained in how to kill tanks with makeshift weaponry (like molotov cocktails, smoke grenades, demolitions, and hand grenade bundles).[24] So, some of those methods undoubtedly reached the regular Hun soldiers in the trenches.

Of particular interest would be whether the German squads of the 1940's were still employing the powerful Stormtrooper assault technique from 1918. Those more recent squads were made up of hand-to-hand fighters.[25] And they did throw a lot of grenades before the final assault of an enemy position—something necessary to mimic a mortar barrage.[26] Because concussion grenades were regularly used during hasty attacks,[27] they would have been expected on a deliberate attack as well. Only at issue would be their intended role.

For a WWI Stormtrooper-like attack, there would have been a mixture of artillery and mortar rounds. Extremely accurate artillery fire would have been necessary to cover the sound of a large bangalore. Then, only the much-smaller mortar rounds could be simulated by grenades. While the WWII Germans would occasionally withhold preparatory indirect fire to attack by complete surprise, they almost always used it against a deliberate defense. Then, those same guns would be partially responsible for keeping their impacts just ahead of the advancing infantrymen.[28] So, shifting their fire forward a little would be easy to arrange.

Any Stormtrooper-like attack in WWII would have been run by a single squad. There is evidence of decentralized control over sister squads in a combined assault. "The assault and penetration are then launched upon the initiative of the squad leader."[29] Thus, lone-squad assaults would be commonplace.

Only still missing is hard evidence of no shooting in the assault. For the German soldier, the final stage of closing with the enemy was "with cold steel (bayonet)."[30] This means a minimum of small-arms fire.[31] The German *Stielhandgranate* grenade was still around from WWI. While this stick grenade could be fitted with a fragmentation sleeve, it primarily relied on a concussive blast.[32] With them in the 1940's, German assault troops could have feigned an indirect-fire attack and then bayoneted defenders who took cover. Thus, WWI Stormtrooper technique was almost certainly alive and well during the next world war, just less often applied.

The Japanese Squad of WWII

Just prior to WWII, the Japanese Army had regularly gained ground against conventional Chinese forces in the Second Sino-Japanese War of 1938,[33] and then been defeated by a more mechanized Soviet force in the Mongolian Nomonhan Incident of 1939.[34] As a result of the latter setback, it had put more emphasis on how riflemen fight tanks and the Samarai code of no surrender—Bushido.[35] Special "tank assault" squads were formed within its infantry who likely shared some of their new methods with the general population of close-combat fighters.[36] Those fighters would have only had mines and grenades with which to contest enemy armor.[37] That may be why the technique of pulling a mine on a string under the treads of an Allied tank became so well documented late in WWII.[38] The same trick was also well known to the German Army.[39] Meanwhile, the bayonet became, in effect, the Japanese soldier's new Samarai sword.

The Japanese squad of WWII was like its German counterpart in other ways as well. Within a "Type A" infantry company were three platoons, each having three 15-man rifle/LMG squads (locally called sections).[40] All "grenade discharge" personnel had been moved into in a separate light-mortar section within the platoon. So, the standard rifle/LMG squad contained a squad leader, an assistant squad leader, eight to ten riflemen, a machinegunner, an assistant machinegunner; and a machinegun ammunition carrier.[41] Clearly, this Japanese platoon was capable of operating alone on offense or defense, while much preferring the former. And like the German Army of 1918 (with its squad-sized spearheads), the Japanese Army of WWII was willing to attack a fortified position with forces others considered insufficient.[42] Much of this capability may have come from its Asian predisposition toward near total surprise and *ninja*-like infiltration. That's why its frontline soldiers had been so heavily oriented toward close-quarters combat.

By doctrine, the Japanese Army only recognized victory to any tactical situation when its troops had closed on the foe with their bayonets.[43] Implicit was a lack of shooting during the final stages of any assault, to include those against fortified positions. In fact, shooting had been specifically disallowed during the final phase of a deliberate night attack.[44]

The Japanese platoon would sometimes close with an enemy bastion through a row of squad columns.[45] At that point, its night attack could be run by complete surprise, or noisy deception. Only necessary for the former would be manual wire cutting and short-range infiltration (recon-pull). Entailed in the latter would be the last-minute shifting of fairly accurate indirect fire.[46] Light mortars from the same platoon could have provided it. Finally, decentralized control had been encouraged during any meeting engagement,[47] so a series of Stormtrooper-like squad assaults was certainly possible in a deliberate attack. The Japanese assaults on Henderson Field at Guadalcanal bore a striking resemblance to Captain Rohr's method. They were comprised of the following steps: (1) sneaking up to the protective wire, (2) bangaloring it during an artillery barrage, and then (3) transiting the breach with bayonets and grenades alone.[48]

Little has been written about Nipponese soldiers using concussion grenades during WWII assaults,[49] but their advisers—the Germans since 1896—certainly did.[50] The Type 98 Japanese grenade was supposedly identical to the German 24 and Chinese 23, though a photograph of its fragmentation sleeve no longer seems to exist.[51] And the charge for the Type 98 is also known to have been weak.[52] For fanatical assault troops, such a grenade—even without that sleeve—would have been adequately safe for close-proximity work.

The Russian Squad of WWII

Right before the Second World War, the Soviet infantry had encountered stiff resistance from the Japanese at the border between Mongolia and Manchuria in 1939,[53] and even more from the Finnish Army in the Winter War of 1939 to 1940.[54] Like the German and Japanese armies, its squads were also built around a machinegun.

The Russian company contained three platoons, of four squads apiece. At first, that squad had 12 men, including a grenadier, assistant grenadier, and sniper. Starting in 1942, those specialty jobs were shifted into a weapons platoon, and the regular rifle squad reduced to 9 or 10 men. It had one leader, another "especially good soldier" (guide), five riflemen, one LMG gunner, and one LMG assistant.[55] During any assault, the LMG personnel accompanied the others.[56] But like the German counterpart, that Soviet squad still had the equivalent of a BOF element and a maneuver element.[57] All members of the latter had been shown how to fight tanks with their bare hands.[58]

The Russian squad also moved forward in much the same way as the German. On patrol or during an approach march, the LMG personnel walked near the front of the column.[59] Then, during any hasty attack, separate parts of the maneuver element advanced on either side of the BOF element. At the squad leader's direction, they could move forward by "team" or individual bounds.[60] Rushing soldiers would often flop down near hollows, shell holes, or other cover.[61] At the end of their dash, they dropped like stones and then crawled to one side.[62] This was to give their opposition the impression they had been killed.

Only during a totally silent night attack (or one through heavy smoke) was the final assault conducted without any shooting.[63] Ordinarily, the Soviet squad would try to keep up with a rolling artillery barrage. And then in the assault, it would do some firing of small arms.[64] One might therefore conclude that the Soviet Army had failed to assimilate the fancy German assault technique from WWI. Yet, it had fully incorporated the Stormtroopers' defensive method. And Model 1914 Russian concussion grenades were still in regular use. Not all would have had their fragmentation jackets afixed.[65]

The Chinese Squad of WWII

The Chinese National Revolutionary Koumintang or KMT) Army had German advisers between 1933 and 1937, and Soviet advisers before this. Those Germans ended up training eight full divisions of that Chinese army.[66] In fact, "Germany . . . was instrumental in modernizing . . . the armed forces of the Republic of China prior to the Second Sino-Japanese War."[67] Then, at some point during WWII, the Chinese Red Army became loosely joined with the National Revolutionary Army to help resist the Japanese occupation.[68]

The rifle company of those German trained divisions had three platoons, with three squads apiece.[69] Each squad carried an LMG.[70] Meanwhile, its Chinese Communist counterpart had three fireteams with three men each (a fighter and two conscripts), but no evidence of its own LMG.[71] Nor was there any deputy squad leader.[72] (Since 1984, each dismounted PLA squad has consisted of 12 men—the squad leader, a deputy squad leader, six riflemen, a light machine-gunner, one or two LMG crew members, and one or two Rocket Propelled Grenade [RPG] men.[73])

All members of those German-trained Chinese divisions were probably good at disabling tanks with their bare hands. There had been special tank-killing detachments (sometimes called suicide squads) in the KMT during Sino-Japanese War.[74] And their members had shared some of the methods with frontline infantrymen. "The men in the trenches waited till the tanks came close, then jumped out and threw bundles of hand-grenades under their wheels and into their ports." Up to nine Japanese tanks were put out of action this way at the Battle of Taierzhuang.[75] The term "grenade bundle" also appears in a Nazi film about fighting armor with makeshift weapons.[76]

The German stick grenade would be used in WWII by the Japanese as a Type 98 and Chinese Nationalists as a Type 23. The Chinese Communists would then provide a later, locally manufactured version—the "Type 67"—to the People's Army of Vietnam (PAVN).[77]

Whether any of the Chinese troops had been shown how to run a Stormtrooper assault by the start of WWII is unclear, only that the Communists eventually figured it out. Grenades did precede every one of their assaults. The most logical kind would have been concussion, and no Chinese soldier was apparently photographed tossing a Type 23 with fragmentation sleeve attached.

> [When not facing barbed wire, attacking] platoons, with each of their squads divided into three teams, advance in a skirmishing formation with 3 to 5 paces between individuals and 7 or 8 paces between teams. They follow their own artillery concentrations very closely. . . .
>
> The assault is made in a continuous rush. As soon as the squads are within range, hand grenades are thrown to cause confusion, smoke, dust, and casualties.[78]
>
> — *Handbook on Chinese People's Liberation Army*
> U.S. Army, DA Pamphlet 30-51

It's now clear that PLA squads regularly used a Stormtrooper assault variation during the Korean War, and so did PAVN squads in the Vietnam Conflict.[79] In both cases, medium mortars probably took the place of artillery—because less artillery was available and its loud impacts were hard to mimic through grenades and satchel charges.

Trends So Far in Eastern Squad Utilization

That the Germans had helped to train both the Japanese and Nationalist Chinese armies prior to WWII would explain some of the same squad structure and methods. The Soviet Red Army had come into close contact with their Hun counterpart until March of 1918.[80] So, it too had gotten a considerable look at the German way of doing things.

The most obvious similarity between the German, Japanese, Russian, and Chinese infantry squads of the WWII era was the organic LMG. German and Japanese squad leaders were both allowed to initiate their part of a parent-unit assault. And Japanese platoons would close with an enemy objective in a row of squad columns—something the Chinese would also be observed doing in a later war.[81]

With mutual access to concussion grenades, all four infantries began every WWII assault with a barrage of grenades. All four also encouraged bare-handed tank killing. It would thus appear that every rifle squad knew how to contest armor without any special weaponry; and perform something like a WWI Stormtrooper assault. Meanwhile, the squads of all "free" Western nations would be equipped and operate in a very different fashion.

The British Squad of WWII

Immediately preceding WWII, England's army had helped to put down an Arab revolt against the British Mandate in Palestine from 1936 to 1939, and Irish Republican Army activity in Northern Ireland from 1939 to 1940.[82]

Unlike the armies of Germany, Japan, Russia, and China, its standard rifle squad had no LMG. By the outbreak of WWII, the British platoon had been reduced from four to three parts—each still squad-sized and called a section. The specialized sections of 1918 were gone, and in their place were all-purpose sections. For each, the normal battlefield maneuver was "a flanking [move] by the rifle team with the Bren [gun] providing cover." That would suggest two teams—one dedicated to maneuver and the other to a BOF, but still able to occasionally shift roles. The Bren team had three men, while the rifle team contained the rest of the unit under the section leader.[83]

Two specialized methods of attack were also developed in the British battle schools: (1) the pepper-pot method; and (2) the lane method. The former involved splitting each section into three groups (instead of two)—with one moving forward 20 yards while the other two covered its movements, and then all somehow "leapfrogging" onto the objective. However, critics felt the Bren remained too idle during such an exercise. So, the "lane method" of attack was also envisioned.[84] It likely involved separate lanes for each of the three groups to lessen their chances of shooting one another. This way the Bren gun could have assumed the best place in line to enjoy an unimpeded view of the heaviest source of enemy fire. However, such a maneuver was nearly impossible to coordinate, and the official historian knew of only one time it was successfully performed in combat.[85]

Regardless of the infantry's method of advancing, a major concern remained. Once the individual soldier had conducted his appropriate battledrill, he often had no visible opponent to shoot at. And because any amount of small-arms fire only partially kept the defenders' heads down, there continued to be an over-reliance on artillery support.[86] Additionally, all supporting fires still had to be ceased right before the final upright assault. "In the end, while the importance of the squad [section] as the basic unit of maneuver was well known by 1944, the best methods for training and utilizing those squads [sections] were never fully realized."[87]

While the British did have a shrapnel-free (bakelite) No. 69 concussion grenade in their WWII inventory, there is no evidence of it ever simulating mortar fire. Introduced in 1940 as a light offensive grenade, it was intended for use in the open without any protective cover.[88]

The American Army Squad of WWII

The U.S. Army had a 12-man squad in 1944. (See Figure 3.3.) It consisted of a squad leader, assistant squad leader, two riflemen scouts, a BAR carrier, two assistant BAR men, and five more riflemen. The assistant squad leader often carried an M7 grenade launcher on his M1 rifle, as did two riflemen. Later in the war (and contrary to the official Table of Equipment), two BAR's were authorized per squad in some theatres of war as were a few (probably Thompson) submachineguns. The squad was usually divided into two teams. They were not symmetrical fireteams, but two that had each been specialized. Normally, the squad leader would lead one contingent, and the assistant squad leader the other.[89]

Figure 3.3: GIs During Battle of the Bulge

(Source: "Infantry/Battered Bulge Village," by Robert N. Blair, U.S. Army Ctr. of Mil. Hist., from this url: https://history.army.mil/images/reference/bulge/9-28-90.jpg.)

For a while early in World War II some of the U.S. squads had a sniper who normally joined the BAR team. That would have made it and the rifle team both four men in size.[90] And there was some experimentation with three teams right at the end of the war, with trained scouts anchoring the extra team. No matter what the arrangement, internal buddy teams were still considered very important.[91]

This late-war 12-man squad was broken down into a two-man scout team (Able), three-man BAR team (Baker), and five-man maneuver and assault team (Charlie). The squad leader was supposed to stay with Able until the enemy was located, while the assistant squad leader accompanied Baker. Then, the squad leader would signal Baker to provide covering fire and make his way to Charlie to lead the assault by short rushes. However, every step was not always possible. It was thus concluded that 11 men were difficult for a single leader to control.[92]

The MK3 was an American concussion-oriented explosive first introduced during WWI—as the MKIII Offensive Blast Grenade.[93] The MKIII was designed for use during fortified position assaults to knock out bunkers and clear trenches without producing fragmentation that could injure the user or any friendly forces nearby.[94] Its WWII successors were the MK3A1 with a water-resistant laminated-paper body and the MK3A2 made of waterproof asphalt-impregnated fiberboard. While both were called offensive hand grenades, they were no longer intended for protecting assault troops. They had been specifically designed to create havoc within an enclosed enemy space—like a building or bunker. "The lethal over-pressure created by the detonation will penetrate twisted confines where fragmentation grenades will not."[95] So, once again, it's doubtful that GIs ever conducted a Stormtrooper-like assault.

Meanwhile, the U.S. Marine Corps had developed its own way of doing things. Much was quite different from what the U.S. Army found useful.

The American Marine Corps Squad of WWII

At the beginning of WWII, the Marine infantry platoon had a seven-man headquarters, eight-man BAR squad, and three nine-man rifle squads. Each rifle squad consisted of a squad leader, a

BAR man, six riflemen, and a rifle grenadier armed with a grenade launcher. But such an arrangement soon proved unsatisfactory. First, the BAR squad disappeared from the platoon. Then, the rifle squad was increased in size to 12 men (a squad leader, an assistant squad leader, six M-1 riflemen, two BAR men, and two assistant BAR-men with M-1 rifles). This rifle squad could now be broken down into two six-man fire units, each with an automatic rifle and five semi-automatic rifles.[96]

Of note, what had sparked such developments is now quite relevant to recent HQMC decisions. With the onset of WWII, the nine-man squad had been found to be sub-optimal for jungle and island fighting. So, that squad was increased to 12 men. Then, experimentation continued at Camp Pendleton based on lessons learned in the Pacific. Three options were tested: (1) a two-BAR, 13-man squad; (2) four three-man "fire groups;" and (3) three four-man fire groups. The last was deemed optimal because it better absorbed casualties and was easier to control. In 1944, the USMC would adopt a 13-man squad, with three four-man fireteams, each built around a BAR.[97]

In effect, the Corps had decided to follow the Raider concept of three fireteams per squad. But, these fireteams would have four men instead of three (allowing for two internal buddy teams).[98] One of those four men would carry a BAR, and another an M-7 grenade launcher.[99] But, the new squad still had no organic LMG. So, only with the help of a parent-unit machinegun, could it go after an enemy bastion with the "blind 'em, burn 'em, and blast 'em" technique. There were a couple of short-range infiltrations late in the war, and some impromptu grenades-only attacks, but no known Stormtrooper-like assault.

The French Squad of WWII

The French infantry company of 1940 had four rifle platoons, with three squads apiece. Each squad had a leader, assistant leader, LMG gunner, assistant LMG gunner, three ammunition carriers, four riflemen, and a rifle grenadier.[100] This so-called LMG was a 7.5mm Châtellerault M24/29. Top fed with 25-round magazines, it was not capable of a high rate of fire. Judged inferior to the BAR in testing, it more precisely qualified as a machine rifle.[101]

The Free French infantry squad of 1945 consisted of two parts and a single BAR. In combat, it mimicked its American sister. "French infantry forces employ the same standard 'fire and maneuver' tactic used by the U.S. Army. . . . [T]his typically involves the assistant squad leader setting up a base of fire with the BAR and half of the squad, while the squad leader takes the other half of the unit and maneuvers to assault the enemy position."[102] The French soldiers of either stage of WWII used only the F1 fragmentation grenade.[103]

How Western and Eastern Squads Differed

Clearly, the British, American, and French armies had placed less emphasis on close combat than their Eastern counterparts. This must be why the Western squads weren't given their own machinegun, concussion grenades, or tank-fighting skills. The logic behind such a decision is simple. The principal Allied strategy of overwhelming force had removed the need for much in-fighting. Meanwhile, the Eastern armies allowed semi-autonomous squads to fully practice 3GW against a better armed adversary. That's how they could penetrate his security screen to get at command and logistics networks.

But, why those Western armies gave their squads machine rifles, instead of a true—tripod-mountable—LMG is harder to explain. (See Figure 3.4.) For one thing, too greatly acknowledging the power of the machinegun would have forced those British, American, and French armies to drastically alter their traditionally 2GW (and very exposed) way of attacking. Plus, tall "top-down" Western bureaucracies tend to resist any change to established procedure, however useful.

Weaponry Details for Squads from the East

The LMG carried by each German Army squad in WWII was the MG34. With only a bipod, it weighed 27 pounds. So, an additional tripod with traversing and elevation (T&E) mechanism could have been easily carried. Such a gun under any circumstance would be much more deadly than a machine rifle.

On any squad assault, the LMG gunner went along.[104] The average German squad also carried M24 offensive blast (concussion) grenades. By 1944, all mortars were at least 81mm in size and consolidated at battalion.[105] Two out of three platoons within a Volkgrenadier Battalion carried submachineguns. But, there is no indication of any WWII German platoon ever having its own mortar squad, so all mortar support for a Stormtrooper-like assault would have come from battalion.[106]

Meanwhile, the average Japanese rifle squad of the era was equipped with the 6.5mm Type 96 Nambu LMG. With a tripod often available, reduced bullet charge, and very little recoil, this LMG could be fired more accurately (at about 550 rounds per minute) than the later (and heavier) 7.7 mm Type 99 Nambu.[107] A bayonet could also be attached to the Type 96 for hand-to-hand fighting. With a top-of-the-barrel handle for from-the-hip firing,[108] it was almost certainly carried on all squad assaults. Within the same infantry platoon, the "grenade discharger" squad carried 12 dischargers of which three were 50mm Type 89 knee mortars.[109] Through experimentation between the wars, the Japanese Army had come up with a family of grenades with great adaptability. Introduced in 1931, the Type 91 fragmentation grenade could be thrown by hand, fired from a cup-type grenade launcher (Type 100), or discharged by a lightweight mortar-like projector (Type 89).[110] It could also be fitted with tail-fin assembly and fired from a spigot-type rifle grenade launcher.[111] Throughout WWII, Japanese rifle squads also carried Type 98 offensive blast (concussion) grenades. In other words, the Japanese rifle platoon could have provided its own indirect fire for a Stormtrooper-like squad assault.

At the beginning of WWII, each Soviet rifle platoon also had an internal mortar squad with a single 50mm mortar. Then, in July 1941, all such mortars were consolidated at the company level, and in early 1942 at battalion.[112] So, while the early platoons may have realized what type of attack their own shifting mortar barrage made possible, they didn't have enough mortars to support it. For whatever reason, the emphasis then shifted to automatic weapons. Some Soviet rifle companies of this era had five rifles, 38 submachineguns, 18 LMGs, six sniper rifles, and two 50mm mortars. If there had been three rifle platoons of three squads each, then each squad would have had two LMGs, instead of one. What set this Soviet rifle company apart from those of other armies was the number of submachinegunners—up to four per squad. According to the U.S. War Department, such a unit was well-suited for "outflanking and [long-range] infiltration tactics."[113]

Most early Chinese LMGs also had a handle over the barrel that would have permitted their firing from the hip.[114] Such a gun could have accompanied every Communist squad assault, but probably didn't because of their limited numbers. Both kinds of squads were also equipped with the Type 23 offensive blast (concussion) grenade. During WWII, the Communist Chinese may had a few improvised light mortars within their infantry platoons. But, the KMT infantry platoons were supported by M2 or Type 31 mortars (probably from a separate company).[115] By 1984 in the PLA, all light (60mm or 61mm) mortars had been consolidated at the company level.[116] Yet, such guns had T&E mechanisms that permitted enough accurate shifting of fire for a grenades-only ground assault.

Which Maneuvers Those Eastern Weapons Made Possible

While equipped with concussion grenades and organic light mortars, the infantry companies of Japan, China, and Russia were certainly capable of running their own Stormtrooper-like squad assaults. The sound of an exploding hand grenade more closely approximates that of a light-mortar impact. Yet, it was not only the Japanese assault troops' concussion grenades,[117] but also their bangalore torpedoes,[118] that made possible the simulated indirect-fire attacks (normally of mixed caliber) at Henderson Field on Guadalcanal.

Carrying an organic LMG also helped the Eastern squad to complete its assault. There can be unexpected automatic-weapons fire during any move into an enemy position. It may come from a flank or totally hidden frontline bunker. Then, its exact location becomes only obvious to the assault troops themselves. Complete fire superiority over an enemy machinegun takes a friendly machinegun. If a bunker aperture is the source of the fire, that aperture must be subjected to a continuous stream bullets to discourage its use. This latter reality was indisputably demonstrated during the Tarawa bunker assault in the well-researched movie, "Sands of Iwo Jima."[119]

Finally, those squad LMGs made it possible for the Eastern

armies to practice the UW part of 3GW. They could now use an array of machinegun ambushes (in the form of squad strongpoints) for their defensive formation. And they could more easily cover a "grenades only" or "quietly crawling" (short-range-infiltration) type of attack.

The LMG that was carried in on every Soviet, German, Japanese, and Chinese squad assault also gave its participants another advantage. In addition suppressing unexpected enemy fire, it made possible a deception involving telltale sounds. Any enemy machinegun burst, however small, will lead an American defender to believe its source is a stationary BOF outside his lines. On level ground, he then looks for the final assault to come from somewhere else.[120] He makes this error in judgment because U.S. ground pounders are rarely allowed to crawl in an assault, nor have friendly machinegun

Figure 3.4: U.S. BAR Man in the Pacific
(Source: "Machine Gun Position," govt. poster, by Andy Pratt, U.S. Army Ctr. for Mil. Hist., from this url: http://www.history.army.mil/art/Posters/WWII/1-15-49.jpg.)

bullets streaming in just above their heads. The gun must be slightly elevated and just beyond the wire (like in the crook of a tree) to be this accurate.

Levels of Alien Army Expertise at Short-Range Infiltration

The WWII Germans and Russians had become skilled at long-range infiltration, not the interpersonal variety (sneaking between enemy holes). Yet, they could still closely approach a deliberate enemy defense.

Meanwhile, the German soldiers of WWII were actually encouraged by their manuals to crawl in the attack.[121] Their Stormtrooper forefathers had been able to sneak right up to the barbed wire of a Doughboy line through the shallow communications trenches of a heavily contested battlefield. In fact, during the first few months of the war, German sappers had created new shell holes to do likewise at the Belgian equivalent to a Maginot Line.[122] In both cases, armed force would eventually become necessary to penetrate the position.

For the Soviet Army, an "infiltration" type of assault was something of a misnomer. It actually consisted of "reduc[ing] the [defense] zone pillbox by pillbox,"[123] as opposed to secretly entering that zone. Yet, the average Soviet combatant was still fairly good at sneaking around.

> In World War II, as in preceding wars, the Russian soldier demonstrated that he was closer to nature than his West European counterpart. This was hardly surprising since most of the Russian soldiers were born and raised far from big cities.... The Russian was able to move without a sound and orient himself in the darkness.... [He] performed particularly well as a night observer. Stern discipline and self-constraint enabled him to lie motionless for hours and observe the German troops at close range without being detected.[124]
>
> — *Historical Study—Night Combat*
> U.S. Army, DA Pamphlet 20-236

While the Germans and Russians were able to slip through a

lightly held enemy sector (long-range infiltration), Asians could sneak through one that was heavily defended (short-range infiltration). As WWII drew to a close, the Japanese less often resorted to stand-up "banzai" charges. A full week after Iwo Jima was declared secure, there was a large counterattack through this island's tunnels against a key airfield.[125] Then on Okinawa, the first major counterattack was one of short-range infiltration. On 12 April 1945, tiny elements from four battalions snuck between U.S. holes, hid for a while in caves and tombs, and then attacked those lines from the rear. The least successful of these battalions still managed to penetrate over 500 yards.[126] A large-scale, last-ditch infiltration of U.S. lines was also planned for the thousands of Japanese naval troops at the southern tip of the island.[127]

Before long, the Communist Chinese would become known as the masters of short-range infiltration. In fact, the official U.S. Marine Corps history credits Chinese soldiers with infiltrating at night better than any other soldiers on earth.[128]

> The Chinese Communists . . . made frequent and effective use of infiltration. . . .
>
> Small units often infiltrate their members individually under cover of darkness and regroup them at a previously designated point [sometimes behind Allied lines].[129]
>
> — *Handbook on the Chinese Communist Army*
> U.S. Army, DA Pamphlet 30-51

Asians Had Realized Link Between Artillery and Satchels

Indisputable proof of Stormtrooper technique may not exist for WWII, but there is mathematical evidence of at least one major army hiding infiltrator-caused blasts among incoming shells. Some of the most convincing comes from Guadalcanal.

Historians generally agree that there were many Japanese soldiers inside the Henderson Field perimeter at any given time. But, what were they all doing there? This is the ongoing question. Gen. Vandegrift's Chief of Staff estimated that hundreds of Japanese had gotten through friendly lines, but saw no incongruity in only one Marine being killed by a sniper.[130]

While Edson's Raiders were making their famous Bloody Ridge

"stand" in mid-September 1942, Sheffield Banta was evicting enemy sappers from the Division Command Post (almost a mile behind the front lines).[131]

> Small groups of enemy that have infiltrated may appear any place. On Guadalcanal a three-man enemy patrol attacked the First Marine Division CP [Command Post].[132]
>
> — U.S. Marine Corps,
> FMFRP 12-9, *Jungle Warfare*

Those infiltrators were also attacking other strategically important targets inside the perimeter in less obvious ways. Some of the activity was by supporting-arms forward observers. The NCOs had told Chesty Puller of intruders using radios and rifle shots as signals.[133] On 13 October, Pistol Pete (an enemy long-range artillery piece) was "registered . . . with slow and methodical precision."[134] But too much precision can mean concurrent sabotage. The airfield had come under aerial or naval bombardment during almost every day and night (at predictable hours). Well dispersed and fully revetted aircraft, ammunition, and fuel had routinely fallen victim to these attacks. After American sentries dove for cover, CPs, equipment, and stores would have been much easier to approach along the ground. That means Japanese sappers may have been responsible for some of those "direct hits."

> On the night of October 14th [actually October 13-14], a Japanese naval task force . . . swung into "Sleepless Lagoon" off Henderson Field and began firing salvos. . . . Then the Japanese ships withdrew, leaving more than half of the ninety planes on the airfield wrecked, the gasoline supply almost all destroyed.[135]
>
> — Richard Tregaskis
> news correspondent on Guadalcanal

> Before anyone in the Perimeter could organize damage-control parties, a chain of Japanese night bombers [aircraft] arrived to make matters worse. A direct hit on Texas Switch, the garrison's main radio station, prevented word of the disaster from going out until nearly dawn.[136]
>
> — *Guadalcanal: Starvation Island*
> by Hammel

That some of that Japanese ordnance was fairly large should not have made much difference against pinpoint targets enclosed by thick walls of sandbags. One has only to play ring toss at the county fair to estimate how many shells it would have taken for each direct hit. Therein lies a strong indicator of deception.

> In twenty-four hours on October 13 and 14, [only] fifty-three bombs and shells hit the [mile-long] Henderson airstrip![137]
> — *Green Hell: The Battle for Guadalcanal*
> by Owens

After all this damage, such a report should constitute proof—albeit mathematical—of a mixing of bombardment with sabotage. Even for closely observed and then carefully adjusted fire, the limits of probability had been exceeded by this many direct hits on pinpoint targets. One can thus conclude that unseen enemy sappers—with satchel charges and possibly timers—had been blowing up key U.S. assets during the nighttime shellings. Wars are won by destroying a foe's logistics and control centers (not his people). This, after all, is the primary rationale behind 3GW. And sappers can play a major role, providing their methods are well enough masked.

Western Squad Weaponry

British, American, and French squads of the 1940's carried machine rifles, but no real LMG. While English and U.S. soldiers had limited access to concussion grenades, the American version had been mostly designed for the overpressure it would produce in a confined space.

The British made only limited use of a two-inch (51mm) mortar during WWII. U.S. Army and Marine rifle companies had a platoon of M2 60mm light mortars,[138] but there is little chance of any being used for a small-arms--free assault. Nor can many modern-day GIs describe the various steps of the evolutionary Stormtrooper method.

Overall Effect of the Variation in Structure and Armament

Only the infantry squads from Germany, Russia, Japan, and

China had access to their own fully functioning machinegun during the Second World War. So, they alone were able to follow the tactical precedent set by the WWI German Stormtroopers—a defense matrix of tiny mutually supporting forts. Those squad machineguns also made possible a safer short-range-infiltration attack (something only the Asians would much utilize). In combination, those two capabilities meant only the Eastern participants of WWII had taken advantage of the tactical advances that would later come to define UW.

Meanwhile, all Free-World armies had continued their continuous-line defenses and stand-up assaults from WWI. Ambushes were occasionally risked beyond friendly lines, but all outposts immediately withdrawn without contact whenever a large enemy attack force showed up. The approach marches to offensive targets were often stealthy (to include some last-minute crawling), but only rarely did they lead to trying to sneak between the enemy's foxholes. In other words, the Western armies had virtually ignored the two most important aspects of UW. To practice its inclusive warfare style of 3GW, one must covertly penetrate the foe's security screen (however dense). Yet, most American infantry outfits had no interest in doing anything involving a disadvantage in firepower (however temporary).

Painfully evident from America's subsequent "expeditionary adventures" has been the effect this lack of UW and 3GW has had on not only their final outcome, but also their friendly casualty counts. WWII would be the last big conflict to be decisively won by the U.S. and its Allies. The Soviet Union had more to do with that victory than most Western analysts like to admit. So, any Russian-trained adversary must now be considered much more dangerous than previously thought.

4 Squad Activity During the Korean War

- Were frontal Chinese assaults what they seemed in Korea?
- How were the Communist probing attacks conducted?

The U.S. squad had no organic machinegun in Korea.

(Source: "The Sunshine Division in Korea," by Rick Reeves, poss. ©, from url: http://www.nationalguard.mil/resources/photo_gallery/heritage/images/sunshinedivision.jpg.)

The Second World War Had Just Ended

The war in Korea began just five years after the end of WWII. Though many smaller countries would participate in this United Nations (U.N.) "police action," there were two major players—the Red Chinese and Americans. So, it is their squads that will be studied. Only the U.S. Army contingent seems to have entered the war with different structure and armament than in 1945.

While it has not been possible to prove Stormtrooper assault technique by the Chinese Communists in WWII, a close variant may have appeared in Korea.

The Chinese Played a Big Part in the Initial Invasion

"[B]attle-hardened Koreans from the PLA" had constituted up to 80% of the North Korean force to invade South Korea in June of 1950.[1] Later that year, a Chinese army of " volunteers" entered South Korea to counter a U.N. offensive and then help build up the border defense zone.[2] In fact, the People's Republic of China (PRC) may have simply redesignated the PLA's North East Frontier Force as the People's Volunteer Army (PVA).[3] The PLA is also known to have trained the North Korean People's Army (NKPA) in the early 1950's.[4] Mao had been fighting a German-trained opponent since the early 1930's. So, this many of his troops now in Korea virtually assured his Communist allies were aware of the evolutionary changes to small-unit tactics from WWI.

PLA Troops Clearly Knew About the Stormtrooper Method

During the first big Chosin Reservoir battle in late 1950, U.S. Marine defenders were attacked by Chinese squads that were still in column formation. There's even a Communist photograph (from behind) of a single file in the final stages of its assault.[5] First came the probing of Marine lines by squad-sized "sticks," and then an all-out attack involving other "sticks." A row of loosely knit squad columns would have looked to a Western observer like successive waves of enemy soldiers. But, these seemingly on-line soldiers did not attack all at once. Instead, separate individuals (and the parent-unit files behind them) took turns punching their way through the Marines' frontline positions. Whenever one succeeded, adjacent files came in behind them.

Such a human-wave deception was possible in the rugged Chosin terrain, because the approaching Chinese "cavalcade" had already split into parallel company columns.

> [Chinese Communist Forces (CCF)] regiments, attacking in columns of battalions [then] deployed in[to] columns of companies.[6]
>
> — *Chosin,* by Hammel

Quickly to create an assault formation of any width, each of those company columns would have to subdivide into a row of platoon columns, and then of squad columns. Each of the 200-man companies in the original string could not have followed the old U.S. Civil War custom of marching to one side and then facing the objective. The resulting motion signature in the barren landscape of North Korea would have been far too great for any semblance of surprise. And, throughout this dispersal process, teams of scouts would have been forward deployed from the larger units. But, these were not just ordinary scouts; they were also skilled "infiltrators." After arriving at the attack objective, their first job would have likely been to act as guides for all arriving subunits of their parent command. Then, a few might have started looking for a spot in Marine lines weak enough for a main attack or covertly entered to destroy crew-served weapons.

> It [3rd Battalion, 236th Regiment, CCF] . . . sent out the usual screen of *infiltrators. [Italics added].*[7]
>
> – *U.S. Marine Operations in Korea*
> History Branch, HQMC

A separate "skirmisher" squad had also preceded each company column. Its job would have eventually been to force its way through enemy lines.

> The first *files* of Chinese skirmishers crept down from the heights opposite the slumbering Marine lines along the northwest, north, and northeast arcs of the Yudam-ni perimeter. *[Italics added].*[8]
>
> – *Chosin,* by Hammel

Such an arrival progression is not the figment of someone's imagination. At the very front of every CCF battalion is known to have been at least one infantry squad that had been specially trained at probing U.S. lines.[9] To do so, it would have needed short-range infiltration skills (how noiselessly to sneak between defender foxholes) or Stormtrooper technique (how by noisy surprise to close with such holes through protective wire). So, at some point, those initial infiltrators and later skirmishers may have come together to perform a joint mission.

After initially helping to probe for gaps in the Marines' lines, those specially configured squads may have tried to divert attention from the sector chosen for the main push, or just sneak

Figure 4.1: U.S. Lines Were Regularly Infiltrated in Korea
(Source: "Corporal Hiroshi N.Miyamura, Korean War," by George Akimoto, U.S.Army Center for Military History, from this url: http://www.history.army.mil/art/A&I/0507-3.jpg.)

a few members in to go after U.S. mortars, rocket launchers, or machineguns. (See Figure 4.1.) All probing progress was then reported to higher headquarters, so that the final assault location could be chosen.

The Possible Chinese Use of WWI Assault Technique

As the large enemy force rolled silently down the rocky and vegetation-free ridge containing the Marines three hours before midnight on 27 November 1950, it fanned out into a long line of extended squad columns. Then came the standard probing of U.S. lines and concentrated assault on a weak spot. To this assault, the Chinese had added overhead machinegun fire and a rolling mortar barrage.

Those Red squad members had access to concussion grenades and bangalore torpedoes made out of bamboo.[10] So, all ordnance was available for a few Stormtrooper-like assaults. Yet, there was probably not much barbed wire around those U.S. hilltop positions, so few identical attempts may have been necessary.

One of the best indicators of the Stormtrooper capability was the formation in which the Red troops had arrived at the objective. A string of company columns could not have secretly marched right up to the foe position and sent hundreds of men off to one side to form an orderly succession of assault lines. Only through a row of squad columns, could it have shown up undetected and ready to attack.

Overall headquarters command and control virtually disappears during any multi-unit assault. However, all the senior Communist commander really needed was an on-line array of semi-autonomous squads, each authorized to breach enemy lines whenever it had the opportunity. (See Figure 4.2.) To forcibly attack while still in column, those squads would have needed a well-thought-out method. While its precise details must remain hypothetical, there are clues in the battle chronicles. They indicate something other than Stormtrooper technique, but still based on the same deception.

> This [the probing and infiltration] was a skillful series of ruses and deployments. . . . Satisfied in time that he had found all that could be revealed, the PLA commander ordered his assault. . . .
>
> [G]renadiers hurled bunches of *concussion stick grenades* [to safely surround his assault troops with supposed 81 mortar impacts] while machineguns on the heights . . . probed the night sky with . . . green tracer [fire]. . . . [It and a] sustained mortar barrage caught many Marines in the open. *[Italics added].*[11]
>
> — *Chosin,* by Hammel

Separate Squad Assaults Against Any Stiff Resistance

Luckily, there is ample evidence of separate Communist squad initiatives after the mortar barrage had been shifted slightly forward. The members of each Red file would have decreased their march interval upon reaching Marines' front line. Only after transiting any barbed wire might they have spread out a little to lessen their chances of being all shot at the same time from the front. However, the night was still quite dark, and they hadn't yet been

Figure 4.2: American Defenders During Rare Dawn Attack

(Source: "American Soldier, 1951," by H.C. McBarron, U.S. Army Ctr. for Mil. Hist., from this url: http://www.history.army.mil/images/artphoto/pripos/amsoldier/5/1951.jpg.)

detected. So, to maintain more control, they may have remained in column formation. Then, to create the impression of mortar rounds still impacting around American foxholes, they tossed concussion grenades.

> At 2125, the mortar eruptions began to walk toward the Marine rear. Whistles screeched, enemy machineguns fell silent, and [thin segments of] the first Chinese assault waves hurled themselves against the juncture of Companies E and F. The enemy attacked *on an extremely narrow front* in order to maintain control. His troops advanced in column within grenade range, then [once through the wire] deployed abruptly into skirmish lines that flailed the Marine positions ceaselessly. . . .
>
> Ultimately, the Reds broke through . . . where the two units were joined. They poured troops into the gap [one squad at a time], and as they attempted to roll back the newly exposed [Marine] flanks, they overran part of Fox Company. *[Italics added].*[12]
>
> — *U.S. Marine Operations in Korea*
> History Branch, HQMC

An attack column would have been already in the right formation to detach segments to assault either flank in a skirmish line. So, any skirmish line activity may have been directed sideways. After the probing or a successful breach, there would have been no more reason for any Red soldier to withhold his small-arms fire. Only, his long-range machineguns would have had to stop shooting into a targeted sector.

> Massed PLA infantry, led by ranks of submachinegunners, tore into the Marine lines, the forward-most three hundred of them driving a wedge at the point where Fox and Easy Companies were joined. . . . [T]he Chinese [subsequently] went [sideways] right after the machineguns supporting the right Fox Company platoon. . . .
>
> . . . First there would be an attack by [concussion] grenadiers, then a lull, then an attack by submachinegunners, then a lull, then another grenade assault.[13]
>
> — *Chosin,* by Hammel

What Continued to Occur at Perimeter Edge

The same routine with grenades and burpguns was also being applied by the Communist squads still in column formation outside the Marines' lines. The grenadiers and submachinegunners may have been one and the same man or just from the same three-man fireteam. One threw concussion grenades, so the other[s] could move forward while defenders had their heads down. Then, the burpgun fire would have discouraged any incoming streams of enemy fire (including that from a bunker aperture).

While this more conventional, "grinding stage" of the attack was undoubtedly designed from above, it was still reliant on frontline opportunism. This is why all assaults had come from slightly different sectors after what amounts to continuous feints. Plus, the long-range BOF machinegunners on the high ground overlooking the Marine position somehow knew when to stop shooting at the start of each surprise assault. It's probably because the battlefield was by now so well illuminated by U.S. flares that they could see the assault get underway. All battlefield signals need not be electronic.

> [T]he nearest heavy machinegun quit firing, and the Chinese mounted another attack.[14]
>
> – *Chosin,* by Hammel

At the Chosin, hilly terrain made overhead machinegun fire possible, whereas flat ground had kept the original Stormtroopers from using it. Those elite German assault troops nevertheless had their own organic LMG nearby.

Other Evidence of the Stormtrooper Capability

At the Chosin Reservoir, the Chinese volunteer army had little artillery of its own.[15] It did, however, have 81mm or 82mm mortars and a full view of the target. So, a mortar barrage could have taken the place of artillery in the Stormtrooper assault method. Grenade bundles would have closely simulated exploding mortar rounds. The Communists were also proficient enough with their mortars to rapidly provide and then shift pinpoint fire. In a later poll of all American defenders in Korea, it was determined that the foe's mortar fire was extremely accurate.[16]

As already noted, the Chinese had bamboo bangalores at Chosin. By this time, they may have also re-engineered the metallic Western version.[17] Yet, some 15 years later, the North Vietnamese Army (NVA) would also find the less noisy bamboo variety more appropriate.[18] Its sound would have more closely matched a mortar impact.

The Chinese Also Helped to Build the New Border Defense

The PVA most certainly showed their North Korean allies how to use the other tactical advance of the WWI Germans—defense in depth through mutually supporting strongpoints. In Korea's mountainous terrain that took fortifying a hilltop as in Figure 4.3. Notice how all the covered trenchlines would have made it difficult to locate the bunkers from the air.

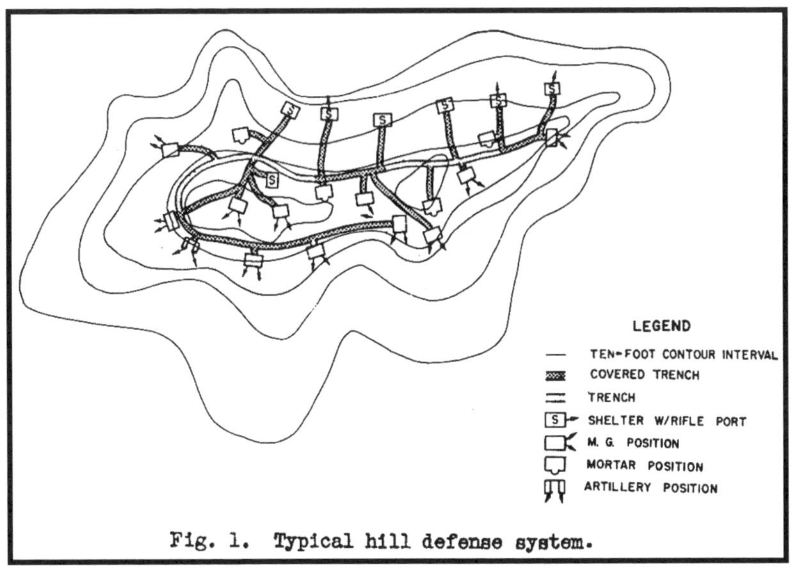

Figure 4.3: The Underground Portion of Every Red Defense
(Source: Excerpt from "Chinese Manual on Field Fortifications," in "A Historical Perspective on Light Infantry," U.S. Army Combat Studies Inst.Research Survey No. 6, p. 85.)

The Chinese Squad in Korea

Each of the erstwhile PLA battalions taking part in the initial NKPA invasion of South Korea had its own heavy machine gun and heavy mortar companies. It was also armed with up to 35 LMGs, 97 submachineguns, and 17 light mortars.[19] This would mean up to 12 LMGs, 32 submachineguns, and two light mortars for each rifle company. That's enough for one LMG and three submachineguns per 10-man squad.

The Chinese PVA later entering the war also had squads consisting of three fireteams, each with three men. However, there had not been enough LMGs for every squad to have one.[20] Luckily, Stormtrooper assault technique didn't require it. But, according to the above annals of Chosin Reservoir combat, some of the men in each PVA squad were carrying a submachinegun. It was probably the Soviet PPSh-41 that had been widely distributed after WWII (and then redesignated by North Korea as Type 49 and by PRC as Type 50).[21] And the stick concussion grenade being thrown was of Chinese Type 23.

U.S. Marine Squad in Korea

The USMC fielded the same 13-man squad in Korea that it had used in WWII. Each fireteam still carried its own M1918A2 BAR.[22]

The U.S. Army Rifle Squad in Korea

The outbreak of hostilities on the Korean Peninsula came too soon after the 1946 Infantry Conference for the Army to have followed through on all suggestions regarding squad composition and utilization. But, similar changes would not be far off. The Conference had recommended that both the squad's size and tactical doctrine be different. The new "improved" squad was to have nine men.[23] The change in its tactics was to be less randomly generated fire and maneuver by internal elements than in WWII.[24] Both modifications would enhance the squad leader's degree of control. Thus implied was a partial return to the unified squad management of WWI. There would now be less risk of internal elements being distracted from their mission by local circumstances. And, every squad member would be more likely to do precisely as directed by tactical doctrine and his chain of command.

Then, early in the Korean deployment, it was determined that a squad with no machinegun lacked sufficient firepower. A single BAR was not getting the job done. With no LMG prototype on the horizon, the U.S. Army decided to increase the number of BARs in each squad to two. Many observers then felt that the nine-man squad organized around two BARs performed well. Those automatic rifles were thought to be effective against Red troops because of the ease with which their 24-pound weight could be carried over the rugged ground of the new war zone.[25]

However, this perceived success of the better-armed squad did not stop the impending refinement of its organization. The ultimate changes would be largely based on the written observations of now famous B.Gen. S.L.A. Marshall and Korean War experiences of Maj. Gen. J.C. Fry.[26]

Marshall had found that U.S. Army units in Korea were often separated—by the broken landscape—into dissimilar and smaller elements. This made command and control difficult. And, there had been more tiny-element engagements than in WWII. As a result, he made three observations: (1) the squad could not function as a unified entity, and often broke up into separate teams; (2) the infantrymen close to the BAR fired their rifles more often than those away from it; and (3) when the BAR was moved tactically from one location to another, a lull occurred in the intensity of combat. Marshal ultimately wanted the nine-man squad subdivided into two four-man teams, each armed with a BAR. In 1953, a change in the Table of Organization and Equipment (TOE) authorized this increase to squad armament.[27]

The combat lessons of Maj.Gen. Fry were then to shape how those two teams would be regularly employed. When Fry was the commander of the Second Infantry Division on the Korean Peninsula, he had instructed his infantry squads to form into two "battle-drill teams" to more easily fire and maneuver. One team would act as a BOF while the other moved forward. And then, by both having their own BAR, they could switch roles. After the war, Fry would claim in the *Combat Forces Journal* that his introduction of "fire-and-maneuver" teams had eliminated those soldiers who would have otherwise not moved forward due to being pinned down by enemy fire.[28]

Though Marshall's observations and Fry's modifications had been acted upon by Army Headquarters, they would also ensure an ongoing debate on squad dynamics after the Korean War.[29] Their ideas on the adoption of identical fireteams would ultimately suggest an enlargement of the squad.[30] And, in 1997, the Chief of Infantry for the U.S. Army declared that the nine-man squad was inflexible and not able to withstand attrition as well as the 11-man squad.[31] Yet, up to the present time, there has been no change to the nine-man format or its tactical contribution to the "bounding-overwatch" strategy.[32]

Thus, the U.S. Army squad has gone from eight men in WWI, to 12 in WWII, back to nine in Korea, up to 10 in Vietnam, and now finally settled on nine. Before the Korean War, various conferences had determined that the larger squad could not fire and maneuver on its own, nor could it be adequately controlled by the squad leader.[33] So, how those two fireteams were to be utilized in combat would be largely dictated by doctrine. Everyone was to do nothing more complicated than a bounding overwatch.[34] In other words, the U.S. Army squad was never to become a dynamic maneuver element—Stormtrooper-like spearpoint, or otherwise.

5 THE VARIOUS SQUADS IN VIETNAM

- Did foe squads in Vietnam use the Stormtrooper method?
- How was it different from the WWII version?

Still no internal machinegun for the American rifle squad.

(Source: FMFM 6-4 [1978], p. 247.)

NVA Using State-of-the-Art Assault Technique

No U.S. military participant of the Vietnam War was ever warned of their enemy using more advanced maneuvers than their own. But afterwards, it became painfully clear that their "underprivileged" foe had routinely applied a close variant of the Germans' evolutionary "noisy-surprise-assault" procedure from WWI.

> Success in the [NVA] attack is dependent on being able to breach the perimeter undetected. The assault is violent and invariably from more than one direction. It begins with a

> preparation, usually mortar and RPG fires. . . . Small arms are not employed except to cover the withdrawal in order to avoid disclosing the location of attacking forces. Once defending troops are forced into the bunkers, penetration of the perimeter is effected. Mortars cease firing, but the illusion of incoming fire is maintained through the use of RPGs, grenades, and satchel charges.[1]
>
> —*NVA-VC Small Unit Tactics & Techniques Study*
> U.S. Department of Defense

The Enemy Assaults Only Appeared to Be Inept

In Vietnam, there were many "seemingly futile" tries by enemy soldiers to loudly break into American bases (as opposed to quietly sneaking in). After U.S. close defensive fires had been briefly applied in the middle of the night, one or two enemy bodies—normally of non-uniformed Viet Cong (VC)—would be found in the perimeter wire the next morning.[2] That's when some blast damage to strategic assets inside the base would also be noticed—like to U.S. command posts, equipment, or supplies. But, because the penetration attempt had been preceded by a brief mortar barrage, no particular significance was attributed to those interior explosions (however suspicious). The guerrilla opposition had failed to get in, and any harm to base property had been the coincidental result of his preliminary bombardment.

This would be the end of the story for a "weapon-focused" society, if not for occasional writings about evolutionary advances to infantry tactics by the German Stormtroopers of WWI. The U.S. military (a victim of the Huns' 1918 Offensive) has never officially acknowledged the power of that new squad assault procedure. But, several of America's subsequent adversaries have. The Japanese applied it on Guadalcanal during WWII, and the Chinese used a maneuver based on the same deception at the Chosin Reservoir in Korea.

Then, some 50 years after the world had first become aware of this tactical milestone, most NVA/VC satchel charges in Vietnam were found to contain no shrapnel.[3] They—like the German and Chinese concussion grenade bundles of previous wars—could have easily created the impression that a U.S. position was only under

82mm mortar attack.[4] The NVA/VC also had at their disposal a bangalore torpedo that was considerably less noisy than its U.S. equivalent. Some made out of bamboo were photographed after the NVA assault on Con Thien in May of 1967.[5] So, one wonders if the Communist Vietnamese had developed a nearly identical variant to the famous Stormtrooper technique.

In the "War to End All Wars," the lone Stormtrooper squad had secretly entered Doughboy lines by first bangaloring the protective wire during a precision artillery barrage and then slightly shifting the barrage.[6] To covertly widen the subsequent penetration, the German assault troops had only to bayonet more U.S. foxhole occupants (as opposed to shooting them) while moving to the left and right.[7] Because there had been no small-arms fire, the majority of American defenders would never realize they were under ground attack.

Years later—with the help of a nearby 61mm mortar—"Chicom" concussion grenades could have accomplished the same secretive entry of a barbed-wire-free U.S. perimeter. And, for the American watchstanders behind a protective barrier, satchel charges could have imitated the 82mm impacts that had just covered the sound of a small bangalore. So, all U.S. personnel headed for Vietnam should have been told about the ongoing state of the art for a "noisy surprise assault." But, no veteran of this war remembers such a briefing. It would take many years of painful experience to relearn the lesson.

The U.S. Air Force Police Discovery

The war in Vietnam was finally forfeited, when Congress realized it could no longer pay for all the materiel being destroyed by enemy action. The total number of parked planes and ammunition dumps lost throughout the conflict would sufficiently quantify the drain on U.S. funds. But, such statistics are hard to find. What is known is that indirect enemy fire had damaged more aircraft than was mathematically possible at Biên Hòa Air Base in 1964 and Da Nang Air Base in 1967. Then, it had destroyed both the ammunition dump and "too many" aircraft at Camp Evans in 1968. While all of this was going on, sappers are known to have gone after aircraft at Camp Holloway Airfield in 1962, Da Nang Air Base in 1965, Marble

Mountain Air Facility in 1965, and Kontum Airfield in 1968. At the Chu Lai Air Base and Marble Mountain Air Facility in 1965, Chu Lai Air Base again in 1968, and Cu Chi Army Airfield (near the tunnels) in 1969, VC indirect fire had landed while the sappers attacked.[8]

Still, any official recognition of an enemy indirect-fire ruse took a long time coming. At Chu Lai in 1965, the planes had not been pre-rigged with explosives, but rather sprayed with "Tommy Gun" fire as satchel charges were tossed up their tail pipes.[9] The foe's use of timed satchel charges did not become apparent until around 1968. That's when the in-country "Stars and Stripes" newspaper carried a story of six or seven helicopters all being destroyed at the same time at Da Nang's Marble Mountain Air Facility by a "lucky string of mortar rounds."[10] The odds of such an occurrence are, of course, astronomical. Either a detonation cord daisy chain or series of timed charges would have been necessary to accomplish such a feat. Timed ordnance was also likely when the An Hoa ammunition dump finally went up around dawn on 23 February 1969 after mortar shells had ineffectually landed by the hundreds atop its heavily reinforced bunkers throughout the night.[11]

U.S. artillery and their pallets of unprotected shells were also a favorite target of the VC and NVA. Satchel-charge-throwing sappers were involved in their destruction at Firebases "Maury I" in May 1968, "Airborne" in May 1969, "Henderson" in May 1970, and "Mary Ann" in March 1971. At Henderson and Mary Ann, all incoming mortar rounds are known to have been preceded by enemy sappers.[12] In all other cases, opposition commandos had supposedly snuck through a screen of fully alert U.S. perimeter guards while preparatory mortar fire masked their wire clipping or other penetration sounds.

Then, came the official realization of what had been happening. At Biên Hòa Air Base in 1972, after witnessing several "overly effective" mortar attacks against American aircraft over the years, U.S. Air Force Police finally connected the dots. On this particular occasion, it was the bomb storage area theoretically under bombardment, but without any indirect-fire impacts being reported at that location.

> A sapper attack took place on 12 Jan. 1972, resulting in the . . . [nearly total destruction] of the ammo dump at Biên Hòa Air Base. On that fateful night, explosions began at the

> bomb dump. . . . We initially thought it was another rocket attack but no one reported [rocket] impacts . . . except in the ammo dump. [Thus, there had been explosions of some other origin at the bomb depository.] [13]
>
> — U.S. Air Force,
> 3rd Security Police Squadron report

The Never Fully Explained Events at Cam Lo

During the early morning hours of 26 August 1966, a U.S. Marine outpost at Cam Lo was partially overrun just south of the Demilitarized Zone (DMZ). (See Map 5.1.)

> At 260340H [0340 on 26 August]. Company A, located at the artillery positions at Cam Lo, began to receive heavy incoming mortar and S/A [small arms] rounds. During the next 1-1/2 hours, Company A's lines were penetrated by an estimated 2 Companies of VC and NVA.[14]
>
> —"1st Bn., 4th Marines Command Chronology"

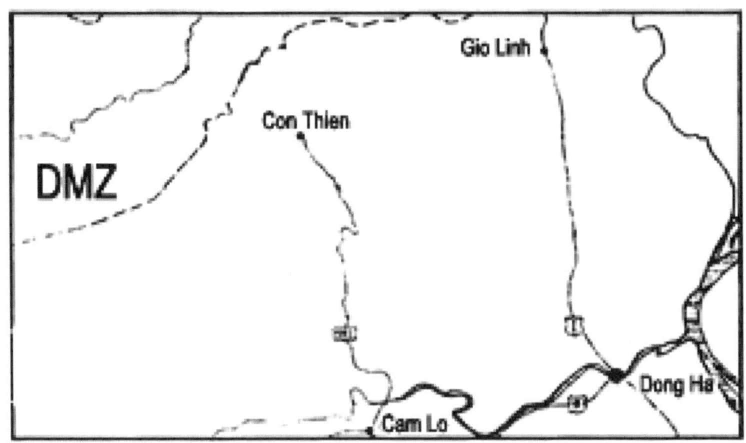

Map 5.1: Cam Lo Was Only Nine Miles from the DMZ
(Source: Map based on illustration designator "amtrac.org - bullalo03.jpg," from official website for 1st Amtrac Battalion.)

The official battle chronicle admits to some "infiltrators" tossing satchel charges at the center of the base (near the artillery's Fire Direction Center [FDC]) before their parent unit was able to force its way through the outer perimeter.[15] How this paradox was resolved at the time is only partially correct. According to the Battalion Commander, the first wave had been so skilled as to pass unseen around the fighting holes of his fully alerted frontline infantrymen. A few had passed through his perimeter alright, but probably on the side expecting attack. That, after all, is the Chinese way of taking this kind of objective. (Look back at Figure 1.3.)

> They [the NVA] snuck on through before we even illuminated the area. . . . [A]s you know, they're real[ly] proficient at moving at night . . . very silently, very slowly, and very patiently. . . . [The NVA] did get through even though our people were waiting for them. They crawled in between the holes, and our people never really realized that they passed through their positions.[16]
>
> —1/4 Battalion Commander, right after the attack

But, there would also be hand-held explosives thrown at the frontline positions. From a distance, they too looked like preparatory mortar fire. But, two enlisted Marines had already learned of the trick.

> At 0300 hours, I woke [Mike] Strickland who took over the watch [at the machinegun position on the north end and highest part of the camp]. . . . I was just laying there . . . when I heard a blast followed quickly by a second and third blast. . . . [S]everal more blasts went off . . . near the center of the perimeter. . . . Mike realized that the blast was not mortar rounds impacting as they were throwing an inordinate amount of sparks; they were grenades or satchel charges.
>
> Suddenly, trip flares started going off, mostly on the southern and southeastern edges of perimeter. . . .
>
> . . . The NVA and VC attack [on that sector of the lines] was supported by heavy automatic weapons fire.[17]
>
> — Pete Mancuso, A/1/4 machinegunner at Cam Lo

> [Now legendary Sgt.] Price . . . also mentioned that the NVA

> would take these blocks of C-4 and as they came close to the perimeter . . . throw them at the fortifications. The Marines in the fighting positions would believe it was incoming 82mm mortars rounds and crouch down and not see the NVA coming into the lines. Sergeant Price explained that is what the NVA did in the early part of the attack. It was not mortar rounds that were hitting the perimeter. . . . He was right. I do not remember the popping sound the mortar makes as it leaves the tube.[18]
>
> — Larry Schorr, 2nd Platoon member of A/1/4

Further Details of the Battle

Of note for all Western tacticians, the successive steps in this NVA battle plan weren't coordinated through electronic transmissions. The sight and/or sound of one milestone had simply signalled the next. What subsequently developed can best be described as a natural (and completely logical) flow of events. (See Table 5.1.) This means every participant (of whatever rank) could have easily followed its progress, and thereby insured a timely contribution.

MAIN ASSAULT FORCE COMES NONE TOO SECRETLY FROM THE SOUTH
SAPPERS USE THE DIVERSION TO SNEAK INTO TARGET FROM THE NORTH
INTERIOR SATCHEL CHARGE EXPLOSIONS SIGNAL SOUTHERN ASSAULT
A FEW MORTAR ROUNDS COVER SOUND OF BANGALORES IN THE WIRE
ASSAULT TROOP SATCHEL CHARGES SIMULATE MORE MORTAR IMPACTS
ELEVATED ENEMY MACHINEGUNS FIRE ONLY AT RED-TRACER SOURCES

Table 5.1: The Natural Flow of What Happened at Cam Lo

The enemy's only initial small-arms fire had been from long-range machineguns. Those guns could accurately counter the Marines' close-defensive fires, because the main part of the attack had come down from higher ground. From there, the origin and impact of all U.S. red and NVA green tracer streams would have been clearly visiblc.

At Cam Lo, 82mm mortar fire had covered the sound of bangalores, and satchels simulated other mortar impacts. However, the attackers had also made good use of smaller grenades. In fact, they may have had access to the latest Chinese concussion grenade. (See Figure 5.1.) It and a bayonet or rifle butt could have proven lethal in close combat. Only Western forces had yet to acknowledge the "surprise-and-shock-producing" relevance of such a grenade to offensive combat.

Some 10 months after the Cam Lo struggle, events just to the north of there would again confirm the use of Stormtrooper-like assaults from WWI. (Look back at Map 5.1.)

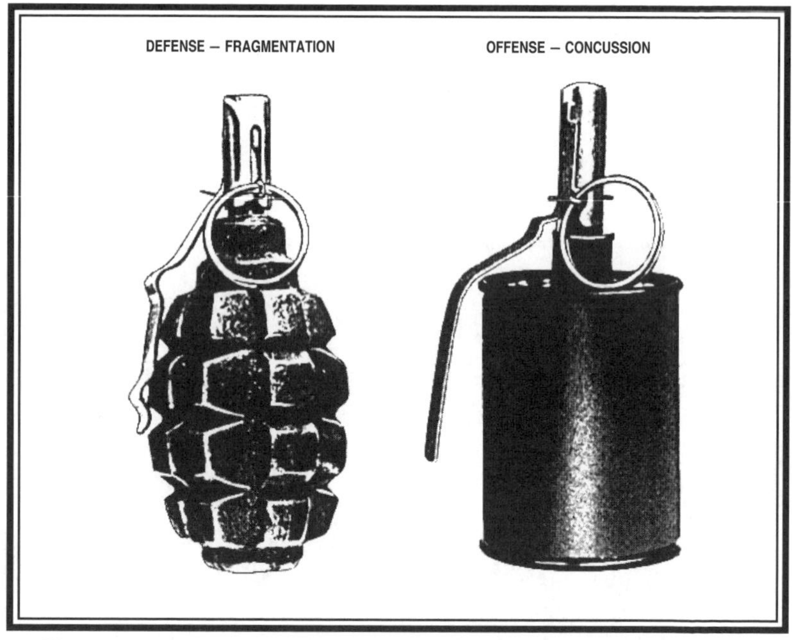

Figure 5.1: PLA Had New Grenades for Separate Purposes
(Source: "Handbook on the Chinese Communist Army," DA Pamphlet 30-51 [1960], U.S. Army, figure 72, p. 74.)

The Major Attack on Con Thien

Missionaries had called this place the "Hill of Angels." In May 1967, far too many men of 1st Battalion, 4th Marines (1/4) found out just how badly the NVA wanted it on the anniversary of Dien Bien Phu.

Con Thien Combat Base was on a 158-meter rise some 10 miles northwest of the big U.S. installation at Dong Ha. Each could be just barely seen from the other. Only two miles below Vietnam's DMZ, Con Thien sat within a small indentation to that invisible boundary. It was surrounded by elephant grass and three types of trees growing in clumps no taller than 12 feet. The camp sat atop a squat pile of red mud. This was to be the key U.S. bastion along the McNamara Line—a bulldozed firebreak to limit enemy incursion. In May 1967, this firebreak was 200 meters wide and 10,600 meters long. It ran all the way from Con Thien eastward to Gio Linh on Route 1.[19] (See Map 5.2.)

Brief Summary of the Battle

At 0255, a green flare lit up the sky south of Con Thien. Then, the base was hit by hundreds of 82mm and 61mm mortar rounds. Under cover of this bombardment, tiny enemy elements with bangalore torpedoes and satchel charges gained entry to the northeastern part of the perimeter at two separate locations.[20] Killed in those penetrations had been many frontline defenders and the U.S. 81mm mortar crew.[21] Then, around 0400, parts of two NVA battalions came flooding through those two breaches in the protective wire. As desperate hand-to-hand fighting ensued, the battalion Executive Officer (XO) sent a relief force to Delta Company via Amtrac. Unfortunately, that tiny mechanized column would come under lethal attack from enemy flame throwers.

Long before those large-scale penetrations, most of the base's ability to light up the battlefield had been removed. The only artillery with enough range to reach Con Thien was the 175mm guns at Gio Linh, but they lacked an illumination round. So, until a C-47 "flare ship" showed up, the fight went on in the dark.[22] There had been no overhead enemy machinegun support, because Con Thien's low hill mass sat just barely above a fairly level plain.

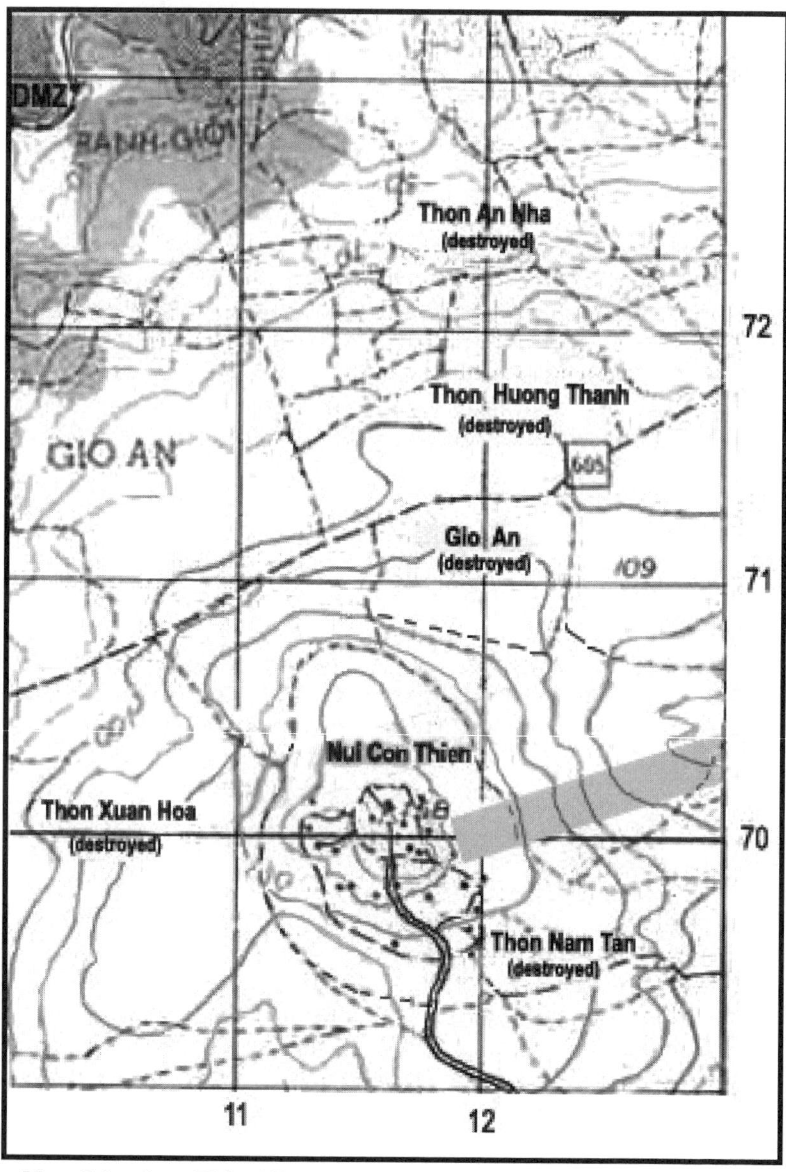

Map 5.2: Con Thien Base and Likely Trace of McNamara Line
(Source: Map based on "1:50,000 USGS, Vietnam Series L7014, Map Sheet 6342-1" and Lt. McDonnell's "Hill of Angels" article at official website for 1st Amtrac Battalion.)

This life-or-death struggle continued until well after dawn. When the last tiny groups of enemy attackers had finally been driven from the perimeter, at least five pieces of heavy U.S. equipment were found to be totally destroyed. There were 44 Marines dead (almost half from Delta [23]) and another 110 injured. The enemy had lost 197 killed and eight captured (probably after being wounded). He had also left behind 72 weapons of various kinds.[24] This had been a concerted effort by the NVA, but Con Thien was still in Marine hands.

Preliminary Details

In the final analysis, squads of enemy soldiers had once again broken through American lines to facilitate a larger assault. Their diminutive bangalores had been masked by 82mm mortar fire, and then their shrapnel-free satchel charges had imitated continuing mortar impacts. While such a ruse came largely as a surprise to Con Thien's leaders, it had been previously experienced by Marines in WWI, WWII, and Korea.

> At 0245H on 8 May, Companies A and D with the Alpha [more likely Bravo] Command Group at Con Thien came under an intensive 82mm mortar attack, followed by a ground attack from the east in Company D sector. Sapper units breached the wire under cover of a mortar barrage with bangalore torpedoes and moved small units inside the wire. These small elements were heavily armed with satchel charges and TNT charges and used them to blow bunkers and trench lines. At approximately 0400H, two battalions of NVA attacked the perimeter through the breach made by the sapper units armed with flamethrowers, RPG [rocket-propelled grenade] . . . launcher and various assortments of small arms, explosives, etc. . . . Company A was directed to send a platoon reaction force to assist Company D as well as escort two LVTs [Landing Vehicles Tracked] and two M-42's [Army self-propelled 40mm anti-aircraft guns] with ammo resupply. *En route* to Company D's right flank, the right rear sprocket of the leading LVT became enmeshed in barbed wire, freezing and stopping the vehicle. The vehicle

> came under fire and the M-42's and one LVTH [probably just a plain LVT without the howitzer] were struck by RPG rockets and set afire trapping personnel inside. The other LVTH was set afire with a satchel charge. The penetration was limited and the breach in the perimeter was closed just prior to daylight.[25]
>
> — "1/4 After-Action Report for 8 May 1967"

Of note was how many satchel charges had been carried to simulate mortar fire and Chicom grenades to kill U.S. foxhole occupants.

> 080245H to 081100H–the Con Thien perimeter vic YD 117-701 was attacked with a coordinated mortar attack and infantry assault by an estimated NVA Bn (rein). The Con Thien position received 250 to 300 rounds of 82mm/60mm mortar fire. The enemy assault troops breached defensive wire with bamboo Bangalore torpedoes and satchel charges, scattered pockets of resistance were driven out of the position as late as 080730H with some enemy stragglers still in contact as late as 081100H. Retreating NVA were taken under fire by Arty, air and friendly ambush (D/2/1/4). . . .
>
> Weapons [captured]: 42 AK47's, 5 SKS, 19 B-40 (RPG), 3 flamethrowers (LPO), 3 RPD [light machineguns], *100 Chicom grenades,* 5,000 rds. 7.62mm ammo, 470 lbs. TNT (taken from satchel charges and bamboo Bangalore torpedoes). . . .
>
> Conclusion: the NVA attack on Con Thien was well planned and rehearsed. . . . *The assault troops, to a man, carried satchel charges*. . . . Small pennant shaped paper-flags, stuck in 6-inch-long reeds and then stuck into the earth were used to mark the lanes through the barbed wire. *[Italics added.]* [26]
>
> — "1/4's Intelligence Summary for 7-8 May 1967"

There Had Been a Pair of Stormtrooper-Like Penetrations

Some of those initial mortar impacts had actually been bangalores in the wire, RPG hits on bunkers, and then shrapnel-free satchel charges along the perimeter trench. As Delta Company personnel hunkered down to escape the apparent shelling, those at the point of attack may have been consecutively grenaded from the side. Retired CWO-4 Guthrie remembers many being later found dead in their holes.[27]

Con Thien's perimeter assignments for that night can now be fairly accurately ascertained. (See Map 5.3.) The Amtrac lieutenant who accompanied the counterattack force remembers the initial enemy mortar sheaf being "extended" to the south side of the base. This could mean the initial barrage had been shifted forward to protect the assault troops. They, in turn, had been throwing explosives to keep up the impression of nearby mortar impacts. The lieutenant's statement also reveals the location of the second line breach. It was where Delta Company tied in with the northern contingent of ARVNs (Army of the Republic of Vietnam). According to the "1/4 After-Action Report," the first had occurred in the eastern part of Delta's sector (near the Strip).[28]

> The defense of Con Thien consisted of Delta Company 1/4 and a company of ARVN regulars with attached regional paramilitary irregulars [around the northern part] . . . . [W]e [the Amtracs and Alpha 1/4] set in on the south side of Con Thien. . . .
>
> . . . Delta's lines tied into the ARVN on their left and with the Strip on the right. The ARVNs [also] held the [small segment of] line from Delta . . . to the Strip. . . .
>
> About 0300 on the 8th of May, an extremely intense and sustained mortar barrage hit Delta's lines. Soon after, as we monitored the net, we heard Captain . . . [Juul] advise the 1/4 XO that he had NVA in the wire. . . .
>
> Over the next ten to fifteen minutes, as the mortars kept coming—*now on us as well,* it became evident that Delta was being penetrated. The NVA were through the wire and throwing satchel charges in Delta's bunkers and trenchlines. . . . *Captain . . . [John F. Juul] reported . . . he thought the NVA had breached the line where they tied in to the ARVNs.* He was also asking for reinforcements [of personnel] and ammo.
>
> . . . By the time I got to Delta's CP [(Command Post) around dawn], *Streck [and his subsequent Amtrac relief column] had moved west to where the Delta lines had met the ARVNs. His action was credited with sealing the [second]*

> *breach* and trapping many NVA in the lines where they were now being slaughtered. *[Italics added.]* [29]
>
> — Lieutenant Patrick J. McDonnell
> Commander of 4th Plt., Bravo Co.,1st Amtracs

The enlisted commander of the lead Amtrac during the initial counterattack confirms that opposition troops had been coming into the Allied base from the northwest.

> [T]here was lots of gunfire and explosions about 0300 hours. . . . We were to take ammo and Marines to the other side of the perimeter. I was informed that my Amtrac was to take point and that Lt. McDonnell was riding with me and taking command of the relief convoy. . . .
>
> As we were moving northeast toward Delta Company positions there was big flash of light and a[n] explosion and we were stopped. . . .
>
> The NVA came from the left front (northwest direction—from inside and outside of the perimeter). . . .
>
> The NVA occupied the fighting positions . . . which the ARVN had vacated on the 7th of May. The NVA was to our front, to the left and the right.[30]
>
> — Cpl. Aldo Betta
> Commander of lead counterattack Amtrac

Concussion grenades had also played an important part in the proceedings. They would have simulated 61mm mortar fire and been easier to carry than satchels. That's why the "1/4 After-Action Report" had distinguished "TNT charges" from "satchel charges,"[31] and an enlisted Amtracker called them by their more formal name.

> French told me later that he had seen me fall among the small-arms fire and *concussion* grenades.[32]
>
> — Lieutenant Patrick J. McDonnell
> Commander of 4th Plt., Bravo Co.,1st Amtracs

Chicom fragmentation grenades had also been available in considerable quantity, according to "1/4's Intelligence Summary."[33] They were almost certainly reserved for dropping from close range into a defender's dugout. Only in this way could they have safely taken the place of bayonets in a Stormtrooper-like assault. Like

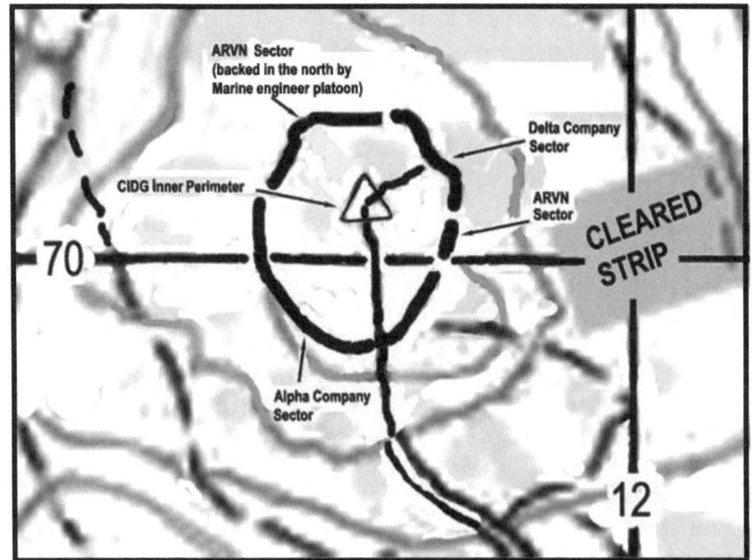

Map 5.3: How Security Sectors May Have Been Assigned
(Source: Map based on "1:50,000 USGS, Viet.Series L7014, Map Sheet 6342-1"; McDonnell's article; Guthrie's e-mails; foxco-2ndbn-9thmarines.com/ConThienFSB.gif.)

RPG hits, those "frag" grenades would have looked and sounded to a distant watchstander like precision 61mm mortar fire. But, for the poor Marine and ARVN troops on the receiving end, they had unexpectedly arrived from a flank. In the dark, a dull "thunk" would have been indistinguishable from all the other noise. From each penetration site, a few enemy soldiers must have crawled both ways along the front lines to roll a frag into each successive hole or bunker.

Likely Overall Scenario

The Amtrac lieutenant had acknowledged ARVN defenders on either side of Delta Company. And, the Delta commander had reported "NVA . . . [breaching] his lines where they tied in to the

ARVNs." That there had been two separate breaches by different battalions was heavily inferred by the A/1/4 historian, official battle chronicle,[34] and "1/4 After-Action Report."[35] A full-strength NVA battalion would have contained about 350 men. According to the Amrackers, one breach had been to the east near the Strip and the other at the northern end of the base.[36] (Look once again at Map 5.3.)

Both breaches had come at the junction of Marine and ARVN lines. So, like in the Chinese effort at Chosin, battalion infiltration scouts had located the weakest spots in Con Thien's perimeter defense. Then, they or other infiltrators had snuck in to destroy the U.S. 81mm mortar position (stopping all far-reaching illumination for a while).

Next, came the main push against the Allies' front lines. While still in column formation, "sapper units" (the equivalent of "company skirmisher squads" in Korea) had bangalored the perimeter wire during a mortar barrage. They had then closed with the closest Allied foxholes by throwing enough satchel charges to simulate a continuation of the now shifted shelling. Those successfully penentrating squads were soon joined by sister squads intent on widening each breach.[37] All members of a column have only to face to the left or right to assault sideways on line. (See Figure 5.2.) After any line breakthrough, Chinese assault doctrine heavily encourages exploitation of the opposition's now unprotected flanks.[38] And at Cam Lo, one frontline defender had been knocked in the head by an NVA who had come at him from the side.[39]

The enemy's assault technique had been so ingenious that it really didn't matter the base had been forewarned of attack by one of its ambushes. Grandfathers of those young Leathernecks' had been similarly tricked during the German Offensives of 1918, but its significance to future combat had never been fully assimilated in the West.

After the initial fighting had subsided, one could see that the enemy had been hurt. However, he had still done fairly well under the circumstances. Besides capturing sizeable portions of the Allies' lines, his "small elements" had removed the Americans' illumination capability. Then, follow-on forces from two separate NVA battalions (and carrying flame throwers) had destroyed two U.S. Amtracs, two (or three) Army Dusters, a quarter-ton truck, and an ONTOS (six 106 mm recoilless rifles mounted upon a tracked vehicle).[40] In addition, three Marine tanks and a road grader had been damaged.[41]

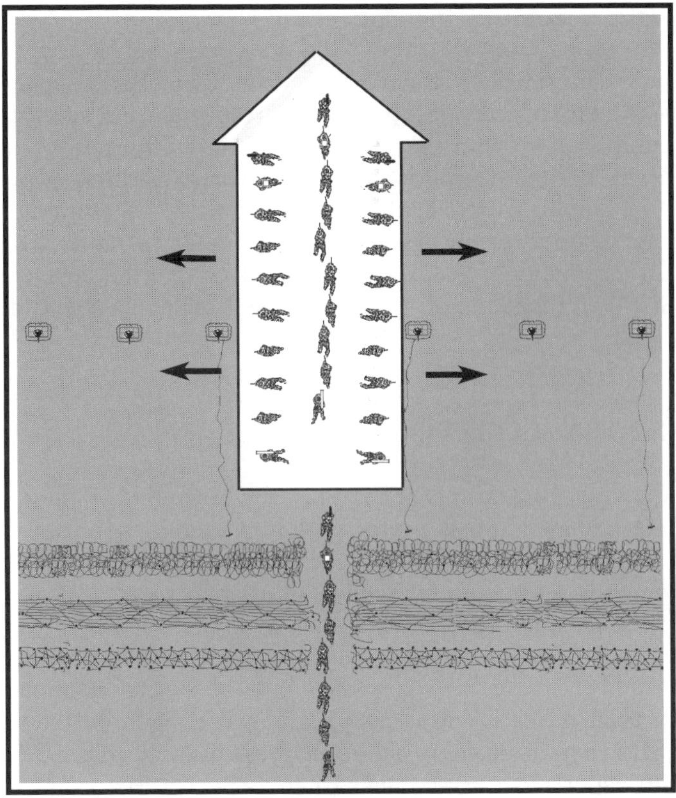

Figure 5.2: How Successive Red Columns Broaden a Wedge

So, one has to wonder how this many enemy soldiers got close enough to expensive U.S. equipment to require its replacement. The ARVNs and their irregular attachments cannot be singularly blamed for what happened at Con Thien. Perhaps, the real problem lay in enough enemy expertise at light infantry tactics to conduct 3GW against 2GW-focused Americans.

What Has Become of the Battlefield Lesson

Most contemporary U.S. infantrymen and special operators have now heard of Stormtrooper assault technique, but cannot fully describe its steps. That may be the result of willful negligence on the part of various leaders. Because surprise and firepower are interchangeable in battle, those who regularly bolster the U.S. economy through firepower will seldom defer to its substitute. Nor will a command in search of total control over all subordinate elements dwell for long on what a semi-autonomous squad might accomplish.

The Enemy Squad in Vietnam

Following the example of the PLA, the NVA likely fielded a 10-man infantry squad in Vietnam. It had a squad leader and three fireteams of three men apiece. All members were exceptionally well versed in light infantry tactics. Most had spent a whole year training militiamen before being allowed to head south.

> The typical North Vietnamese regular fighting in the South was twenty-three years old—four years older than his U.S. counterpart. . . . [H]e had already logged three years of compulsory service, undergoing military training and also instructing local militia.[42]
>
> — *Vietnam Experience: A Contagion of War,* by Maitland and McInerney

Those NVA fireteams were probably all armed in the same way and thus good at fire and movement.

> On Operation Buffalo in Vietnam, the North Vietnamese used fire team rushes. Their three-man fire teams were so well camouflaged as to become almost invisible when they stopped in the waist-high elephant grass.[43]
>
> — *Operation Buffalo,* by Nolan

This means the average NVA squad didn't have its own LMG,

only one sometimes attached.[44] That gun would have been the Chinese version of a Soviet RPD and fire around 650-750 rounds per minute.[45] With built-in bipod, it only weighed 17 pounds empty.[46] Then in 1967, the Type 67 with a tripod attachment may have become partially available.

Meanwhile, the Main Force VC infantry squad was organized somewhat differently. Consisting of only nine men, it had a squad leader, assistant squad leader, LMG man, and two three-man fireteams.[47] So, it did have its own LMG.

The Chinese Communists had already provided the PAVN with a refined version of the Type 23 stick concussion grenade.[48] The PAVN and VC would have used it, a more modern equivalent (as in Figure 5.1), or a satchel charge to simulate indirect fire. All grenades would have sounded like a light mortar, and the satchel charge like an 82mm.

An NVA command specializing in assault technique must have been providing the "special-assignment squads," which were attached to VC regional forces during the Vietnam War.[49] That these "special units" cooperated with artillery suggests Stormtrooper technique. According to VC sapper Nguyen Van Mo, personnel from these special units would often personally cut or bangalore the enemy's protective wire.[50] Local VC fighters had already performed much of the interior reconnaissance for NVA attacks,[51] so most had a good working knowledge of short-range infiltration.[52] But, after the heavy losses suffered by the VC during the Tet Offensive, all sapper operations in South Vietnam became closely supervised by the NVA's 429th Sapper Group. This Group reported directly to a tiny offshoot of the NVA High Command. And few of the subsequent VC operations were conducted without special training at Group camps.[53]

All the while, regular NVA infantrymen were also being shown how to perform perimeter penetrations through sapper technique.[54] During Operation Buffalo in 1967, NVA soldiers were observed assaulting segments of a Marine column by throwing TNT charges following a mortar and artillery barrage.[55]

The U.S. Marine Squad in Vietnam

HQMC switched to a 14-man infantry squad for the Vietnam War.

Figure 5.3: On-Line GIs During Typical "Search and Destroy" Sweep

(Source: "American Soldier, 1966," McBarron, url: https://upload.wikimedia.org/wikipedia/commons/8/8e/The_American_Soldier%2C_1966_-_H._Charles_McBarron.jpg.)

An M79 grenade launcher man had been added to three four-man fireteams.[56] Within every fireteam, the role of the machine rifle was now filled by an M16A1 that could be fired on full automatic.[57]

The U.S. Army Squad in Vietnam

After Korea, the U.S. Army again changed its infantry squad size. Despite the agreement of four more studies with the 1946 conference, Army leaders increased the squad's size from nine men to 11, thus returning to the 1940's doctrine of fire and maneuver. Now present were a squad leader and two five-man fireteams (Alpha and Bravo), each having its own BAR. Such a structure was thought to absorb casualties while still permitting an internal fire-and-movement capability.[58]

Then, under the ROAD (Reorganization Objective Army Divisions) structure in 1963, that infantry squad was reduced to 10 men. There would now be two fireteams (each missing the scout), and an extra rifleman with whom the squad leader could do what he wished.[59] But, his maneuver options during a multi-unit on-line sweep would be few. After being deployed to Vietnam, he had to hope his sweep segment would not be the one to stumble upon a prepared enemy position. (See Figure 5.3.)

At first in Vietnam, U.S. Army infantry squads were equipped with the M14 rifle. However, certain design features of the M14 troubled frontline soldiers. Chambering a 7.62x51mm NATO (North Atlantic Treaty Organization) round, it weighed nine pounds and was thus hard to carry. The large caliber bullets also gave the M14 a tendency to climb when fired on automatic (difficult to keep on target). Such factors limited its effectiveness on patrols in the jungle.[60] Then, in 1965, the much-lighter M16 rifle replaced the M14 as the infantry's primary weapon. This new rifle's problems with jamming were largely resolved in 1967, with the issuance of the M-16A1.[61] Still, its close manufacturing tolerances would not permit much mud.

In 1973, the U.S. Army once again increased the size of its rifle squad to 11 men. The infantry experience in Vietnam had been the contributing factor. The extent of small-unit action had resulted in too many casualties for proper squad functioning. And the smaller structure had not well enough facilitated fire and maneuver. In

1975, a second study recommended the U.S. Army retain an 11-man squad with two five-man fireteams.[62] (As the infantry become more motorized, that number has since be fallen to nine.[63])

U.S. Army infantry squads had long suffered from a deficiency in firepower, because the BAR couldn't adequately take the place of an actual LMG. During the Vietnam War, veterans had wanted an M-60 carried by every infantry squad to ensure its fire superiority over an enemy counterpart. However, many of the studies and experiments had warned the gun would slow down the squad's movement.[64] So, in 1973, the recommendation to add an organic Stoner 63A or M60 machinegun was not adopted. Some M16A1's could be fired on full automatic and thus function as a machine rifle. The M249 SAW (Squad Automatic Weapon) was not to appear on the scene until the mid-1980's.[65] It too would lack the accuracy of tripod-mounted machinegun.

Moving On

How each squad is configured and armed will largely dictate how it can be utilized in the future. If its dimensions and weaponry have been largely based on strict compliance with orders and a firepower agenda, then it may have difficulty functioning semi-autonomously at some later date. The lethality of modern-day weaponry has made further dispersion of the infantry a nonnegotiable requirement. The next part of this book will investigate how each squad should be composed to singularly perform the most common battlefield missions.

Part Two

Squad Use Largely Dictated by Structure and Arms

"In most Marine infantry units today, the squad is regarded as merely a subset of the platoon." — William S. Lind

(Source: Attributed to William S. Lind, tactical adviser to 29th Marine Commandant.)

6 Deliberate Attack

- What exactly is a deliberate attack?
- Which squad configuration best facilitates one?

What a U.S. sweep segment may encounter well hidden.

(Source: FM 7-8 [1984], p. 3-28; MCO P1500.44B, p. 14-18.)

The Poorly Obeyed Attack Axiom

Safely to occupy a prepared enemy position (one with protective wire, land mines, and/or interlocking machinegun fire), an infantry outfit must conduct a "deliberate attack." This is one that has been carefully preplanned—minimally through reconnaissance of the target location and rehearsal of how sequentially to counter its various defensive aspects.[1]

Yet, in Vietnam, most of the foe's stationary strongpoints had been so well camouflaged they only became visible after contesting a broad U.S. sweep. Herein lay the problem. The standard Yank sweep was considered so powerful by its designers it could never bog down. Its path had been under Harassing and Interdiction (H&I) artillery fire for months, helicopter gunships continuously overflew it, and member units were allowed to reconnoiter by fire. (Look back at Figure 5.3.)

So, what normally ensued upon contact with a hidden enemy bastion was the rapid transition by part of the U.S. sweep line into a "hasty-attack" mode. That's why the unit involved could seldom succeed without excess casualties.

> In practice, the [hasty] attack by "fire and movement" often failed miserably....
>
> The fact is that open-order tactics of "fire and movement" were sometimes appropriate in mobile warfare, if the defender was caught unprepared and could not coordinate fire effectively. . . . However, in World War I, trench warfare on the Western Front proved that linear frontal attacks against prepared defenses did not work.[2]
>
> — U.S. Marine Corps, MCI 7401

One U.S. Marine company commander in the An Hoa area remembers never even hearing of a deliberate attack in eight full months of intermittently heavy contact. Might U.S. forces have become so impressed with their firepower-induced freedom of movement, that they forgot about their occasional need for a deliberate attack? The principal U.S. Army manual on the subject goes so far as to imply that any pre-recognized enemy stronghold should first be tested with a hasty attack.

> The deliberate attack is a fully coordinated operation that is usually reserved for those situations in which the enemy defense cannot be overcome by a hasty attack.[3]
>
> — U.S. Army, FM 3-21.8 of March 2007
> (predecessor to FM 7-8)

Only if this hasty attack on an opposition bastion could be partially launched and then immediately withdrawn, would it serve any useful purpose (as in a probing attack). However, American sweeps are thought to generate valuable momentum. And they are difficult for their overall commander to slow down, much less back up a little.

The Generally Accepted U.S. Way of War?

The hasty attack against stiff resistance took one of three forms in Vietnam: (1) all members shooting during a stand-up frontal assault; (2) a whole unit advancing though small-unit rushes; or (3) part of the unit outflanking the main source of enemy fire while the rest attempted to achieve fire superiority ("bounding overwatch.") Because all three options had only been previously tried under different circumstances, their current participants suffered unexpected casualties.

There is a more rapid type of deliberate attack that was used by the German Stormtroopers of WWI. It involved "recon pull" and enough experience to know defender tricks. Why then had the Stormtroopers' singular assault procedure worked? It had gotten the job done, because all quarries had been following the same MLR model, and the Germans' attack method had been so deceptive as to be never fully understood by their Western opposition. The U.S. military won't be able to match the feat with its standardized deliberate-attack procedures, because they are so highly publicized and devoid of surprise.

When up against an enemy of any proficiency, a steady diet of hasty attacks could thus prove quite debilitating. And repeatedly placing U.S. troops into this compromising a situation did not just come from having to operate in someone else's backyard. After regularly conducting multi-unit "pushes" throughout two world wars and Korea, the occasionally ill-fated hasty attack had become an inescapable part of the American way of war. Its origin had been fairly obvious: trying to overwhelm everyone in the way with economy-enhancing firepower.

What U.S. Commandos Have Generally Managed to Avoid

American special operators are good at what they do, but normally able to bypass the more unpleasant aspects of a frontline defense. They are deposited by parachute or helicopter behind enemy lines, and then only occasionally asked to penetrate a "softer" rear-area position. Their normal mission is to reconnoiter that position from a distance or adjust the bombardment. Yet, of late, SOCOM has been given most of this nation's expeditionary assignments.

The U.S. Infantryman's Lot

Meanwhile, America's infantryman have been held mostly in reserve. During the Operation Desert Storm, one whole Marine task force was left to languish aboard ship as a high-level feint. While "the grunts" are still thought to a home for slow thinkers, the light infantry field is actually the most complicated of all occupational specialities. Infantry personnel additionally face the most danger in combat. Their risk comes not from wandering around alone in a hostile area, but from regularly having to move upright through enemy machinegun fire. That's why surviving veterans of the Korean and Vietnam Wars so often talk about going "high-diddle-diddle-up-the-middle." And with America's growing aversion to combat casualties, this is also why U.S. "ground pounders" are so seldom summoned.

The Various Problems Involved

While the U.S. infantry manuals do offer one or two deliberate-attack options for both daylight and nighttime, they generally skip any mention of opposition wire, mines, or interlocking machinegun fire. (See Figure 6.1.) Only part of this oversight is justifiable. To stay hidden since late in WWII, America's adversaries weren't able to erect much barbed wire. However, they do continue to use claymores,[4] and continuous streams of grazing fire from rearward positions.[5]

So, though American units almost never run a deliberate attack in actual combat, it would still be nice to know which U.S. squad configuration might best facilitate one. And of specific interest would be how to get through the wire, mines, and band of bullets. Among other pitfalls would be forward-deployed enemy ambushes or roving outposts. And, once a Western-looking "defensive line" had been penetrated, there is also the little problem of dealing with the firesacks in each apparent gap between actual squad strongpoints.

Because America's Eastern adversaries have placed more emphasis on infantry utilization than the Pentagon, their ways of handling the various impediments to a deliberate attack will also be considered. They need not ever be adopted by GIs for their lesson to be useful.

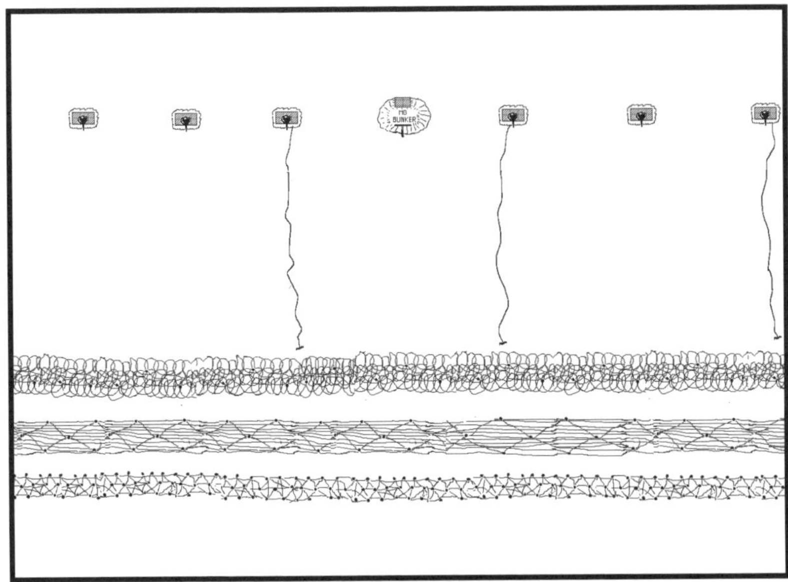

Figure 6.1: What Only a Deliberate Attack Can Handle
(Source: "The Last Hundred Yards," Posterity Press, 1997, © 1994, 1995, 1996, 1998, by H.J. Poole, figs. 18.7, 19.3, 20.9.)

Getting Through the Wire

Where a barbed-wire barrier has been erected to the front of an objective, the attacking unit will need more than just impromptu cutting to get through it. To simply be delayed near it could mean getting cut to pieces by enemy fire. There are several ways to breach or cross such an obstacle. (See Figure 6.2.) Then, the transiting unit must make as wide, irregular, and shifting a target as possible to keep from every member getting shot at the same time. (See Figure 6.3.)

Claymores or Land Mines

There are several ways to handle a claymore: (1) turn it face down; (2) remove the blasting cap; or (3) snip the detonator wire.

Figure 6.2: Ways of Dealing with Protective Wire

(Source: "Podgotovka Razvegchika," ©, pp. 278, 279; FM 7-11B1/2 [1978], p. 2-II-A-5.2; FM 21-75 [1967], p. 32; FMFM 1-3B [1981], p. 4-19; FM 90-10-1 [1982], p. B-4.)

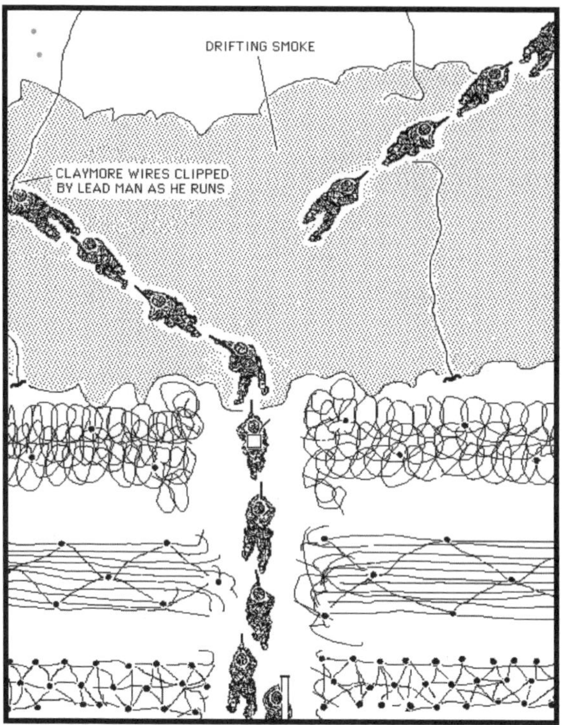

Figure 6.3: Moving Through the Hole
(Source: FM 5-103 [1985], p. 4-6.)

(See Figure 6.4.) Only after moving to the inside of any barbed wire can all three be accomplished on the spur of the moment. (Look more closely at Figure 6.3.)

Anti-personnel land mines are harder to spot. Normally, they project a three-prong pressure fuse just above the ground. (See Figure 6.5.) In a deliberate attack, an NVA assault force wouldn't try to remove them, just mark a safe path through them with little flags.[6]

Figure 6.4: U.S. Claymore's Size in Relation to a Grenade
(Source: FM 23-30 [1988], p. 1-8; MCO P1500.44B, p. 14-18; FM 90-5 [1982], p. 4-13); FM 7-11B1/2 [1978], p. 2-IV-B-1.2.)

Figure 6.5: Telltale Prongs of an Anti-Personnel Device
(Source: FM 21-76 [1957], p. 38)

Figure 6.6: The Final Assault Must Be Roughly on Line
(Sources: FM 23-30 [1988], p. 5-3; FM 7-8 [1984], p. 3-28.)

Spreading Out into a Ragged Line Formation

Once through the wire obstruction, American troops must quickly maximize their firepower while being careful not to shoot each other in the back. From a 2GW background, they will invariably stop to realign. This is a very bad habit. By simply running in column to the left or right and then echeloning forward, they could all cross the enemy line of foxholes in a lazy "W" formation—thereby lessening the threat of automatic-weapon fire from a flank. (Look again at Figure 6.3, and then at Figure 6.6.)

Trip Flares at Night

The deliberate night attack is actually safer than its daytime counterpart. But, it does have some pitfalls. Among them is the inevitable trip flare. (See Figures 6.7 and 6.8.) All surprise is not lost when one gets triggered, because the culprit may have been a small animal or even the wind. In fact, intentionally popping a flare on one side an objective, might make attacking its opposite side more likcly to succeed.

Other Reduced-Visibility Considerations

While smoke in the daytime makes unobserved movement possible (as in Figure 6.3), crawling will accomplish the same thing after dark. By simply wriggling through the assault sequence, most members of an attacking unit could escape the first burst of (normally high) enemy fire. Creepers could more easily detect claymore wires, escape detection by thermal imaging, and acquire the protection of overhead fire from their own machinegun.

Unfortunately, U.S. infantry forces have become so obsessed with proper alignment and sectors of fire, that they almost never attack at night. Nor do they enjoy any of its advantages.

Figure 6.7: The Inevitable Trip Flare
(Source: FM 7-8 [1984], p. 3-57.)

Figure 6.8: Trip Wire
(Source: Courtesy of Sorman Information and Media, from "Soldf: Soldaten i falt," © 2001 by Forsvarsmakten and Wolfgang Bartsch, Stockholm, p. 370.)

Squad Configuration to Best Facilitate a Deliberate Attack

The German Stormtroopers of WWI had shown the world that a deliberate attack by any size of unit can only achieve surprise through the actions of a lead squad. So, how each American infantry squad is now structured and armed should be the same as if it were being asked to attack alone.

Three fireteams (instead of two) would help the squad move through a narrow breach in the wire. One team could go slightly left, one right, and the last spread out between them. Two fireteams might mistakenly leave a few enemy soldiers unopposed in the middle. Yet, the squad leader and a combined gun team might also be able to fill this center portion.

To prevent any devastating machinegun fire from a flank, each squad would need its own LMG. The M249 SAW cannot produce an accurate-enough stream of fire from an attached bipod. This is also true of its replacement, the M27.

> [T]he M249 [SAW] . . . is primarily used as an automatic rifle. . . .

> The M249 in the bipod or hand-held mode moves too easily off its point of aim after three rounds and automatic riflemen must readjust their aim . . .
>
> When used as a machinegun, the M249 requires a tripod, a T&E mechanism, and a spare barrel. These items increase the stability, the ability to make minute adjustments in aiming, and the ability to fire greater than three-round bursts.[7]
>
> — *Federation of American Scientists*
> *Military Analysis Network*

Those bipod-mounted SAWS fire at a high enough rate to temporarily fill the aperture of a fortified enemy position. But to penetrate its walls, a SMAW (Shoulder-Launched Multipurpose Assault Weapon) would have to be regularly carried by each squad. The Multi-Role Anti-Armor Anti-Personnel Weapons System (MAAWS) may soon take its place.

Thus—to retain the highly useful pairs of riflemen—each squad must minimally have 13 or 14 people. It could have two four-man fireteams, a two-man LMG team, and a two-man MAAWS team; or three fireteams and a tripod and T&E for at least one of its M249's.

But neither arrangement would make the squad leader of a U.S. Marine unit very happy. He needs three fireteams to continue the freedom of maneuver he has come to enjoy since 1944. He also needs his own separate LMG to establish a consistently effective base of fire. As such, a far better option for the future squad would be all three fireteams, an LMG man, and an MAAWS man (with riflemen sometimes serving as assistants or ammunition carriers). That way, the squad leader has only five direct subordinates. Neither an assistant squad leader, nor a systems man would be necessary during a deliberate attack—because the overall effort would have been fully rehearsed.

With More Equipment Comes Certain Trade-Offs

Because U.S. commanders are constantly trying to limit their casualties, they frequently overestimate what each man must carry "to remain safe." Only once in recent history have U.S. infantrymen gone into combat with a light enough load to remain agile—some

45 pounds per soldier while landing in the Aleutians during WWII. Many studies have since confirmed that 45 pounds is near the optimal burden.[8] According to S.L.A. Marshall, if a soldier's load in the approach march is more than one-third his body weight, he must be rested before attacking.[9] Most of the time (including the stifling heat of Vietnam), American infantrymen have been carrying loads that sometimes exceed their own body weight.[10] That makes it almost impossible for them to dodge enemy fire.

After studying all major armies, it should now be evident for deliberate attacks that grenades constituted a more productive load than small-arms ammunition. How that weight was carried is also important. The WWI Stormtroopers wore lighter footwear and uniforms with leather patches on knees and elbows for crawling. For their grenades, they had special bags instead of ammunition pouches on a belt. The *Gewehr 98* rifle was soon abandoned for the lighter *Karabiner 98a,* and the 9mm *Lange Pistole 08* with drum magazine occasionally carried to increase their short-range firepower. Their long *Seitengewehr 98* bayonet was replaced by a shorter model, to

Figure 6.9: Earliest Wearing of Stormtrooper Gear
(Source: "Bild eines Sturm-Pioniers vom Sturm-Bataillon 5 Rohr," by L.Dettmann, https://commons.wikimedia.org/wiki/File:StB5_%E2%80%93_Sturm-Pionier.jpg#filehistory.)

be used in conjunction with trench knives, clubs, and other melee weapons.[11] By 1918, the *Berman MP18* submachinegun with drum magazine had taken the place of a carbine. (See Figure 6.9.)

If all GIs must keep their helmets, flak jackets, weapons, and web gear (to include ammo and electronics) with them at all times, they won't ever be able to infiltrate a prepared enemy position. Nor will they covertly reach an "attack point" close enough to do a relatively safe stand-up assault. In other words, their basic load will prevent them from ever fulfilling the deliberate attack responsibilities of 3GW (and their parent command from fully practicing that more advanced style of warfare).

Of course, each squad having its own machinegun would also create certain problems. The guns are hard to carry while crawling, and their moving parts difficult to quiet. That's why the German Stormtroopers undoubtedly left their organic machinegun slightly behind during their initial trench clearing activities. From just inside the wire, that gun could have still suppressed any unexpected fire from up the line.

An Inescapable Truth About the U.S. Way of War

Much has been said about how America's Eastern foes allow more initiative from their lower ranks, more greatly rely on small-unit maneuver, fully rehearse each attack, and perform bottom-up training. Most U.S. citizens attribute those extra activities to not enough technology and firepower. They also blame them on less regard for troop safety.

But this chapter has shown that U.S. forces generally attack across a wide frontage in full daylight and with little regard for any defensive anomalies. They utilize "heavy" infantrymen whose principal job it is to follow orders and shoot their weapons. And every rifleman has to remain upright until specifically told not to. That, like it or not, is the U.S. way of war. And it automatically shifts most of the "thinking" onto the higher echelons. Frontline units are not allowed to slow down for increased resistance, nor are their individual members encouraged to follow anything but established procedure.

Thus, one has to wonder which side has been trying harder to avoid casualties, or even to gain the final victory. The American military hasn't decisively won an extended ground conflict since

WWII. Might always attempting to enhance the national defense through more spending be the reason? Perpetual warfare would best support the U.S. economy. And advanced "light-infantry" training could be conducted within each U.S. unit for free (with the help of Posterity Press or its publications).

7 ENEMY BUNKER SEIZURE

- What are the steps to capturing a defended bunker?
- Which squad configuration best facilitates them?

Enemy gun bunkers are more difficult to assault.

(Source: FM 5-103 [1985], p. 4-1.)

How Opposition Methods Have Evolved Over the Years

America's adversaries in WWI, WWII, and the Korean War were mostly armed with rifle grenades lacking the power to punch through a bunker wall. So, having considerable light-infantry skill, many tried instead to sneak up on a fortified U.S. position—get close enough unseen to toss in an explosive. By the time the Vietnam War rolled around, the foe had RPGs—tiny shaped charges that could penetrate an aggregate-dirt wall. And the noise of those RPGs could—like small bangalores—be easily covered by an initial mortar barrage.

Non-Traditional U.S. Attacks on Enemy Bunkers

When used against a fortified enemy position, the Marines' famous "blind 'em, burn 'em, and blast 'em" procedure from WWII often left a lot to be desired. It wasn't always possible to place more fire into a bunker's aperture than it could spew forth. Lugging a bulky flame thrower around within full view of the enemy wasn't all that healthy. And neither could the demolitions man easily run up to the pillbox opening. So, on several occasions, individual Marines attempted to set a slightly different example.

William Dean Hawkins and His Short-Range Infiltration

By November 1943, U.S. Marine units had come to depend on this standardized assault method. Unfortunately (as confirmed by the Tarawa reenactment in "Sands of Iwo Jima" [1]), the first part of the technique was overly optimistic. During the initial suppression phase, bunker occupants could too easily shoot back for the napalm and demolitions men to safely approach them. That may be why a former enlisted scout sniper—William Deane Hawkins—went on "a one-man rampage [on Tarawa], attacking pillbox after pillbox" by himself. He did so by "crawling up to them [through the tiny folds] in the ground, firing into the gunports, and [then] tossing grenades inside." He was finally killed by mortar fire and later awarded the Medal of Honor (MoH).[2]

Tony Stein and His More Pronounced Shot Pattern

Part of the problem in the "blind 'em" step was that the Marines of this era had no easily carried automatic weapon with a high enough rate of fire to completely fill a bunker aperture with bullets. While preparing for the Iwo Jima landing, a former armorer by the name of Cpl. Tony Stein decided to personally rectify the situation. Stein had been an apprentice toolmaker before enlisting in 1942, and so could use those skills to modify a gun taken from the wing of a wrecked Navy fighter plane.[3] This weapon was probably an AN/M2 Browning aircraft gun from a Dauntless dive bomber. The infantry version may have had an M1 Garand buttstock, BAR bipod, Browning M1919A4 sight, and modified trigger. It became a man-portable, belt-fed machinegun that could fire an astounding 1200 rounds per minute. Stein's new "stinger" soon earned him a place in Marine Corps history. After hitting the beach on Iwo Jima, he used it to knock out several pillboxes in a row. By intermittently carrying wounded men back to the beach while on an ammunition resupply foray, Stein won the MoH. Sadly, he was killed a couple of days later while on a patrol near Hill 362A.[4]

> For conspicuous gallantry and intrepidity at the risk of his life above and beyond the call of duty while serving with Company A, 1st Battalion, 28th Marines, 5th Marine Division, in action against enemy Japanese forces on Iwo Jima, in the Volcano Islands, 19 February 1945. The first man of his unit to be on station after hitting the beach in the initial assault, Cpl. Stein, armed with a personally improvised aircraft-type weapon, provided rapid covering fire as the remainder of his platoon attempted to move into position. When his comrades were stalled by a concentrated machinegun and mortar barrage, he gallantly stood upright and exposed himself to the enemy's view, thereby drawing the hostile fire to his own person and enabling him to observe the location of the furiously blazing hostile guns. Determined to neutralize the strategically placed weapons, he boldly charged the enemy pillboxes 1 by 1 and succeeded in killing 20 of the enemy during the furious single-handed assault. Cool and courageous under the merciless hail of exploding shells and bullets which fell on all sides, he continued to deliver the fire of his skillfully improvised weapon at a tremendous rate of speed which rapidly exhausted his ammunition. Undaunted, he removed his helmet and shoes to expedite his movements and ran back to the beach for additional ammunition, making a total of 8 trips under intense fire and carrying or assisting a wounded man back each time. Despite the unrelenting savagery and confusion of battle, he rendered prompt assistance to his platoon whenever the unit was in position, directing the fire of a half-track against a stubborn pillbox until he had effected the ultimate destruction of the Japanese fortification. Later in the day, although his weapon was twice shot from his hands, he personally covered the withdrawal of his platoon to the company position. Stout-hearted and indomitable,

> Cpl. Stein, by his aggressive initiative sound judgment, and unwavering devotion to duty in the face of terrific odds, contributed materially to the fulfillment of his mission, and his outstanding valor throughout the bitter hours of conflict sustains and enhances the highest traditions of the U.S. Naval Service.[5]
>
> — MoH Citation for Tony Stein

The Details of Stein's Method

Stein had successfully assaulted several bunkers with his new weapon before being killed some other way. In other words, his bunker-killing procedure had worked well enough to do safely. While the specifics of that procedure are now largely lost to history, they did involve another Marine.

> Stein spotted a pillbox holding up the advance and went for it. His weapon was a one-of-a-kind machinegun fired from the hip....
>
> The husky corporal called it his "stinger," and it was [quite] unique. . . . Spewing bullets in rapid bursts, the "stinger" and its gung-ho triggerman [Stein] pinned the Japanese inside the pillbox while Savage finished them off with a demolitions charge.[6]
>
> — *Iwo Jima,* by Ross

The significance of Stein's achievement was recognized by his immediate chain of command, but its recommendation to headquarters that each infantry squad be given a true LMG never accepted. Stein's stinger had possessed a high rate of fire but no tripod. It was therefore not as well suited to other forms of combat.

> [I]t was requested that one Stinger LMG to be issued per squad, replacing a BAR man. However, the war ended before this was ever implemented.[7]

Why Hawkins and Stein Had Taken Such a Risk

In effect, a pair of low-ranking Leathernecks had tried to show their immense bureaucracy how better to dismantle the building block of every Japanese defense. Stein had been a Paramarine (a special kind of Leatherneck created about the same time as Carlson's Raiders). As such, he had probably been allowed more initiative than the average infantry NCO. Hawkins had been a scout/sniper, and thus also accustomed to working alone. Yet, they were probably not the only "Gyrenes" to have realized the assault procedure's limitations. By a simple show of hands, any commander could have discovered the necessary refinements from a random group of ordinary riflemen.

Thankfully, Hawkins' and Stein's "demonstrations" were not lost on those who had witnessed or heard about them. Their courageous examples would eventually add firepower to the method. In future years, young Marines wanting to take down a machinegun bunker would have a rapid-firing SAW, more accurate way of launching grenades, and more powerful bazooka-like weapon. No longer would a young Marine try to approach such a bunker with a napalm bomb strapped to his back. However, the other part of Hawkins' lesson—that of microterrain making a crawling approach possible for the demolitions man—would go largely unheeded into the modern era. Exactly why is the question.

Not only can those little ripples in the ground near a pillbox protect assault troops from its fire, but also from that of sister positions. In an advanced defense matrix, the front of every strongpoint will be crisscrossed by a grazing stream of bullets from either side and behind it. This makes any kind of an upright attack extremely dangerous. 4th Raider Battalion had done a lot of crawling at Bairoko, and its redesignation—2/4—again at Okinawa's Sugar Loaf Complex.[8] In Vietnam, 2/4 and 3/4 would both opt for the incremental "prone-fire-team" approach over the fully engaged upright onslaught.[9]

> To get at one bunker [at the Battle of Dai Do in Vietnam], you had to take the fire from another. By teams and pairs, the Marines would throw grenades, then flank the bunker, and fire up the trench.[10]
>
> — *Marine Corps Gazette,* April 2004

Yet, most modern-day U.S. infantry battalions still practice a heavily populated, fully standing, and everyone-shooting style of offense. That they continue to ignore what a few people might accomplish through the landscape irregularities must be due to overemphasis on fire superiority. Ordnance-rich commanders wouldn't see much need for self-protection. Only their frontline fighters would realize it, and they (because of their rank) would seldom be polled for an alternative solution.

In Defense of the Technique

Modern day infantrymen might wonder why the WWII Marines did not also blind the bunker occupants with smoke. Smoke grenades would have made it harder for them to keep the bunker aperture full of bullets. They might have obscured the side sources of criss-crossing machinegun fire. And they send a very distinct message that someone is attempting to assault. So, total surprise (without any smoke) may have better helped the flame and demolition elements.

The Contribution of Douglas T. Jacobson

In the Pacific campaign, as in North Africa, the first U.S. bazookas to be sent into combat had reliability issues. The battery-operated firing circuit was easily damaged by rough handling, and the rocket motors often failed as a result of high temperatures and exposure to moisture, salt air, or humidity. But, with the introduction of the M1A1 and its more-reliable ammunition, the American bazooka became quite effective against the small concrete bunkers and pillboxes of the Japanese.[11]

About this same time, a Marine PFC who had won a Navy Commendation Medal as BAR man on Saipan got the chance to do something rather extraordinary on Iwo Jima. He had apparently figured out a way to improve—with the bazooka—on the blind 'em, burn 'em, and blast 'em technique. No longer needed was the flame component. So, when the bazooka man in his unit was killed on Iwo, he grabbed the weapon and went on a one-man rampage. He then lived through destroying at least two enemy strongpoints—complete with central blockhouse and outlying machinegun positions—on one of the main Japanese defense belts.[12]

For conspicuous gallantry and intrepidity at the risk of his life above and beyond the call of duty while serving with the Third Battalion, Twenty-Third Marines, Fourth Marine Division, in combat against enemy Japanese forces during the seizure of Iwo Jima in the Volcano Islands, February 26, 1945. Promptly destroying a stubborn 20mm. anti-aircraft gun and its crew after assuming the duties of a bazooka man who had been killed, Private First Class Jacobson waged a relentless battle as his unit fought desperately toward the summit of Hill 382 in an effort to penetrate the heart of Japanese cross-island defenses. Employing his weapon with ready accuracy when his platoon was halted by overwhelming enemy fire on February 26, he first destroyed two hostile machine-gun positions, then attacked a large blockhouse, completely neutralizing the fortification before dispatching the five-man crew of a pillbox and exploding the installation with a terrific demolitions blast. Moving steadily forward, he wiped out an earth-covered rifle emplacement and, confronted by a cluster of similar emplacements which constituted the perimeter of enemy defenses in his assigned sector, fearlessly advanced, quickly reduced all six positions to a shambles, killed ten of the enemy and enabled our forces to occupy the strong point. Determined to widen the breach thus forced, he volunteered his services to an adjacent assault company, neutralized a pillbox holding up its advance, opened fire on a Japanese tank pouring a steady stream of bullets on one of our supporting tanks and smashed the enemy tank's gun turret in a brief but furious action culminating in a single-handed assault against still another blockhouse and the subsequent neutralization of its firepower. By his dauntless skill and valor, Private First Class Jacobson destroyed a total of sixteen enemy positions and annihilated approximately seventy-five Japanese, thereby contributing essentially to the success of his division's operations against the fanatically defended outpost of the Japanese Empire. His gallant conduct in the face of tremendous odds enhanced and sustained the highest traditions of the United States Naval Service.[13]

— MoH Citation for Douglas T. Jacobson

Somewhere between what Hawkins, Stein, and Jacobson had demonstrated, lay the answer to future bunker fighting. It is most efficiently done through tiny elements armed with grenades, a rapid-firing LMG, special demolition charge, and shoulder-fired bazooka-like weapon.

The German Method from WWII

In May of 1940, the Germans again employed what they had learned from WWI. All they really needed to defeat Fort Eban-Emael—the linchpin of the Belgian defense line—was a few well placed artillery rounds and some combat engineers.

> The German heavy artillery fired, not in a vain attempt to destroy the fort, but to create craters in the flat terrain. . . .
>
> When darkness fell, the German engineers crossed, in rubber boats, an artificial lake that separated them from Eban-Emael. Using the shellholes made by their own guns for cover, they crept forward. At dawn, flamethrowers sent streams of burning oil onto the embrasures from which the machineguns responsible for the close defense of the fort were expected to fire. Reeling from the heat and blinded by the smoke, the machinegunners failed to see the small team that had rushed forward with a huge shaped charge. A few seconds later, the charge went off. . . . Other explosions followed. . . . By the end of the morning, the fort was defenseless and surrendered.[14]
>
> — *Stormtroop Tactics,* by Gudmundsson

The use of flame is duly noted, but the Belgian defenders had not previously suspected foe attackers this close to their position. Once the initial element of surprise was lost, the key elements of the Germans' plan were short-range infiltration—through intentional cratering—and some special explosives.

Shortly after the war, a very interesting training film would surface showing how German squads were supposed to attack a lone opposition pillbox in lightly vegetated terrain. One fireteam was to move to its immediate right, and the other to its immediate left, while the squad leader and his LMG team advanced up the middle. All movements were of team size, covered by smoke, and preceded by participant shooting. That way, all return fire would land harmlessly where an attacker had previously been. The final assault was then made with grenades only by whichever flanking team was able to get close enough.[15] Needless to say, this "quick type" of deliberate attack would have required major modification against a belt of mutually supporting bunkers in more open terrain. But its resemblance to what had worked for the former Raiders at Okinawa's Shuri Line is still interesting. (Look back at Figures 1.3 through 1.5.) What proves useful for one world-class army should also work for a dedicated competitor. Unfortunately, where U.S. forces are concerned, pride has often gotten in the way of learning.

The Various Versions of Bunker

Covered gun positions need not be clearly identifiable as such. On low ground, they can look like piles of dead vegetation (as in Figures 7.1. and 7.2.) They can be in a hollowed out hummock of soft rock, like at Iwo Jima. (See Figure 7.3.) Or they can be below ground on a hillside with interconnecting passageways, as in Figure 7.4. During the Korean War, they were often part of a covered trenchline.

Figure 7.1: WWII Japanese Bunker on Flat Ground
(Source: TM-E 30-480 [1944], p. 159.)

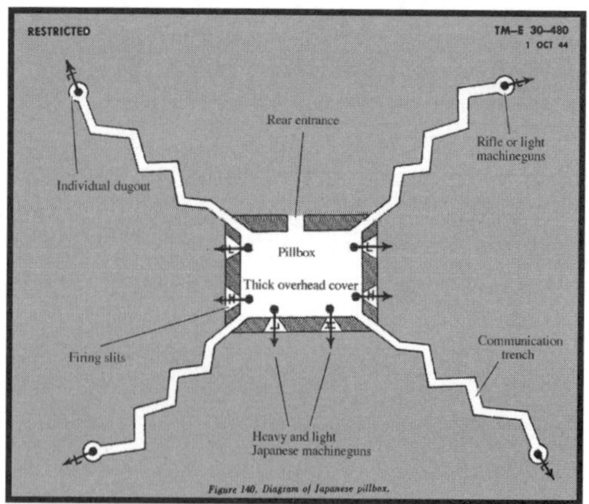

Figure 7.2: Gun Pits Protecting Hidden Japanese Pillbox
(Source: "TM-E 30-480" [1944], p. 160.)

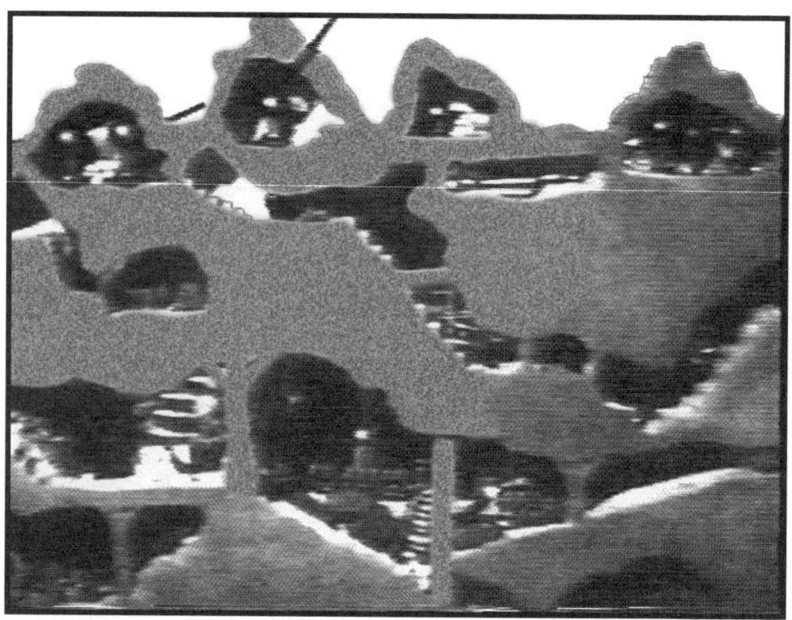

Figure 7.3: Guns Inside the Hummocks of Iwo Jima
(Source: "A Tribure to WWII Combat Cameramen of Japan," Nippon TV videocassette.)

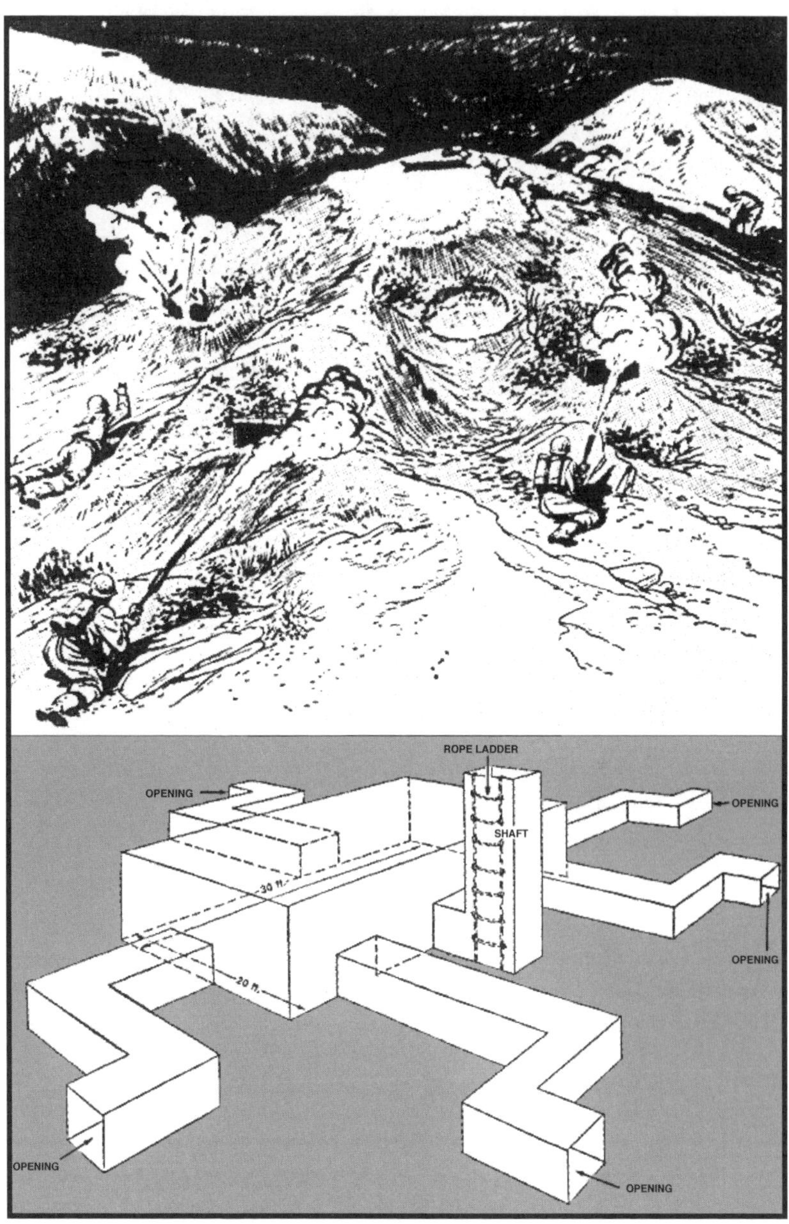

Figure 7.4: Interconnected Nipponese Bunkers on a Tiny Hilltop
(Source: Courtesy of Osprey Publishing from U.S. War Dept. sketch in "Japanese Army of World War II," by Philip Warner, © 1972 Osprey Publishing Ltd.)

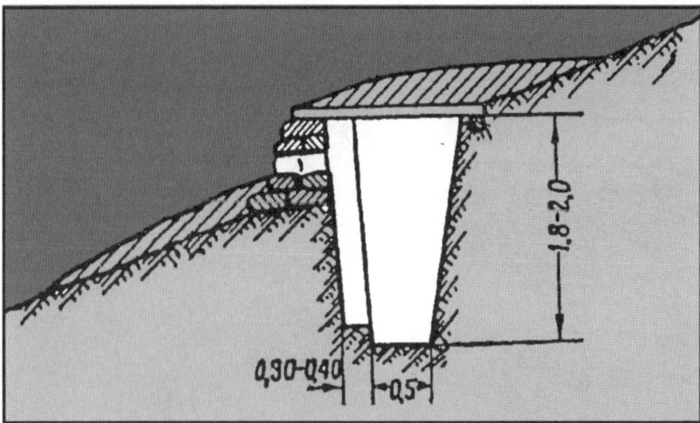

Figure 7.5: MG Bunker in Covered Trench During Korean War
(Source: "Voina v Koree: 1950-1953," by A.A. Kuryacheba, © 2002 by Polygon Publishers, p. 585.)

(See Figure 7.5.) And during the jungle fighting of WWII and the Vietnam War, they were beneath large trees or within paddy dikes. (See Figures 7.6 and 7.7.) They were even on the first-approached side of bomb craters, and thereby able to shoot passing attackers in the back.[16]

Because many Eastern armies have given their infantry squads an LMG, they often surround their gun bunkers with fox or spider holes. (Look again at Figure 7.2.) Anyone wanting to destroy such a bunker thus faces a multiple threat. It may not only have covering fire from elsewhere, but also a full array of nearby protective measures. That's why, if possible, this fortified enemy position should be outflanked (as the Marines did at Dai Do earlier in this chapter).

Figure 7.6: Forest-Concealed Bunker in WWII and Vietnam War
(Source: FM 7-8 [1984], p. B-1.)

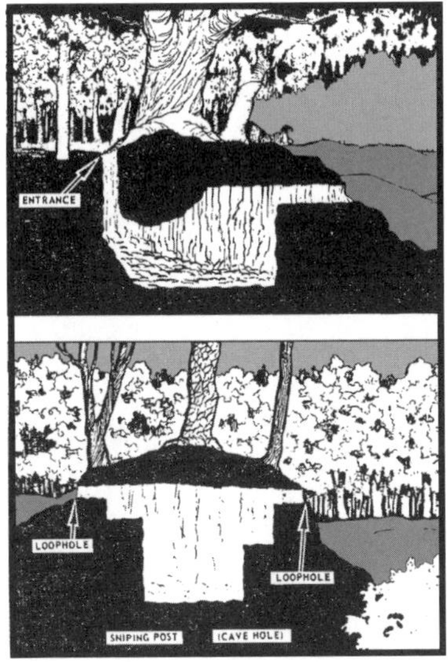

Figure 7.7: Ingeniously Dug Firing Position
(Source: TC 23-14 [1988], p. 90.)

The Best Squad Configuration for a Bunker Take-Down

The present-day U.S. squad seems fairly well armed for its own attack on a "hardened" gun site. No flame weapon appears necessary. But, only with an attached SMAW (or MAAWS), would its M320 grenade launcher and three SAWs barely satisfy the weapons requirement. And how the SMAW discharge fit in with the rest of the attack would have to be well practiced to insure an empty backblast area. Of course, enough grenades of all types and some other demolitions would also be necessary. If fired accurately enough, those extra SAWs might even stifle some of the grazing fire across the bunker's front. But to do so, they would have to shoot into an adjacent squad's lane. And such fire might put that squad at risk. So, as in Figure 1.6, such suppression would normally be the job of the adjacent-lane occupant.

Yet, the American squad's internal structure is still at issue. As in the German outpost-taking method from WWII, three small teams could most easily get the job done in lightly foliated terrain. But, on barren ground, the center team could not easily move forward—just capture the enemy's attention. As such, it might more usefully have a machinegun.

8 Deliberate Defense

- What role do grunt squads play in an advanced defense?
- Which squad configurations work best?

There's more to a defense than just watching outboard.

(Sources: FM 100-5 [1994], p. 39; FM 5-103 [1985], p. 4-5.)

What Other Countries Have Discovered

Germany, Russia, Japan, and China have all adopted the evolutionary refinement to defensive tactics pioneered by the German Stormtroopers of WWI. That's a mutually supporting matrix of squad strongpoints. To participate, each squad needs an LMG. To preserve ammunition, its rate of fire cannot be too high. And it must have a tripod and T&E to lay down an interlocking stream of grazing fire.

Those foreign armies have often tried to make this in-depth matrix of tiny bastions look like a standard U.S. defense line.

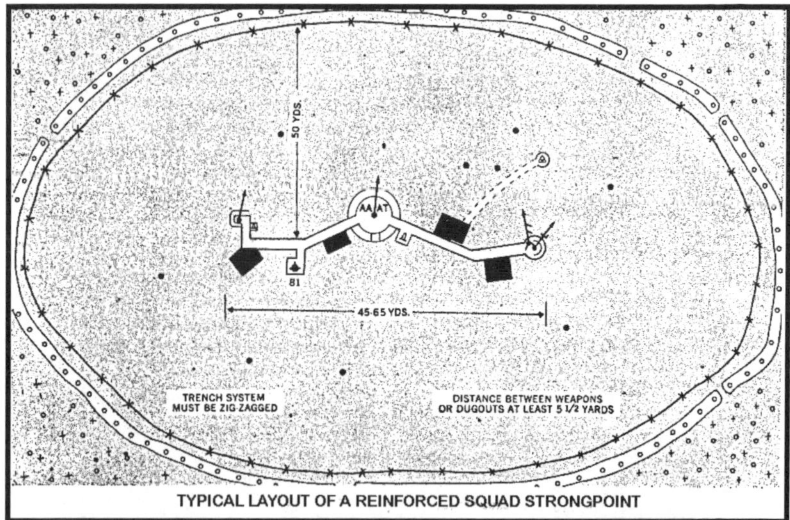

TYPICAL LAYOUT OF A REINFORCED SQUAD STRONGPOINT

Figure 8.1: Interior of a German Squad Strongpoint
(Source: "Handbook on German Military Forces," TM-E 30-451 [1945], p. 230.)

Germany

In WWII, the Germans once again relied on squad-sized strongpoints, but these tiny bastions were not randomly sprinkled throughout the existing shell holes as in WWI. They were carefully grouped into parent-unit arrays and hidden within an extensive system of communications trenches. (Look back at Figure 3.1.) Like the bigger arrays, each of these "moveable" squad positions was then surrounded by barbed wire and mines. (See Figure 8.1.)

The Union of Soviet Socialist Republics (USSR)

The platoon-sized elements of a Soviet defense matrix were similarly made up of squad strongpoints. That's evident from the Soviet tactics manual for the period.[1]

But, the Soviets didn't try to ring every progressively larger component with barbed wire like the Germans had done—possibly because of its telltale signature from the air. They opted instead for a little deception—by creating something that would look to a Western observer like one of his own string of emplacements fronted by a row of wire. And they further added dummy positions leaving the frontal center and rear flanks of each composite formation unmanned. This would cut down on the extent to which their overall defensive array could be damaged by indirect-fire or aerial bombardment. (See Figure 8.2.)

Still, within each occupied Soviet platoon fortress lay the same three squad trench segments in a "two-up-and-one-back" formation the Germans had used.[2] That's why each Russian squad regularly dug a "combat trench (man-deep), shell-proof covered position, communications trench, and alternate positions."[3] (See Figure 8.3.) Those tiny Soviet detachments were then responsible for covering by fire all unoccupied areas between them (including those in the fake strongpoints). So, to any Western attacker, those areas may have looked like gaps to be exploited, but were really preplanned kill zones. By 1986, the Soviets were calling this deadly type of arrangement a "firesack defense."[4] It has since been copied by client states as well as South Asian adversaries.[5]

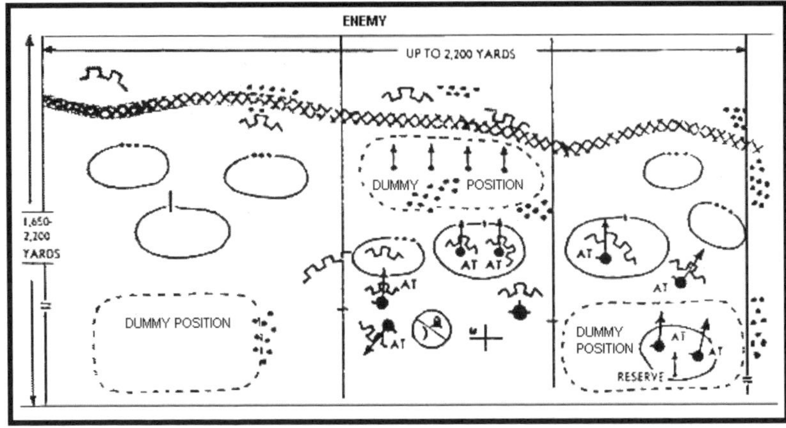

Figure 8.2: Soviets Make Bastion Matrix Look Like Western Line

(Source: "Handbook for U.S.S.R. Military Forces," TM 30-340 [1945], p. V-47.)

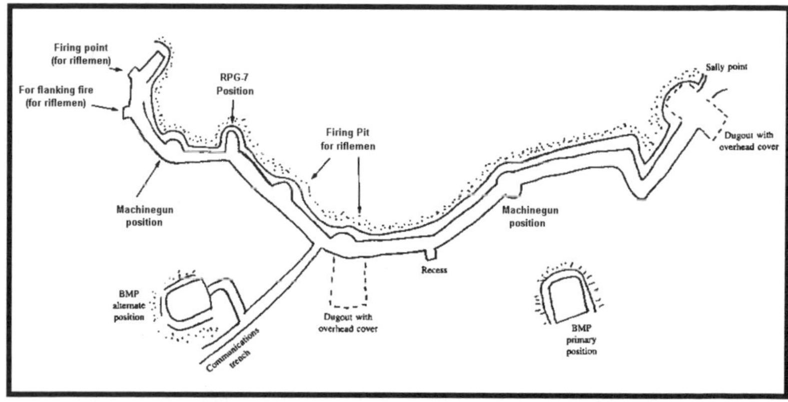

Figure 8.3: Two Squad Strongpoints in This Bit of Soviet Trench
(Source: Courtesy of Presidio Press, from "Soviet Airland Battle Tactics," by William P. Baxter, © 1986 by Presidio Press, p. 137.)

Like the Germans, the Soviets had also occupied both forward and reverse slopes of any low ridgeline. By U.S. admission, their firing positions were staggered elevation-wise as well as in depth.[6] In other words, there were several tiers of squad-sized perimeters on both sides of any sharp rise in the ground. And it was not long before someone thought of connecting such closely deployed fortresses by tunnel.

The Japanese

Across Iwo Jima's northern half stretched three separate bands of tiny strongholds.[7] Each had, as its building block, a squad-sized position with a dozen or so riflemen closely ringing a crew-served weapon. At the center of this tiny perimeter was a cave or tunnel into which everyone could escape bombardment or fall back to an obscure reverse-slope opening. (See Figure 8.4.) The east-west ridgelines just north of Shuri Castle on Okinawa were also defended in this fashion.

> [A Japanese] POW [prisoner of war] can recall . . . tactical recommendations made in the [32nd Army] Battle Lesson(s):

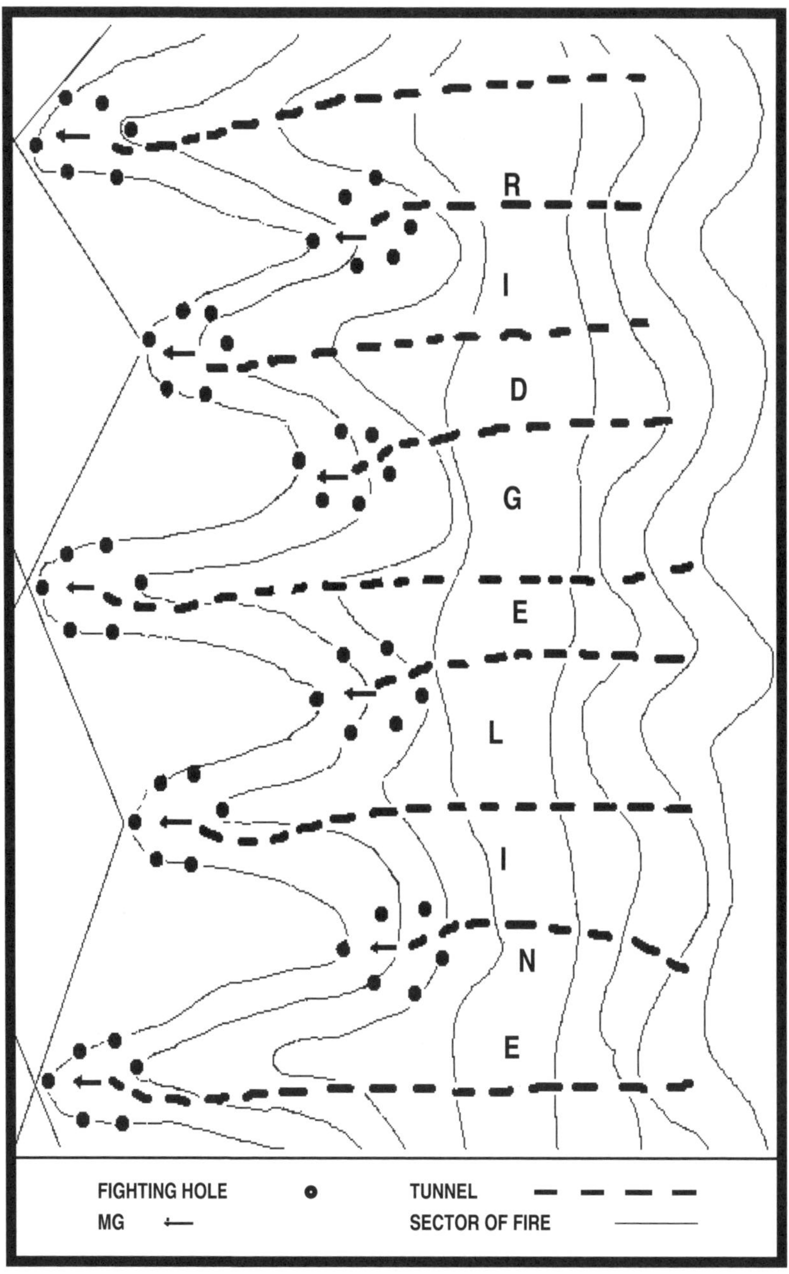

Figure 8.4: Japanese Connect Squad Forts to Reverse Slope

> one [was] . . . that they increase the distance between the so-called "octopus pots" *(Kakutsubo)* foxholes in preparing defensive positions in front of caves and similar entrenchments.[8]
>
> — Col. Hiromichi Yahara
> Imperial Japanese Army survivor of Okinawa

The Okinawan terrain was different. Whereas the ridgelines on Iwo had been closely bunched, those on Okinawa could be easily subjected to direct, long-range fire by the Americans. For this reason, Okinawa's defenders placed only observation posts on the forward slopes and all fighting formations underground on the immediately adjacent reverse slope. Doing so served a dual purpose. Central to the Asian style of war was encirclement and close combat.[9] When attackers were allowed to pass through those well-hidden reverse-slope strongpoints, they became automatically entrapped by the defending Imperial Japanese Army (IJA) unit. Nothing achieves annihilation as well as multi-directional crossfire.

The Chinese

The Chinese "volunteer army" in Korea operated in much the same way.[10] (See Figure 8.5.) By placing many of their most important defensive positions on the reverse slope of each defended hill mass, they could cover them by fire from the rear. They could also escape any low-trajectory preparatory barrages. Undeniably, the Chinese were using the same strongpoint system as the Germans, Russians, and Japanese had before them. Even the "two-up-and-one-back" firesack arrangement may have been the same.

> CCF defensive works exploited the terrain and followed an irregular shape, often triangular or ladderlike, so that rearward positions could fire in the gaps between the forward positions.[11]
>
> — U.S. Army, *Leavenworth Research Survey No. 6*

Like the Russians, the Chinese had tried hard to hide all squad-sized strongpoints. After erecting very little barbed wire, they incorporated them into a maze of dirt-roof-covered trenchlines. To a distant observer, the resulting spiderweb perimeter was then almost impossible to distinguish from the surrounding countryside. (Look back at Figure 7.5.) At various places, tunnels then led from those gun bunkers to a bomb-proof shelter deep in the hillside.

> During the last two years of the [Korean] war, the Chinese defense assumed a positional character of remarkable strength. By the end of 1951, the extensive trench network ran fourteen miles in depth (attributed to Marshall). As time passed, the works became more and more impregnable. By hand labor, using ordinary tools, CCF troops fortified the reverse slopes of hills and dug tunnels all the way through to the forward slopes for observation (attributed to Ridgway).[12]
>
> — U.S. Army, *Leavenworth Research Survey No. 6*

The North Vietnamese and Their Lowland Variant

With the same firesack arrangement the Japanese protected beachfront bomb shelters in WWII (look again at Figure 7.2), a Chinese protege would fortify patches of jungle after the Korean War.

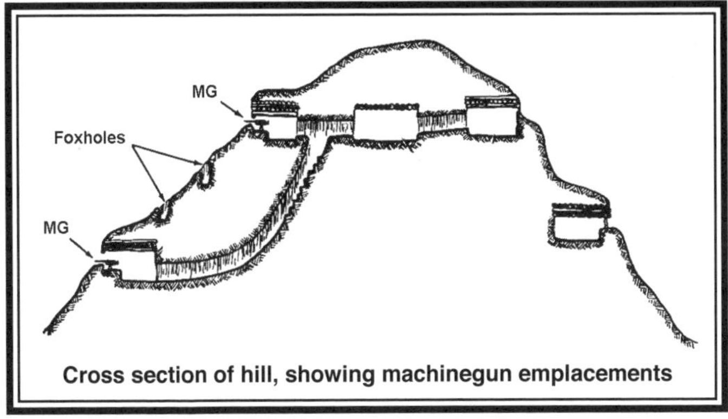

Figure 8.5: Fortified Chinese Hill Mass in Korea

(Source: Excerpt from "Chinese Manual on Field Fortifications," in "A Historical Perspective on Light Infantry," U.S. Army Combat Studies Inst.Research Survey No. 6, p. 88.)

Figure 8.6: Viet Cong "Wagon Wheel" Outpost
(Source: "The Tiger's Way," chapt. 12.)

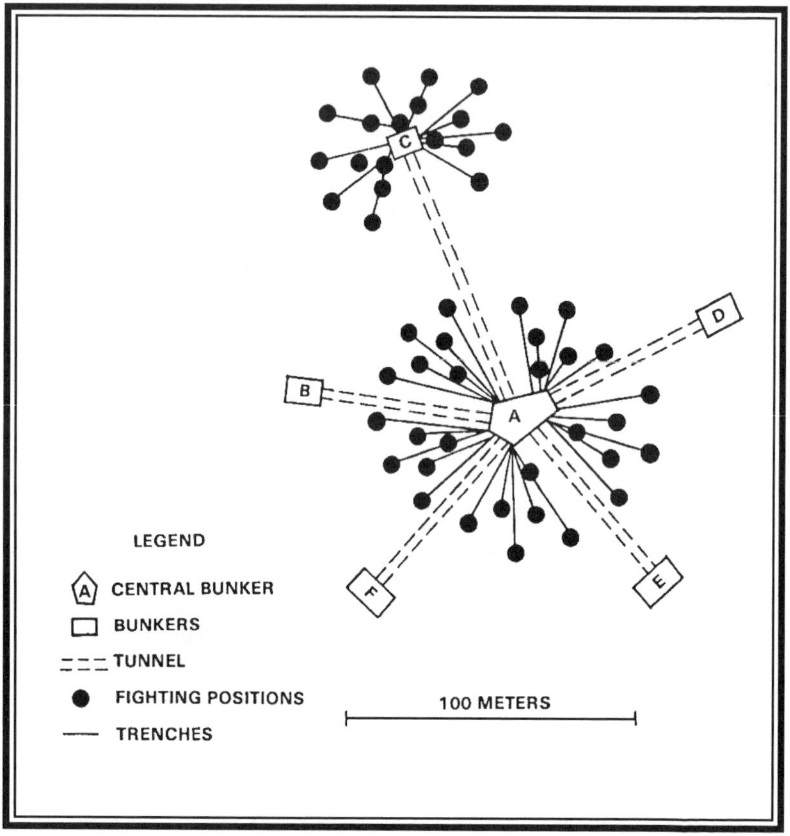

C
D
B
A
F
E

LEGEND

CENTRAL BUNKER
BUNKERS
TUNNEL
FIGHTING POSITIONS
TRENCHES

100 METERS

Figure 8.7: Likely Vietnamese "Military-Fortress" Design
(Source: "Counterguerrilla Operations," FM 90-8 [1986], p. A-6.)

(See Figure 8.6.) This other Communist entity then repeated this same basic design to create a nearly impregnable "belt of resistance" for partially vegetated level ground. (See Figure 8.7.) Where there were no hill masses to get behind or burrow into, it placed a series of underground bunkers—each with its own sunburst of outlying fighting positions. Somewhere within this defensive array lay a large central bunker that could be used as bomb shelter, rally point, and headquarters. It was connected to all the other main bunkers by tunnel. Such a formation sported not only large firesacks between platoon-sized clusters of foxholes, but any number of smaller firesacks within each separate cluster. In effect, each main bunker had been given an intentionally porous perimeter. When widely combined, this new kind of defensive building block could have as easily protected flat terrain as its "squad strongpoint" predecessor did hilly. In reality, all the trenches in each sunburst would have followed the interior hedgerows of some hamlet and not presented as symmetric an aerial signature as portrayed by Figure 8.7.

> Each village of the district is to become a "combat village," . . . and all the districts together . . . a grand Military Fortress. Villagers are armed, and all have combat duties. . . . Each villager spends part of each day training and working on fortifications, for which he gets extra rations. The work includes digging the usual combat trench foxhole, trench, bunker, underground food and weapons storeroom, and the *ever-present "vanish underground" installation,* the hidden tunnel complex. These are within the village. Some distance out, usually two to three kilometers, is what is called the "distant fortification," a second string of interlocked trenches, ambush bunkers, manned by well-equipped paramilitary troops serving full time. Several villages (usually about five) are tied together by communication systems and fields of fire into "combat clusters" (about seven per district), and the whole becomes a single strategic entity *[italics added].*[13]
>
> — *PAVN: People's Army of Vietnam,* by Pike

Figure 8.7 may depict the Vietnamese "Military Fortress" concept that—when applied by poorly armed local militia alone—would stymie a fully supported Chinese invasion of North Vietnam in 1979.[14]

Another rather amazing tactical similarity between Eastern armies also appeared during the Vietnam War. Just as the Japanese had done on the Iwo Jima ridgelines, NVA soldiers created hidden

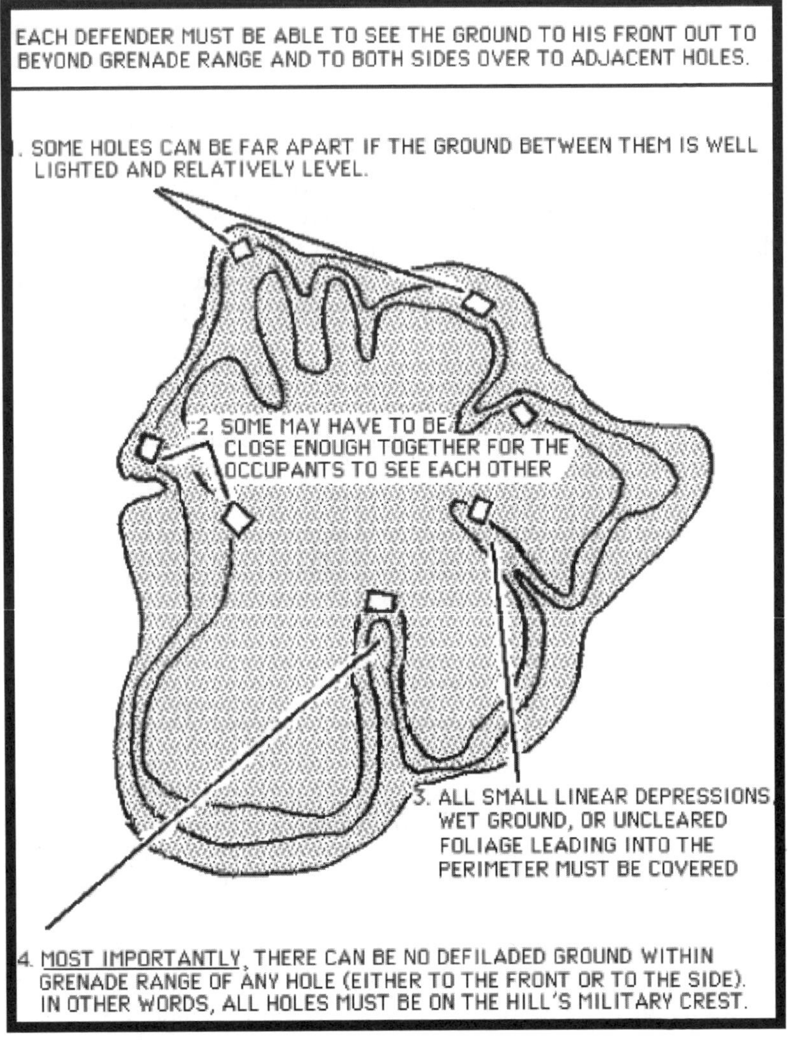

Figure 8.8: A Perimeter That Can Stop Infiltrators
(Source: "The Last Hundred Yards," chapt. 21.)

dugouts on the flatlands of Vietnam to shoot GIs in the back who had just overrun their first defensive line. Those tiny firing positions were hard to see—just below the lip of bomb craters and facing in the same direction as the attackers were moving.[15]

The Sentry Posts for Any Strongpoint Array

Forward-deployed sentry posts are vital to any defense, linear or otherwise. In heavily vegetated terrain, this defense can be as stealthily attacked in the daytime as at night.

Among the drawbacks of a tiny bastion array is its greater chance of being infiltrated. That may be why the Pentagon has been so hesitant to move beyond its continuous line of foxholes. But, such a line—or even a succession of lines—cannot curtail a more "concentrated" form of attack. It didn't stop the German Stormtrooper squads of 1918, nor their successors at the Battle of the Bulge. It also allowed enemy sappers in Vietnam to destroy enough materiel that Congress could no longer fund the war. This is why a completely different style of defense was originally designed in the East. A somewhat flexible matrix—in which squad fortress occupants can fall back at their own discretion—can more easily absorb the shock of a giant or highly deceptive attack. This is particularly true when it is combined with a skirmisher screen.

There are ways of limiting the susceptibility of a tiny-fortress network to infiltration. One is through the same profusion of interior barbed wire and mines as was used by the WWII Germans. (Look back at Figure 3.1.) Another is by so well placing the strongpoints as to achieve total domination over all intervening areas. The Japanese accomplished this at the north end of Okinawa's infamous Shuri Line.[16] Of course, how well the perimeter holes of each bastion are positioned with regard to the micro-terrain is also important. (See Figure 8.8.)

At night, a seasoned attacker will normally avoid the main avenue of approach to his objective and attempt some less-obvious route. That's why sentry posts (SPs) are needed along all possible paths.

SPs are always at risk. For this reason, their exact locations must be kept secret. Their occupants must go out, be relieved in place, and come back—all without being observed by the enemy. A security patrol can initially find the best SP site and then easily

Figure 8.9: Only Way LP Occupant Can Return to His Unit
(Source: FM 5-12B3 [1977], p. 2-308.)

drop off or pick up its two-man team. Without counting heads, the enemy will never realize what has been happening. Or, the SP occupants can exfiltrate out of their parent-unit perimeter using all available diversion, cover, and concealment.

While on defense, all units must do the following: (1) nightly move all SPs closer to friendly lines, (2) regularly relieve them to preserve their vigilance, and (3) periodically shift their locations to keep the enemy guessing. While concealed by low light, folds in the ground, and vegetation, the SPs can move around fairly well on their own. But, to withdraw under pressure, they will need a defiladed route through the various ground depressions back to their parent unit. (See Figure 8.9.)

Because defensive lines often curve around a bit, a two-man security team can easily become visible from more than one sector and then get mistakenly shot. For outpost personnel, most dangerous will be the leaving and reentering of friendly lines. Watchstanders within every sector must be continually reminded of all SP movements and signals.

With radios, SPs cannot only alert their parent unit of impending attack, but also adjust indirect fire onto the approaching intruder. Those radios can be placed on squelch with the volume turned down. With a handset-keying code, there will no longer be any need for talking. Field phones are a poor substitute. Enemy scouts can backtrack along communications wire.

The Use of Roving Sentry Posts

While on defense against a world-class opponent, the American unit must be as devious possible. The WWII Germans often used two-man "reconnaissance and visiting" patrols within each row of defensive sentry posts. Their job at night and in broken terrain was to observe the intervening areas not occupied by posts, and perform liaison.[17]

The Japanese of that era did likewise. In fact, the 1913 Japanese night-fighting manual had listed not staying stationary as one of the conditions for a good listening post (LP).[18] As the night sentinel often had to shift location, he was further trained in night reconnaissance.[19] At one point during the Nomonhan Incident of 1939, Japanese defensive scouts were able to shadow Russian infiltrators.[20] While on the move, night sentinels were taught not to: (1) make noise or cast shadows, (2) move quickly, (3) go in the wrong direction, (4) approach another sentinel unannounced, or (5) compromise a passing patrol.[21] In fact, the patrols and entire sentinel line were required to share with one another everything they had learned about the enemy.[22] This is a perfect example of how much more can be accomplished by decentralizing control. Western commanders would never dream of operating this way. The Russian infiltrators must have been equally skilled in the Russo-Japanese War of 1904-05, because the subsequent Japanese manual warned of Russian interference during the relief of a sentinel.[23]

During WWII, the daytime Russian sentry post was normally manned by two stationary pickets. But in Afghanistan, the Russians operated differently. According to a DoD-published study, "the security outposts functioned around the clock. During the day, one man per squad or tank was on watch while a two-man patrol worked the area."[24]

In Manila near the end of WWII and again in Seoul during the

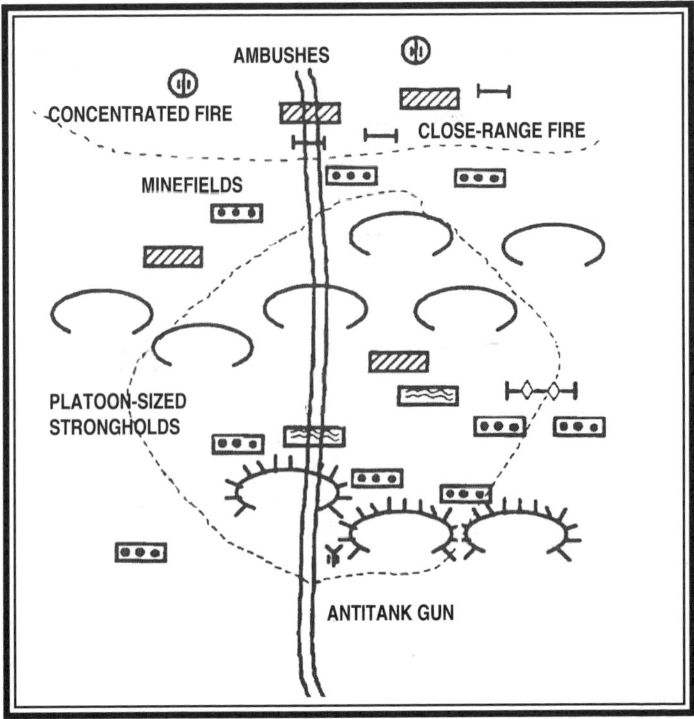

Figure 8.10: NKPA "Defensive Stronghold" Includes Ambushes
(Source: *North Korea Handbook*, DoD PC-2600-6421-94 (1994), p. 3-99)

Figure 8.11: North Vietnamese "Double-Line" Defense
(Source: "The Tiger's Way," chapt. 12.)

Korean War, U.S. troops encountered lone enemy sentries inside otherwise empty buildings.[25] Those sentries would have regularly moved around their respective structure, and the ones in Seoul were likely trained by the Chinese.

The Use of Preliminary Ambushes

Ambushing is the principal means through which a 3GW-consistent defense is conducted. The attacker will be eventually subjected to deadly surprise fire in the firesacks between separate bastions of a hidden matrix, but he can also be forced to encounter it before even reaching the matrix. A preliminary ambush may cause him to deploy too soon for the final assault—thereby making his unit more susceptible to artillery fire. Figure 8.10 from a U.S. government publication shows ambushes out in front of a North Korean battalion-sized strongpoint. Those nearby indirect-fire concentrations may have served a dual purpose—allowing the ambushers to escape and raining down pinpoint fire on the approaching enemy unit. At that point, the attacker may just turn around and go home without ever encountering the matrix.

The North Vietnamese "double-line defense" was yet another version of the same surprise effort. After quickly firing, the entire first row of combatants fell back to join the second. (See Figure 8.11.)

Squad Configuration Issues

To create the most tactically powerful belt of resistance, separate American squads must rapidly establish a mutually supporting defense matrix. They won't be able to do so until each has its own LMG with a tripod and T&E. However, any squads assigned instead to a forward-deployed ambush may find that same LMG a bit of an impediment. They must accomplish their mission without any shooting and then quickly crawl away to keep from being overrun. This takes calling for a single mortar round on a preregistered nearby target and then detonating claymore mines. Nor would leaving that LMG alone at an ambush rendezvous site be a good idea. In fact, its fire under almost any circumstance might warn of the upcoming defense matrix.

To maximize the number of emplacements and SPs every U.S. squad can man, that squad will need two buddy teams for each of three fireteams. And because more fighting holes may be necessary to protect some gun sites from infiltration (as in Figure 8.8), one can build a good case for a larger squad. That may be why the rifle/LMG squad of a Japanese "Type A" infantry company of WWII contained 15 men.[26] (Look again at Figure 8.4.)

9 Anti-Armor Capabilities

- Can a standard infantry squad defend against armor?
- What if it has no steel-piercing anti-tank weapon?

All infantry accompanying foe tanks must first be targeted.

(Source: FM 17-1 [1966], p. 179)

Tank Killing by the Grunts of Other Nations

Even with no antitank gun, ordinary soldiers can still contest armor. Among their most common methods over the years has been to place one man in a spider hole right next to a narrow trail. When no enemy infantrymen are looking, he drags a mine—by string or wire—under the tread of the approaching tank and then again disappears below ground. That trick has been reliably reported in two widely separated parts of the world and heavily suspected in a third: (1) the Finns in 1939;[1] (2) the Japanese during WWII;[2] and (3) the VC in Vietnam.[3]

The Germans of WWII

At the start of WWII, there were special tank destruction teams in the German army. They used plate mines, molotov cocktails, jerry cans of gasoline, *geballte ladungen* (massed load) grenade bundles, hand grenades, smoke grenades, satchel charges, and sometimes even axes. What they lacked was any kind of armor-piercing anti-tank ordnance. Wherever opposition armor might become channelized, they deployed mines on a swinging board. As a moveable mine barrier, one end of the board was anchored and the other pulled by string across the tank's path. Other variants were one or more mines on the same string. Such teams normally had a security element, smoke element, and demolition element. However, the smoke element did not always get involved because total surprise better helped the demolition element. The security team's job was to direct small-arms fire at the tank's observation slits and machinegun ports.[4]

As early as 1941, those tank killer teams were issued the *panzerwurfmine (l),* an extremely lethal close-quarters anti-tank grenade. This grenade contained a shaped charge. After it was tossed far above a tank, three canvas fins came out to stabilize its downward flight. The *panzerwurfmine* looked like the later *panzerfaust* warhead with launch tube attached. So, one had to heave it high enough to make a completely vertical landing upon a horizontal surface. Because the *panzerwurfmine* was so hard to throw accurately, a shorter version was subsequently developed with a single canvas flap. Direct hand placement of either grenade would not have been possible.[5]

Another German attempt at a man-portable antitank weapon was the *hafthohlladung* (attachable shaped charge). It was a little larger than a grenade and equipped with three magnets, so it would adhere to a flat metal surface. Too heavy to be thrown, it had to be hand placed on a vulnerable part of the tank.[6]

In addition, the Germans had a few other ways to disable armor after closely approaching it. They included the following: (1) a "blinder grenade" full of sticky white powder; (2) satchel charge to throw under the tank's treads; (3) plate mine to place between turret and main body; and (4) two smoke grenades attached by string to toss around its gun tube and thus blind the occupants.[7] That the world's most tactically advanced army spent this much time on manual tank killing adds to its credibility.

The Japanese of WWII

The Nipponese were not as good at noisy surprise attack as the Germans, but quite skilled at short-range infiltration and close combat in general. As a result, they trained somc infantrymen to be "bare-handed" tank fighters. Only armed with antitank mines and smoke grenades, they would attack enemy armor in three ways: (1) one soldier crawling close enough to throw and then pull a mine on a string under its track; (2) several pairs of tank fighters placing a number of mines in its path; or (3) two men hiding and then pulling many mines on a long line directly in front of it. At some point in the war, tanks were also delayed by driving thick metal rods between the spokes of their wheels, or with magnetized armor-piercing mines. Suicidal effort was a part of the Japanese methodology.[8]

> The tank-fighter is also taught to attack the tank by jumping on top, usually from the rear, and damaging guns or rotating mechanism of the turret with picks. . . . Another method is to blind the tank crew by throwing a shelter-half over the turret, covering the slits with mud, or "smoking it out."[9]
>
> – *Handbook on Japanese Military Forces*
> U.S. War Dept., TM-E 30-480

At first, the Japanese army only had a hand-thrown anti-tank grenade consisting of a 100mm-wide cone-like charge. Tank skin penetration of this grenade was only around 50 mm. Then, a second grenade nicknamed the "lunge mine" appeared. It had a larger shaped charge at the end of a five-foot stick. Its operator would ram the warhead into the tank. This, in turn, broke a shear wire allowing a strike pin to impact a primer and detonate the explosive. Unfortunately, both the soldier and target were usually affected. While crude, this Japanese lunge mine had six inches (150mm) of penetration, the greatest of any anti-tank grenade of the era.[10] Such a discussion gives more meaning to the wartime footage of a famous movie. From inside a U.S. tank in the Pacific, *Sands of Iwo Jima* shows a Japanese soldier crawling around to its direct front.[11]

The Russians of WWII

While apparently concentrating on rocket-propelled-grenade

development, the Soviet Army of WWII did not formally develop as many single-handed tank killing techniques as the German special units had.[12] However, its ordinary soldiers may have done so on their own accord, because they were still expected to fight tanks without any antitank weapons.

> The Soviet soldier must know how he (personally) can fight tanks.
>
> If the tanks attack without infantry, they are to be attacked with antitank grenades and flame bottles, the vision blocks (slits) taken under fire, ball charges and antitank mines thrown under the tracks. . . .
>
> If the tanks attack together with infantry, only designated soldiers will fight the tanks, while all the rest attack the infantry at close quarters.[13]
>
> — *Soviet Combat Regulations of November 1942*

Chinese of the WWII Era

Chinese troops in the Second Sino-Japanese War also employed suicide tactics against armor. After strapping grenade packs or dynamite to their bodies, they sometimes threw themselves under a tank to blow it up.[14] During the defense of Taierzhuang in 1938, the KMT dug a series of narrow trenches. When the IJA tanks rolled up to those trenches, Chinese soldiers jumped out to throw hand grenade bundles under their tracks. On this occasion, the Chinese infantrymen were able to neutralize their Nipponese opposition's entire tank force.[15]

During the Korean War, Chinese PVA liked to attack U.S. armor while still in column moving up to or away from the combat zone. They would approach that column from both sides on a narrow mountain road, damage the lead tank's tracks, and then have their way with the others. PVA fireteams knew how to finish off an immobilized tracked vehicle. A single soldier normally jumped up on each vehicle while his comrades watched for ground opposition. He had at his disposal two antitank grenades. One was of normal size and possibly for concussion or burning. (See Figure 9.1.) The other was bigger and looked like a small shaped charge. It almost certainly had to be hand positioned in an upright position on a flat surface.[16]

Figure 9.1: PVA Soldier atop U.S. Tank in Korea
(Source: With permission of IISH/Stefan R. Landsberger Collections at Leiden Univ. in the Netherlands, ©, from ChinaPosters.net image designator "E13-860.jpg.")

Tank Crew Trepidation

When armor first appeared on the battlefield in WWI, it was thought to invoke great fear among opposing infantrymen. But half way through WWII, after the major Eastern armies had experimented with various bare-handed tank-fighting methods, much of that fear was shifted onto the tank crews themselves. In Vietnam, American armor had to move to support an infantry firefight quickly and along no obvious route. Those attempting to do so along existing trails routinely blew off a track coming up from the back of U.S. sweeps.[17] Since then, America's various opponents have only been intimidated by modern armor in a flat and sandy environment. (See Figure 9.2.)

Two or three factors had prompted the change. One was that infantrymen can escape the biggest tank in average soil by simply digging a narrow, man-deep, and zigzagging trench. This trench

Figure 9.2: Current Foes Don't Worry Much About U.S. Armor
(Source: http://search.usa.gov public-domain image from this url: http://www.dia.mil/images/history/military-art/1980s-series2/field_laser_9.jpg.)

cannot, however, be easily distinguishable from the surrounding terrain. Otherwise, the tank may stop and alternately spin its treads. Once a tank has passed overhead, it is relatively easy to attack by up-close and personal means.

The Other Unconventional Methods

There are other popular ways to stop a tank bare-handed. Its most vulnerable areas are the treads, ventilation ports, observation ports, and narrow (blast-enhancing) space between turret and main body. *Hezbollah* and its Sunni allies in Southern Lebanon have made large buried ordnance into a virtual art form. The many culverts in any road network makes such ordnance easy to install. The tank

Figure 9.3: Outposts Can Fight Without Revealing Their Presence
(Source: FM 20-32 [1976], p. 151.)

may not be damaged by the blast, but its crew will still die through concussion. Anywhere American troops are operating, there will always be an abundance of large unexploded shells and bombs. So, with very little ingenuity, those GIs could easily employ the same defensive method. Any number of other jury-rigged tank-killing devices exist. Figure 9.3 appears to show an electrically triggered foo-gas launcher. Figure 9.4 depicts another spider hole variant from the Orient.

Actually, the only limit to armor neutralization is one's own imagination. Tank/infantry assaults only work well in the desert. In any kind of broken terrain, those tracked vehicles can be somehow channelized. Once they have been forced into a narrow pathway,

Figure 9.4: Eastern Way of Disabling a Tank

(Source: Courtesy of Michael Leahy, from preliminary drawing for "Phantom Soldier"; FM 20-32 [1976], p. 57.)

many things can so immobilize them as to make them virtually defenseless. Good examples would be a deepened hole full of water in a dirt road closely bordered by trees or tangles of barbed wire in the bushes along a far too narrow trail. Tank engines and operators still have to breath. This makes any air vent a prime target. So too, can vision ports be blocked with as little as a balloon filled with paint.

The Most Recent Urban Lesson

The tank's only real value in the city is to provide standoff bombardment of a contested building. Any armored vehicle venturing beyond a friendly area becomes susceptible to flame bottles from the rooftops and multisided attack. While those flames may not hurt the tank, they could cause a panicky crew to open a hatch. (See Figure 9.5.) In 1994, a Russian armored column trying to enter Grozny was swarmed and virtually destroyed by tiny groups of poorly armed Chechens.[18] Within how they did it lies several important lessons.

Figure 9.5: Every Man Is a Tank Killer in the City
(Sources: FM 90-10-1 [1986], p. H-7; MCI 03.66a [1986], p. 3-11.)

[T]he 6,000 Russians troops ran headlong into approximately 15,000 urban guerrillas. . . . The Chechens waited until the armored columns were deep into the confines of the urban sprawl before initiating their ambush with a hail of hit-and-run rocket-propelled-grenade (RPG) attacks. Within 72 hours, nearly 80 percent of the Maikop Brigade were casualties, while 20 of their 26 tanks and 102 of their 120

Figure 9.6: First Shot Had to Be Well Aimed to Do Any Good
(Sources: FM 5-103 [1985], pp. 4-4, 4-7; FM 7-11B3 [1976], p. 2-III-C-4.2.)

> armored vehicles were destroyed. The 81st Motorized Rifle Regiment also came under ambush as it entered the town from the direction of the northern airport. . . . For the next 20 days and nights, the Russians fired up to 4,000 artillery rounds an hour into the city while they struggled to extract their remaining troops.[19]
>
> — *Marine Corps Gazette,* October 2001

Some of the Chechen's tank killing methods may seem old-fashioned, but they still worked.

> Vehicles are fired on at point-blank range from [rocket- propelled] grenade launchers [in series]; view ports are covered with tarpaulins; vehicles are set on fire.[20]
>
> — Gen. Mikhail Surkov

Grozny was defended in much the same way that Stalingrad had been by the Soviets in WWII. It had been subdivided into tiny sectors. Each sector was then defended by several, loosely controlled maneuver elements. Those elements did not confront the armored column head on.

> The Chechens would position small teams behind the Russian forces to harass their progress through the city's 100 square miles of urban high-rise sprawl. The Russian Army planned to fight in a traditional, linear style, but the Chechen defense would force them into a noncontiguous and nonlinear fight.[21]
>
> – *Marine Corps Gazette,* October 2001

Thus, one of the best ways to get U.S. infantry squads to contest enemy armor in rural areas is to give them separate Tactical Areas of Operation (TAORs). By then decentralizing control over their actions, one could indirectly force all to come up with a viable way of keeping tracked vehicles out of their respective defense sectors.

The Current Generation of Antitank Rockets

The North Koreans now have a laser-guided AT-4,[22] and the Israelis possibly a hand-held and laser-guided armor penetrator packing white phosphorous.[23] That means accurate man-packed tank killing from a distance. (See Figure 9.6 for what it previously took to hurt a tank with a shoulder-fired weapon.) If either of the new armaments were regularly carried by infantry squads, armor would be at a great disadvantage. Maj.Gen. R.H. Scales—a well-respected reformer—goes so far as to say that with arms from the Second Precision Revolution, "skilled infantrymen will make mechanized warfare a relic of the Machine Age."[24]

The Best Squad Configuration for Tank Fighting

Three separate teams within each American infantry squad would permit security, smoke, and demolition elements (like in a WWII German special tank destruction unit). The U.S. squad should be carrying not only an assortment of grenades, but also magnetized shape charges and the harder-to-find ingredients of a molotov cocktail.

The U.S. infantry squad should further be armed with a laser-guided successor to the AT-4. That's because all enemy armor should first be contested from a distance. This same launcher must also have a bunker-busting round. Occasionally attaching its owner to the squad would not permit its members to adequately rehearse the joint battledrills. In combat, this could result in friendly backblast casualties and an aborted attack.

In tank fighting, machineguns have always helped to remove accompanying infantrymen and keep the target buttoned up. That, in turn, limits its degree of observation and can cause operator panic from a small bit of well-placed flame. More subordinate elements within each infantry squad would help it to attack a tank from many directions at once.

10 Roving Ambushes and Fighting Outposts

- Must outposts always be pulled in when attackers arrive?
- Couldn't an ambush be made to look like something else?

It's not all that hard for a tiny contingent to remain hidden.

(Source: FM 7-8 [1984], p. 5-22.)

The Ultimate Significance of Ambushing

Ambushes are the building block of a modern 3GW defense for a reason. Enough of them in depth can slow down and eventually stop a major enemy thrust. If the initially sprung ambushes can relocate, they will need fewer "companions" to get the job done. But, as with the Communists in Korea, ambushes can also supplement the "firesack defense" of a strongpoint belt. (Look again at Figure 8.10.) When positioned just to the front of a Western MLR, they can so confuse an attacker as to their exact location that he will prematurely launch (and thus squander) his deliberate-attack sequence.

Former Use of Small Elements Beyond U.S. Lines

While Yank forces undoubtedly did some ambushing in WWII and Korea, the battle chronicles don't discuss it much. Vietnam was a different story. There, all American infantry outfits regularly sent out nighttime patrols. Before long, trends began to surface regarding their degree of success at ambushing. Normally, those squad-sized patrols saw no action at all. But, this did not necessarily mean the lack of an enemy presence. West of An Hoa in late 1968, a squad of Marine ambushers one night had small rocks thrown in on their site.[1]

If movement in the kill zone were met with the standard burst of U.S. automatic-weapons fire, one body would be later found (likely that of an enemy scout).[2] Only when those U.S. ambush squads used only things that go "boom" against a larger enemy force was there much chance of more kills. Believing itself in a minefield or mortar barrage, such a force would first "hit the dirt" and then wriggle off. One can only guess at the reasons behind those unexpected U.S. trends.

What a Few Americans Were Able to Accomplish in WWII

The opposition in the South Pacific was good enough at jungle fighting that the Americans protecting Henderson Field on Guadalcanal were at one point forced to put out platoon-sized listening posts (LPs).[3] The Japanese liked to crawl during a patrol near the U.S. base.[4] This made manning a smaller LP with its own land line telephone exceedingly dangerous for the Marines. They could be easily attacked from the perimeter side. On the night of 24 October 1942, Sgt. Mitchell Page heard Japanese chatter from where his three-man LP had been. He was then forced to plaster the area with grenades.[5] The foe's ability to spot Marine outpost sentries had exceeded their ability to stay hidden.

Except during Carlson's "Long Patrol," neither were many small contingents dispatched to where the enemy was likely to be on Guadalcanal. There were exceptions, of course. At the east end of Henderson Field in September 1942, Lt. Joe Terzi one night asked for volunteers to conduct a "suicide mission." He and six stalwart young Marines were going to single-handedly confront an approaching

Japanese attack force. With providential insight, the good lieutenant had correctly surmised that 3rd Battalion, 1st Regiment's only real chance lay in disrupting the enemy horde's momentum. (If the Nipponese unit had reached the Marines' lines without incident, it could have easily breached them with "German-Stormtrooper-like" squad assaults.) When enemy skirmishers finally showed up after dark, all seven Americans began wildly shooting their Thompson submachineguns. The Japanese commander, believing his lead elements had stumbled upon the Marines' MLR, became bewildered but resolute. His assault squads then tried to penetrate the supposed row of U.S. emplacements. But, all this wasted effort only made them more vulnerable to the close defensive fires of U.S. artillery. Meanwhile, Terzi's overcommitted Leathernecks did something one must have seen in an old cowboy movie. They all jumped into a deep stream and began breathing through hollow reeds.[6] That's what ultimately saved them from enemy bayonets and "friendly" shrapnel.

The Germans may not have been as good at spotting human sign as the Japanese, or at night fighting as the Russians,[7] but they were quite skilled at surprise attacks. So, in North Africa and Europe, U.S. Army units probably didn't establish many SPs to the front of their nighttime lines. Those units depended for their protection on overwhelming firepower, and any forward-deployed personnel would have only gotten in the way.

U.S. Forays of Limited Size in Korea

The amount of short-range infiltration by the enemy in Korea would have also made American LPs quite dangerous. Yet, some were still deployed just beyond U.S. lines, because veterans remember the smell of garlic emanating from unseen scouts. With hordes of Chinese volunteers roaming the area, it's doubtful that U.S. ambush patrols wandered very far from their home bases.

Vietnam's Greater Opportunity for Small-Unit Action

Vietnam provided a better testing ground for U.S. squad action. The enemy there was thought to be mostly VC and thus backward in the ways of war. As a result, ambushes were heavily utilized by American forces. They seldom carried a machinegun, because it was heavy, hard to quiet, and a key part of base defense. (See Figure 10.1.) Sometimes, ambushes wouldn't go out as far as directed. However, in a randomly bombarded area, so doing could result in nonjudicial punishment. And just taking too long going through friendly wire was a good way to get grenaded by an overly ambitious watchstander.[8]

Of course, the enemy continued to pose a risk as well. The two Leathernecks manning an LP in the tiny hamlet next to the 27th Marines compound south of Da Nang were both wounded one night in the summer of 1968. Their post had been in the same spot for months, and its entry/exit route not hard for the locals to determine.[9]

In Vietnam, U.S. ambush patrols occasionally encountered an enemy force they thought too big to shoot at. It happened at Con Thien on the night in May 1967 that the NVA attempted another Dien Bien Phu. Luckily, the ambush squad's corpsman didn't follow instructions, thereby possibly disrupting the timing of the enemy's planned attack on the base.[10]

Figure 10.1: Too Much Machinegun Ammo Can Be a Problem
(Source: " Perimeter Patrol, by SP4 Michael Crook, U.S. Army Center of Military History, posters, illustration designator "p_3_4_67.jpg,)

The Reasons Behind Those Non-Productive U.S. Trends

The platoon leaders of most Marine units in Vietnam picked all ambush sites for their squads. Usually, those sites were at one entrance to a trail junction that had been on the maps for years. No self-respecting enemy unit would have wandered through such an obvious kill zone.

Local VC also followed most U.S. ambush patrols into position. Their job was to keep track of all enemy activity in their area. That's how they protected NVA and Main Force VC units in transit. Those local guerrillas had also found (or created) subtle gaps in the barrier systems of any resident American base. They often followed up such an effort with: (1) personally reconnoitering the base's interior; (2) making the sabotage of U.S. equipment look like an accident or lucky mortar hit; or (3) guiding in a visiting attack unit.

But the facts of life do not easily alter traditional habits. American squad leaders should have been allowed to choose their own ambush sites during previous security patrols. By simply preregistering a mortar round nearby, they could have then precluded the successful counterattack of any quarry. By further looking—through their binoculars— for how each site could be covertly entered from the rear, they would have guaranteed full surprise of the victim. At that point, the world's best light infantry would have known they were fighting someone equally capable.

The Same Tactical Precepts Apply to Any Setting

While ambushes to the front of a strongpoint belt may serve to disrupt the timing of a deliberate attack, they can also discourage passage where no belt exists. In great enough depth, they can stop an over-extended attacker dead in his tracks. Once mobile ambush elements have engulfed him, they can swarm in for the kill. There were no defensive strongpoints, *per se,* in Grozny. By subdividing that city into tiny sectors, and assigning several hasty ambush teams to each, the Chechen leader had created a swarm environment. How those teams were armed made them capable of dispatching tanks.

> [T]he Chechens' standard "hunter-killer" team consisted of an RPG gunner, machinegunner, and sniper. Three to

> five hunter-killer teams would together work the same sector.[11]
>
> – *Marine Corps Gazette,* April 2000

Surprise was the Chechens' standard method of engagement. They would attack an armored quarry from every direction at once. Under random small-arms fire from sewer openings, ground level, and rooftops, each Soviet tank's crewmen had trouble acquiring a target and became quickly confused. At this point, their tracked vehicle was subjected to the same thing U.S. armor had been in Hue City—a barrage of RPG rounds from all sides.[12] Thus, was the practice of "roving ambushes" first applied to an urban environment. Of note, each contact element in Grozny always had a preplanned escape route.[13]

Roving Ambushes in a Rural Environment

The idea of a roving ambush is not new. This was how the Combined Action Platoon villages were protected in Vietnam, in the absence of close defensive fires.[14] But any lesson that flies in the face of the "overwhelming-firepower" approach to warfare gets easily superseded. An Israeli patrol of elite special operators got into serious trouble in Southern Lebanon right before the turn of the century. A roving ambush had almost certainly been responsible.

> For 10 days, . . . the MK drone—a pilotless reconnaissance plane—had flown over the fields and orange groves at the northern end of Insariyeh. . . .
>
> The naval commandos silently emerged from the water onto a rocky beach. . . . The team had to sneak across the road and pass through a gate in a 3-meter-high concrete wall running along the east side of the highway to reach the cover of banana plantations and orange groves before continuing up the hill to Insariyeh. . . . Under the cover of a banana plantation, the team began the hard uphill march to the cliff-top village. . . .
>
> The "Israeli" [commando] team approached the lane between Insariyeh and Loubieh cautiously. Kurakin, the radio operator and one other soldier led the rest of the team

> by a few meters. As they reached the gate near the lane, Kurakin motioned them to halt. He and his two companions darted across the road and crouched beside a pile of garbage. Kurakin turned to order the other commandos forward. As he did so, a massive explosion engulfed the commandos, killing several of them instantly. Barely having time to recover from the shock of the blast, the team was hit by a second bomb which exploded in a huge bubble of orange flames with hundreds of steel ball bearings ripping through the "Israeli" unit. Kurakin raced back across the road to help the survivors. Then the machineguns opened up from the orange grove to the north. A bullet struck Kurakin in the head, killing him instantly. . . .
>
> An "Israeli" Army commission of inquiry concluded that the commandos were the victims of a chance guerrilla ambush.[15]
>
> – *The Daily Star* (Lebanon), 9 June 2000

A high-level Israeli probe later determined that there had been no intelligence leak.[16] The commandos would have been visible on radar coming ashore. Then, they had probably picked up a stalker at the hole in the beach wall. After watching them enter the natural lane between orange grove and windbreak, the stalker had relayed their route to a hilltop command post by cell phone. By the time the commandos reached the intersecting road, a roving claymore team had moved in to stop them. Or, upon seeing black shapes crossing the whitish-appearing road, the hilltop observer had remotely detonated prepositioned claymores and finished up with a long-range machinegun. Whatever the case, the rest is history. The loss of this entire squad of special operators so shook Tel Aviv's confidence in its own Armed Forces that no Israeli military personnel were allowed into South Lebanon after May 2000. (This may have now changed.)

A Properly Executed Claymore Ambush

The whole key to successful ambushing is going to where the enemy is sure to be. Then to do well against a woods-wise opponent, the U.S. squad must: (1) leave the parent-unit perimeter without being seen; (2) carefully move to the back of its planned site (following shadowy hedgerows and crawling across openings); and then (3) enter that site without any noise. Those GIs may still be detected

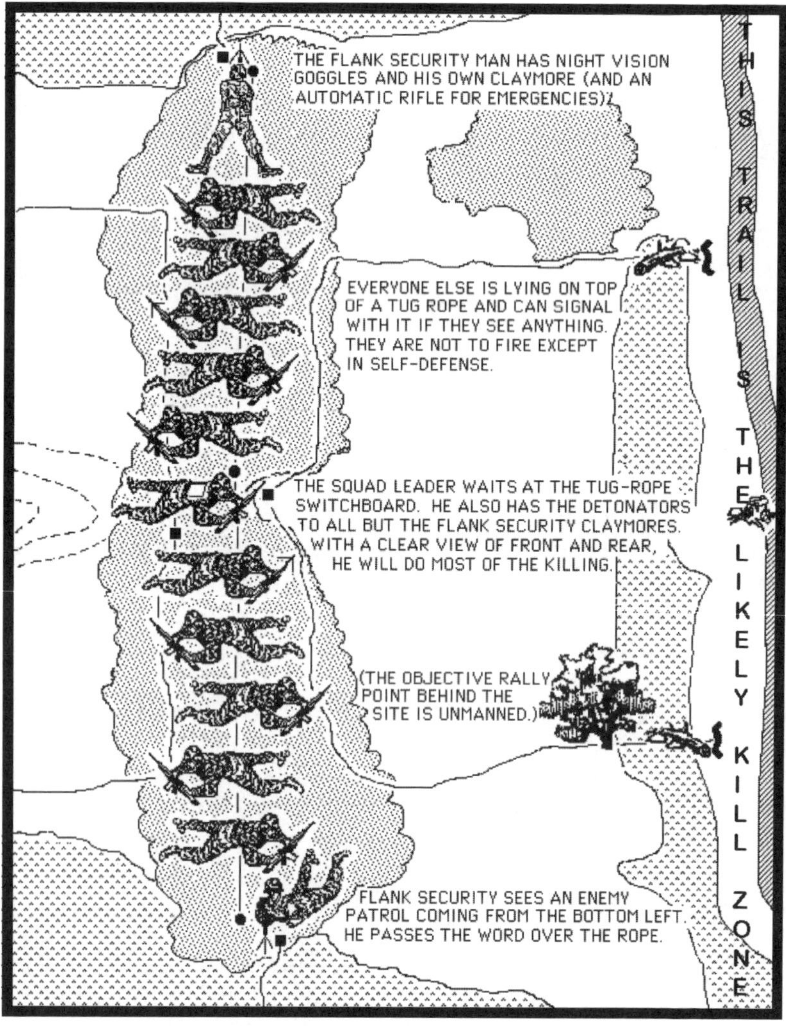

Figure 10.2: The Ambush to Handle Any Contingency
(Sources: FM 22-100 [1983], p. 66; FM 7-70 [1986], p. 4-20; MCI 03.66a [1986], p. 2-8; FM 7-11B1/2 [1978], pp. 2-II-A-5.2, 2-III-E-8.2.)

en route or by an approaching quarry. If that quarry is big and skilled, the Americans' ambush technique must be well thought out and thoroughly rehearsed.

America's Eastern foes aren't stupid. They also use established trails only as a navigational aid. That's why they may show up right behind the ambush site. Most dangerous will be their point men. To get at the main body, those scouts must be initially allowed to pass. Then, they must be heavily grenaded as soon as they reach far end of the U.S. formation. (See Figure 10.2.)

A tug rope is the most secure way of passing the "word" between ambush occupants. However, those scout-killing grenades will be the signal to set off all claymores. Every U.S. squad member then immediately crawls out of the site in the same order he came in, some dragging claymore wires behind them. If the squad leader deems it appropriate, he can call for a single mortar round on the nearby concentration. Later rounds will further the ruse or augment the damage. Providing no small arms fire was necessary throughout the entire process, the enemy may never realize what had been inflicted on him.

To prepare completely for this ambush, the squad leader must have accomplished several things during a previous patrol to the area: (1) preregistered a target just beyond the kill zone; (2) picked a thick enough island of brush to set up in (so no enemy scout tries to walk through it); (3) stayed well away from the site; and (4) made sure it had a below-ground exit route (like a watershed ditch at its back). Ideally, there are also swampy or unobstructed areas to the front and both flanks of that island of brush. No site will ever be perfect. But, as many favorable terrain features as possible will help to limit the danger.

At this point, the American squad leader is ready to tackle a skilled enemy of any size. By alternating the direction his men are facing, putting them atop the same tug rope, and having them lie close together, he has allowed for every other man to quietly sleep. Somebody will see the enemy coming and alert everyone else through tug rope signal.[17]

There is no adversary too large for such an ambush. It will believe itself either in a minefield or under mortar attack. Even if it suspects the truth, it has no way of knowing which way to assault. Should the enemy guess that direction correctly, the terrain and Yanks' automatic weapons will easily defeat the attempt. Provid-

Figure 10.3: Amateur Shadow Walker Against Light Background
(Source: MCRP 3-02H [1999], fig. I-5.)

ing all Americans leave the site immediately after the claymores have been blown, have good crawling muscles, and come back after dawn to search the enemy bodies, they should be able to get home unscathed.

Figure 10.4: Any Mound Can Produce Sky Silhouettes
(Source: FM 19-95B/CM [1978], cover; MCRP 3-02H [1999], fig. I-3.)

Further Development of the Roving Ambush

During any period of limited visibility, two to four men can more easily traverse a battlefield than a dozen. By being careful to avoid lighter backgrounds, military crests, elevated microterrain, and standing water, they can better avoid being spotted. (See Figures 10.3 and 10.4.)

While a roving ambush might better hide its presence from enemy infantry through claymores, it can operate more conventionally against a mixed target like the one in Grozny. In fact, there are many similarities between a roving ambush and the legendary "hunter-killer team." Enough stealth will also hide the instigators of any strike. At Stalingrad, Soviet scouts did more than reconnoiter the German lines. They often formed tiny, noiseless killer contingents. And their more personal approach to things would have worked better than explosives for gathering human intelligence.

> Parties of three to five scouts used the . . . ravines . . . to infiltrate enemy lines . . . [and] pounce on outposts.[18]
>
> — *Red Army Resurgent,* by Shaw

After all, a single Moslem extremist with one well-placed claymore may have annihilated that Israeli commando presence in Southern Lebanon. The claymore is as destructive as it is easy to install. Initially to conceal its use, the operator has only to confiscate the detonation wire.

Fighting Outposts

Outposts need not keep totally quiet and then run for home at the first sign of an enemy attack force. Antitank and anti-personnel mines can both be rigged in series and then remotely detonated. (See Figure 10.5.) That means any place within full view of a likely kill zone should also be considered for a mine control team hide. This includes the top of any bushy tree. If those trees had grown in any abundance, their human occupants could easily escape a determined search. Only a few Far East Asian armies look for anything but birds in trees.

Any well camouflaged below-ground outpost could also safely adjust indirect fire onto the approaching foe, whereas unobserved

Figure 10.5: Remotely Controlled Interdiction
(Source: "Counterguerrilla Operations," FM 90-8 [1986], p. C-22.)

fire might miss him. The 27th Marines Headquarters Company LP spotted a large enemy force in transit at the rice paddy edge of its adjoining hamlet one dark night in the summer of 1968. An artillery spotting round was requested well out in the paddy from the 27th Marines command post (CP), but never received. Had this "systemic inertia" been foreseen, things might have still worked out for the good guys that night. Under LP direction, a tracer stream from the Headquarters Company .50 caliber atop the base observation tower could have also been brought to bear on the target.[19]

Best Squad Make-Up and Load for These Types of Missions

To become a "hunter-killer team" of mechanized vehicles (like in Grozny), each U.S. squad will need not only an LMG and advanced SMAW, but also a sniper.

To counter a ground infantry attack while on patrol, it will need one claymore per man. In broken terrain, this weight would prove far more productive than extra bullets. And a claymore's noise won't disclose either the operator's presence or location. In fact, for any 3GW-like defense against infantry, one needs as many roving ambushes and fighting outposts as possible. That takes squads with the maximum number of two-man teams. If each squad also had its own LMG with tripod and T&E, it could further cover (from a distance) a few unmanned areas.

11 Security Patrolling

- Do Eastern units patrol the same way as Western units?
- How are their squad weapons employed on patrol?

Not all security patrols are as aggressive as others.

(Source: FM 7-8 [1984], p. 5-22.)

Other-Nation Patrols Have a Different Order of March

While American security patrols have an LMG team attached on occasion, the WWII German, Japanese, and Russian squads all carried their own. The Germans and Russians regularly put this organic LMG near the front of each patrol.[1] This, after all, would have been the quickest way to establish fire superiority over an enemy contact. Meanwhile, U.S. patrols continue to place any heavy weapon near the back of the column.[2]

At some point after the Korean War, the Chinese added one or two RPG men to each squad.[3] Its Russian counterpart also carried an RPG-2 as of 1956, and an RPG-7 as of 1961.[4] As will soon be evident, NVA/VC patrols in Vietnam often initiated contact with such a weapon. That rocket launcher was either being carried by a scout, or someone next to him. (See Figure 11.1.) Its purpose was to counter opposing point men with a noise the rest of their unit wouldn't automatically associate with a human presence. In other words, the same sound could have more easily come from a booby-trap. Meanwhile, the U.S. patrol—that places much less emphasis on surprising its opposition—continues to position any attached SMAW man well back in its order of march.[5]

The Other Side's Encounter with a Larger Unit

When an Eastern security patrol spots a bigger enemy force on the move, it makes just enough contact to delay it. If the two are moving along the same trail, the Eastern unit will set up a hasty ambush and then quickly withdraw, as the Japanese did on Guadalcanal.[6] If the two are not using the same trail, the Eastern unit will sneak up a little closer and somehow harass the other. (See Figure 11.2.)

In the latter situation, the WWII German squad would work as far forward as possible without shooting.[7] As soon as it took fire or ran out of cover, it would open up with its LMG.[8] Whether this attack by fire was followed by a ground assault would depend on local circumstances.[9] Either way, the gun's operator would have to move elsewhere after divulging its location.[10]

Upon sighting a larger unit, the squad-sized Soviet security patrol of WWII was only slightly less aggressive than the German. If undetected, it reported its sighting to headquarters and kept the enemy force under surveillance. This would give its parent unit the option of indirect fire. If the Soviet patrol had actually collided with the larger unit, its instructions were to assault and break through.[11] If the enemy force were close by, the assault would take the form of a stand-up rush. Or, if that force were farther away, the attack would be by fire and movement.[12]

To disrupt an enemy maneuver force, the Asian Communist patrol would either snipe—with a single shot—a unit leader or loft a short string of mortar rounds. Even when not preregistered, such a sheaf could be amazingly accurate. Neither event gives away the Oriental perpetrator's exact location.

Figure 11.1: Some NVA Point Men Carried RPG Launchers
(Source: Courtesy of Osprey Publishing Ltd. from "Armies of the Vietnam War 1962-75," Men-at-Arms Series, © 1980 by Osprey, Plate C, No. 2; FM 21-76 [1957], p. 68.)

Enemy Use of Mortars During a Meeting Engagement

By 1944, all German mortars were at least 81mm in size and consolidated at battalion.[13] At the start of WWII, each Soviet rifle platoon had its own mortar squad with a single 50mm mortar. Then, in July 1941, all such mortars were consolidated at the company level, and in early 1942 at battalion.[14] But, the major Asian armies continued to make good use of a light mortar at the small-unit level.

During WWII, the Communist Chinese may have had a few improvised light mortars within their infantry platoons. But, by 1984, all light (60mm or 61mm) mortars had been equipped with search-and-traverse mechanisms and consolidated at the company

Figure 11.2: The Eastern Scout Is Elusive
(Source: FM 5-20 [1968], p. 14.)

level.[15] (See Figure 11.3.) Only some of China's regional proteges may have maintained a "direct-lay" light-mortar tradition at the lower echelons.

The Japanese, on the other hand, had made full use of the light mortar since the beginning of WWII. That's when "grenade discharge" personnel were moved into in a separate light-mortar section within the Japanese infantry platoon.[16] They carried 12 dischargers of which three were 50mm Type 89 knee mortars.[17] So, a mortar team could have been easily attached to each squad-sized Japanese patrol.

All 81mm or 82mm mortars would have been carried by a company-sized maneuver element from Asia. But, these larger mortars were not fired from a traditional "gun park." When a VC mortar platoon commander switched sides in January of 1971, he revealed how he could hit certain types of targets so accurately and quickly. He operated his 82mm mortar in much the same way the Japanese had employed their smaller-caliber "knee" mortars in WWII.

> [The VC] told how he had mortared Dat Do earlier in the year. His rounds had landed in a string that stretched across both sides of the [ARVN] District Headquarters to the hospital . . . He carried the tube and his few soldiers carried the baseplate and the mortar rounds. No tripod was needed. At a given point he stood, legs apart, behind the baseplate, held the tube in his hands and raised his thumbs to be used as sights.[18]
>
> — *Conscripts and Regulars,* by O'Brien

By direct laying his mortar from somewhere along the same axis with a linear target, he was quickly able to hit it. To cover the entire target, he had only to tilt his mortar a little more between rounds. In Vietnam, one U.S. Marine lieutenant experienced mortar rounds that could walk up and down either a march column or front lines

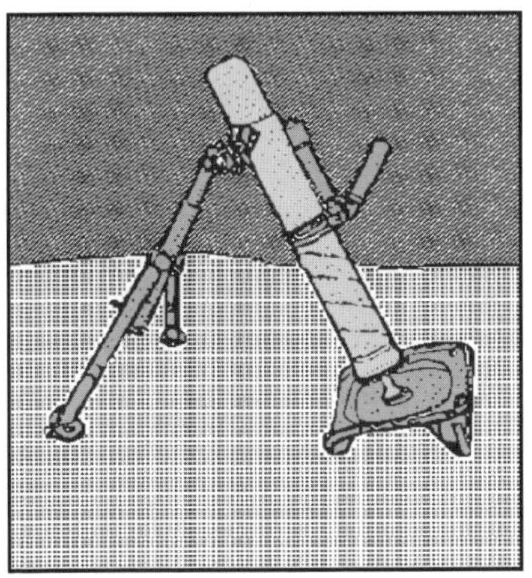

Figure 11.3: 60mm or 61mm Mortar
(Sources: FM 23-30 (1988), p. 1-8; MCO P1500.44B, p. 14-18; FM 90-5 (1982), p. 4-13.)

as if they had eyes.[19] The tube for the first kind of rounds had to be up the road from him, and for the second at one end of a linear portion of his parent-unit's defensive formation. But the Japanese and North Vietnamese may not have invented this technique. Pictured in Moscow's Armed Forces Museum is also an 82mm mortar without a sight.[20]

The Meeting Engagement with a Same-Sized Unit

The WWII German squad would rush an opponent of equal size. It tried to do so with bayonets and grenades only,[21] but still brought along its LMG.[22] The WWII Russian squad did the same thing initially, but left behind the machinegun to cover the ensuing maneuver.[23]

During an unexpected engagement, the Oriental squad also preferred a "boom" to a "bang." Whereas one connoted mortar or mine, the other telegraphed an enemy presence. The North Vietnamese patrol often initiated contact with an RPG. U.S. Marine Sergeant Lester "the Rock" Ford had an RPG fired at him at the start of a chance encounter.[24] He was not the only Allied soldier to experience this.

> The enemy's quick reaction contact drill [in Vietnam] was excellent, firing an RPG round immediately on contact. I remember it fly past my right shoulder and thinking how beautiful it looked at night, just like a large firecracker.[25]
>
> — 2nd Lt. Karl Metcalf,
> Royal Australian Regiment

Special operators—like Russian Spetznaz—are now equipped with a hand-held automatic grenade launcher.[26] When all fired in a row, its four grenades would sound like a short string of small mortar rounds. On the other hand, thermobaric RPG rockets could be as noisy as heavy artillery.

Rationale Behind This Alternate Choice of Weapons

The RPG was effective up to 300 meters,[27] whereas the Type 89 knee mortar could only shoot accurately up to 120.[28] Yet, the first was good against exposed targets, whereas the second could reach those in partial defilade. So, both types of weapons were appropriate for initiating contact without automatically summoning enemy reinforcements.

An RPG round fired point blank at an opposing point man many not have hit him, but its launching noise and approaching size would have definitely made him duck. Then, it would have gone on to make a much-bigger impact noise behind him. The two sounds would have been close enough together that only the apparent location of the second would have been remembered.

It is almost impossible to tell from which direction mortars have come without inspecting a crater, and this can be a very risky endeavor where a highly accurate gun is involved.[29]

The Potential for Other Tricks

What makes an explosion such a good feint when fighting a rich Western army is that army's fondness for stand-off bombardment. All U.S. sweeps/pushes are preceded by a heavy barrage, and defensive positions preregistered with indirect fire. Then, any perceived enemy movement is countered with long-range artillery, and the ammunition supply refreshed through H&I fires. For every artillery shell expended, there will be 10 mortar rounds. Such noises carry a long way. What results is an intermittent series of "booms" that have nothing to do with a direct man-to-man confrontation. When a single boom is heard by a U.S. infantryman, an impending ground attack is the last thing he suspects.[30] This gives America's foes the deception opportunities already mentioned, and perhaps a few more.

In Vietnam, as in Iraq and Afghanistan, there were many IEDs (improvised explosive devices) exploded. Called boobytraps in those days, these devices were strictly for anti-personnel use. They could have been either tripped by the quarry, set off with a timer, or remotely detonated. Satchel charges rigged with an old-fashioned alarm clock to go off during a subsequent mortar attack has already been proven circumstantially.[31] A grenade rolled along the ground from a spider hole would have had a better kill rate than an unmanned boobytrap. If tossed with a little wire around it, its nearby controller would never have been suspected. Yet, there was rarely a detailed search of the area after a boobytrap had harmed an American in Vietnam.[32] Considering one of the Asians favorite ways of killing tanks, such a search would have been fully justified. (Look back at Figure 9.4.)

Nor would such a play on sound work for just Asians. Even normally stealthy Communist armies will occasionally employ massive indirect fire. So, they too could be fooled by an adversary known to discourage lower-echelon initiative. U.S. security patrols need no longer run from an enemy maneuver element. Like the Germans, they could sneak into its way, and then disrupt its momentum with what mimics a mine or boobytrap. That's how most productively to conduct any kind of defense.

The U.S. Equivalent Against a Unit of Unknown Size

The Communists in Vietnam reacted to chance contact with a "boom-producing" weapon because they didn't know how large the opposing force would turn out to be. Japanese and German patrols dealt with the same uncertainty during WWII by moving closer to an enemy sighting without doing any shooting. In both cases, the degree of noise helped to conceal their presence.

A mobile U.S. security element could capitalize on both lessons at once. While its members quietly "covered and stalked" toward the target, their leader could call in an indirect-fire mission 600 meters behind it. (See Figure 11.4.) When the American squad leader then walked lone mortar rounds (100 meters at a time) up to the enemy's rear, his own troops would be less obvious at the enemy's front. Only when the U.S. riflemen were finally noticed would they start firing their small arms. Whether to continue with their hasty attack would then depend on the enemy's size.[33] Too large an adversary could be plastered with a precision mortar barrage while the U.S. squad reversed its direction and broke contact. Against a foe of equal size, the mortar mission could be temporarily halted while the Yank squad added grenades to the end of its fire and movement exercise. Most enemy squads would flee under such an intimating mixture of ordnance.

The Ideal Squad Composition

It takes four elements of at least two men each to provide all-around protection to any patrol. Only a squad with four-man fire-teams can produce that many. Having its own LMG would keep it from being overrun during a chance contact.

Figure 11.4: Covert Approach to a Chance Contact
(Sources: FM 7-8 [1984], p. 3-28; FM 7-70 [1986], p. 4-20; FM 7-11B1/2 [1978], p. 2-II-A-1.2; MCI 03.66a [1986], p. 2-9.)

12 The Hasty Attack Options

- How often did U.S. units hastily attack targets in Vietnam?
- What were other-nation hasty attacks like in WWII?

Heavy brush offers no protection from grazing MG fire.

(Source: "Indiana Rangers," by Mort Kuntsler, poss. ©, from this website location: http://www.history.army.mil/art/225/INRGR.jpg.)

Some Hasty Attacks Are More Productive Than Others

An honest critique of the Vietnam War reveals continual misuse of the non-deliberate (or hasty) form of attack by U.S. forces. Such an attack was conducted every time one of their on-line "sweeps" met resistance, but seldom when a security patrol made chance contact. Nor was it generally run when an American ambush patrol got ambushed itself.

The routine failure to use this form of attack under appropriate circumstances may have helped to lose the war. Why will take only a brief explanation.

A fully deployed infantry outfit doesn't have to "open up" with every weapon it has and then march dutifully forward every time it gets shot at. (Look back at Figure 5.2.) That's how U.S. units in Vietnam often found themselves painfully exposed to carefully hidden enemy bastions. What happened next was not to their advantage, just statistically disguised.

Safely to enter any enemy-occupied area, the American unit (of whatever size) must do something unexpected. Only for a small patrol can it be an immediate (and not necessarily upright) assault. Anything larger than a squad will be far too predictable in its actions. An instantaneous assault may be the most obvious path to momentum, but its failure will result in many unnecessary casualties.

In other words, only a squad-sized unit is sufficiently small to do something quickly enough on "autopilot" (without the intermittent direction of leaders) to surprise a woods-wise quarry. Bigger units are too slow and methodical. But whatever the tiny U.S. patrol attempts on autopilot must be well thought out, and then fully rehearsed ahead of time. To remain unexpected, it cannot be taken verbatim from a public-domain tactics manual. For example, one wouldn't want to "bum rush" an ambusher 50 meters away who knew this to be standard USMC procedure.[1] With good cover and automatic weapons, this quarry would intentionally position itself on the other side of perfectly level and sparsely vegetated ground. And ay GI to enter it would wish he hadn't.

Thus, properly organizing and equipping the contemporary American infantry squad will take additional research into this specific set of circumstances.

Job of the Security Patrol

A security patrol is supposed to do more than just spot a large intruder. In some way, it must try to disrupt the intruder's intended actions. Calling for indirect fire while "high tailing it" for home is not going to get the job done. As suggested by the last chapter, such a task can be most reliably accomplished by moving directly toward the target, however large. While such a move may seem foolhardy, it's nonetheless proper. One the most highly respected U.S. combat commanders—Chesty Puller—used to do this all the time.[2] Patrols from the world's best Eastern armies do it as well. In the process, they try to remain quiet and unseen for as long as possible. That would take some way of advancing incrementally without much of a motion signature.

Eastern Units May Double Envelop After Chance Contact

When an Eastern patrol first spots a smaller enemy counterpart, it will try silently to annihilate it. The WWII Russian contingent fell (with bayonets only) upon a group of fewer opponents and then took as many prisoners as possible.[3]

If that sighting is simultaneous, the Eastern contingent will often make a feint toward the tiny prey's center and then send people around both flanks. So doing is an example of the "encirclement and annihilation" thread running throughout Asian, Russian, and German tactics (but violates U.S. doctrine).[4] Attacking a quarry from every direction at once will lessen the effect of his direct fire. Then, to avoid his indirect fire, the Eastern unit tightens the noose ("hugs"). For an Oriental patrol, the encirclement response may apply to a contact of equal or greater size.

> [T]he Japanese are willing to try a double envelopment without any . . . numerical superiority and regard it as possible . . . by an inferior force which relies on surprise and deception.[5]
>
> — *Handbook on Japanese Military Forces*
> U.S. War Dept., TM-E 30-480

And not only the 1940's Nipponese were willing to take such a chance. The Communist Chinese and their regional proteges have also tried to encircle victims of any size. During Maoist-Chinese-trained Evans Carlson's famous foray into Japanese controlled territory on Guadalcanal, his tiny patrols routinely sent a few fighters around both flanks of whatever they bumped into. Those fighters had been told to make their loop a little wider than that of any enemy counterpart.[6]

The Eastern Ambush Can Also Involve Encirclement

For armies that are fully adept at 3GW, the difference between security and ambush patrols blurs. So, anywhere in Communist Asia, one easily converts into the other. Not all ambushes are stationary. A notable exception is the famous "Closing-V" or *Haichi Shiki* Battle Array, where parts of the ambushing unit close in for the kill. (See Figure 12.1.) This maneuver is believed to have come from ancient China despite its Japanese name. The opening of the "V" faces the foe. Normally for counterattacking a pursuer, the *Haichi Shiki* can be applied to anyone following a well-marked trail.

The *Haichi Shiki* was first chronicled during the Korean War, but something similar soon appeared in a PLA tactics manual. (See Figure 12.2.)

> [T]he Chinese Army . . . planned attacks to strike from the rear, cutting escape and supply routes and then sending in frontal waves. The basic battle tactic was the *Haichi Shiki*, a V formation into which they allowed opposing troops to move. The Chinese then would close the side of the V while another force moved below the mouth to stop any attempts at escape and to block relief columns.[7]
>
> — *Korea,* by Goulden

Where the approaching victim is rather large, an Asian Communist ambush may try to cut its linear formation in one or more places and then encircle tiny segments.[8] This was done to a road march of U.S. Marine "ground pounders" (B/1/9) on Operation Buffalo in Vietnam. It had previously happened to several Soviet motorized columns during the Finns' 1939 Winter War.[9] Thus, the whole idea of encircling a moving target predates WWII and extends far beyond the Orient. Yet, other kinds of hasty attacks are more commonly applied by an Eastern patrol experiencing a chance encounter.

The German Response to a Meeting Engagement

After any surprise contact with an opposition unit in transit, the German patrol conducted a hasty attack. Half of its maneuver section fell in on either side its LMG team, and then all three elements alternately moved toward the foe in answer to the squad leader's whistle.[10] Or, any number of riflemen took turns advancing at the

Figure 12.1: The *Haichi Shiki* Ambush
(Source: "Phantom Soldier," by Poole, chapt. 4.)

direction of the squad leader. Where there were not enough objects or depressions along the way to provide cover, all squad members simply crawled. That's because WWII German infantrymen had been encouraged by their manuals to crawl in the attack.[11] Where

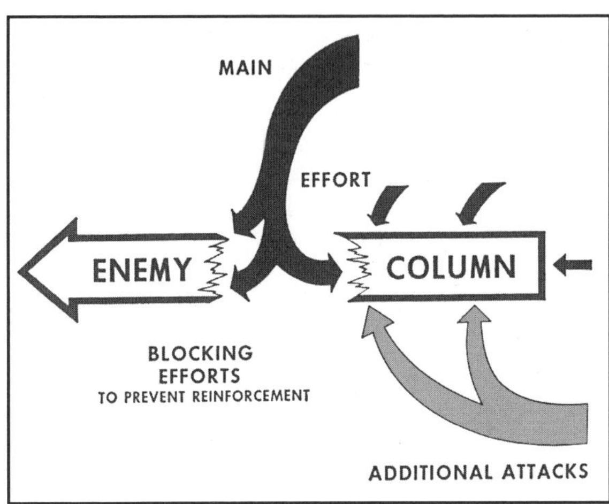

Figure 12.2: PLA "One-Point, Two-Sides Attack" on Foe Column
(Source: "Handbook on the Chinese Communist Army," DA Pam 30-51 [1960], p. 24.)

there was sufficient ground cover, all three elements moved mostly upright. After each dash, participants "hit the dirt" and rolled to one side. That was to confuse the enemy as to where they might reappear.

Smoke and concussion grenades were then used during the final assault by whichever flanking element could get close enough to the target. If that final assault were to fail (or be deemed impossible), the squad leader had the authority to withdraw his unit.[12] But, he needed permission to depart prematurely (after the initial machine-gun burst and before any attempt to close with the opposition).

The Japanese Patrol's Reaction to a Moving Unit

During any surprise enemy encounter, the Japanese patrol almost certainly attacked as well. It parent organization had become convinced that the key to successful warfare was offense, and had trained all frontline soldiers in close-quarters combat. In fact, by doctrine, the Japanese army only recognized victory to any battlefield situation when its troops had closed with the opponent using bayonets.[13]

The Russian Contact Scenario

The Soviet patrol was just as aggressive. In fact, it was obligated to "assault and break through" any moving target it bumped into.[14] During this hasty attack, the BOF element could be either in the middle or to one side of the maneuver element halves. Then, all three alternately advanced.[15] At the squad leader's request, any internal part could also move forward by "team" or individual bounds.[16] Rushing soldiers would try to flop down near hollows, shell holes, or other types of cover.[17] At the end of their dash, they often dropped like stones before crawling to one side.[18] This gave their immediate foe the impression they had been killed and would not be back. Archival film footage in Moscow's Armed Forces Museum also shows individual Soviet soldiers getting down every time enemy small-arms fire comes anywhere near them. Then, they jump back up as soon as the fire moves elsewhere. This connotes a far greater degree of individual initiative than might be expected.

As previously mentioned, the Russians tried not to use small arms during the final stages of their hasty attack. In this way, they were like the Japanese (with their bayonets} and Germans (with their concussion grenades). Their mutual intent, of course, was not to sound like an infantry encounter to any other enemy force in the area.

The Asian Communist Meeting Engagement

Where enemy supporting arms threaten, speed can act as a type of security. Like the NVA and VC in Vietnam,[19] the Chinese would often jog in column formation while on patrol or an approach march. Their scouts then provided all the command and control that was necessary.[20] To this day, Guerrilla Warfare remains an equal part of every PLA unit's triple capability.[21] So, what happens during a chance contact isn't hard to imagine. In this kind of warfare, tiny elements regularly infiltrate the opponent's flanks and rear before any assault.[22] It's called penetration-envelopment.[23] The chance contact equivalent of this would necessarily entail encircling the quarry.

In July 1968, NVA regulars were seen leapfrogging forward in fire-team size (three men at a time) on Operation Buffalo near the DMZ.[24] But two months before and a few miles to the south, they may have been using individual rushes. On the first night of the Battle of Dai Do, G/2/4 witnessed the following:

> The NVA . . . came at the grunts there as shadows that leapfrogged forward in the moments of darkness between illumination rounds—darting, dropping down, then popping up to fire AK47's.[25]
>
> — *The Magnificent Bastards,* by Nolan

It wouldn't have been hard for those separately moving NVA soldiers to occasionally join up with adjacent squad members. Such groups could then have mounted alternating assaults (like the Chinese did at Chosin). Those squads in Korea had preceded each assault with concussion grenades.[26] So, what happened at Dai Do 18 years later should have come as no surprise. During the first counterattack against Hotel and Echo 2/4, the enemy force came "rushing out of the brush in squad-sized groups."[27] There were many opposition grenades and bayonets then employed in the ensuing melee.

> Cpl. Richard R. Britton engaged in close combat, killing four NVA who attacked him in concert. He shot one with his Colt .45 and another with his M16; another he bayoneted in the throat, and the last man he killed with his issued K-Bar knife. Britton suffered a slashing wound to the inside left thigh for his effort; then a grenade landed near him, and it was over. He passed out from his wounds.[28]
>
> — E/2/4 Company Commander in his memo

Thus, for another Oriental adversary, the final stages of its hasty attacks had involved an absolute minimum of small-arms shooting.

Sufficiently Decentralizing Control over a Hasty attack

Whether the hasty attack occurs during a chance encounter or ambush, the most effective ways of advancing will depend upon terrain and distance (but be otherwise the same). Only when a small infantry unit is allowed to move forward without any interference from internal leaders, might those ways be quick enough to generate surprise. And they will work best for a unit of squad size that has previously practiced them. (See Figure 12.3.) Against a prepared enemy position, however, only a deliberate attack is going to succeed with minimal casualties.

"Firing and moving on line" and "stalking on line" are very similar and easily combined maneuvers. Both entail lone combatants running forward while prone buddies cover them with their rifles. The only difference is that all friendly fire is withheld during a stalking evolution. For either option to succeed, all movements must be individual, well thought out, and random. The military world has long recognized the advantages of decentralizing control to this extent.

> At the Imperial Maneuvers of 1902 [at the height of the interest in Boer tactics], German infantry was observed

Figure 12.3: Most Effective Way to "Fire and Move"
(Source: "Strategic Rifleman," by Poole.)

Figure 12.4: Individual Rushes Create Lowest Motion Signature
(Sources: FM 22-100 [1983], p. 84; FM 7-70 [1986], p. D-24.)

> working... in... skirmish lines, each rifleman moving from one covered position to another as an individual.[29]
>
> — *Stormtroop Tactics,* by Gudmunddson

In a previous paragraph, Russian soldiers had been allowed to get down whenever enemy fire got close as long as they were willing to jump back up as soon as that fire was shifted. Such a rule also connotes a random and individually based style of fire and movement. A lone soldier cannot move forward against resistance without someone covering him by fire. Most logical is the person who knows his every idiosyncrasy—namely, his assigned buddy. (See Figure 12.4.)

The maneuver depicted in Figure 12.3 is really just two-man technique separately conducted in parallel lanes, as opposed to a squad method. As a result, it could be run by something as big as a platoon or company. And, it would have worked in Vietnam during any sweep that was not heavily contested. Lack of cover in one lane could have been easily resolved by the affected buddy team crawling across the open area. Then, as long as no team allowed itself to get more than a few yards ahead of the others, a fairly linear formation could be maintained. But, one of the rules of such a maneuver is that everyone stops advancing if anyone encounters the following: (1) well directed enemy machinegun fire; (2) fresh dirt indicating recent fortification; (3) claymores or barbed wire. At this point, the composite array on autopilot grinds to a halt and again falls under the tactical control of its overall leader.

When Something "Hard" Is Unexpectedly Encountered

The meeting engagement may turn out to be more than that. A machinegun nest may be discovered dead center in what had previously appeared to be a moving enemy column. Then, the advancing U.S. line must halt and wait for instructions from its leader. He may decide to return fire at the center and only continue forward on the edges. (See Figure 12.5.)

That's how the U.S. Marines did so well during their on-line hasty attacks at the Battle of Dai Do in May of 1968.[30] Any enemy machinegun bunker is likely to have a lateral trenchline behind it. Such a trench would give flanking U.S. buddy teams the chance to engage any enemy group at target center with long-range fire. During E/2/4's brilliant move through the outlying hamlets of Dai Do in Vietnam, "several times . . . Marines gained the flank of trenchlines and placed killing enfilade fire on large numbers of NVA soldiers."[31]

As long as the front of the enemy bunker isn't protected by crisscrossing machinegun fire from others behind it, the enemy's defenses are only hasty in nature.

The Successful Conclusion of a Hasty Attack

To prevail over a foe defender's greater firepower, the lead

Figure 12.5: What to Do with a Hidden Machinegun Nest
(Source: "Strategic Rifleman," by Poole.)

elements of an Easterner's hasty attack must get—unnoticed—to within grenade range of the first row of Western soldiers. This was what the Japanese were able to do on the night of Chesty Puller's famous defense of Henderson Field at Guadalcanal in 1942.[32] And this is what the Chinese Communists did 18 years later at the Chosin Reservoir.[33]

Both of these Oriental military units are known to have previously identified their best grenade throwers. And such soldiers would have been placed at the front of their formation. The same thing would apply for a hasty attack. Some GIs are so inept at grenade throwing that they shouldn't do so in combat. Others can throw farther and with greater accuracy than most.

Then, during the assault phase of a hasty attack, some members of the German squad throw only concussion grenades to prevent friendly casualties from shrapnel.

How Eastern Units Dealt with Being Ambushed

In WWII, all Japanese enlisted men had drilled on how quietly to accomplish the following at night: (1) route march; (2) cross rough ground; and (3) attack.[34] While crossing rough ground, changing from column to line formation was stressed.[35] During a chance encounter at night, closing with the foe silently would still have helped. If that encounter were an enemy ambush, the need to remain silent or even withhold small-arms fire would be less apparent. But, any degree of surprise will increase a counterattack's odds of succeeding. Unless the ambusher is only feet away, the smart move is a disguised envelopment. Those in the kill zone crawl behind any available cover and return fire, while those just outside the kill zone quietly crawl back down the trail to outflank and then surprise their tormentor. (See Figure 12.6.)

An Eastern ambusher would not expect this complicated a response from a Western quarry. He has come to expect the rote execution of a head-on Immediate Action (IA) Drill, or nothing at all.

The Most Appropriate U.S. Squad Make-Up

During any hasty attack, an organic LMG would greatly help

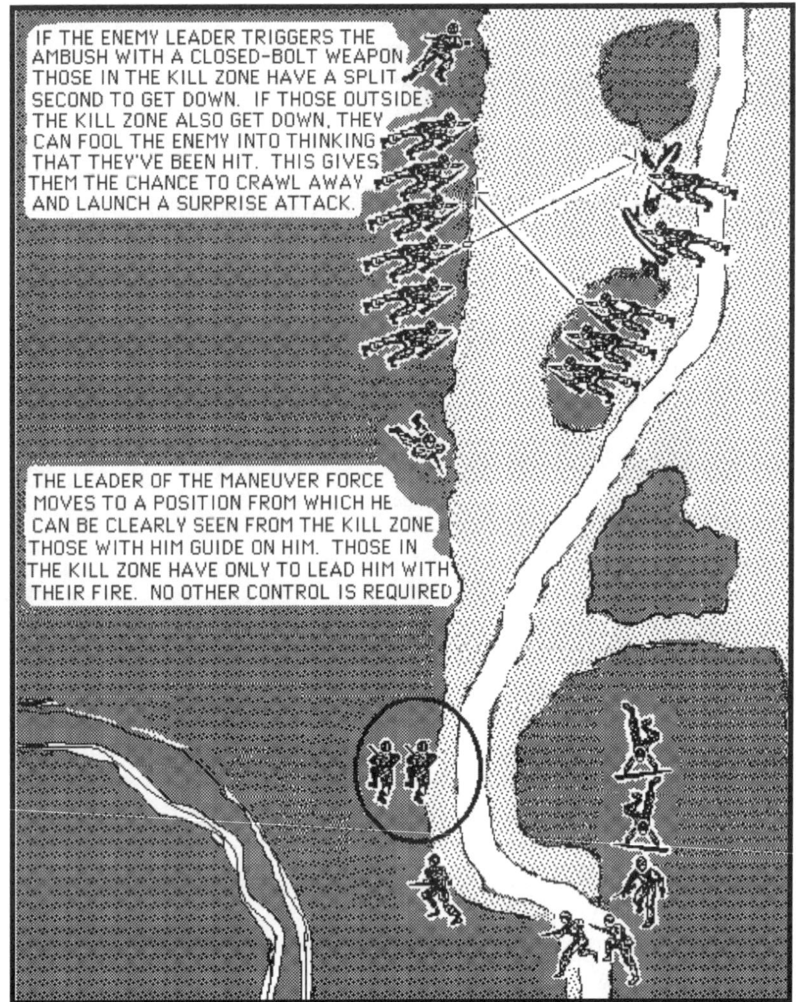

Figure 12.6: The Counterambush Technique at Night
(Sources: FM 7-70 [1986], p. 4-20; FM 5-103 [1985], pp. 4-6, 4-38, 5-10; FM 90-10-1 [1982], p. B-4; FM 7-11B3 [1976], p. 2-VII-C-4.4.)

the American infantry squad. It would come in particularly handy, if that attack were contested by an enemy machinegun. While the center of the U.S. formation would then remain in place, its flanks would have greater freedom to advance.

The most efficient version of fire and movement is provided by buddy teams—with one man rushing while the other covers. Every member of a three-man team would have to advance at the same time, while another whole team covered (like the NVA did on Operation Buffalo). Under no circumstance would three-man fireteams do as well at fire and movement as two-man teams. There would be less accurate cover fire and a much-greater motion signature. Because a fireteam leader would now be making decisions and providing instructions, no longer would the random flow of individual initiative be possible (or the speed it generates). Nor could the formation extend across as wide a frontage.

In other words, the Asian Communist armies may not be the world's best at fire and movement. The WWII Russians routinely relied upon two-man "pickets."[36] Both Japanese and German armies utilized two-man "reconnaissance and visiting" patrols within their respective strings of picket posts.[37] So, the other big Eastern militaries may have better recognized the tactical legitimacy of a "leaderless" two-man contingent under adverse circumstances.

Summarized Assessment for Squad Structure Specialists

Only with an LMG could a U.S. squad establish immediate fire superiority over the opposition in a chance encounter. Two man buddy teams would help it to perform any fire and movement toward the quarry.

13 URBAN OFFENSE

- Which armies have the most urban-attack experience?
- How are their maneuvers similar at the squad level?

U.S. infantry squad entering a building in Iraq.

(Source: "Capture at Ar Ramadi," by Don Stivers, poss. ©, from this url: http://www.nationalguard.mil/resources/photo_gallery/heritage/hires/arramadi.jpg.)

Eastern Armies Have Done More Street Fighting

Because of the extreme risk in frontally assaulting a built-up area, Eastern armies have developed alternatives. By the end of the WWII era, five trends had surfaced. The Soviets, Chinese, and other Asian Communists had isolated parts of cities through encirclement. The Japanese and Soviets had first sent a spearhead to its middle. The Japanese, Soviets, and Asian Communists had infiltrated at some stage of the assault. The Japanese, Soviets, and Germans had advanced through the buildings alongside streets.[1] And all four Eastern armies had concurrently attacked through sewers. Nations less well armed than America have had to rely more on maneuver. So, their tactical trends should interest the Pentagon. Within them may lie a safer way for U.S. troops to occupy a contested city.

The Germans

The Germans were able to seize many cities during WWII, but only in Warsaw and Stalingrad did they experience many problems. In Warsaw, they were forced to burn and flood the ghetto to put down the second Jewish uprising.[2] During the Battle for Stalingrad, a fully supported German army was kept from reaching the Volga River by a series of independently operating Russian squad-sized elements.[3]

Tanks and direct-fire assault guns accompanied all German infantry outfits into urban combat. Mortars were used against well-screened enemy strongholds, because they could drop rounds almost straight down through overhead openings. Antitank weaponry covered all intersecting side streets to prevent counterattack. (See Figure 13.1.) And then elevated long-range machineguns engaged enemy snipers on rooftops.[4]

The German urban assault unit's immediate objective was segmenting the area held by the foe, to limit his ability to reinforce the various parts. That unit's troops were divided into separate columns to advance along parallel axes (but never from different directions). Within each column were assault and mop-up elements. Where possible the assault elements then blasted holes in the walls of adjacent buildings to create a covered avenue of advance. Each house along the way was then cleared with small-arms fire. When possible, cellars and attics were occupied first. Machineguns were left atop tall buildings to cover all movement along backyards and rooftops.[5]

When compelled to enter a street, the Germans moved in parallel files along opposing storefronts. Each file member had been instructed on which floor or type of opening to watch. Some captured buildings were immediately converted into defensive strongpoints. Others were occupied by tiny observation posts. Along with the surface advance came one through all underground conduits and sewers. If clearing or smoking them out were not possible, then entrances were barricaded, blown up, or guarded. All German tanks and direct-fire artillery pieces were protected by infantry. After a captured area had been adequately sealed off, the mop-up units would conduct a detailed house-to-house search. Specifically inspected would be all rooftops, attics, basements, courtyards, and staircases. All Germans had been told of the secret rooms and passageways in Warsaw. At night, elevated searchlights quickly illuminated all that had been so far "neutralized.".[6]

Figure 13.1: *Panzerfaust* Was Also Good for Wall Penetration
(Source: Courtesy of Cassell PLC, from *World Army Uniforms since 1939*, © 1975, 1980, 1981, 1983 by Blandford Press Ltd., Part II, Plate 193; *FM 90-10-1* (1982), p. B-9.)

The Japanese

Within the WWII period, the Japanese captured many defended cities. How they did so is best chronicled for Shanghai in 1937 and Singapore in 1942.

During the first urban assault of the Sino-Japanese War, the Nipponese initially sent a column into Shanghai's downtown area to capture several strategically important points. Soon ensued a vicious house-to-house battle involving amphibiously landed Japanese reinforcements. There exists photographic evidence of them blowing holes in building walls to keep from having to advance up a fire-swept street. Barricades also played a role in their offensive effort (possibly by protecting their flanks from counterattack).[7] Much better armed than the Nationalist Chinese defenders, the Japanese attackers eventually captured the city.[8]

At Singapore on a dark night in early 1942, some 23,000 Japanese troops boarded tiny barges and collapsible boats to cross the narrow strait separating Singapore Island from the Malay Peninsula. They easily snuck between the 3000 shoreline defenders, and seven days later 80,000 British, Indian, and Australian troops were ordered to surrender the city.[9]

For urban combat, the Japanese had at their disposal all the ancient techniques of *ninjutsu*. Such methods would have helped them to infiltrate a stronghold before any full-fledged attack. "Entering an Enemy's Fortress" *(chiku jo gunryaku heiho)* included ramparts crossing (through sewers, air shafts, and other seemingly inaccessible openings). "Entering an Inaccessible Structure" *(shinobi-iri)* offered both effortlessly moving through a window opening and noiselessly climbing stairs next to a wall.[10] With skills such as these, the Japanese rear guard at Manila was able to exfiltrate the fully surrounded the Intramuros fort in 1945.[11]

The Russians

Of the major Eastern armies, the Soviets left this period in history with the most experience in attacking (or counterattacking) through built-up areas. During WWII, they fought for several big cities between Stalingrad and Berlin. However, much of what they learned may have then failed to make it into their organizational memory. By 1995, they were reported to have little street-fighting expertise left. In the aftermath of the Chechen disaster, Gen. Mikhail Surkov admitted that "street fighting tactics are absent from the manuals of the Russian armed forces."[12] Still, erstwhile knowledge is never completely absent. Much of it may still reside amongst the rank and file.

The WWII Soviets liked to surround and isolate a city before thoroughly reconnoitering it. By Soviet doctrine, the most rapid and economical assault on a built-up area was then through occupying its "centers of resistance."[13] To reach one, the Soviet assault group often mounted an accelerated attack against a weak defensive sector.[14]

By U.S. admission, the WWII Russians not only reconnoitered each block before assaulting it, but used short-range infiltrators as part of their lead element.[15] At first in the war, this infiltration had been of a slightly different nature. After a support group raked the targeted block with fire, tank and artillery rounds were directed at its middle. Next, through concurrent smoke, an infiltration group dashed to that same mid-block location. Then, an assault group systematically captured the remaining buildings. And finally, a reserve group provided flank-security patrols. If that entire sequence went well, the reserve was instead committed to taking the next block (after further support and infiltration phases). A typical assault subgroup was composed of seven submachinegunners, five engineers, three heavy machinegun crews, and two antitank riflemen.[16]

By the time the Soviets got to Berlin, they could apply all the refinements to house-to-house fighting they had acquired in every *festungsstadt* (fortress city) since Stalingrad.[17] At the German capital, the Soviet army deployed smaller combat groups—mixed-arms units of about 80 men closely supported by direct-fire artillery. Each assault group was, in turn, divided into subgroups of six to eight men. Those groups moved between adjacent houses instead of directly up any street. They went through apartments and cellars after blasting holes in parent structure walls. Many German *Panzerfaust* anti-tank weapons had became available to the Soviet Army at the start of 1945 and were thus available for this purpose.[18] (Look again at Figure 13.1.) In Berlin, other combat groups fought across rooftops and through attics.[19] There is even evidence of how successive rooms were taken. Stalingrad replacements had been told to do the following to any small space: (1) throw a grenade; (2) enter; (3) throw other grenades into every corner; and (4) direct submachinegun bursts toward any other possible threat while moving forward.[20]

For fear of counterattack from the subways or sewers, all below-ground conduits were also secured as the Soviet assault groups advanced.[21]

The Chinese

At the Battle of Shanghai in 1937, the Nationalist Chinese had difficulty countering the Japanese thrust into the center of the city. They had mostly small caliber weapons, whereas the Japanese enclaves were soon fortified with concrete thick enough to resist 150mm howitzer shells. Chinese troops had only one way to advance toward such a bastion. Under the cover of machinegun fire, they crawled close enough to kill its defenders with hand grenades. Lacking the heavy weaponry to destroy the Japanese bunker complexes directly, the Chinese commander decided to encircle them. He ordered his men to take the streets around each Japanese beachhead. Every time such a street was successfully cleared, the Chinese would set up a sandbag blockade. In that way, they were able to gradually isolate each stronghold. But when the Japanese brought in their tanks, such a strategy no longer worked, and the Chinese were eventually defeated.[22]

Every modern-day PLA unit (of whatever size) is trained in Guerrilla Warfare (GW). GW would help with the initial infiltration of a targeted city, as well as the inherently decentralized process of room clearing. Thus, all modern-day Chinese Communist soldiers are well suited for urban offense. During China's fully supported punitive expedition into North Vietnam in 1979, its soldiers were finally able to capture all five of the originally targeted provincial capitals. While those troops had been badly attrited in the rice paddies on the way in, they were nevertheless to gain valuable urban-assault experience.[23]

All *ninjutsu* technique had originated on the Asian Mainland, so Chinese troops would likely be as skilled at entering an opposition fortress and inaccessible structure as their Japanese counterparts.[24]

The Other Asian Communists

To avoid the casualties of openly assaulting a city, the Oriental will secretly enter it. He covertly moves in via all available means and then blends with the local population. After all key bridges and chokepoints have been secured, he may then send in conventional reinforcements.

Of all the Asian Communist nations, North Vietnam has the most recent experience with such a maneuver. The NVA easily captured Hue City in 1968 and several other South Vietnamese cities (to include Saigon) in 1975. It did so from the inside out.[25] Only after supplies had been staged, commandos positioned, and key buildings seized, did their spearhead battalions strike toward the city's center.

Most built-up areas provide a veritable maze of underground rooms and passageways. Within those subterranean spaces can be hidden hundreds of commandos and tons of ammunition. That makes possible what the North Vietnamese call their "Blooming Lotus" maneuver. Many infiltrators quietly penetrate any Western-style defense. Then, they have only to attack from its center outward.

In the Japanese attack on Shanghai and probable predecessor to the Blooming Lotus in Vietnam, the center of town is not initially seized by infiltrators. Instead, striking columns intentionally bypass perimeter strongpoints.

> This methodology was developed in 1952 in an assault on Phat Diem. Its key characteristic was to avoid enemy positions on the perimeter of the town. The main striking columns move[d] directly against the center of the town seeking out command and control centers. Only then were forces directed outward to systematically destroy the now leaderless units around the town. . . .
>
> This approach contrasts sharply with Western doctrine, which traditionally would isolate the town, gain a foothold, and systematically drive inward to clear the town. This sets up a series of attrition-based battles that historically make combat in built-up areas such a costly undertaking.[26]
>
> —"'Urban Warrior'—A View from North Vietnam"
> *Marine Corps Gazette,* April 1999

At the outset of the 1968 Tet Offensive, NVA spearhead battalions had little trouble night-marching into Hue City. That's because the bridges, intersections, and gates along their avenues of approach had already been captured by infiltrators or commandos disguised as pilgrims. Those battalions went on to consolidate infiltrator gains at most of the key buildings and compounds in the city.

The Tet attack on Saigon in 1968 followed the same theme. To sneak up on the South Vietnamese capital, the NVA undoubtedly used the Cu Chi infiltration route from Cambodia. It provided no shortage of underground passageways, rest stops, and storage areas. Then, infiltrators attempted to seize nine key objectives in the South Vietnamese capital and hold out until their spearhead battalions could arrive. Among them were Independence Palace, Army General Staff, Navy Command, Tan Son Nhut Airfield, U.S. Embassy, Police Headquarters, Capital Special Zone, and Chi Hoa Jail.[27] All the while, other main-force units had attempted to keep the majority of U.S. and ARVN forces busy at the outskirts of town. But, the Communists had lacked both the timing and wherewithal to pull off such a grandiose takeover. Unfortunately, they had still learned from the experience, while their Western-minded adversaries hadn't.

Seven years later in 1975, the VC/NVA were to dispatch commandos and spearheads against only five key targets within Saigon and then fan out to capture other important facilities. For the inside effort, they had a larger and more sophisticated "special task force."[28] Its elements launched surprise assaults against the following: Tan Son Nhut airfield, Army General Staff, Presidential Palace, Saigon Special Military Sector, and General Police Headquarters. Others seized bridges and intersections along the spearhead column approach routes. Still others reconnoitered and then helped spearhead elements to capture secondary targets. Of note is how easily thousands of personnel and tons of supplies had been prestaged within the confines of city.[29] Without extensive space below ground, this would not have been possible. Through it all, the South Vietnamese never suspected the buildup. If they had, they could have better defended Saigon's center.

For the 1975 spearheads, the North Vietnamese used armored columns with embedded infantry and artillery support. On 30 April, those spearheads attacked Saigon from all four of the cardinal directions. Among the VC/NVA ruses in the final assault were regular soldiers wearing civilian clothes, special task force personnel dressed like ARVN soldiers,[30] and Communist pilots bombing with South Vietnamese planes.[31] It was no coincidence these ruses reinforced the impression that a popular uprising was underway. The "Blooming Lotus" had become the state of the art for urban offense.

The Tactical Differences Between Eastern Armies

Only the Asian Communists had attempted to occupy the center of a city through secretive infiltration before any concerted attack. And only they would then send in conventional spearheads from different directions.

During WWII, both the Soviet and the German infantrymen seemed to carry more submachineguns than their Asian counterparts. From 1944 on, German rifle platoons had about 11 submachineguns.[32] Some Soviet rifle companies also had up to four per squad.[33] Of the 20 or so people in a typical Russian assault subgroup, all the short-range fighters were submachinegunners.[34] And in the little pamphlet issued to all replacement Soviet troops at Stalingrad, a submachinegun was specifically needed to comply with its instructions.[35]

Early in the Korean War, the Chinese would also employ many "burpguns" during their rural assaults.[36] So, the urban-warfare correlation would not have escaped them for long.

Control over Urban Combat Is Necessarily Looser

Within the heavily compartmentalized terrain of a city lies the most isolating of all battlefield environments. No more than a fireteam can easily seize a room, nor more than a squad comfortably clear a small building. Even in larger structures, each hallway or floor must be ultimately assigned to a separate (and semi-autonomous) squad.

The counterattacks of reinforced Russian squads had kept a whole German army from reaching the Volga in Stalingrad. Then, at Grozny, the same size of unit had swarmed and destroyed a mechanized Soviet column.

Just staying alive while changing location in built-up terrain takes advanced individual movement skills and the leeway to use them. So, it should be evident that any urban offense will require some decentralization of control. This is why the lower-echelon combatants who have been formally trained in GW have the best chance of doing well in an urban attack. At present, this would only be those of the Communist Asian armies, and any Eastern rebels who happened to be following the Maoist method.

> In handing the Russian military a humiliating defeat [in 1995], the Chechens adapted to modern [urban] conditions their traditional forest guerrilla tactics. . . .
>
> For a force of guerrillas, the new urban "forest" provides many . . . opportunities for sniping, mines, boobytraps, and ambushes, while it negates the enemy's superiority in . . . armor, artillery and . . . air power. Urban fighting also cruelly exposes the shortcomings of an army accustomed to relying on major units acting together under a rigid hierarchy of command. Even more than in modern warfare in general, units operating in cities get separated and broken down to the section and even subsection level, throwing tremendous responsibility on junior officers, noncommissioned officers (NCOs), and individual soldiers.[37]
>
> — *Armed Forces Journal Internat.,* August 1998

Which U.S. Squad Could Best Utilize Such Knowledge

For the present-day U.S. Marine squad to have more rifles capable of fully automatic fire now seems well justified where urban combat is concerned. However, its three SAWs will still not take the place of the true LMG (with tripod and T&E) that every major Eastern army has in each infantry squad. For fighting in a built-up area, this LMG can provide pinpoint or long-range fire under several important circumstances: (1) suppressing defender fire from any tiny aperture; (2) overwatching the rooftops of the avenue of advance from a tall building; or (3) successfully countering long-range enemy machinegun fire. (See Figure 13.2.) After the Eastern armies of WWII had made countless holes in walls to advance safely, the American squad will also need either special demolitions or an organic SMAW equivalent.

Urban momentum is ordinarily achieved by moving through structures more quickly than expected. That takes the absolute minimum of noise and personnel. Only with a trio of four-man fireteams, can a single squad easily clear a small building. Required will be one fireteam per floor, and well-acquainted buddy teams working along opposite sides of every hallway.

Figure 13.2: Only a MG with Tripod and T/E Can Cover Rooftops
(Source: FM 90-10-1 [1982], pp. 3-14, E-18.)

14 Urban Defense

- How did the North Korean Army defend Seoul in 1950?
- Did it have advice from the PLA?

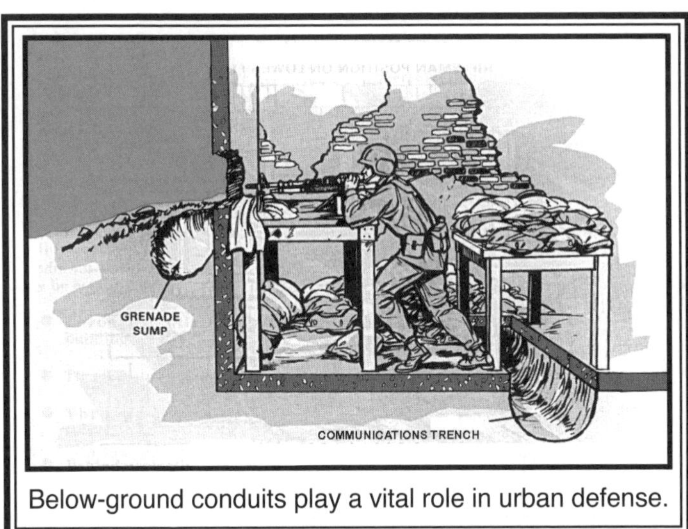

Below-ground conduits play a vital role in urban defense.

(Source: FM 90-10-1 [1982], p. E-4.)

How Important Is the Consensus Opinion of Other Armies?

If the more-maneuver-oriented Eastern armies had similarly defended built-up terrain in the mid-20th Century, shouldn't future U.S. squads be wise to do the same kinds of things? Or has the latest U.S. gadgetry effectively negated all tactical lessons so far learned about urban combat?

Not since the machinegun's invention has close combat greatly changed in any arena. Because technology only slightly affects how wars are waged, there's no need to follow a strict time frame when discussing how those Eastern armies have tactically improved.

The Japanese

At the last minute, the Nipponese decided to defend Manila in 1945. So doing may have created some very effective ways of countering an urban invader. Beginning 3 February, the 9500-man Japanese Naval Defense Force (skilled Japanese marines) made a concerted stab at holding the city. Those few combatants were then able to resist the U.S. juggernaut for four weeks. To do so, they had no armor or aircraft, and little artillery, communication, or overall control of detachments.[1]

Yet, those naval troops were still the product of excellent tactical doctrine and training.[2] So, within the 15-square-mile city, they created semi-independent matrices of mutually supporting strongpoints. To hide the location of these matrices, they created the illusion that the entire city was being defended. They did so by assigning a single combatant to many structures and then widely patrolling in gun trucks.[3] As well as a supposed defender, that building's lone occupant probably functioned as a forward observer for artillery or mortars.[4] At the center of many matrices were important buildings—e.g., the New Police Station, the Philippine General Hospital, City Hall, the General Post Office, Philippines University, Rizal Stadium, the Manila Hotel, and the Legislative/Finance/Agriculture Complex.[5] So, while the matrix did not necessarily lie along one of the U.S. Army's avenues of advance, it was probably near its end.

During the subsequent defense of Manila, tiny detachments of those Japanese marines exercised considerable initiative. They cut firing slits through the foundations of buildings at ground level.[6] To hide and protect crew-served weapons, they placed their bunkers deep inside rooms.[7] Such an arrangement could also make the building's interior easier to protect.[8] To keep the Americans from assaulting their structures from the top down, they placed machinegun nests on flat roofs,[9] tossed aerial bombs or molotov cocktails from upper stories,[10] destroyed stairs,[11] dropped grenades from holes in ceilings,[12] and fired rifles upwards through holes in the floors.[13] Just to move forward, U.S. troops often had to rubble the next building to their front.[14] In effect, the Japanese naval security forces had turned all contested streets into kill zones and the lower floors of many buildings into "firesacks."

Just as the Soviets had done with Stalingrad's industrial sites, the Japanese decided to most heavily defend the Provisor Island

Electricity Plant and Paco Railroad Station. With no intention of finally abandoning the city, they tried to make capturing it so costly that U.S. forces would have trouble occupying the rest of Luzon. All around the train station, the Nipponese marines established machinegun posts. As at Iwo Jima, each machinegun was, in turn, surrounded by "foxholes with riflemen."[15]

> [In the Paco district] Japanese observers were present in almost every building. At street intersections, machinegun pillboxes were dug [recessed] into buildings and sandbagged so as to cover their approaches. Artillery and anti-aircraft weapons were placed in doorways or in upper-story windows. Most streets and borders of streets were mined. . . . The streets were a fireswept zone forcing Americans to move between streets and within buildings.[16]
>
> — U.S. Army Combat Studies Institute research

Those fireswept streets, in turn, forced the American soldiers to move through some very dangerous structures along them. Not only were those structures full of firesacks, but at least some had been pre-rigged for complete demolition by the Japanese.[17] At the time, this may have been a fairly new defense strategem. Not until the 21st Century wars with Muslim extremists would intentionally collapsing a previously occupied building become regularly expected behavior.

Like the Germans and Russians, the Japanese had also composed their defensive arrays out of embedded subordinate units. On open ground, the final component was then the self-sufficient squad-sized fort. Within each building, this unit hierarchy may have extended all the way down to semi-autonomous two-man teams. In other words, the occupants of each room may have been allowed to develop their own fire, barrier, and withdrawal plans. This much freedom of action would have made those buildings virtually impossible to seize.

> Sandbags and barricades blocked all ground-level doors and windows. Interiors were also fortified as in other strongpoints.[18]
>
> — U.S. Army Combat Studies Institute research

But the Japanese marines in Manila were not just good at defending buildings. To channelize U.S. armor and/or blunt forward momentum, they also built roadblocks. Such a travel barricade normally consisted of a minefield, roadbed-driven steel rails, and wire-attached trucks. The whole arrangement was then covered by the interlocking fire of four heavy machineguns.[19] Those guns may have been situated in the buildings in a nearby strongpoint matrix.

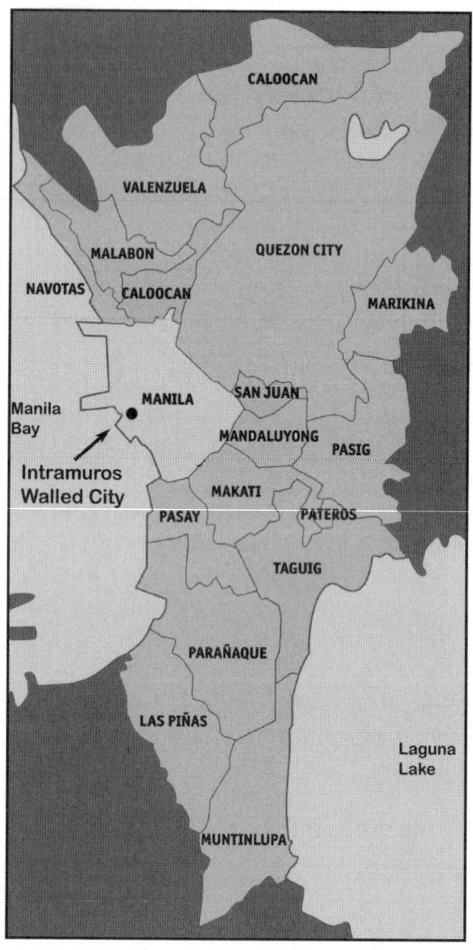

Map 14.1: Last Stand at Manila's Fort Santiago

(Source: "Political map of Metro Manila, Philippines," by Adkranz, reprinted under Creative Commons Attribution-Share Alike 4.0 International license, © 2014.)

What has just been described comes quite close to advanced Maneuver Warfare procedure. Only lacking is a way for individual strongpoint occupants to escape encirclement and an overall rearward motion toward previously established fallback positions. The sole proof of a tactical withdrawal from Manila is the previous report of "intentional demolition or incineration of defended buildings." But to so well defend a city of this size, that few Japanese defenders must have additionally manned a succession of fallback positions along the Allies' main routes of entry. As long as all living defenders ended up near the urban center, their backwards movement would not have constituted an abandonment of the city. As it turned out, a "last stand" of sorts did occur in the subterranean rooms and tunnels of the 16th Century Fort Santiago on the northwest corner of the old walled city of Intramuros. (See Map 14.1.) That was right before 2000 refugees came flooding out of the place.[20] Forts of this vintage had secret passageways leading from royal chambers to some point beyond their walls. In this case, that point would have been right where the Pasig River entered Manila Bay.

The Chinese

Shanghai was mostly protected by the Nationalist Chinese in 1937. Yet, their more mechanized attacker still encountered "isolated snipers behind every window and on every rooftop" during its final-mopping-up operation.[21] If there had been some Communist troops contesting the city, GW might have helped them to thwart the initial Japanese thrust to its center (just as it would later do for Chechen rebels in Grozny). In March of 1951, PVA "volunteers" from China would abandon Seoul without a fight and never get the chance to demonstrate their proficiency at urban combat.[22] A large portion of the North Korean force that attempted to keep the Allies from retaking Seoul the year before had been formerly part of the PLA.

How a Chinese-Assisted Army Defended Seoul Initially

Some 20,000 members of the NKPA ended up fighting for the South Korean capital in the autumn of 1950. Among them were several infantry battalions that had been part of a PLA Frontier Force.[23] Because Maoist Mobile Warfare involved some intentional backwards movement, the attacking U.S. Marines at first could not tell how resolutely Seoul would be contested. But as their Gen. O.P. Smith had suspected, his North Korean counterpart would "soon change from delaying tactics to hard-nosed, stand-and-deliver defense."[24]

While the North Koreans then made the Marines "fight for every inch of ground" and launched several determined spoiling attacks inside the city,[25] their overall motion was nonetheless rearward. Just as the Japanese had initially done in Manila, Seoul's defenders first blunted American momentum through hastily erected roadblocks. But, only in outward appearance were these roadway obstructions the work of a rear guard during a general skedaddle.[26] The attacking GIs also encountered buildings turned into strongpoints.

Just as "retreat combat" had become Japan's most formidable rural defense method near the end of WWII,[27] so too had tactical withdrawal come to signify Maoist Mobile Defense. This was not a retreat in the Western sense of the word at Seoul, but rather a carefully choreographed attempt to overextend a more heavily armed opponent. That would explain the rash of spoiling attacks. Some were actually "counterattacks" after stringing out a U.S. unit. A closer look at the eventual North Korean pullout from South Korea's capital city reveals a fairly orderly event.[28]

Simply to enter the sprawling metropolis in September 1950, the 5th Marines had been forced to cross a fireswept river (the Han).[29] Next, they had fought through an NKPA battalion to reach the first high ground on Hill 125. Then, enemy resistance stiffened abruptly, and it would take the 5th Marines another full week of desperate fighting to advance the final four miles into Seoul. Much of that resistance would be encountered around Hill 296.[30] (See Map 14.2.)

Meanwhile, a little to the southeast, the 1st Marines *en route* to the suburb of Yongdungpo successfully ambushed a Communist tank-led spoiling attack with their new 3.5 inch rocket launchers. But, the unsuccessful Reds did not leave the suburb. "The surviving North Koreans withdrew to their prepared defenses within Yongdungpo."[31] After a bloody crossing of the Kalchon Canal, the Marines moved through dry rice paddies without much trouble. Then, A/1/1 found itself entering the main street of Yongdungpo

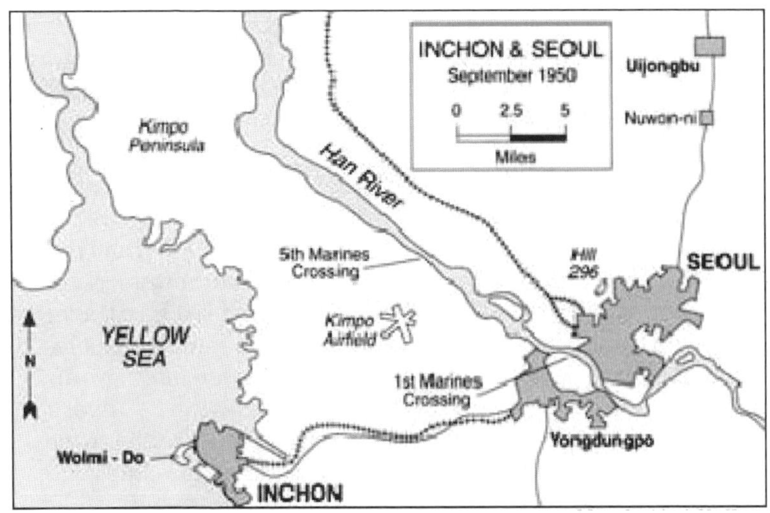

Map 14.2: U.S. Marines' Approach to Seoul
(Source: Map by Mary Craddock Hoffman, "Battle of the Barricades: U.S. Marines in the Recapture of Seoul," by Col. Joseph H. Alexander USMC (Ret.), p. 5.)

totally unopposed. Before dark, it had cut the Seoul suburb in half. (Look at Map 14.2 a little closer.) The NKPA attacked Company A shortly after sundown with five Soviet-built T-34 tanks. Once again, the Marines' 3.5 rockets saved the day. Later that night, there were four separate NKPA infantry assaults—all successfully repelled. The road to Seoul now lay open for the 1st Marines as soon as the 5th Marines could move far enough east to cover another Han River crossing.

The enemy had left this corridor into Seoul relatively undefended.[32] He counterattacked when the Americans began to outdistance their source of resupply and reinforcement. That's when the details of his battle plan also became apparent. To save manpower and materiel, much of his defense would be hurriedly established along the Allies' main axes of advance. Then, it would be sequentially dismantled and re-established farther along their route. This defense would have five successive stages: (1) minefields; (2) anti-armor ambushes; (3) intersection barricades; (4) mutually supporting buildings as strongpoints in a matrix; and (5) occasional counterattacks.

> The North Koreans defending Seoul lacked the numbers to occupy every building or side street, so they concentrated instead on the major avenues and thoroughfares [that the Marines were using]. By now each significant intersection in [that part of] the city featured an improvised barricade, typically protected by rice bags filled with sand or rubble, piled eight feet high by five feet wide, and defended by antitank guns, heavy machine guns, and mines. . . . "Every [such] intersection was [hastily] barricaded after the fashion of the Paris Commune: carts, earth-filled rice bags . . . furniture, and rubble."[33]
>
> — *Battle of the Barricades,* by Alexander

Such barricades had only been constructed along the Marines' entrance routes, and not throughout the massive metropolitan area. Otherwise, there would not have been as many in the Marines' way, and the heavily defended ones as easy to spot.

> In Seoul, the Marines encountered barricaded roadblocks every 200 to 300 yards along the main boulevards.[34]
>
> — *Battle of the Barricades,* by Alexander

Only some of those closely arrayed barricades may have been accompanied by the other four defensive features. Yet, all roadblocks seemed to be contested by upper-story snipers. That was to keep actual strongpoints safe from preparatory bombardment. In Seoul, there was likely a strongpoint matrix just beyond any combination of mines, molotov cocktails, and roadblock. As at Manila, machinegun pillboxes had been hidden in its composite buildings to cover a key intersection.[35]

> Now NKPA barricades mushroomed at each intersection. Enemy snipers fired from blown out windows. Other NKPA troops [occasionally] lobbed molotov cocktails from the rooftops onto the Marine tanks in the street below.[36]
>
> — *Battle of the Barricades,* by Alexander

Eventually, one forward-positioned Marine commander got a good look through his binoculars at what was concurrently happening up ahead of him. Here's what he saw.

> For once he [the Marine commander] could clearly see the enemy troops moving into new positions, building fresh barricades, and preparing future ambushes.[37]
> — *Battle of the Barricades,* by Alexander

As the Marine columns moved slowly through Seoul, the anti-armor ambushes, fights for each barricade, and strongpoint captures all took place in close succession. In effect, those things had all confronted the lead U.S. infantry element and its accompanying armor at about the same time—in what has since come to be known as standard Oriental practice. The GIs' only option was then to attack all sources of fire at once.

> Street fighting in Seoul involved forcibly uprooting the NKPA troops from either their roadblock barricades or their isolated strongpoints within or atop the buildings.[38]
> — *Battle of the Barricades,* by Alexander

Then came more of the so-called "spoiling attacks" wherever U.S. forces seemed a bit overextended. Many involved loosely coordinated tank-infantry assaults. Others were by non-supported infantrymen at night or just sappers.

> Far from fleeing the city, the enemy—at least this particular battalion of the 25th NKPA Brigade—was charging due south down Ma Po Boulevard with six to 12 tanks and self-propelled guns, accompanied by infantry [on the night of 25 September]. . . .
>
> The North Koreans executed a third major spoiling attack [in a different sector] at 0500.[39]
> — *Battle of the Barricades,* by Alexander

> In downtown Seoul on 26 September, . . . [a] nimble-footed North Korean darted out from the rubble, caught 2d Battalion, 1st Marines' riflemen by surprise, and flung a satchel charge atop a passing flame tank, then vanished in

> the blast and smoke. The crew escaped unscathed, but the tank was destroyed. Angered and embarrassed by this bad luck, 2d Battalion's NCOs forcibly reminded their men to watch the adjacent alleys and rubble piles, not the tanks. This paid off. The NKPA launched a dozen more sapper attacks against Marine tanks operating in the center of the boulevard; Lieutenant Colonel Sutter's troops cut each one of them down.[40]
>
> — *Battle of the Barricades,* by Alexander

Large numbers of NKPA troops were obviously being held in reserve just beyond all such "key defense zones" to take advantage of any lapse in the attackers' due diligence. Most likely they would have been from the same units as had manned the myriad of tiny outposts and defensive positions along the way. As the Marines moved through the city, so did this enemy manpower pool somewhere to their front. The job of its members was not to die in place, but rather to wear down their opponent enough while moving backwards to make him possible to defeat.

> Thousands of North Korean Peoples' Army (NKPA) troops lay waiting for them behind barricades or among countless courtyards and rooftops.[41]
>
> — *Battle of the Barricades,* by Alexander

The overall NKPA defense had also involved a lot of "snipers" not associated with any particular strongpoint. Their role had been to make each building appear fully defended. And their existence kept the GIs from developing any forward momentum. Each edifice along the way would have to be fully searched.

> The Marines fought two enemies in downtown Seoul—those who defended behind the barricades and the snipers seemingly hidden in every other window.[42]
>
> — *Battle of the Barricades,* by Alexander

As at Manila five years before, U.S. troops discovered many buildings occupied by a single enemy soldier in the South Korean capital. While this soldier occasionally fired his rifle, his role in the overall scheme of things had to be more comprehensive than just sniping. As the Japanese at Guadalcanal, he may have been keeping his parent unit informed of opposition progress through some sort of code based on rifle shots.[43]

> It seemed like every building in Seoul housed an enemy sniper.[44]
>
> — S.Sgt. Lee Bergee, Seoul veteran

There are other similarities between the battles for Manila and Seoul. In both places, U.S. troops encountered hordes of civilians at inopportune times.

> Suddenly, in trying to get away from a firefight in their neighborhood, hundreds of women and children would mob into our area, blocking us off.[45]
>
> — PFC Win Scott, Seoul veteran

And as during the fight for Manila, U.S. troops had trouble locating the source of some of the most destructive enemy fire in Seoul. They soon discovered the reason. They were again facing extremely narrow fields of fire from recessed positions.[46]

On the rocky barrens of Iwo Jima, the Japanese had routinely taken U.S. Marine assault units under fire from all sides at once.[47] In the built-up terrain of Seoul, the North Koreans tried to do likewise. That's when "buttoned-up" U.S. armor came in handy for heavy-caliber stand-off shooting.

> There was no front and no rear. Thank God we had tanks with us. Without them we'd still be fighting there.[48]
>
> — PFC Win Scott, Seoul veteran

"The Soviet Union's official newspaper *Pravda* soon compared the situation in Seoul to the Russian defense of Stalingrad in WWII: 'There is firing behind every stone.'"[49] But, no direct evidence exists of semi-autonomous NKPA squads working together between tiny islands of resistance in South Korea's capital. So, *Pravda* may have meant that well-placed and mobile ambushes had made Seoul look like it was fully defended.

There had been a minimum of subterranean activity in Seoul.

Its subway would not be constructed for another 20 years. The Korean War chronicles only mention a few caves beneath Hill 105 in the 5th Marines' sector.[50]

Another Maoist Inspired Army at Hue City

The Chinese PLA offered little tactical advice to the NVA infantry during the Vietnam War, but the smaller of the two had

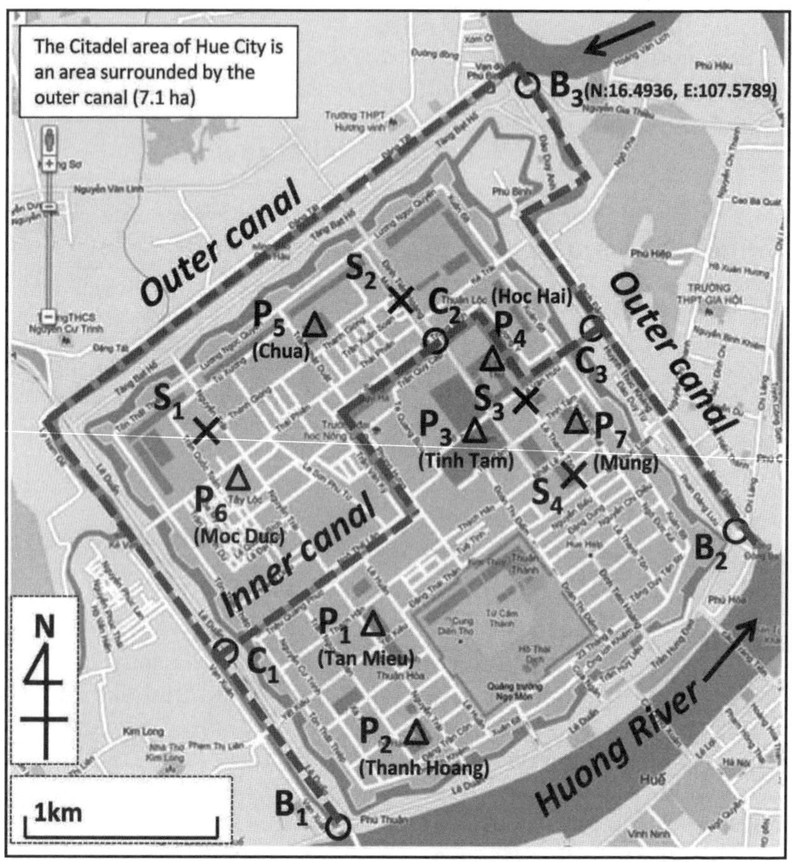

Map 14.3: Water Features in and Around Hue's Citadel

(Source: Courtesy of researchgate.net and iwapublishing.com for use of the map in "Characterization of Water Pollution in Drainage Networks ... in the Citadel area of Hue City," by Y. Nagano, T. Teraguchi, P. K. Lieu, and H. Furumai, from "Water Science & Technology," 70(4): 612-619, August 2014, ©)

still been based on Maoist principles. That's why at Hue City in 1968, the urban equivalent of a Maoist Mobile Defense once again appeared.

After the North Vietnamese had captured the center of city in February 1968, they were able to hold on to it for almost a month. Within the ancient Citadel's walls, they established—on alternating streets—strings of strongpoints.[51] So, U.S. forces could not tell which buildings were being heavily defended, those between were occupied by roving shooters.[52] The occupants of one such street—the narrow Mai Thuc Loan (or "Phase Line Green")—were subsequently able to keep a fully reinforced U.S. battalion from crossing for four days.[53] To do so, they used preregistered, long-range machinegun and mortar fire from both ends of the street. And they employed narrow, overlapping bands of random small-arms and RPG fire from bunkers between the houses, within the rooms, and sometimes even behind the Americans. The whole arrangement provided Phase Line Green's defenders with the kill zone for a 360° ambush and enough close-defensive fires to discourage an attack.

The NVA invaders of Hue City then made good use of the Japanese-dug passageways within the dirt-filled Citadel walls. Mai Thuc Loan exited the old fortress at the Dong Ba Gate. That's where some of the NVA's long-range machineguns were located. Every time the Marines would bomb or capture this gate, more North Vietnamese soldiers would emerge from its interior passageways.[54] Mai Thuc Loan's defenders could also have moved between strongpoints through its covered sewage trenches. In fact, that may also be how the NVA's rear guard was able to carry casualties from the Imperial Palace and southern corner of the Citadel on the nights of 22-23 February 1968.[55] The rest of the contingent would leave—a few at time—by grabbing onto flood refuse in a darkened river. Thus, subterranean and watery activity would prove vital to their defense plan.

At Hue, the Communists had first captured the city center and then moved outward in their "Blooming Lotus" maneuver. When their presence was contested, they did not conduct a fighting withdrawal from the entire city, but only back to its center. From the Imperial Palace within the Citadel had undoubtedly existed an old below-ground escape route to the river. (See Map 14.3.) So, from the walled Citadel, they—like the Japanese at Intramuros in Manila—had managed to exfiltrate an Allied cordon. Both Asian armies would do better at this ploy than Berlin's final defenders.

The Germans

During WWII, the Germans fought by far the hardest for their capital city. The Soviet armies that had closed in on Berlin in the Spring of 1945 were no strangers to urban attack. Before crossing the Oder River, Zhukov had insisted on special instruction in street fighting for all assault troops.[56] Yet, to take the city, those armies would suffer 305,000 casualties from 16 April to 8 May 1945.[57] While some of those losses may have occurred along the city's approaches, the total is still mind boggling. By this late in the war, Berlin was being protected by hastily trained *Volksgrenadier* (people's infantry) battalions,[58] a hodgepodge of understrength support units, *Volksturm* (home guard) volunteers, and Hitler Youth. To the *Volksturm,* the Fuhrer had assigned the job of defending the city street by street.[59] It was comprised of men over 60, boys between 16 and 18, the "medically unfit," and possibly women.[60] By some accounts, only half had small arms with which to confront the Russian armor.[61] For the final battle, one military force would be well organized, trained, and supported, while the other would not. From the Soviet casualty total comes strong evidence of the power of decentralized control and innovative technique during an urban defense. Against a veritable cascade of Russian bombs, shells, and tanks, the German citizen soldiers would have little else going for them.

> As dawn broke on the morning of 25 April [1945], 464,000 Soviet troops, with 12,700 guns and mortars, 21,000 *Katyusha* multiple rocket launchers, and 1,500 tanks and self-propelled guns, stood ready and waiting to begin the final assault on the heart of Berlin. To the north, south, east and west, the Soviet spearheads were within four miles of Hitler's chancellery and the Reichstag. Supporting them [were] . . . thousands of planes.[62]
>
> — *The Fall of Berlin, by* Read and Fisher

Of the 1500 tracked vehicles (from the Soviet First and Second Guards Tank Armies) to enter the built-up area initially,[63] two-thirds may have been lost. Just before the final assault on the Reichstag, another entire tank army (the Third Guards) had to be committed.[64] At first, the tanks operated in columns, and then in pairs, but seldom with infantrymen to their front.[65] This was to cost them dearly. The

Russians were adhering to a favorite tactic—tank assaults preceded by bombardment.[66] Although the hastily assembled neighborhood defenders possessed few heavy weapons of their own,[67] they did have an ample supply of durable buildings, underground conduits, and *Panzerfaust* antitank rockets. While climbing the piles of rubble unprotected by infantry, many a Russian tank must have been subjected to a close-range belly shot. The defenders were also good at ambushing Russian armor. The *coup de grace* was normally antitank munitions from every direction at once. Such fire so confused the quarry that he couldn't accurately respond to it. In this same way, a Soviet infantry unit had once destroyed a German armored column on the grassy Steppes of Russia.[68]

> The [Soviet] tanks, in particular, started out disastrously, moving along city streets in columns. The defenders had only to knock out the leading tank with a well-aimed *Panzerfaust,* and the others, strung out in line behind it, were trapped, easy prey with their sides exposed to fire from the buildings on either side.[69]
>
> — *The Fall of Berlin, by* Read and Fisher

With three apparent rings of fortifications around the city,[70] and Berlin's waterways forming concentric circles around the Reichstag, the Russians became convinced that the inner city had its own security plan. More likely were thousands of small loosely controlled contingents simply exercising enough initiative to attempt a combined stand.

> Never before in the experience of warfare had we been called upon to capture a city as large and as heavily fortified as Berlin. Its total area was almost 350 square miles. Its subway and other widespread underground engineering networks provide ample possibilities for troop movements. The city itself and its suburbs had been carefully prepared for defense. Every street, every square, every alley, building, canal and bridge represented an element in the city's defense system.[71]
>
> — Soviet Field Marshal Zhukov

Thus, it would be more accurate to say the Soviets met some resistance at almost every street, square, alley, building, canal, and bridge. But, much of that resistance had been coming in an impromptu fashion from temporary defenders who had been gradually withdrawing toward the city's center. The under-trained and under-equipped *Volksturm* would not have been able to make a concerted effort throughout every corner of this large a metropolitan expanse.

No longer hypothesis, most of the above is confirmed fact. To canalize the Russian armor, the Germans are known to have built a lot of tank traps and barricades.[72] German snipers had also been assigned to some buildings,[73] and whole units to others. So, strongpoint matrices had been sprinkled throughout probable attack corridors through partially defended buildings. Where those corridors crossed the so-called defense rings received the most attention. Most likely to have been heavily fortified were the structures around canal bridges, flak towers, and subway stations.[74] Yet, many would be only temporarily occupied. Was that by design or necessity? The Russians did discover an abundance of "cellar escape routes."[75] On the subway walls were the German inscription: "We withdraw but we are winning!"[76] So, this had unmistakably been the same type of retreat combat already conducted by a German ally at Manila.

> Under fire from Soviet advance units, Skorning's combat group was soon in danger of being surrounded. The regimental commander ordered them to pull back to the northern side of the canal, where Skorning set up his strongpoint at a narrow bridge. . . .
>
> Soviet troops soon crossed the canal, and Skorning and his men were forced to retreat under fire, back through the graves of St. Luke's and Emmaus churchyards toward the S-Banh [tunnels] skirting the airport, part of the city's inner defense ring.[77]
>
> — *The Fall of Berlin, by* Read and Fisher

So far in the battle for Berlin, the makeshift German units had been doing quite well with the hand-to-hand tank-killing methods detailed in Chapter 9. But, then their magnificent *Panzerfausts* began to run out.

> With no more *Panzerfausts* left, Skorning's men had no chance of holding them [the Russian tanks] off. Under fire from Soviet gun positions, they escaped along the S-Bahn

> [tunnels] to Tempelhof Station, where his regimental command post was situated in a public air-raid shelter.[78]
> — *The Fall of Berlin, by* Read and Fisher

The battle chronicles show some of the German defenders blowing up the canal bridges as they were forced to retreat farther into the city's central area.[79] One would assume they were always doing so out of necessity. But, on occasion, they may have been intentionally pulling back to soften up their immediate foe for counterattack. In certain neighborhoods, the Germans had already taken some offensive action.[80] In others, the degree of fortification was the only thing to worry their opposition.

> From his vantage point [Gen.] Chuikov had a clear view of the rings of defense works built along the canals and railway lines which curved around the city centre, where every building seemed to have been transformed into a fortress. The most powerful defenses appeared to be in the area of the old city walls, built in the eighteenth century. . . . The Landwehr canal and the sharp bend in the Spree [River] with its steep, concrete-lined banks, formed a protective screen around the government buildings, including the chancellery and the Reichstag—the bull's eye in Chuikov's target.[81]
> — *The Fall of Berlin, by* Read and Fisher

Most of those brave young defenders of Germany's capital city fought on to the bitter end. Then, some may have evaded the tightening Russian noose—through the city's vast subterranean networks. While many German units had their command posts in S-Bahn and U-Bahn tunnels,[82] Hitler's last-minute decision to flood those tunnels near the Landwehr Canal did little to improve their chances of escape.[83] Yet, when all seemed lost, Hitler forbade their surrender and suggested his frontline troops "break out in small groups" to join the forces still fighting outside the city. He issued a formal order to that effect before committing suicide.[84] Before long, many of the *Volksturm* started throwing away their rifles and melting into the civilian population.[85] On 2 May 1945, all that remained of the Berlin garrison—some 70,000 men—surrendered to the Soviets at the center of city.[86] Still alive below ground were some two million other Berliners.[87]

How fewer than 100,000 under-prepared defenders with only

hand-held weaponry could do this well against 2.3 million seasoned urban assault troops backed by 6250 tanks would not be of much interest to the prideful West.

The Russians

At Stalingrad, the Soviet Army had already discovered how urban terrain can be made virtually unassailable through "killing zones" and tiny mutually supporting counterattacks. With reinforced infantry squads separately operating from adjoining enclaves, they were able to keep a whole German army from reaching the Volga River. Those tiny "shock groups" had been organized and outfitted like a smaller version of the Soviet assault unit in the previous chapter. Of particular importance were their armaments.

> But, the Russians, though still heavily outnumbered remained their [the Germans] masters in the technique of house-to-house fighting. They had perfected the use of "shock groups," small bodies of mixed arms—light and heavy machinegunners, tommy gunners, and grenadiers usually with antitank guns, who gave one another support in lightning counterattacks; and they had developed the creation of "killing zones," houses and squares heavily mined to which the defenders knew all the approach routes, where the German advance could be canalized. . . . By the end of October the Russian positions at Stalingrad had been reduced to a few pockets of stone, seldom more than three hundred yards deep, bordering on the right bank of the Volga. . . . But these last islets of resistance, hardened in the furnace of repeated attacks, were irreducible. Paulus's VI Army was spent.[88]
>
> — A.J.P. Taylor, as quoted in
> *Stormtroop Tactics,* by Gudmundsson,

Such funneling of enemy soldiers into kill zones was a distinct indicator of the same kind of "retreat combat" that would be later practiced by the Japanese at Manila and Germans at Berlin. But, from Stalingrad had come the first hint of its details. The kill zones had apparently been houses, courtyards, and squares laced with explosives. Of course, for the latter two locations, a concentrated mortar barrage could have accomplished almost the same thing. All open kill zones may have been additionally swept by Soviet machinegun fire.

To draw the attackers into such zones, some Russian soldiers may have visibly retreated along their approaches. Whether all shock groups had then attacked at the same exact spot as the explosions is doubtful. They more probably showed up nearby. Their job would have been to cut off and destroy the segment of the German column that still existed outside of the kill zone. To do so, several Soviet groups would have swarmed in from different directions. Like the Asian Communist *Haichi Shiki* in rural terrain (refer back to Chapter 12), such a group counterattack would have first prevented retreat/reinforcement and then tried to annihilate all trapped Germans.

Those reinforced Russian squads had played a big part in keeping a fully supported German division from reaching the river, and thus provided a salient to which reinforcements could safely boat. Because such an impromptu maneuver had constituted a major milestone in the evolution of small-unit tactics, modern-day grunts should pay particular attention to shock group specifics.

The Soviet Strongpoint Matrices in Stalingrad

It isn't likely the above-mentioned shock groups operated within TAORs that were completely devoid of other personnel. The Soviets had plenty of manpower, and the best-dug-in defenders within each TAOR could not have switched over to the offense quickly enough to intercede in an adjoining area.

Within each Soviet TAOR had been matrices of "strongpoint buildings" connected by trench. Relatively flat areas between the buildings were covered by antitank and submachinegun fire from basement or first-floor apertures. Uneven areas between the buildings were protected by mines, mortars, and plunging machinegun fire from upper-story windows. Until the heavier fire was needed, Soviet snipers kept the Germans at bay (from elsewhere) while stronghold defenders remained hidden. Each little matrix of bastions then created an impenetrable island. Protected by interlocking fields of fire from rearward positions, small bands of resolute Russians could and then did hold off much-larger German forces "almost indefinitely."[89]

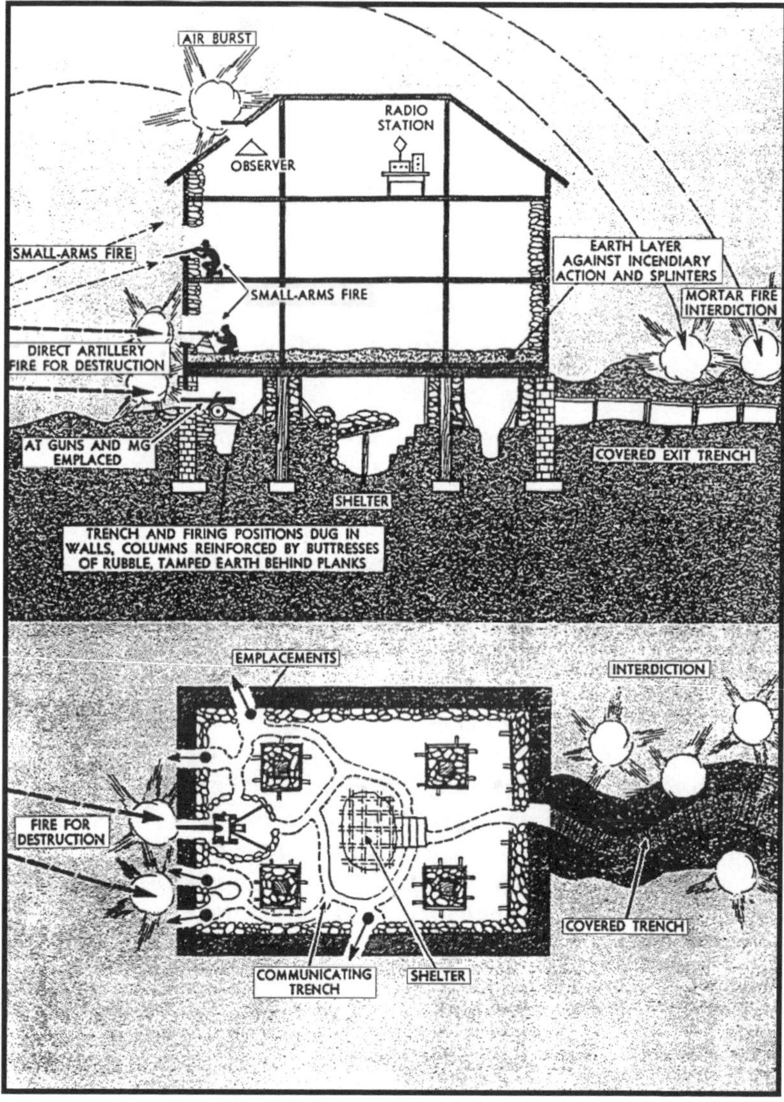

Figure 14.1: Strongpoint Within "Soft" Soviet Defense Matrix
(Source: "Handbook on U.S.S.R. Military Forces," TM 30-340 [1945], U.S. War Department, p. V-124.)

Chuikov expected his troops to turn every occupied house into a fortress, complete with barrier plan and covered routes of reinforcement or egress. His men subsequently seeded the surrounding areas with mines and dug trenches between the buildings. Then, they occupied positions most advantageous to their particular weapon. Artillerymen watched the distant approaches, while heavy machinegun and mortar crews covered the closer avenues. Submachinegunners defended each structure's immediate access to its lower floors. And all defenders withheld their fire until a German unit had entered into their prescribed kill zone. On one occasion, two Soviet machinegunners at a crossroads house managed to bring a whole German battalion under fire (apparently along the entire length of its formation).[90] All defended buildings also had an underground escape route. (See Figure 14.1.)

The Overall Soviet Counterattack at Stalingrad

Every Russian replacement in Stalingrad had received a list of the individual methods with which Lt.Gen. Vasily Chuikov's 62nd Army had successfully contained the vastly superior German 6th Army. Chuikov had been an adviser to the Nationalist Chinese in he early 1940's. Then, at Stalingrad, he had allowed his men to use their own initiative in cleverly improvised small-units that took advantage of the heavily rubbled terrain. The initial pamphlet's instructions had been concise: (1) to neutralize German artillery, "get close to the enemy"; and (2) to escape German observation and small-arms fire, "move on all fours, make use of craters . . . , and dig trenches." [91]

In fact, it was at Stalingrad that Chuikov first developed the now famous tactic of "hugging the enemy." With it, his soldiers could keep their attackers close enough to restrict the use of Wehrmacht airpower.[92] During the battle, the Soviet Commander ordered his men to get as near to enemy lines as possible, so close that "every German soldier . . . feel[s] . . . he is living under the muzzle of a Russian gun." Here are the specifics of Chuikov's advice on how to "get [that] close to the enemy's positions: [1] move on all fours, making use of craters and ruins; [2] dig your trenches by night, camouflage them by day; [3] make your build-up for the [counter]attack stealthy." The distance between the Soviet and German combatants was often only 10-20 meters. So, German artillery and aircraft couldn't bombard Red Army positions without hitting their own people.[93]

The subsequent effort to evict the German invaders from Stalingrad was not always the do-or-die charge that one might expect from a tightly controlled unit of recent Soviet conscripts. It was more often performed through widely dispersed, loosely controlled, and initiative-reliant small-unit raids. Their initial target was the German outpost line. Each night, small packs of Soviet snipers would creep forward to do their damage. In the morning, they would pull back to secret vantage points. Soviet scouts instead formed killer teams with a more personal approach.

> Parties of three to five scouts used the . . . ravines . . . to infiltrate enemy lines . . . [and] pounce on outposts.[94]
>
> — *Red Army Resurgent,* by Shaw

When German columns advanced, they were at times swarmed by reinforced Russian squads. By necessity, those squads would first get close enough unseen to "physically jump" a momentarily disadvantaged segment. In the below excerpt, "storm groups" may have been one and the same as the previously mentioned "shock groups."

> These [squad-sized] "storm groups" would creep close to their target, wait . . . and then charge.[95]
>
> — *Red Army Resurgent,* by Shaw

Again, what tiny under-armed Soviet contingents had accomplished at Stalingrad would never reach the average GI of WWII. With the best equipment, he had little need for maneuver or initiative.

What the Big Eastern Armies Had in Common

To a Western observer, all Eastern defenses may have looked linear since WWI, but most were actually made up of strongpoint arrays (even in the city). While under urban attack, the Japanese, North Koreans, North Vietnamese, Germans, and Russians depended upon them. For all but the Germans, areas to the front of those arrays were mined and/or covered by fire, so some may have also contained the preliminary ambushes of 3GW. For all (including the Germans), an observer had been left in non-strongpoint buildings to conceal those being fully defended. And for all, these lone sentries conducted some sniping.

Such Eastern strongpoints were mostly established in buildings. The Japanese, North Koreans, and North Vietnamese had placed recessed firing positions inside of rooms to better obscure their muzzle flashes. The Russians, Germans, and North Vietnamese had created sub-surface exit routes from urban bastions. When trapped, the Japanese, Asian Communists, and Germans had tried to blend in with a horde of refugees.

All Eastern armies conducted a rearward moving urban defense (retreat combat). For the Japanese, North Koreans, and Germans, such a defense included not only temporarily occupied strongpoints, but also preliminary minefields, ambushes, and street barricades. The whole idea of moving backwards was to whittle the attacker down to a size that could be successfully counterattacked. It would have ideally involved his channelization (through barriers and other means) into preplanned kill zones. The Japanese, Germans, and Russians all tried to alter the foe's path in the city, whereas the Asian Communists quickly established kill zones he couldn't avoid. In other words, they made full use of limited assets by placing almost all in the foe's way. (See Figure 14.2.) Both the Asian Communists and Germans also made good use of underground spaces and conduits.

Then, at an appropriate time, the Japanese, North Koreans, Germans, and Russians counterattacked with what closely resembled a tiny assault group. Only for the Russians did that counterattack occasionally take the form of a "swarm" by semi-autonomous squad-sized elements. At other times, the lead enemy tank was engaged by antitank weapons from every direction. The Japanese and North Koreans liked to drop molotov cocktails from rooftops, whereas the North Vietnamese and Germans preferred antitank rockets from window and door openings.

With a little more research, one could probably show all big Eastern armies to be using almost identical defensive strategies in urban terrain. That's because they have been mutually striving to counter the technology and firepower of a Western opponent. Meanwhile, this opponent has seen little need to add much small-unit maneuver to its limited bag of noisy tricks. Lining up every weapon at the edge of a town might seem a logical way to defend it. But such logic quickly falls away when a few enemy attackers are able to gain entry. At that point, most American defenders would be outflanked.

A Defining Moment in the Research

This study has delved into how major Eastern armies fight in more detail than any before it. Its conclusions were not predetermined and then supporting evidence gathered. Instead, every reported tactical technique was listed (along with its associated maneuver) to make a more comprehensive comparison between nations possible. From the beginning, Posterity Press has noted "trends" in how Eastern armies fight, but remained ready to attribute them to coincidence. Meanwhile, armchair tacticians and well-respected reformers alike have scoffed at the idea that a joint capability might exist. They have insisted every country develops its own way of fighting, and that similarities are bound to exist. Many still believe U.S. small-unit tactics to be as good as the others.

But, everyone realizes that America's traditional adversaries from the East have been less well funded than their own military. So, why couldn't all major Eastern armies have been trying whenever possible to substitute cost-free surprise for expensive firepower? Over time, their ways of fighting would then become very much alike.

Again, the naysayers would object. Most think once an army has been surprised by a particular ruse, the same ruse will never work on it again. But, if that army were prideful, controlled by a top-down bureaucracy, and fully dependent on firepower, such a learning experience may not occur. Should a foe's initial formation look like something American and be followed by a firepower simulation, the resulting attack may never be recorded as anything out of the ordinary. That's when GIs could again be fooled by apparent rows of assault troops tossing shrapnel-free explosives.

So, all Eastern armies may be in pursuit of surprise and readily share ways of achieving it. Those ways would become the 3GW state of the art and have to be only slightly modified to fight another Eastern opponent. That Western armies don't operate this way would in no way disturb them, because their respective legislatures may get tired of funding endless wherewithal.

The Inescapable Conclusion

From past chapters, U.S. infantry veterans should now see that the major Eastern armies have been relying on more small-unit maneuver than their own in rural terrain. For example, no rearward movement on their part has ever been "doctrinally encouraged" under any circumstance. Now, the Germans, Japanese, Russians, and Communist Asians have all been defending cities with a complicated rearward maneuver involving the same five building blocks. That's too much of a coincidence to be ignored. It likely means all four have been operating about the same way in every aspect of combat. This unfortunate reality combined with another could lead to a very unsettling conclusion. The other, of course, is that the U.S. military hasn't decisively won an extended ground conflict since WWII. Assuming America's war planners have been monitoring the battlefield progress of other world powers, one cannot help but conclude something quite disturbing. The Pentagon has been consciously ignoring the tactical trends with which those powers have been succeeding in battle.

Only by trying to resolve every military shortfall through another expensive defense contract could such an oversight be possible at DoD. That's because enough squad preparation to start winning again would cost the taxpayers nothing. By utilizing the fully tested and non-copyrighted Posterity Press methodologies,[96] such training could be conducted in-house by existing personnel. This is, after all, where the ultimate truth regarding such matters

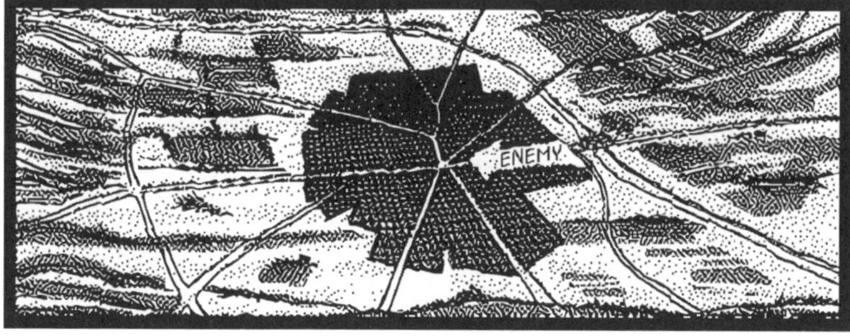

Figure 14.2: Only Standing in the Way of Actual Enemy Thrusts
(Source: FM 90-10 [1979], p. 1-9.)

should reside—not with some well-connected business enterprise. And because that supplementary training would be "bottom-up," it could be done with little, if any, additional effort by each unit's already overworked command echelon. In other words, only the routinely "waiting" troops would become more busy.

The Appropriately Structured U.S. Squad

To defend an expansive urban area with a minimum of manpower, one has little choice but to use highly mobile reinforced squads. Such squads must then move from barricade to barricade, ambush to ambush, and strongpoint to strongpoint as the attacker continues to advance. Any other way of contesting 200 square miles of built-up terrain would be cost exorbitant, in both material and manpower.

Most of those ambushes would be directed at enemy armor. That's why the U.S. squad must have a reliable shoulder-fired antitank weapon. Sisters squads may be called to destroy enemy infantry through pre-arranged kill zones and close-defensive fires. This would require each to have its own LMG with tripod and T&E.

Machineguns have always been most helpful on defense. Because urban terrain is largely comprised of long flat openings, this is particularly true in the city. Even to consider replacing an outmoded linear defense with a strongpoint belt of tiny forts, each squad must be allowed its own LMG. And just as the Soviet "shock groups" at Stalingrad each needed their own machinegun, so too will the modern-day U.S. infantry squad just to change location in what has become increasingly urban terrain.

To defend more rooms and create enough sentry posts to hide a defense bastion amongst other buildings, that Yank squad should also be composed of two-man buddy teams. The U.S. Army infantry remains heavily committed to the concept, while its amphibious cousin has now made a monumental mistake by abandoning it.

Part Three

What Proper Squad Composition Makes Possible

"Uncommon valor was a common virtue (on Iwo Jima)!"
— Admiral Chester Nimitz

(Source: Attributed to Admiral Chester Nimitz after the battle of Iwo Jima.)

15 Context in Which to Assess These Findings

- What has Part Two of this book demonstrated?
- Do all Eastern small-units fight about the same way?

Similar results from research lead to joint conclusions.

(Source: FM 10-76Z/CM [1977], cover.)

The Heritage of Overwhelming Firepower

To bolster the U.S. economy, Washington has—since WWI—attempted to win all foreign conflicts via the liberal application of American-made ordnance. Whenever possible, that ordnance has been given or sold to local nations, so their soldiers might do the fighting. But, wherever enough allied soldiers were not available, the Pentagon made sure deployed GIs had ample amounts of the most advanced wherewithal. It was trying to limit the number of U.S. casualties through sufficient supplies and equipment for all "friendlies" involved.

To further limit the loss of U.S. life, Washington has also asked its Armed Forces to conduct as much long-range "neutralization" as possible. That's what the massive pre-assault bombardments have been all about. Unfortunately, too much standoff firepower automatically results in too little ground maneuver. Because the quarry has already been pulverized, there's no longer any need to sneak up on him. Then, physically closing with the enemy becomes little more than an administrative march in the minds of senior officials. Yet, most participants share a different outlook. The most dangerous aspect of this final approach may be the standard U.S. linear attack formation. Should a few enemy defenders still be alive, bad things can happen. But, being fully "on line" is the best way for every U.S. unit to bring to bear all of its weaponry. And it could wield less firepower if any subordinate element were still out in the front of the main formation. So, U.S. units routinely pull in all reconnaissance elements before any full-fledged attack, and U.S. troops move slowly forward in a fully exposed upright row while finally assaulting a prepared enemy position.

The same mindset affects every American defensive stand. All listening posts are withdrawn as soon as an opposition force shows up, despite their ability to adjust close defensive fires, remotely trigger mines, or further report enemy maneuvers.

In short, U.S. commanders have been required by superiors to fight in the most simplistic ways to achieve maximum firepower. But what may have been gained through parade-field precision, has since been lost to enemy learning and initiative. In short, the American battlefield forays have become so predictable that the quarry has little trouble evading their bombs and shells.

The Warfare Style Most Conducive to Weaponry Use

America's over-abundance of firepower has, in turn led, to its Armed Forces primarily conducting 2GW (killing as many enemy soldiers as possible). This takes maximum firepower—followed by a mopping up operation—on the enemy's forward-most deployed manpower. In return, America's under-armed adversaries have had to wage 3GW (bypassing an enemy's first line of defense to more easily get at his command and logistics networks). That this required a greater degree of small-unit maneuver should be evident from Part Two.

For every aspect of modern combat, Part Two has further described the sophisticated small-unit stratagems with which those foes have managed to wage 3GW. That they are about the same for all Eastern armies is no accident. Getting behind someone's first line of defense requires a great deal of surprise. Only a tiny element can generate that much. It takes pre-practiced procedure based upon recent reconnaissance.

By suggesting the possibility of an Eastern and Western way of war, Posterity Press has been accused of over-generalization. Now, this study has conclusively shown the principal Asian armies, Germans, and Russians to be all fighting in about the same way at the small-unit level. If this Eastern way had not become the state of the tactical art, those foreign armies possessed enough ordnance to do things the American way. Many of the same tactical tricks have probably been tried by nonconforming groups of GIs. But the difference between East and West has been in their quantity and frequency. Most of those tiny element techniques had already been institutionalized. In other words, the Eastern soldiers had been formally trained in how tactically to counter a better-armed foe. And, their parent units were thus able to practice a more advanced form of warfare. Through fewer bombs and bullets, they could cause less collateral damage and fratricide.

Further Evidence of Enemy 3GW

As pointed out in Chapter 2, 3GW largely depends upon the UW methods identified by President Kennedy in 1962—defense by ambush and attack by infiltration. That's why, in 1917, the Germans had used strongpoint defense matrices and noisy surprise attacks to try to salvage WWI. The first consisted of built-in firesacks, and the second resulted in undetected penetration. But the 3GW paradigm is in many ways the exact opposite of its 2GW counterpart. In effect, surprise takes the place of firepower.

As a result, most of the small-unit tactics in Chapters 6 through 14 have never been even considered by GIs, much less tried. Yet, few would violate the rules of war or engagement. And, with most, far less resupply would be required. So, the Pentagon's continuing satisfaction with "pre-machinegun tactics" must be based on over-control and making money.

Figure 15.1: Precision Automatic Weapon Fire Only from LMG
(Source: "Machine Gun Crew in Training," Olin Dows, U.S. Army Ctr. of Mil. Hist., image designator "61_30_45-s.jpg," from url: https://history.army.mil/art/dows/DOWS.htm.)

Future Needs of the U.S. Military

At some point HQMC will come the realization that—to fully practice its new doctrine of MW—it must have infantry squads which can operate in a more semi-autonomous manner. In other words, they will have no parent-unit protection or supporting-arms umbrella. Such a conclusion is clearly indicated from how the biggest Eastern armies were able to conduct 3GW throughout the latter half of the 20th Century. As the Germans demonstrated in WWI, each squad must be able to do two things: either (1) temporarily match in firepower whatever it runs into; or (2) leave some its firepower behind to secretly infiltrate the enemy concentration.

Part Two of this study has shown something else quite extraordinary. For every major combat scenario of all-out war, the ideal U.S. infantry squad would have 15 men: (1) a squad leader; (2) four-man fireteams; (3) an LMG man; and (4) an MAAWS man. The U.S. Marine Corps' squad of the Vietnam era had 14. Only lacking during those years was an LMG man. The Japanese "Type A" infantry company of WWII did contain 15-man rifle squads, each with its own LMG.[1] Chapters 4 and 5 have revealed U.S. Army studies in 1951 and again in 1973 that called for an LMG in each squad. Why this recommendation has yet to be acted upon is anybody's guess.

Might a squad LMG force the U.S. military to adopt all the stealth and humanitarian precision of post-machinegun tactics? (See Figure 15.1.)

Justification for So Big a Squad

Among the best reasons for a 15-member American squad are more room for casualties and tactical innovation. Any fireteam leader could take over the squad, should its leader be wounded. Each fireteam could absorb up to two losses and still function. And all riflemen could be cross-trained on the use of the crew-served weapons.

The bounding-overwatch routine of a two-fire-team squad becomes far too predictable in actual combat for it to work under increasing pressure. The third fireteam creates the opportunity for an occasional feint.

What makes the infantry squad such a unique combat asset is its size-related ability to operate—through rehearsed technique—on autopilot (without any additional instructions from a leader). This, in turn, gives that leader time to study the foe, think, and talk on the radio while his unit has already begun to fight. Radios are light enough now that the squad leader no longer needs a radio operator. Nor—with only five subordinate elements to coordinate—does he require an assistant squad leader. Too many cooks spoil the broth, and more control through a dedicated assistant only serves to nullify the autopilot capability and prerequisite member initiative. Should the squad leader need someone to double-check his target coordinates on a call for fire, any nearby Marine rifleman could do it.

Drones are for gathering intelligence over a broad expanse of battlefield. As such, they are more logically the purview of some headquarters element that is not in constant contact with the enemy. A drone at the squad level would only sacrifice any chance of forward momentum. The squad leader would be double-checking every fireteam leader's report of a new enemy presence, instead of running the play most consistent with the input. All other "vital" electronics—short of ground penetration radar—can be carried by the squad leader himself. For example, only he should be doing any long-range land navigation. Delegating that authority to a point man would jeopardize unit morale every time the unit gets a little disoriented. A GPS-equipped (Global Positioning System) squad leader can instead claim to be "taking a circuitous route" to better deceive a highly proficient quarry.

The LMG and MAAWS men must be part of this future U.S. "super-squad," as opposed to occasional attachments. They can then participate in the rehearsal of all squad battledrills. Without their continual presence, some rifleman will eventually wander into a backblast area during a bunker assault, or a machinegunner fire prematurely during a night attack. At that point, both attacks would have to be aborted. Advanced tactical technique takes continual rehearsal by all participating personnel.

Squad Composition Still a Moving Target

While some infantry squad requirements have been tactical in nature and thus fairly stable since the invention of the machinegun, others have slightly changed with later technologies. Now having both LMG and MAAWS within the squad is totally consistent with what Eastern armies have so far learned about modern combat. Routinely available must be well-aimed automatic weapons fire, antitank fire, and bunker-busting/wall-penetrating fire. Because the MAAWS is laser-guided, it's also of use against opposition close-air support.

Plus, there may be additional future needs. North Korea's semi-autonomous squads already carry their own LMG and assorted RPGs. They may be about to get three more shoulder-fired weapons: (1) a thermobaric rocket (Fuel Air Explosive artillery substitute); (2) an anti-aircraft missile (SA-7 or MANPADS); and (3) a laser-guided version of the American AT-4 antitank weapon.[2] Some 40,000 so equipped squads—each with their own tiny adjoining TAORs—could pose quite a problem for the Western invader.

In short, the future U.S. infantry squad must be able to do two widely differing things depending on the situation: (1) outmaneuver any size of adversary through advanced tactical technique; and (2) temporarily outgun that adversary through organic weaponry. In the past, they could do neither. They had no short-range infiltration skills (to sneak between enemy holes); and they could only take on a better-armed foe through a time-consuming call for (long-range) indirect fire.

A Little Advanced Tactical Technique Would Also Help

When MoH winner Wesley Fox first took over his rifle company in Vietnam, he noticed its squads had no "technique" whatsoever.[3] By this, he had meant no "tailor-made operating procedures" for recurring situations. While his men did have M-79's, this weapon was not accurate enough to put a round through a tiny bunker aperture. What those Marines had really needed the day Fox won his medal was a few LMGs (with tripods and T&Es) and some heavier bunker-busting rockets. Then, much less heroism and personal sacrifice would have been necessary to seize the "prepared enemy position." After a short delay in the proceedings, a deliberate attack utilizing an advanced assault technique might have also been possible. Unfortunately, most Marines of that era had never heard of the noisy surprise assault of WWI Germans. Something like it could have been run in the daytime jungle under a "dry" airstrike—at the loss of many fewer U.S. lives. (See Figure 15.2.)

To this day, most young Leatherneck grunts only regularly practice the one tactical procedure for each category of enemy encounter in their manuals. And those methods have been in no way modified. Too many standardization-oriented leaders have regularly seen to that.

U.S. Tactical Doctrine Is Largely to Blame

America's tactical doctrine was originally designed for 2GW. It is far too restrictive to allow for the more sophisticated small-unit maneuvers of 3GW and 4GW. HQMC officially switched over from Attrition Warfare (2GW) to Maneuver Warfare (3GW) in the late 1980's. But because most missions still require some 2GW procedure, it never loosened its tactical parameters (like that restricting double-envelopment). Until those parameters permit it, Marines won't be able to fully practice their new doctrine. The final part of this study will cover the U.S. infantry commander's expanded options once this doctrine has been relaxed.

Maneuver, by itself, produces no fratricide. Only how one's firepower is employed during the maneuver can do that. Because 3GW involves less shooting than before, it lessens the chance of death by friendly fire.

Figure 15.2: "Dry" Airstrike Makes a Better Diversion
(Sources: MCI 03.10M, p. 5-10; FM 90-10-1 [1982], pp. B-3, B-4; FM 5-103 [1985], p. 4-38; FM 22-100 [1983], p. 22.)

16 Contributions of Other Ordnance/Equipment

- Which part of the traditional load is no longer necessary?
- What should the U.S. infantry squad be carrying instead?

A few GIs carried Thompson submachineguns in WWII.

(Source: Courtesy of Osprey Publishing Ltd., from "The Korean War 1950-53," Men-at-Arms Series, © 1986 by Osprey, Plate A, No. 1; FM 21-76 [1957], p. 150.)

Some Tasks Are Made Easier with the Latest Ordnance

The American super-squad will have to conduct more of the missions of 3GW—staying hidden until a truly lucrative target can be reached. This takes additional surprise—attacking more by infiltration, and defending more by ambush. Among its most-helpful procedures in rural terrain will be a quiet sapper-like entry, noisy surprise assault, and various kinds of ambush. The first takes an easy-to-silence rifle. The second calls for concussion grenades, a light-weight bangalore, and good bunker buster. The third can be most easily accomplished through claymore mines to handle personnel or magnetized shape charges, thermite grenades, anti-tank mines, and armor-piercing rockets to handle tracked vehicles. Luckily, 3GW technique involves less shooting of all small arms (to attain total surprise). So, much of the individual squad member's load previously dedicated to extra rifle and automatic-weapon ammunition can now be used for other things.

Among that new squad's most vital capabilities in urban terrain will be wall-breaching, strongpoint producing, and swarm-like counterattacks. The first takes special demolitions. The second is only possible through an LMG (with tripod and T&E) of its own. (See Figure 16.1.) And the third requires all the heavier weaponry of a Soviet "shock group" in Stalingrad. Minimally needed would be the LMG, a good antitank rocket launcher, molotov cocktail detergent and wick alcohol, and some submachineguns.[1] Of course, to lower the U.S. infantryman's overall weight, gear that had previously proven useful would still be acceptable.

The Submachinegun Issue

Though now satisfied by the addition of M27 rifles to the U.S. Marine rifle squad, its need for submachineguns has been long recognized. In fact, during WWII, up to three Thompson submachineguns were sometimes carried by both U.S. Marine,[2,] and U.S. Army, squads.[3] One of the first such weapons—the *Berman MP18*—was effectively utilized by German Stormtroopers in late WWI. Once their artillery deception had been recognized as a ground assault, bayonets were not nearly as effective as a stream of close-range bullets. Then late in WWII, the Germans created *Volksgrenadier* divisions that emphasized defensive over offensive strength. Those divisions also carried a higher proportion of submachineguns and thus more short-range firepower.[4] In fact, two out of three platoons within each *Volksgrenadier* battalion carried more submachineguns than the other.[5] That those platoons would be protecting urban terrain may have been responsible for the increased number. Those *Volksgrenadier* outfits did subsequently play a major role in the defense of Berlin.[6]

Many Russians units in WWII were also nearly half armed with submachineguns. In fact, the regular Soviet army may have had more submachinegunners per squad—up to four—than even its Ger-

Figure 16.1: Each U.S. Squad Will Need Its Own LMG
(Sources: TC 90-1 [1986], p. 3-23; FM 90-10-1 [1982], pp. 3-35, 5-7; FM 22-100 [1973], p. 2-4.)

man counterpart. According to the U.S. War Department, this made such Russian units well suited for "outflanking and [long-range] infiltration tactics" in rural terrain.[7] According to Zukov, they were also perfect for counterattacking in urban terrain. That's why his pamphlet for Stalingrad replacements had recommended the following actions in every small contested space: (1) throw a grenade; (2) enter; (3) throw other grenades into every corner; and (4) direct submachinegun bursts at anything left while moving forward.[8] And at Stalingrad, each urban assault subgroup contained seven submachinegunners.[9] Of course, submachineguns were vital to the defense as well. As per Chapter 14 and Figure 14.2, relatively flat areas between the building strongpoints were covered by submachinegun fire from basement and first-floor apertures. Submachinegunners additionally defended each structure's immediate access to its lower floors.

Then, when formerly PLA battalions took part in the initial NKPA invasion of South Korea, each of their 10-man squads may have had three submachineguns.[10] And the Chinese PVA used a lot of submachineguns at the Chosin Reservoir. After the element of surprise had been lost during one of their attacks on a Marine position, the squad-sized assaults became a repetitive grinding motion, with each thrust composed of concussion grenade barrage and burp gun rush.[11] Please note the similarity between such a move and Zukov's Stalingrad advice. During the first defense of Seoul, North Korean troops had on at least two occasions counterattacked with submachineguns.[12]

Other Tasks Are Complicated by the Latest Weaponry

One might assume the average U.S. squad only totes enough ordnance and equipment on each separate mission to complete it, but that's not what happens. Through some parent unit's over-emphasis on standardization and security, the squad carries enough ammunition on patrols to fight WWIII single-handedly. This may make possible a longer firefight after any enemy encounter, but it also sacrifices the mobility to win it. As a result, S.L.A. Marshall pointed out that the soldier (when expected to fight) should not be carrying any more than one third of his own body weight.[13] Anything over that can, however, be "staged in place" after the first enemy machinegun burst. If all the mandatory gear has been properly stowed, this should in no way limit the GI's ability to win the contact. In 3GW, he will come to rely more on maneuver than firepower. And in 3GW, a tactical withdrawal when too badly outnumbered/outgunned will be acceptable.

To a rifle squad, fancy equipment can be like a crutch. Its mandatory amount should be kept to an absolute minimum. Only one GPS should be allowed per squad, and it be carried by the squad leader. He may need it to double-check his exact location during land navigation by terrain association or a call for fire. Otherwise, he will regularly fail to take advantage of the tactical attributes of the landscape. He will also need a compass, 1:24,000 map, and binoculars. Then, no laser rangefinder or drone will be necessary (as later explained).

Every member of the squad can have his own miniature radio or cell phone as long as no "texting" takes place. In combat, as in driving, any visual distraction can prove fatal. Besides grenades for fragmentation, smoke, and concussion, each man should carry a claymore mine and trip flare. Only in the city would a wall penetrating demolition be appropriate, or around tanks a magnetized shape charge, thermite grenade, antitank mine, and molotov cocktail

Figure 16.2: 3GW Takes Much More Crawling Than Before
(Source: FM 21-75 [1967], pp. 26, 77.)

ingredients. Night vision equipment for everyone's helmet is only appropriate when the unwieldy attachment can be left behind on particularly stealthy missions. Nor is the flak jacket always necessary. Under one commander in Vietnam, the men of 3/5 never wore one in combat.[14] In short, enough agility can produce as much safety as physical protection. Only a fool would automatically reject what used to work. Every Marine Raider of the WWII era carried a "toggle rope." This eight-foot line had a loop on one end and a small peg on the other. It could on a dark night be strung between individuals to maintain unit integrity, or be easily combined for stream crossing and cliff scaling.[15]

Each squad should additionally have a few specialty items (but never the heavy wall or ground penetration radar). For some missions, it might find wire cutters, a grappling hook, or mirrors useful. Because the heaviest items are about to be temporarily jettisoned, where everything gets carried becomes quite important. In general, the things to be retained are attached to the web belt or harness, and the things to be left behind on the pack. For example, the gas mask and e-tool belong on the belt, whereas extra ammunition should be tied to the pack. Disregard for this old battlefield axiom could cause key gear to be unavailable at critical times. Of course, anything at the very front of the belt may also impede crawling. (See Figure 16.2.) Normally only flat ammunition pouches are carried in that location.

Just as the German Stormtroopers of WWI, all modern infantrymen need heavy pads on the knees and elbows of their uniforms. Crawling is an inherent part of 3GW, because post-machinegun tactics will often call for it over long distances. Non-reinforced uniforms will also wear out during the rapid window entry that so often occurs in urban warfare.

Old-Fashioned Range Estimation [16]

There are several ways to estimate range without an extra electronic gadget. The most useful is the map inspection method. First, the map is oriented. Then, one looks downrange for a terrain feature near the target that is also depicted on the map. The distance to the target is now fairly evident from the map. Another variation on this theme is to choose a known object beyond the target, and then estimate what fraction of the distance to this object constitutes the range to the target.

Additionally, there is the flash-bang method. It is based on the speed of sound between target and observer (330 meters per second). There must be only a distinct noise corresponding with a visible action. Any combination will do; it need not be the report and muzzle flash of a weapon.

Another way of estimating range is to imagine how many multiples of a well-known distance would be needed to fill the void. The distances between firing lines at the rifle range are those most familiar to infantrymen.

Antitank gunners rely on a variation of the WERM rule to estimate range. They use the number of mils displaced by a target and what they guess to be the target's width. In other words, they insert a known angular deviation and width into the WERM formula to find an unknown range. All armor is about 3 meters wide and 10 meters long. If the base of an upright finger at arm's length (displacing about 30 mils) covers the entire breadth of a sideways moving tank, the tank is approximately 330 meters away:

W (10) = Range x Mils (30)
10/30 = Range (in increments of 1000 meters)

The following technique can also be used under a number of circumstances. The height of a tree line can be estimated from the known size of a man standing at its base. The height or width of a building can be estimated from the standard dimensions of a door. In either case, however many fingers are needed to cover the height or width of the object will disclose its range. In other words, the number of mils an enemy soldier is tall on the reticle of standard binoculars will also reveal how far away he is using the WERM rule. (See Figure 16.3.)

Figure 16.3: Binoculars Still Good for Distance Estimation
(Source: Corel Gallery Clipart, People, image designator "34H008.")

17 Complying with Infantry Conference Conclusions

- How many studies have there been on squad dynamics?
- Can the new super-squad accomplish all of those goals?

Infantry conferences conduct after-action assessments.

(Source: Drawing by Donard L. Dixon, "First Offensive: The Marine Campaign for Guadalcanal," by Henry I.Shaw, Marines in WWII Commemorative Series, HQMC, 1992, p. 16.)

U.S. Army's Experience with Infantry Squads in WWII

In the Second World War, the U.S. Army infantry squad had 12 men organized into three teams. It had one leader and an assistant. In theory, Alpha team scouts deployed forward under control of the squad leader. The assistant squad leader directed Baker team, the fire support element. And then the squad leader eventually supervised Charlie team, the maneuver element. But in actual combat, the squad leader rarely got to do all this. His high likelihood of being wounded resulted in someone else trying to control all three teams with no previous experience doing so. And the heavy attrition of other squad members caused constant changes to team composition. When the ABC interaction was attempted, the squad leader often became pinned down with his scouts and unable to control his fire support, much less the maneuver element.[1]

The 1946 Infantry Conference

In 1946, infantry leaders gathered at Fort Benning to discuss what had been learned from WWII. Four changes to the doctrine of the infantry squad were recommended. The most telling had to do with tactics:

> Limitations of squad tactics
> Attendees of the conference conceded that the pre-war doctrine of a [single] squad conducting "fire and maneuver" was not possible. They found that achieving fire and maneuver required at least two squads: one to be the firebase, while another maneuvered.[2]
> — *NCO Journal,* March 2018

The attendees of this conference had actually drawn several conclusions. The first was that the infantry squad should be defined as the smallest combat element consisting of as many soldiers as one leader could control. Second, the highest number of soldiers a single leader could control in favorable conditions was eight. Third, a squad of this size could not employ a BOF element and a separate maneuver element simultaneously. Finally, the squad must expect to operate at 25% below authorized strength. Based on these conclusions, the conference wanted to reduce the 12-man squad to nine and to eliminate the Alpha-Baker-Charlie concept altogether.[3] In 1947, the Army leadership accepted these recommendations, and so changed the Tables of Organization.[4] The squad would no longer consist of separate elements but only of a group of soldiers meant to close with the enemy as a single entity—in a virtual throwback to WWI.

Conferences Associated with Korea

U.S. Army squads had entered the Korean War without any

internal fire and maneuver capability. However, near its end, their parent organization again altered rifle squad size. Despite the conclusions of the 1946 conference and four subsequent studies, Army leaders upped the unit structure from nine men to 11 and returned to the 1940's doctrine of fire and maneuver [within the squad].[5] That's largely because B.Gen. S.L.A. Marshall had seen U.S. squads being forced by the broken terrain into separate elements in Korea, making their overall control more difficult. Then, he made three formal observations—the most important of which was that the squad could no longer function as a unified entity. Following his advice, the TOE was changed in 1953. This increased the squad's firepower and enabled it to subdivide into two equally balanced fireteams. Because the rugged landscape had caused the infantry squads to fight more frequently alone, many parent units had already been experimenting with two teams. In the attack, their squads would often split into fire and maneuver elements.[6]

Conferences in Conjunction with the Vietnam War

U.S. Army infantry units deployed to Vietnam again following the squad "fire and maneuver doctrine" of WWII. Their 10-man squads were now built around two separate fireteams and a squad leader.

In 1973, the U.S. Army once again increased the size of its rifle squad to 11. Its infantry experience in Vietnam had been the contributing factor. The extent of small-unit action had caused too many casualties for proper squad functioning. And the smaller structure had not sufficiently facilitated enough fire and maneuver within the squad.[7] The two-fire-team setup was to remain basically in tact from then on.

The U.S. Army's Current Squad Doctrine

Suffice it to say, the current Army infantry squad is the product of countless lessons learned and studies conducted. It is built around two fireteams, each with a leader. This supposedly gives the squad the ability to maneuver on its own whenever necessary. Each fireteam is organized and equipped quickly to either close with the adversary, or establish a BOF to cover the other team's movement. Such a configuration in theory comes from the need for more battlefield dispersion (and decentralization of control) due to increased enemy weapon lethality.[8] But, one should not conclude the average squad will enjoy more flexibility of action than before. In reality, the Army squad will be allowed only one offensive maneuver—a bounding-overwatch.

> Maneuver is the ability to move quickly to close with the enemy while under fire. . . . The present squad can only fix the enemy with one team and maneuver to the left or right flank with the other.[9]
>
> — Monograph, School of Advanced Mil. Studies, U.S. Army Cmd. and Gen. Staff College, 1994

Why So Much Emphasis on Standardized Squad Activity?

The 1946 U.S. Army infantry conference on squad structure found fault with all the random maneuver that had taken place within the squad of WWII. Neither did this meeting or its Korean War sequels like Army squads getting pinned down. So, with identical fireteams and no LMG, subsequent studies would virtually mandate the bounding-overwatch maneuver under every circumstance. Instant obedience to an order to move forward may appear to obey all the tenets of 2GW, but it can also lead to unnecessary casualties. If there happens to be a hidden prepared enemy position in the way, the U.S. squad only has two reasonable options: (1) stop for a while to reconnoiter, rehearse, and conduct a deliberate attack; or (2) back up and go around.

Even, the Army's system of promoting some infantry E-3's to Specialist technicians (SP4) instead of NCO leaders (CPL) would tend to limit the amount of initiative that each squad could display. The U.S. Marine Corps does not have this problem. It makes all Lance Corporals into Corporals, and creates no strictly technical infantry ranks until the pay grade of E-8.

The majority of U.S. Army planners must still believe that officers win wars as long as all enlisted personnel do precisely as told. 2GW may be at times waged this way, but not 3GW. Nor can U.S. forces regularly defeat a "bottom-up" Eastern opponent with such a dictatorial regimen.

Key Issue Appears to Have Been Control

Throughout the scores of U.S. Army machinations over squad composition and doctrine, overall control has always been enhanced. When the segmenting effect of terrain called for more fire and maneuver within each squad, the squad was allowed a single standardized method of movement. The only real concession has been a pair of subordinate team leaders.

Within America's traditional way of war (2GW), overall control is an important factor. Firepower is most easily maximized by keeping all personnel on line, whether on defense or offense. But, to perform the latter, units must also move forward. Those widely sweeping displays of firepower cannot be allowed to bog down. So, the U.S. Army has come up with a standard way for the most heavily contested formation segments to continue to advance. Unfortunately, each bounding-overwatch still constitutes a hasty attack. Nor does it achieve enough battlefield dispersion to compensate for any increase in enemy weapon lethality. Sufficient dispersion would require less overall control, so smaller squad parts could adapt to local circumstances (like in the random one-man rushes of Figures 12.3 and 12.4).

In essence, the U.S. Army will be unable to follow a more-maneuver-oriented way of war (3GW) until more tactical leeway has been given to each of its infantry squads.

The Concurrent Shaping of the U.S. Marine Corps Squad

Meanwhile, the Leatherneck counterpart has been triangular in structure (instead of binary) for the last 75 years. Since 1944, it has consisted of three fireteams of four men each.[10] This three-sided arrangement was originally adopted because Mao had used it, the Marine Raiders found it successful, and more tactical flexibility ensued from it. It maximized the squad's firepower (through three automatic weapons) and improved its ratio of leaders to those being led.[11] And, by each squad having six buddy teams, it better handled all the tiny engagements that the inherent compartmentalization of most kinds of terrain—jungly, mountainous, and urban—produced.[12]

While the Corps has probably never run a deliberate attack with a single squad, it still expects squad-sized security patrols to close with enemy units during chance contact. That means more semi-autonomous squad activity than the U.S. Army apparently feels necessary. And, as military expert Ferdinand Otto Miksche had pointed out in his 1942 study of blitzkrieg tactics, "Only a [squad-sized] unit that can fight in three echelons can be considered capable of independent action."[13] He went on to say, "an infantry section of eight to 10 men becomes reduced—during the first stages of action—to a number only just sufficient to defend and serve the light machinegun."[14] He concluded his assessment by stating, "a section of eight to 10 men is too small to fight on its own."[15]

Likely Reception of the New U.S. Super-Squad Structure

Infantry squads of the U.S. Army were authorized three composite teams at the very end of WWII. But the same requirement for internal maneuvering has been formally acknowledged by it throughout that world war, the final part of the Korean War, and the entire Vietnam conflict. The standardized interaction of only two teams has been far too easy for the enemy to counter. As a result, a U.S. Army study concluded the following in 1975: (1) that the average U.S. infantry small unit in Vietnam had taken "excessive casualties"; and (2) and that too few assigned members had "not permit[ted] the squad to both fire and maneuver." The squad size would be subsequently increased, but the fully predictable "two-team" leapfrog maneuver never brought into question.[16] For this reason, the American Army will be unlikely to consider a 15-man squad.

While the existing Marine Corps structure could be easily extended to that of a super-squad, a true combat champion will take more than just additional ordnance. The Corps will have to allow each squad member to at times lay down part of his load to make possible a 3GW maneuver. This degree of surprise will additionally take a full portfolio of techniques—several fully rehearsed options for each expected scenario. Because modern war tends to be more compartmentalized than before, such techniques need only be the same for each parent company. Otherwise, they will become too well known and their users less capable of "independent action" in enemy country. And only in that way might a learning dynamic develop through unit competition.

For the Marine Corps, that means two alternatives will have to be locally developed for each of the standardized methods in the manuals. If the U.S. Army were to follow suit, its bounding-overwatch would become just one of three hasty attack options for non-fortified areas.

The PRC is no longer an impoverished nation forced to rely on incremental small-unit action instead of the latest firepower technologies. Just as the modern-day Chinese infantry squad can quickly transition between Positional (2GW), Mobile (3GW), and GW,[17] so must America's new super-squad.

18 Reducing Foe Firepower Through Maneuver

- Is return fire the only way to counter enemy bullets?
- What else can be done to avoid friendly casualties?

Sgt. York maneuvered to save his squad from enemy MG.

(Sources: FM 22-100 [1983], p. 113; FM 7-8 [1984], p. 3-28.)

Sales Pitches Not the Same As Wartime Strategies

Must every new enemy weapon system be countered by a more destructive one from the Pentagon? Wouldn't dodging the opposition weapon's effects be as helpful as blowing it (and everything around it) away? Yet, U.S. arms manufacturers have so well promoted their products that there seems no maneuver capable of negating the threat.

With more surprise-oriented tactics, American squads could either sidestep the new weapon's fire or close with its operator. Because such techniques could be developed for free at each infantry company, they offer an attractive alternative to the defense contracts for extra equipment. Better tactical technique would also result in less collateral damage and friendly fire casualties.

Dodging shells requires small-unit maneuver. There are two ways to come up with advanced tactical technique (how small units and individuals can still move around safely). One is to develop it—from scratch at the rifle company level—through trial runs against simulated casualty assessment (as in the Appendix). The other is to adjust—for existing circumstances—the Eastern state of the art for the type of enemy contact involved. Then, by adding the singular procedure in the manuals, the squad leader has three well-thought-out maneuvers/formations to choose from. This will make his enemy-fire-avoidance attempt much more difficult to predict.

This Book Reveals State of the Art for Most Foe Contacts

From the first 17 chapters, it has become obvious to U.S. war veterans that the soldiers of big Eastern armies have been using squad tactics more advanced than their own. Because of how those armies arrived at those tactics (to counter superior firepower) and the resulting similarities, a shocking conclusion is possible. Their combined effort offers the nonelectronic state of the art for how best to handle the most common battlefield challenges.

Such tactical advances are not much affected by time—only additional technological innovation (something more profound than night-vision goggles or "eyes in the sky"). For many scenarios, modern surveillance devices make no difference at all. That's because the major Eastern armies have also been studying how to counteract Western technology. For example, just by using a simulated indirect-fire attack, their troops can avoid detection by thermal imaging. All Western defenders will still be at the bottom of their holes. That's why the German Stormtrooper method from WWI remains—to this day—the state of the art for a noisy surprise assault. As such, U.S. squad leaders should be allowed to add it to their portfolios.

Major Contributors to This Consensus Opinion

Squad structure may have been partially responsible for this higher level of proficiency in the East. The Asian Communists have been using a three-fire-team format since before WWII. While the German and Russian squads were both binary in structure (each with its own dedicated maneuver and LMG BOF elements), they often split into three parts. For example, half of their squad maneuver element regularly advanced on either side of the BOF element.[1] Through concurrent focus on close combat and machinegun support, the Japanese squad was inherently binary, but further subdivided at times. Around the edge of each squad-sized strongpoint were several rifleman pits or "octopus pots" *(Kakutsubo)* to protect the LMG at its center,[2] as in Figure 7.2.

What has set the Asian Communist squads apart from the others is their greater reliance on short-range infiltration (sneaking between enemy holes). With six separate buddy teams all trying to sneak in at the same time, the new U.S. super-squad's triangular organization will greatly facilitate its use of this signature maneuver to the UW portion of 3GW.

While mostly sharing this three-sided structure, not all Eastern squads have limited all hasty attacks to only three moving parts. Those from both Germany and Russia have allowed the fire and movement of up to 10 separate elements. Any number of German riflemen could take turns advancing at the direction of the squad leader.[3] And at the squad leader's direction, Russian squad members could move forward by "team" or individual bounds.[4] That's why the U.S. super-squad—through the four-man composition of all teams—will be capable of the random rushing of individuals in Figures 12.3 and 12.4.

More Preparation for Close Combat in the Eastern Armies

For whatever reason, the major Eastern armies have also been better preparing their squads for short-range fighting than those in the West. In WWII, all members of the German squad had been trained as close-combat fighters.[5] By doctrine, the Japanese Army only recognized victory to any tactical situation when its troops had closed on the enemy with bayonets.[6] The Soviet patrol was obligated to "assault and break through" any moving target it bumped into.[7] And through a predisposition toward short-range infiltration alone, Asian Communist infantrymen have gained the reputation of brawlers.

But this still vital aspect of war has not been limited to *mano y mano* confrontations. All four nationalities have been promoting "weaponless" tank fighting. The Germans had special armor-killing soldiers with makeshift ordnance (molotov cocktails, smoke grenades, demolitions, hand grenade bundles).[8] All members of the Russian squad's maneuver element had been instructed in how to fight tanks with their bare hands.[9] The Japanese had special tank-killing squads (using only mines and grenades) within their regular infantry.[10] And there had been special armor-reducing detachments (sometimes called suicide squads) within the Chinese Nationalist KMT during the Sino-Japanese War.[11] Of course, the Chinese Communists were not far behind. Mao had said, "It is people, not things, that are decisive in war."[12] Then, a firsthand observer to the Korean War described Mao's soldiers as "constantly studying their mistakes, and improvising methods to . . . offset modernized [Western] equipment."[13]

Those special units from all four nationalities had undoubtedly passed along some of their makeshift "tracked-vehicle-killing" methods to the rank and file.

The Standard Knee Jerk Reaction

When American military professionals are told that their overwatching government agency has caused them to underdevelop small-unit maneuver, some take great offense at the idea. How could that be even remotely possible? After countless displays of enlisted bravery, their parent commands have been on the winning side of both world wars.

But, what has made contemporary watchstanders mad is the insinuation that their traditional way of fighting (2GW) has been superseded by more advanced forms (3GW and 4GW). Instead of closing with and destroying the foe, they are now supposed to bypass his best fighters and engage a softer target? Red-blooded Americans recoil at the thought of not regularly engaging the best the enemy has to offer. But, sneaking deep into enemy country can be just as exhilarating. And U.S. riflemen will no longer have to march upright into enemy machinegun fire to get near enough to hurt an adversary. In truth, most may come to love a steady diet of the more-challenging (and less-suicidal) missions of 3GW. With the additional combat experience will come a deeper appreciation (by themselves and superiors) for their possible contributions to overall victory.

Of the world's major armies, only the PLA has managed to contain this chronic rivalry between old and new. Instead of completely discounting 2GW, it requires all small units to be able to quickly alternate between it, 3GW, and Guerrilla Warfare. Everything previously learned about fighting remains valid as long as it continues to mesh with current circumstances. For example, all "the fortress entry" skills of an ancient Oriental *ninja* become perfectly legitimate during a modern-day special-operations raid.

Only Eastern Armies Have Pursued State of Offensive Art

With concussion grenades in the assault, only the Germans, Russians, Japanese, and Communist Asians had managed to embrace the evolutionary advance to offensive combat from the WWI Stormtroopers. Most had light mortars at the company level. Their squads all carried an actual LMG in through the wire (and could thus fill any bunker aperture with bullets). And their squad-sized attacks universally involved some initial short-range infiltration. So, with indirect-fire-simulating shrapnel-free explosives, all could perform some variation of the still viable "noisy surprise assault" technique.

This initial sneaking around helped to establish the principal offensive maneuver of UW, and—in turn—how fully to practice 3GW. Left in the hands of the more traditional Western armies, 3GW would not have become nearly as comprehensive a style of battle. In fact, Maoist Mobile Warfare contains a few useful parameters that the original Maneuver Warfare had missed—like how quickly to disperse and reassemble a large maneuver element.[14]

All Four Eastern Foes Also Sought State of Defensive Art

While Western armies doggedly stuck with their firepower-enhancing MLR, those Eastern armies were following through on the evolutionary change to defensive tactics by the WWI Huns. All subsequently developed elastic belts of squad-sized strongpoints.

This was only possible through each of their squads having its own LMG, some "say-so" as to when to abandon their tiny fortress, and in many cases a preplanned fallback position.

The squad-sized positions had open areas between them. To the attacking Allies those areas initially looked like gaps, but soon turned into firesacks. In combination with the extensive camouflaging of manned bunkers, such firesacks then fulfilled the UW requirement for defense by ambush. And the state of the art for 3GW-like resistance was born.

All Four Ended Up Practicing State of Urban Offensive Art

For three out of four Eastern armies, their urban offenses involved a rapid attempt to reach the city center and then fight outward. Through armored columns, this was done by the Japanese at Shanghai and Russians at Grozny. Through infantry spearheads, it was done by the Russians at Stalingrad and the North Vietnamese at Phat Diem, Hue City, and Saigon. For both of the latter armies, some infiltration also took place on a smaller scale. A few Russian soldiers would "infiltrate" through the smoke to the center of each new block after it had been softened up with artillery. There were North Vietnamese supplies and commandos initially smuggled into Hue City to support the later ground thrusts. Such revelations make the North Vietnamese "Blooming-Lotus" maneuver the current state of the art for urban offense.

Three out of four Eastern armies attacked through the buildings at the side of each street instead of along its sidewalks. The Russians, Germans, and Japanese also fought along the rooftops wherever possible—probably because buildings are easier to clear from the top down. The Soviets moved across rooftops and through attics.[15] The Germans used elevated machineguns to watch for enemy snipers atop buildings.[16] And the Japanese liked to occupy the highest part of each structure.[17]

All Discovered the State of Urban Defensive Art As Well

When defending a built-up area, all four Eastern armies liked to turn streets and the lower floors of some buildings into kill zones. They also practiced a rearward-moving combination of minefield,

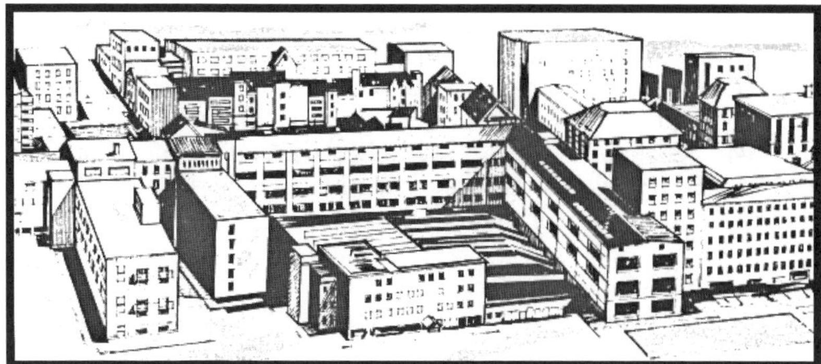

Figure 18.1: Hardened Factory Will Slow Down Urban Attacker
(Source: FM 90-10-1 [1982], p. 2-3.)

ambush, barricade, strongpoint matrix, and counterattack. By funneling most of their manpower and materiel into the direct path of any enemy thrust, they were able to best utilize their limited assets. Something like this "rearward grinding sequence" followed by a "forward correction" has thus become the state of the art for urban defense.

In Russia and the Philippines, the opposition may have been intentionally canalized toward well-hardened targets: (1) the Tractor Factory complex at Stalingrad; and (2) the Provisor Island Electricity Plant and Paco Railroad Station in Manila. Its purpose was to so wear down a better-armed intruder that he could be ejected. At Stalingrad, the strategy greatly contributed to the eventual Russian victory. (See Figure 18.1.)

Not all of this rearward motion was toward the edge of town. Some concluded at its center. Then, if the final counterattack didn't succeed, the remaining fighters exfiltrated their encirclement through either subterranean tunnels or herds of refugees. The Germans at Berlin, Japanese at Manila, and North Vietnamese at Hue all fought toward the city center. Many of the final fighters then escaped through underground conduits at Fort Santiago in Manila, the downtown subways of Berlin, and the Citadel's tunnels in Hue City.

Of course, there were also many integral stratagems shared by Eastern powers. The Japanese, Chinese, and North Koreans liked to leave lone snipers in buildings to make the ones being fully defended harder to spot. In Manila, Seoul, and Hue, there was enemy fire from positions intentionally recessed into rooms (to obscure any muzzle flashes). At Seoul, Hue, and Grozny, there were antitank ambushes involving rocket-propelled grenades from every direction. At Manila, Stalingrad, and Seoul, molotov cocktails got tossed down on armor from the rooftops. So, for almost any defensive need, those may still be the best ways to accomplish them in the city.

Combat Expertise Does Not Incrementally Accumulate

Most elite U.S. fighters firmly believe they have superior combat skills, and that those skills have been meticulously derived from world history and their latest equipment. The gear part of this conclusion is poorly justified. Their new gear may make an enemy combatant easier to target, but it in no way protects the user from detection. The tactical viability of those skills, in turn, depends on how much surprise they generate.

The rest of the story has to do with the passage of time and organizational dynamics. Combat skills tend to be the highest after struggling to win an extended conflict—like, for all participating armies right after WWII. Then, those skills gradually erode as peace sets in. That's not only because of their lack of use, but also the influence of military bureaucracy. Because any change however beneficial challenges established procedure, lessons learned in combat are rarely institutionalized. For example, this chapter has greatly touted Russian expertise at urban warfare—calling some of it the current state of the art. Yet, around 1995, in the aftermath of the Chechen disaster, Soviet Gen. Mikhail Surkov personally admitted that "street fighting tactics are absent from the manuals of the Russian armed forces."[18]

So, to acquire the state of the art in most urban methods, the modern-day Russian soldier would have to study his own WWII history. Of course, some Americans also displayed great small-unit ingenuity during WWII. But, because the Allies were winning, most of their ideas never got into common usage, much less the manual rewrites. That's why it's easier to determine the state of the art from studying all underfunded armies at once.

The next part of this book will address the squad tactics with which U.S. commanders can now pursue a 3GW agenda as hard as the major Eastern armies have.

Part Four

Additional Opportunities for U.S. Maneuver

And when he gets to Heaven, Saint Peter he will tell:
"Another Marine reporting, sir—I've served my time in Hell!"

(Source: Possibly a revised version of "Our Hitch in Hell" found in the book "Mud and Stars - An Anthology of World War Songs and Poetry," by Dorothea York © 1931.)

19 Double-Envelopment of a Small Target

- Can U.S. rifle platoons double-envelop a foe bastion?
- Why not?

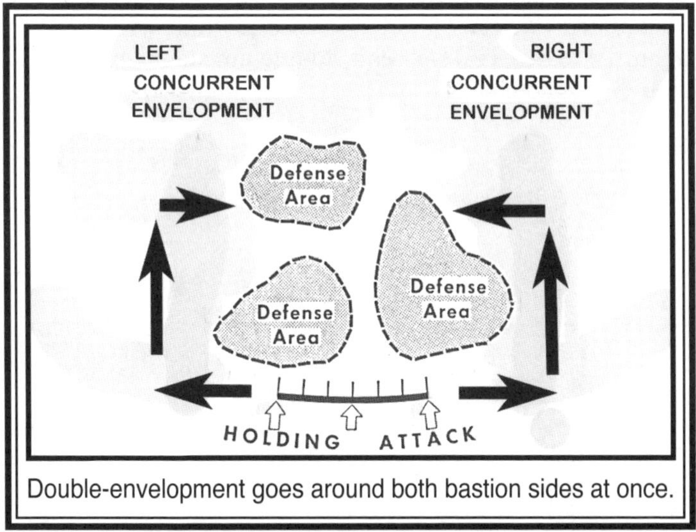

Double-envelopment goes around both bastion sides at once.

(Source: "Handbook on the Chinese Communist Army," DA Pamphlet 30-51 [1960], p. 24.)

Important Precedents

Double-envelopments violate U.S. doctrine. Yet, there had been several such maneuvers by U.S. forces during the latter stages of WWII and in Korea. Where the objective is an enemy-occupied hill mass, the chances of an accidental shooting are remote.

American Forces Use of the Maneuver in WWII

The Maoist U.S. Marine Raider battalions had, of course, conducted some double-envelopments early in WWII: (1) at Wickham Anchorage on Vangunu in the New Georgia group;[1] and (2) at Bairoko Harbor on New Georgia.[2] (See Map 19.1.) Then, 2/4 (formerly 4th Raider Battalion) used a double-envelopment to take the very difficult Half Moon (Crescent) Hill in the Sugar Loaf Complex at the northern end of Okinawa's Shuri Line in 1945.[3] (See Map 19.2.) In the last two examples, there is evidence Marine fireteams liked subdividing to double-envelop each bunker through the microterrain.[4]

Then, at Okinawa's southern end, Col. Shapley—the man who had disbanded Carlson's Raiders—used 2/4 and 3/4 (a more traditional outfit) to run a larger-scale double-envelopment of Hill 72 on Kiyamu-Gusuku ridge.[5]

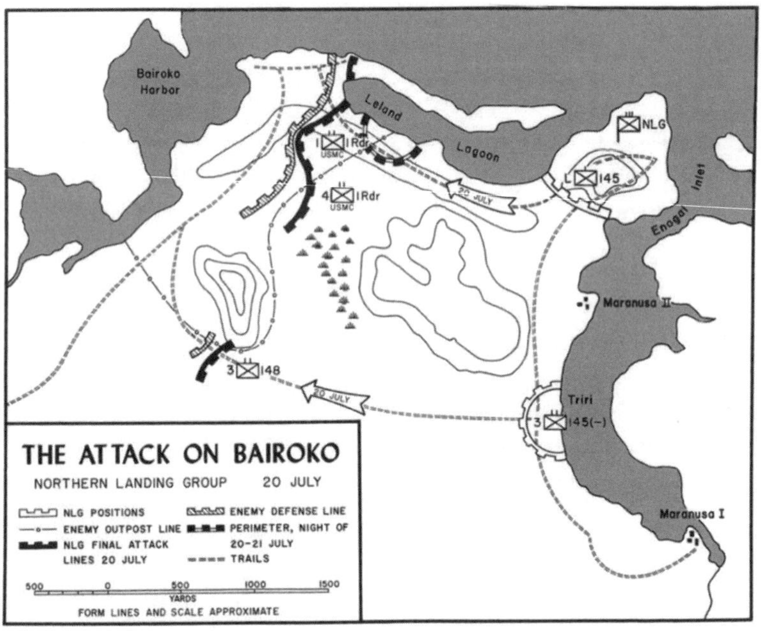

Map 19.1: U.S. Forces at Try Both Ends of Bairoko Bunker Belts

(Source: "From Makin to Bouganville: Marine Raiders in the Pacific War," by Maj. Jon T. Hoffman, Marines in WWII Commemorative Series, HQMC, 1995, p. 34.)

Another U.S. Double-Envelopment in Korea

The 5th Marine Regiment had conducted a double-envelopment of the first high ground after crossing the Han River at Seoul in 1950.[6]

What the World's Other Big Armies Had Been Doing

Meanwhile the Japanese,[7] Germans,[8] Russians,[9] and Asian Communists have all regularly used double-envelopments—even against forces of larger size. Figure 19.1 shows this maneuver to be

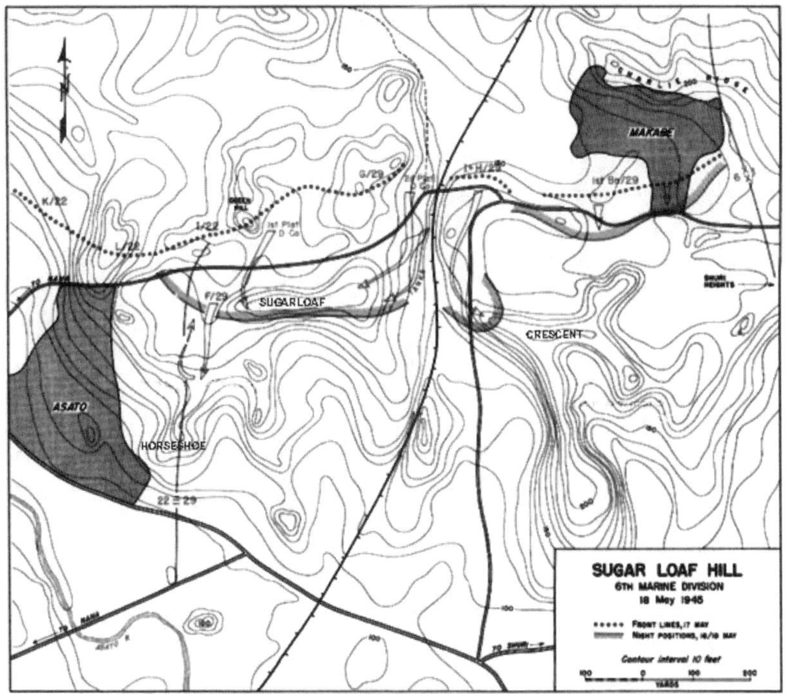

Map 19.2: Just Before 2/4's Attack on Crescent Hill in May 1945
(Source: Map 38, "Okinawa: The Last Battle," by Roy Appleman, James Burns, Russell Gugeler, and John Stevens, U.S. Army Ctr. of Mil. History, 2000.)

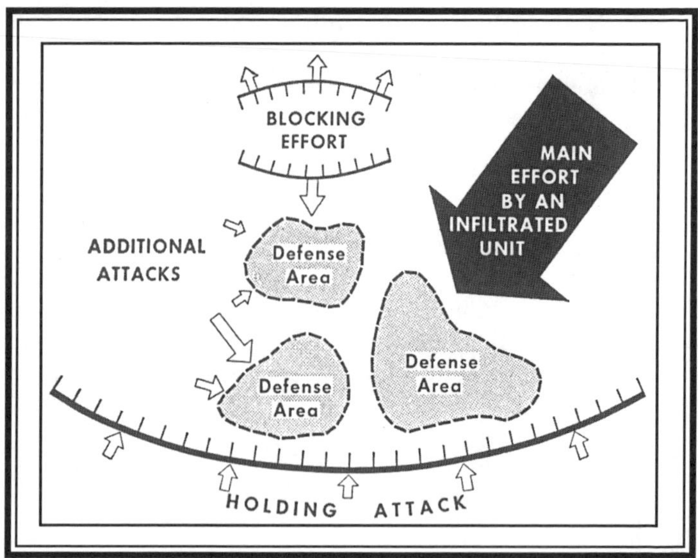

Figure 19.1: Standard PLA Attack on Encapsulated Position
(Source: "Handbook on the Chinese Communist Army," DA Pamphlet 30-51 [1960], p. 24.)

still part of every PLA attack on a self-contained bastion. A further discussion of its particulars may help to alleviate DoD's doctrinal aversion to it.

The Tactical Isolation of a Tiny Target

Most studies of double-envelopment discuss only large pincer movements. To discover the tactical advantages of smaller version, one must find a battle chronicle with enough detail of its composite stages. There aren't many around. Yet, the *Hutier* (infiltration) tactics of the WWI Germans implicitly involved double-envelopment because "pockets of resistance" were automatically formed from multiple breaches of the same Doughboy line.

> The first wave was an infantry probe . . . whose purpose was to identify enemy positions for the next wave. . . . The second wave [elite storm companies] attempted to penetrate the

> enemy zones by pushing through [assaulting] weak areas to *envelop* enemy positions. Supporting these efforts was the third wave [of] . . . support from the division. Behind these three waves followed the remainder of the accompanying division, which reduced *pockets of resistance* bypassed by the storm units *[italics added]*.[10]
>
> — Gen. Erich Ludendorff, as quoted in U.S. Army, *Leavenworth Papers No. 4*

The Only Highly Detailed Description

The Battle of Rorke's Drift occurred a long time ago in South Africa. Lasting only 12 hours, it started with a Zulu attack on a British mission station serving as supply depot in the early evening of 22 January 1879. It went on all night, and concluded with a brief "salutatory" appearance of the attack force at dawn the next day.[11] While this example may seem too dated to be useful, close combat has not changed much over the years. The Rorke's Drift account explains how near-naked African warriors were able to compensate for their almost complete lack of firepower. In fact, 1,300 well-armed British troops had just been overwhelmed by spear-carrying Zulus at nearby Isandlwana.[12] (A similar "ordnance-avoidance" thought process would accompany every close encounter between Eastern and Western forces from then on.)

During the final part of the Zulus' approach march on Rorke's Drift, the rhythmic beating of spears against shields sounded to the British like a steam locomotive. Then, everything went quiet, while separate contingents of the 4000-man Zulu force closed in on the outpost. They did so through small-group rushes in ragged-line formation, swarming quietly ahead through the sparse vegetation to stop/disappear without any signal at each lateral depression in the earth. Soon, those elements assumed their position in the famed "Horns of the Buffalo" maneuver. This is where two bodies of personnel—the head and loins of a buffalo—approach a quarry from the front. At the last moment, all portions of the head disperse around both sides of the prey as along inward-pointing horns. (See Map 19.3.)

At this point, the buffalo's torso becomes a holding attack composed of a series of feints.[13] While the movie "Zulu" depicts the African chieftain initially sacrificing his men to count the guns of

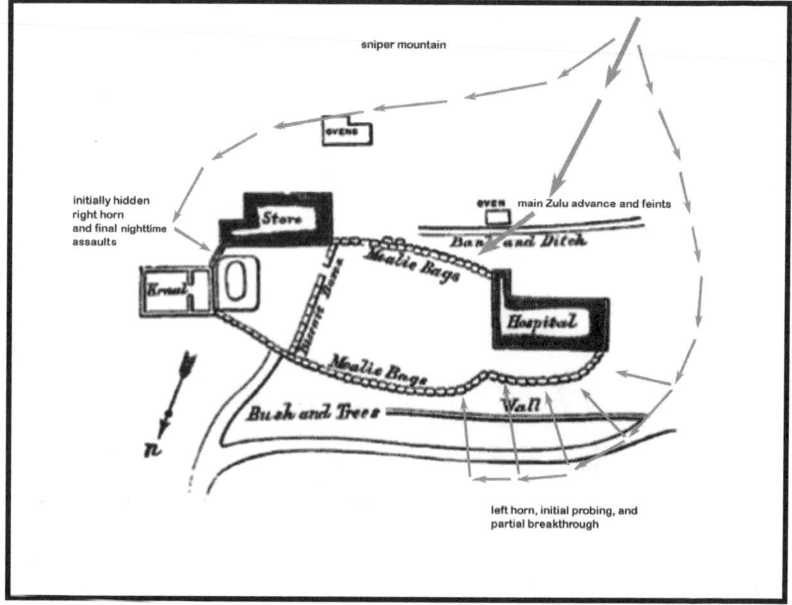

Map 19.3: Zulu Attack on Rorke's Drift Outpost

(Source: Wikipedia Encyclopedia, s.v. "Battle of Rorke's Drift, Hist. of the Corps of Royal Engineers, at https://commons.wikimedia.org/wiki/File:Rorke%27s.Drift.Post.jpg.)

140 defenders,[14] he was more likely probing enemy lines to locate a weak spot. Suffice it to say, the buffalo's loins continued to demonstrate at the front of the outpost while the horns slid along both sides through feeder creeks and watershed ditches. The two horn tips would end up attacking at different times, with the first one being quite attention-gaining at the left rear of the objective—right across from the hospital.[15]

As the Zulus at the front of the compound kept up their illusionary assault to keep the British from reinforcing other sectors, they exercised a lot of common sense. They would get down each time a British rank fired. By dropping to the ground at the command of "fire," they could elude most, if not all, of the bullets. When the Redcoats were allowed to fire at will, the diversionary Zulus simply hid in the grass. This kept the British from taking well-aimed shots. In this way, the Zulus were able to closely approach the British front lines with minimal loss of life.[16] (Such tricks may seem hokey to a contemporary Western commander, but they're smarter than regularly requiring one's people to move upright through a steady stream of machinegun bullets.) By this time in history, most Zulu combatants were armed with a short "stabbing" spear. In a direct confrontation with bayonet-wielding defenders, that funny looking little pointed stick could be unexpectedly thrown a short distance.

All the while, Zulu snipers had been crawling up a hill to the direct front of the outpost. With overhead fire, they intended to cover some of the ground assaults. British sharpshooters were soon able to out-shoot them, because the main Zulu attack would come from the right rear of the compound (just behind the storehouse).[17] (Some 70 years later at the Chosin Reservoir, Chinese Communist forces regularly launched an inconspicuous main attack against the backside of America's defensive positions.)

To find the best place for the all-out assault, the Zulus did a good bit of probing (something almost unheard of in the West). After one or two such attacks at the left rear of the camp unexpectedly broke through the British cordon, scores of Zulu warriors gained entry to the compound. At first, the intruders were driven out by alternately firing ranks or bayonet charges of red-coated soldiers. But, at some point, the British were forced to withdraw behind a makeshift "maize" bag wall at the camp's eastern end. That's when the hospital was stormed, and most occupants escaped through a window.[18]

As soon as the sun set, Zulus closely approached the entire rear portion of the camp and began to probe the remaining pocket, discovering slightly less resistance between storehouse and corral.[19] After the most dramatic of the frontal feints, the Zulus finally launched their main assault at this point on the right rear side of the camp during the night. Their intent had been to confuse the British as to which of the now possible attacks was to be decisive. (This combination of encirclement and segmentation would later be copied by the big Eastern armies. When unexpectedly successful in Korea, Communist holding attacks and probes were sometimes allowed to carry a U.S. position.)

The British did not have smokeless powder in those days.[20] So, the Zulu warriors could temporarily blind their foes by getting them to fire several successive volleys. And thus emerged another detail of their rather amazing assault technique. After the assault element went to ground during two or three fusillades, it could move forward a short way undetected.[21] (See Figure 19.2.) (While bending forward is acceptable for a Western-assault participant, getting down and then catching up with one's brethren isn't. Yet, it would be easy for young GIs to do. While moving forward at Stalingrad, Soviet soldiers dropped like stones, so they could reemerge at the same place without being killed.[22])

As the spear stabbers closed with the British lines, the bayonet thrusters took their traditional defensive stance. It was not long

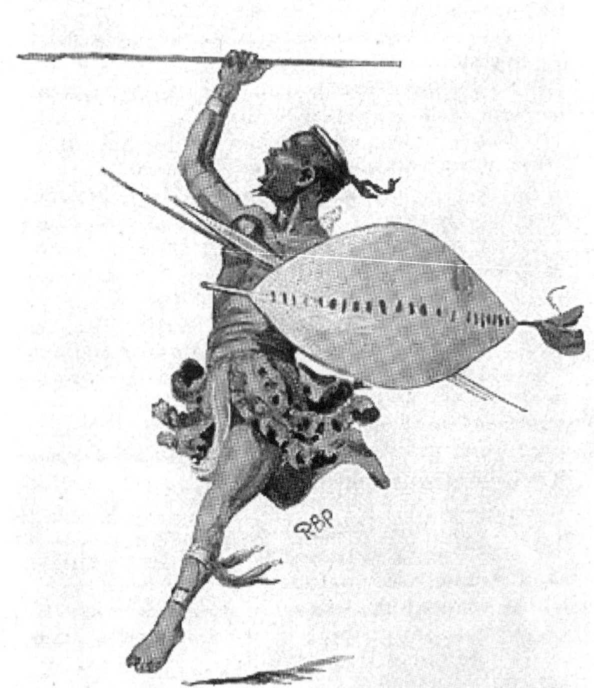

Figure 19.2: Zulu Warrior Knew How to Counter Better Weaponry
(Source: Sketch of a Zulu Warrior, in "My World Tour," by Robert Baden-Powell, Boy Scouts Beyond the Seas, 1913; "Zuluwarriorbp.jpg" from Wikimedia Commons.)

before innovation had gotten the better of standardization. When the Zulus came within feet of adversaries who had expected one thing, they did another. Many threw their *"assegais"* as the Limey to their front dutifully complied with his limited interpretation of close combat.[23] Though designed for stabbing, the short spear's heavy end made it a lethal projectile at short range. By 1888, most Zulu warriors were carrying three short throwing spears and one stabbing spear. Though they had access to repeating rifles, they preferred the lower-tech weaponry.

> They carried huge shields of ox-hide on the left arm . . . while on the right they carried two or three throwing *assegais* [spears] for hurling at the enemy, and a broad-bladed stabbing assegai which they kept for hand-to-hand fighting. In their girdles was slung a club or axe for polishing off purposes.[24]
>
> — *Scouting with Baden-Powell,* by Freedman

The Battle of Rorke's Rift was largely fought at night (another attribute of what would become the Eastern style of war). One can thus conclude that—through common sense or trial and error—the Zulus had come up with some fairly refined night-fighting techniques. (A rifleman's procedure is almost never designed that way in the West; there is no input or trial and error from the low-ranking personnel who must ultimately put such procedures into practice.)

The Obvious Similarity and Its Meaning

The standard PLA attack in Figure 19.1 from the late 1940's closely resembles the Zulus' Horns of a Buffalo maneuver from the 1880's. Yet, it's not likely that any Chinese tactician had ever heard of the African equivalent. Experienced squad trainers know of a connection that is often ignored by their superiors. Over time, advanced tactical procedure can emerge out of field experimentation, without any prior knowledge of world history. Only those armies that have maximized control through discouraging subordinate-unit experimentation may have failed to realize this. Good tactics require only common sense, a search for surprise, and a desire to minimize friendly casualties.

What Is Known About the Battle of Chochiwon

While the next example of double-envelopment happened on a considerably larger scale than the last, it would have a profound effect on the quarry. At 0630 on 11 July 1950, four North Korean T-34's advanced on 3rd Battalion's (21st U.S. Infantry) position. Behind the tanks were 1,000 ground pounders of the North Korean 3rd Infantry Division. They were about to conduct a double-envelopment of the U.S. battalion, and then set up roadblocks at its rear to prevent resupply or medevac. Simultaneously, the battalion command post came under heavy mortar fire, destroying its communications center and ammunition stocks. At that point, the forward observers for the American battalion could no longer summon fire support.[25]

The North Korean attack had been so well coordinated that the American forces were eventually overwhelmed after some desperate hand-to-hand fighting. That was partially because North Korean machineguns had continued to pummel the U.S. position until their American counterparts ran out of ammunition. For an infantry outfit that depends almost entirely on firepower, the complete absence of machinegun or supporting-arms fire could be quite disheartening. Of 667 men in 3rd Battalion, over 60% quickly became casualties. With many of soldiers already captured, 3rd Battalion was forced to break down into smaller groups that attempted to fend for themselves. The smart ones formed a provisional company of 150 men to make the final retreat. In total, 90% of the battalion's equipment, including weapons and helmets, had also been lost.[26]

That's the extent of the battle's written history. One can only imagine its further details. The American battalion had apparently been in a fairly tight formation. That's why the enemy mortars and machineguns had been able to cut it up. At some point the pocket had been penetrated, or there wouldn't have been as many GIs initially captured. Only as a provisional company were any able to break out of the encirclement. Most of the desperation had been born out of a shortage of ammunition and being surrounded.

How Easterners Can Safely Double-Envelop an Objective

Double-envelopment only becomes dangerous when both maneuver elements are fully exposed and shooting towards one another. So, only forces that move around the battlefield in perfect formation and depend almost entirely on firepower worry about that stratagem's potential fratricide. There are several ways to prevent it: (1) shoot upwards, downwards, very carefully, or not at all; and (2) only double-envelop where the terrain itself will preclude accidents. Sometimes, a low ridge exists between opposing elements. More often the curvature of a hillside automatically sends all stray rounds from one over the heads of the other. Even on totally level ground, there is no need for much concern. On Operation Buffalo, some NVA shot downwards from trees after encircling segments of the Marine column. Those on the ground were only allowed well-aimed shots from behind good cover.[27]

Not the Only Sophisticated Stratagem from the East

America's small-unit tactics continue to be so "straight-forward" and simplistic as to be "premachinegun" in format. They were supposedly designed that way to give their users more modification leeway. But, such elementary subordinate unit maneuvers also facilitate parent unit movement, maximization of firepower, and compliance with orders. In addition, a central command often creates so high a tempo of operations that no subordinate unit has time for anything but standard procedure. So, over the years, most of the tiny-element maneuvers tend to remain the same. Eastern armies have attempted to compensate for this syndrome by having more advanced (surprise-oriented) tactical options available to all companies and below.

Part three of this study discussed no fewer than 12 other maneuvers/formations to which tiny Eastern contingents have access (but Western counterparts don't). Without squad spearpoint expertise, total surprise of the enemy won't ever be possible for a big Western unit. Only with a "3GW-friendly" change to current U.S. infantry doctrine can the tactical shortfall be corrected. Squads with more sophisticated stratagems are able to contribute more to a war's final outcome.

20 Tactical Encirclements

- How can a platoon completely surround a foe target?
- Which follow-up attacks are then possible?

Intentionally encircling an enemy concentration.

(Source: Public-domain material, from U.S. Army "War on Terror Images," at this url: http://www.history.army.mil/books/wot_artwork/images/19b.jpg.)

A Widely Misunderstood Concept

Encirclement is a military term for the surrounding and isolation of an opposition force. Normally accomplished on large scale (as in a "flow-around" or pincers movement), it only has tactical significance when applied to a tiny objective—like a foe outpost. For all Eastern armies, encirclement has become closely associated with total annihilation of the quarry. In the West, it can mean as little as a porous blockade around the unit in question to limit its reinforcement and resupply. In neither case is encirclement the same as double envelopment.

Small-scale encirclements are almost never attempted by any DoD unit, because going around both sides of an objective violates U.S. doctrine. The worry, of course, is the same for both—an increased probability of fratricide. In a dual envelopment, friendlies potentially shoot toward each other. In an encirclement, they actually come to close quarters in an enemy infested area. But, fratricide requires bullets or shrapnel. If everyone is either not shooting or shooting very carefully from good cover, the chances of fratricide can be reduced to almost nothing. For example, while encircling the top of foe-occupied hill, all fire from juxtaposed attack elements will be high enough—through ground curvature—to prevent friendly casualties during the union.

Most Encirclements Have Occurred on Offense

Of the major armies, the Asians have been most interested in encirclements. That's because the maneuver is discussed in the famous 36 Stratagems. In fact, "encircle the foe but let him think he has a way out" was one for confused situations. So, within the Orient, the circle formation has long been appropriate. (See Figure 20.1.) A period tactician once remarked, "if attacked from four sides, form a circle and fight from all sides."[1] But Asian Communists do not normally defend from an encapsulated perimeter,[2] so the original formation may have had mostly offensive reasons. Among them would have been to attack a much bigger quarry from the inside out.

Figure 20.1: Ancient Circle Formation
(Source: "100 Strategies of War: Brilliant Tactics in Action," trans. Yeo Ai Hoon [Singapore: Asiapac Books, 1993], p. 17.)

Sun Tzu had only seen danger in big encirclements: "When you surround an army, leave an outlet free. Do not press a desperate foe too hard." He said nothing about the same risk from smaller targets. That's why Asians have so often combined encirclement with annihilation.

The WWII Japanese so revered completely surrounding somebody as not to differentiate it from double envelopment. Nor did they worry about the size of the intended quarry.[3]

> By the 1930's, IJA planners realized more than ever that the Japanese army could not fight a war of attrition against the ever growing might of the Soviet Union. Consequently, they designed and refined their tactics to wage a short war fought to a quick and decisive conclusion.... The [initial] goal...was to encircle the enemy.[4]
>
> — U.S. Army, *Leavenworth Papers No. 2*

> In ascending order of effectiveness, the [Japanese] envelopment may be single, double, or an encirclement.[5]
>
> — *Handbook on Japanese Military Forces*
> U.S. War Dept., TM-E 30-480

The WWII Russians, liked to surround each composite part of a larger objective, before its piecemeal destruction from several different directions at once. Encirclement of an enemy target was doctrinally correct for something as small as a Russian platoon.

> The Soviet encirclement attack seeks to penetrate the enemy defense in two or more sectors and converge on a limited objective; its mission is to encircle or envelop enemy groupings and destroy them by simultaneous attacks from all directions. This scheme of maneuver is fundamental for the offensive operations for units of every size from the platoon to the army group.[6]
>
> — *Handbook on U.S.S.R. Military Forces*
> U.S. War Dept., TM 30-340

The MW-qualified Germans from WWI also used a certain amount of encirclement in WWII. The most obvious was associated with counterattacking. Their "soft defense in depth" was nothing more than a squad strongpoint belt in which some participants were allowed to pull back under extreme pressure. To a Western assault force, that looked like an opportunity. Once it had moved into the resulting "soft spot," defenders on either side of the breach would sometimes close it—thereby effecting an encirclement.

> Encirclement had always been a German specialty.[7]
> — *The Devils Guard,* by Elford

Many years later, the U.S. would face the master of encirclement in Vietnam.

> During these campaigns, our [NVA] army carried out very extensively the strategic splitting and large-scale encirclement of the enemy forces. It . . . [subsequently] attacked their nerve centers to wipe out and disintegrate all their important defense complexes.[8]
> — Gen. Vo Nguyen Giap
> (from "How We Won the War")

Some Encirclements Are Actually Built into a Defense

By letting an attacker pass over the first string of reverse-slope strongpoints, an IJA unit could automatically encircle its attacker. As at the Sugar Loaf Complex at Okinawa in 1945, it would then actively counterattack him through existing communication tunnels.[9]

The Chinese Communists did the same thing in Korea.[10] (Look back at Figure 8.5.) By hiding their fallback positions on the reverse slope of a ridgeline, they could cover them by fire from positions even farther back. They then would take an attack force under heavy fire from every direction at once. Undeniably, the Chinese were simply exercising the same strongpoint belt option as the Germans, Russians, and Japanese had before them.

The Surrounding of a Large Objective

When applied to a sizeable target of strategic import, an encirclement will sometimes be conducted like a siege. The various siege trenches are then gradually moved inward, as at Dien Bien Phu.

> The system of positions of attack and encirclement included the communication axes running around the Muong Thanh [central] sub-sector . . . ; many lines of communication trenches . . . from the surrounding hills to the proximity of the enemy's front line; many cross communication trenches to increase liaison possibilities.[11]
>
> – *Dien Bien Phu*
> The Gioi Publishers, Hanoi

Near the end of the battle, the Viet Minh had ringed Dien Bien Phu with a vast web of ditches that extended to within 100 yards of every French position and, in some cases burrowed beneath them.[12] Many positions had been so closely embraced as to cut off any chance of resupply or reinforcement.[13]

Something similar was attempted at Khe Sanh in first half of 1968. Map 20.1 shows the North Vietnamese version of what happened there. There were no troop movements near the Marine base, but extensive fortifications within 400 meters of it. *Asserchiamento* means encirclement in Italian, and *Ta Con* is the North Vietnamese name for Khe Sanh. As Marine security patrols hadn't encountered any NVA trenching outside their lines,[14] those circular fortifications on the Italian map must have been below ground. In other words, the North Vietnamese had accomplished in one fell swoop with tunnels at Khe Sanh what their fathers had mostly done through gradually encroaching trench lines at Dien Bien Phu.[15]

Frontline defenders had heard digging from the bottoms of their foxholes and seen superiors implant detection devices.[16] So, the tunneling is more than a hypothesis. Had the Marines stayed at Khe Sanh another month, they would have had hundreds of NVA soldiers come pouring up out of the ground some dark night at the center of their base.

The Encapsulating of a Small Objective

When an Eastern unit on the move spotted a smaller adversary first, it attempted silently to close with and annihilate it.[17] When the sighting was simultaneous, the larger Eastern force would demonstrate at its prey's center and send forces around both flanks to encircle it. That's because of the annihilation theme running

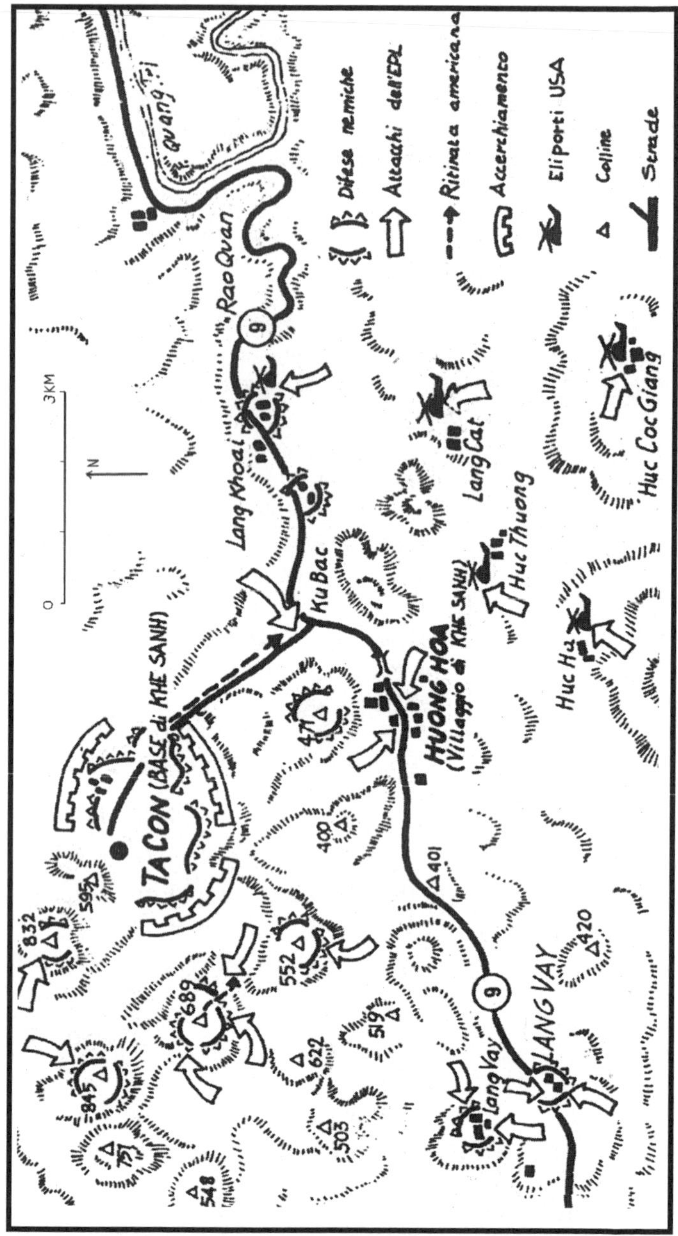

Map 20.1: Sub-Surface Fortifications Around Khe Sanh

(Source: Figure 540,"The War 1858-1975 in Vietnam," by Nguyen Khac Can, Phan Viet Thuc, and Nguyen Ngoc Diep, Nha Xuat Ban Van Hoa Dan Toc Publishers, Hanoi.)

through Asian, Russian, and German tactics.[18] The target's final destruction frequently involved segmenting the quarry, encircling every segment, and then subdividing it.

Interior Encirclements During Operation Buffalo

While applying the *Haichi Shiki* ambush (Figure 12.1), an ambitious Easterner will first block the open end of the inverted "V" to keep his quarry from being withdrawn, reinforced, or resupplied. At an area called the Marketplace just south of the DMZ, that's precisely what the North Vietnamese did in early 1967. A northward moving Marine company-sized column had just been sniped at from the left front. Before it realized there was also opposition to the right, a small NVA contingent was moving down from Hill 70 to shut the back door to an ambush.[19]

The left-side participants of the inverted "V" would close with the road, while the right-side group stayed put in their spider holes. Already on line in the treeline just to the west of Route 561, the left-hand group had only to maintain the same alignment while moving forward. But this was not a fully visible Western-style assault. Its troops were randomly to advance by fire and movement (using three-man fireteam rushes). The NVA soldiers had camouflaged themselves to look like tufts of grass. Every time one of the fireteams stopped, it blended in so perfectly with the savannah that the U.S. troops had nothing more to shoot at.[20]

But it is what happened next that would make the ambush so deadly. At various places along the Marine-occupied road, NVA fireteams crossed over to the other side, thereby segmenting the column.

> They [the Marines] opened fire on the NVA still dashing across the road. They fired on the NVA in the brush on their flanks too, but with elephant grass secured to their pith helmets and bush hats as well as on their packs and web gear, and around their arms and legs, the NVA were almost impossible to see.[21]
>
> — *Operation Buffalo,* by Nolan

To annihilate an entire column of troops, one must first subdivide it—to prevent the cooperation of its various parts. This is the whole purpose behind the Chinese "One-Point, Two-Sides Attack on Enemy Column" in Figure 12.2. At the Marketplace, elements of the NVA's westerly contingent crossed the road to effectively dismember B/1/9. Then, by "hugging" its various parts, they escaped any supporting-arms response.[22]

Once the internal encirclements of Company B had been completed, Oriental soldiers closed in for the kill. Their willingness to crawl and climb had created the method. As long as the target was slightly above or below the encirclers, they could all take it under fire without fratricide. So, the westerly NVA crawled toward the slightly elevated road, shot only at non-observant Marines, wriggled forward before taking another shot, and took turns doing it again. In that way, they could destroy their quarries without hurting the spider hole occupants on the opposite side of the road. Shooting downwards from the surrounding treetops also worked well for similar reasons.

Dual Encirclements

To preclude breakouts, several generations of Russians have used double circles.[23] So doing has facilitated multi-sided attacks on a small scale as well as large. At several battles in Manchuria in 1945, the final Soviet assault then came from three sides at once.[24]

> Their [Soviet] normal methodology called for an inner encirclement force to hold the trapped force in place while an outer encirclement force pushed out from the encircled area to put distance between the trapped forces and an enemy rescuing force. Only after the two forces were in place, would the Soviets fragment and meticulously destroy the trapped force. . . . In Afghanistan, the enemy . . . could usually slip through the Soviet encirclement.[25]
>
> — DoD-published Soviet military academy study

For complete annihilation of an opponent, the NVA would also use a double encirclement. In the initial battle of their 1975 push toward final victory, they used this maneuver against Saigon's 22nd Division at Phuoc An.[26]

21 PROBING AND DISSECTION ATTACKS

- What exactly is infantry probing?
- Why would someone want to subdivide an objective?

The interiors of enemy bastions sometimes favor a split.

(Source: FM 7-8 [1984], p. B-2.)

What's the Connection Between Probing and Dissection?

"Probing" is something one does to an adversary's front lines. Best described as a partial assault, it is used to find the most suitable location for a main attack. In the process, it can achieve several things: (1) determine the extent of the foe's barrier system; (2) get his machineguns to reveal their location; (3) see if his foxholes have been properly placed to cover all approaches through the microterrain; and (4) find where subordinate-unit responsibilities may be shared or unclear (separate sectors abut). All probing comes to a halt where the quarry has extensive barbed wire. Then, a Stormtrooper-like assault at any point along his lines would work as the main attack. But, the major Eastern armies mostly deploy belts of strongpoint matrices, so they have no "lines" *per se* (only an occasional row of Western-looking barbed wire that is partially backed by dummy holes). Such a defense may never be probed at all.

To breach an extended array of squad-sized strongpoints not fronted by barbed wire, Eastern armies would also require short-range assaults. Their purpose would be to dissect this array (possibly from different directions) and then encircle the resulting segments. The process would be repeated on a smaller scale until enough strongpoints had been eliminated to create an opening in the overall defense belt.[1]

> The objectives of infantry attack are to break the cohesive defense of the enemy, to divide him into smaller groups, and then destroy him.[2]
>
> — *Handbook of U.S.S.R. Military Forces,*
> U.S. War Dept., TM-30-340

Thus, both probing and dissection would be most likely accomplished through squad-sized assaults. What each separate attack might look like is the purpose of this chapter. One of its requirements would be for all participants to easily pull back should the resistance it encountered become too strong.

Origin of Probing

Probing has likely been around since the first armed conflicts, but the forerunner of its present-day equivalent surfaced during the Germans first Spring Offensive of 1918.[3] By this time, all Doughboys" lines were protected by plenty of barbed wire, so most probes did not entail any frontline assaults. They instead consisted of an examination of the foe's overall barrier system through long-range infiltration.

> The first wave was an infantry probe . . . whose purpose was to identify enemy positions for the next wave, about 250 meters behind.[4]
>
> — U.S. Army, *Leavenworth Papers No. 4*

Enemy Probing in WWII

The Japanese are known to have probed the Marines' front lines on Guadalcanal where there was only a limited supply of strand barbed wire.[5] (See Figure 21.1.) Before the heavy fighting, very few of those probes actually penetrated the perimeter.

> The Henderson Field defenses were tested almost daily during the first three months of the Guadalcanal Campaign. The Japanese probed, shot indirect fire, and attacked on the ground.[6]
>
> — Marine Corps Command & Staff College thesis

> We did repel probes that occasionally threw in mortar fire before testing the barbed wire.[7]
>
> — *Counterpunch.org*

Figure 21.1: Scarce U.S. Wire Being "Probed" on Guadalcanal

(Source: FM 21-75 [1967], p. 32.)

> The Japanese night attacks, of course, have limited objectives; and sometimes withdrawing after dark as much as [a few] yards will fool them and they won't know where you are.[8]
>
> — *Fighting on Guadalcanal,* FMFRP 12-110

How such tentative assaults were conducted is not quite clear. The more concerted ones at the Nipponese bridgehead on the Matanikau River had the second wave throwing grenades that were likely of the concussion variety. Something similar would be later observed in Korea.

> They attack in bunches, shoulder to shoulder. . . . They came out in a mass formation, 20 abreast, yelling, bayonets afixed *[sic],* automatic weapons working, rear ranks throwing hand grenades.[9]
>
> — *Fighting on Guadalcanal,* FMFRP 12-110

Opposition Probes During the Korean War

Unlike the U.S. forces in Korea, the Communists may have conducted "recon pull" in conjunction with their ostensibly 2GW (but really 3GW) assaults. But, before deciding where—on a U.S. perimeter—to launch the main attack, they still did extensive probing. At the Chosin Reservoir, the only concertina barbed wire was probably around the Hagaru-ri Airstrip.[10] Up on the surrounding ridgelines, only the flimsy strand variety may have been sometimes present, so there would have been more nighttime probing of Marine lines.

At the very front of every CCF assault battalion is known to have been an infantry squad that was specially trained in probing U.S. lines.[11] For Easy Company, 5th Marines, atop a Chosin Reservoir ridgeline in November 1950, such probes were initially done to find the best place for a main attack. Right at 10:00 P.M., there were two distinct rounds of probing against narrow sectors of the lines.[12] Red Chinese squads containing both grenadiers and burpgunners would hit those lines and then recoil.[13] (The Chinese liked to attack with alternating rows of burpgunners and grenadiers.[14]) As at Guadalcanal, most of those grenades would have been of the concussion variety and coming from the second row of attackers.[15] About midnight, the Chinese sent in what appeared to be human waves against Easy Company's position.[16]

If such a probe were unexpectedly to penetrate a U.S. perimeter at Chosin, it just kept coming to go after a center of gravity or support a subsequent main attack from inside the objective. Some of the Chinese probes that got all the way through Marine lines at Easy and neighboring Fox went after mortar pits and command bunkers.[17] Others put pressure on the Marines' perimeter positions from the rear. While beating back the Chinese human-wave assaults, frontline Marine positions are known to have received concussion grenades and "burpgun" fire from the rear.[18]

Probing in Vietnam

During the initial stages of the Battle of Dai Do just northeast of Dong Ha in July of 1968, there had been "two large enemy night attacks and several probes."[19]

On 13 March 1969, M/3/4's position was probed in the vicinity of Landing Zone Sierra northwest of Cam Lo. In this instance, the probes continued until one actually got through the perimeter. Such a thing would be reminiscent of enemy grinding in Korea.

> During the night, the Marines were subjected to a series of probing assaults, which increased in intensity until the early morning hours when the enemy penetrated a sector of the [Marines'] perimeter. . . . He [Lt. Kelley] fearlessly led a bold counterattack resulting in the defeat of the North Vietnamese Army force.[20]
>
> — Navy Cross citation for E.C. Kelley

Dissection

For Eastern armies, the intentional subdivision of an objective serves several purposes: (1) to find out what the objective holds; (2) to make its piecemeal take-down possible; and (3) to keep separate segments from resupplying/reinforcing each other. Such a penetration is considered far too dangerous in the West.

The Roots of Dissection

Dissection of U.S. lines had occurred in WWI during the German Stormtroopers' multiple penetrations of those lines. Otherwise there would have been no pockets of resistance to later reduce.

> Behind these three waves followed the remainder of the accompanying division, which reduced pockets of resistance bypassed by the storm units.[21]
>
> — U.S. Army, *Leavenworth Papers No. 4*

Dissection During WWII

The WWII Russians liked to break an objective into several parts, before attacking each part from several directions at once. In this way, they could fragment and then meticulously destroy a very dangerous trapped force. Of note, the penetrations associated with an encirclement attack were doctrinally authorized for a Russian platoon.[22]

During the Second World War, the German urban assault unit's immediate objective was also to segment an area held by the enemy, to limit his ability to reinforce its various parts. But to do so, its troops only advanced along parallel axes (never from different directions).[23]

The same dissection routine after an encirclement of enemy forces is an important aspect of Chinese Communist infantry tactics as well. This is clear from Figures 1.3 and 12.2 and the following quote from the *Handbook for the Chinese Communist Army*. The Asian version offers more insight into subsequent maneuvers than the Russian. It points out the flanking opportunities that automatically ensue from dissection.

> The isolation and subsequent detailed reduction of individual strong points of a defensive zone are called the *Divide-and-Destroy* tactical method. It is based on the theory that no defensive system can be equally strong everywhere and that weak spots exist which, if captured, will permit an attack from the flank or rear on adjacent strong points.[24]
>
> — *Handbook of the Chinese Communist Army*
> DA Pamphlet 30-51, 7 December 1960

The mutual interest of Russians, Germans, and Chinese in the dissection of an encirclement makes Figure 19.1 the likely state of the art for seizing any encapsulated series of enemy emplacements. That the Zulu "Horns of the Buffalo" followed the same scheme further supports this conclusion.

Dissection During the Vietnam War

In Vietnam, how the various segments of a dissection were subsequently destroyed became clear. It was through a repetition of the same sequence of events on a smaller scale. For the overall objective, the outer ring of enemy forces was first broken by several thrusts. Then ensued the inner encirclements and their piecemeal destruction. Its particulars would have been basically the same as in Figure 12.2—namely further dissection.

> In Hue, our army did not attack the outposts in the outer defense perimeter but rapidly carried out the strategic splitting of enemy forces, made deep thrusts into their rear, upsetting their battle array, then encircled, *split,* attacked and wiped them out in their inner defense perimeter.[25] *(Italics added.)*
>
> — Gen. Vo Nguyen Giap,
> from "How We Won the War"

How Was Such a Squad Assault Conducted?

An Eastern probing or dissection attack would not be exactly like a Stormtrooper assault (because there was no barbed wire to transit). But, it probably followed some of the same principles. Initially in column, the 10 or so members of the participating squad may have fanned out a little to handle particularly stiff resistance. The back row would have tossed concussion grenades while the front row advanced spewing small-arms fire. Then, once the attackers had negotiated the blockage (if that was indeed their mission), they would have returned to column formation for ease of movement and speed.

22 Spearpoint and Button-Hook Attacks

- What's the advantage of a sharp but tiny penetration?
- Can this breach be easily widened?

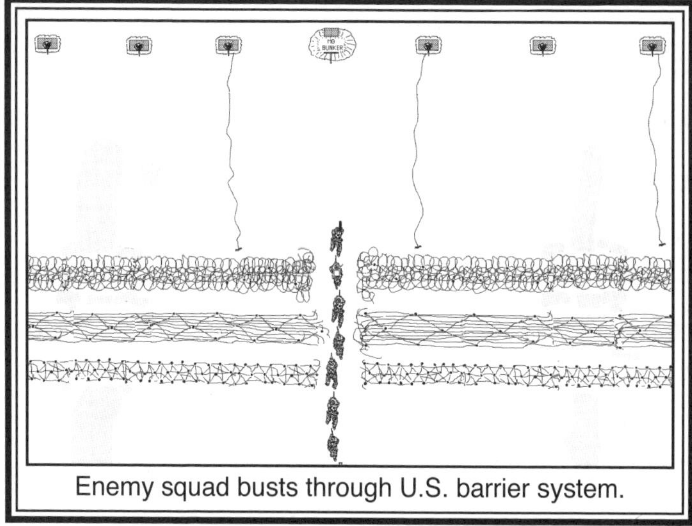

Enemy squad busts through U.S. barrier system.

(Source: "The Last Hundred Yards," Posterity Press, 1997, © 1994, 1995, 1996, 1998 by H.J. Poole, fig. 18.7.)

The WWI Trick of Seizing a Tiny Trench Segment

Occupying a narrow sector of enemy lines is how to get the most out of a few attackers. As the spearpoint for follow-on forces, the 10 or so men of each German Stormtrooper squad from WWI did precisely that. But, then instead of continuing on into the foe's rear area, this squad sent a small team in either direction along the initial trench to secretly clear a wider breach. They did so with bayonets and grenades simulating mortar impacts (no shooting). This subsequent frontline maneuver became known as a "button-hook" attack.

> Instead of attacking the enemy trenches over the whole width, they only assaulted key points, entered the trenches and then fought their way inside and alongside the trenches. Instead of surging against the trenches like a wave, the storm troops opened holes and flowed [laterally a short way] through the trench system.[1]
>
> — *1914-1918 Online*

By 1917, the Russians had developed elite assault units that were similar to German Stormtrooper squads.[2] Several Western European armies also tried late in the war to create the same type of unit, but none were able to do what the Stormtroopers had done. Part of the problem may have been their tactical doctrine. U.S. doctrine specifically disallows moving in both directions along a trench after a single squad has made the initial penetration.[3] So, an overall aversion to double envelopment may have been the problem. Yet, troops moving through sub-surface trenchlines enjoy very good cover from all kinds of threats. Without working in both directions at once along the perimeter excavation, there can be no risk-free widening of a narrow breach.

Japan in WWII

To force open gaps for follow-on forces, the Japanese also employed night attacks across narrow frontages. These attacks were hauntingly reminiscent of German Stormtrooper technique from WWI. Gen. Vandegrift's Chief of Staff at Guadalcanal noticed the following: "When given his choice, he [the Japanese] operates exclusively at night;...he attacks on a very narrow front, practically *en masse.*"[4]

The NVA During the Vietnam War

In May of 1967, the enemy in Vietnam decided to celebrate the anniversary of Dien Bien Phu by trying to seize the U.S. Marine Base at Con Thien. After a night of very heavy fighting, the NVA attack force was finally made to leave. Yet, it had still accomplished quite a bit. After making two narrow breaches in the protective wire, it had captured enough of the perimeter defenses to allow parts of two battalions with flamethrowers to enter. Besides "rolling up" a sizeable portion of D/1/4's frontline trench with grenades and bayonets after a shift in its mortar fire, the initial assault elements had accomplished something else. Like at the Chosin Reservoir in Korea,[5] one had taken out the Americans' 81mm mortar position (and any subsequent illumination). Their follow-on forces then destroyed the following: (1) two Marine LVTH's (amphibious tractors with turret-mounted 105mm howitzers); (2) two (or three) Dusters (Army 40mm self-propelled anti-aircraft guns); (3) a quarter-ton truck; and (4) an ONTOS (self-propelled 106mm recoilless-rifle platform). Three Marine tanks and a road grader were also damaged.[6]

How those forces had managed to get this close to expensive U.S. materiel is ultimately the issue. The initial NVA penetrations had been undeniably like those of the German Stormtroopers of WWI. Instead of precision long-range artillery fire, they had used nearby 82mm mortars. Instead of concussion grenades, they had thrown satchel charges. And an unexploded section of bamboo bangalore was even photographed following the attack.[7] Perhaps, how the follow-on forces were armed had provided the impetus. Those of the German Stormtrooper squads had also carried flamethrowers.[8] And two NVA submachineguns were discovered on the ground after the pre-attack ambush—a real rarity in Vietnam.[9]

Any blow-by-blow account of the foe's initial assault must necessarily be an educated guess based on previous research into his *modus operandi*. After bangaloring the wire during a mortar barrage, two NVA assault squads had gained entry to ARVN (Army of Republic of Vietnam) sectors by tossing satchel charges to simulate mortar impacts.[10] Then, the easternmost of those enemy squads worked to the right along the trench, while the westernmost went left (thereby closing with one another to create sizeable breaches at either end of D/1/4's lines). (Look back at Map 5.3.) So, instead of a classic button-hook at each penetration, the initial NVA assault squads may have tried to clear the entire stretch of trench between them.

Still throwing enough satchel charges to keep up the mortar deception, those assault squads had for a while done all their trench clearing with bayonets and Chicom grenades. Their assault technique had been so highly deceptive that it didn't really matter base defenders had been forewarned of the attack by a preliminary ambush.

Yet, 1/4 still persevered—largely through the confidence of its small units and dedication of its NCO Corps. The Alpha Company ambush squad had provided the 1/4 CP with a two-hour warning and the attack's direction. Its relief squads aboard the Amtracs had prevented too deep a penetration. And, though outflanked at both ends of its perimeter trench, Delta Company had managed to hold on to most of its frontline positions.

> With two tractors and the duster—me in the lead—we headed for Delta. We turned a tight corner . . . and through the flashes and smoke I could see Delta's command post . . . down the road. . . .
>
> Suddenly, we were under fire and I felt the tractor slowing down. . . . At the time, I could not understand why we had stopped, but we were under fire from the trench line [ahead]. . . .
>
> As I came around [fully gained consciousness], it was obvious that crawling toward the [Delta] trenchline was not an option. The incoming fire indicated it was full of NVA. . . . The only alternative was to slide downhill and take cover in a depression. Once out of the immediate area, I could then try to make my way toward Delta's lines [CP]. I recall crawling when I came across a wounded Marine. His leg was in bad shape. . . .
>
> He seemed to come out of it as I spoke with him. He kept telling me that the trench was full of NVA and to not go there. He had been trying to get out of the trench . . . when he had been hit.[11]
>
> — Commander of the LVT Relief Force

Five members of Delta were to end up winning a Silver Star in the struggle—two posthumously. So did a tanker in the Delta Company sector. By wise selection of the relief force route, the 1/4 XO had blocked the adversary's main avenue of approach to the base's highest point and strategic center. All the while, the NVA had been using state-of-the-art squad assault technique and some fairly sophisticated weaponry. Yet, on this particular night, the *Gung Ho* spirit of a Western outfit with a fleeting Maoist background had trumped the *Gung Ho* tactics of a fully Maoist Eastern opponent.[12]

A Rural Button-Hook Still Exists in Eastern Armies

Within U.S. military doctrine, the only legitimate button-hook maneuver occurs during room entry. (See Figure 22.1.) But, Eastern armies regularly send people down both sides of a breach in a countryside enemy position to widen it.

Role of Spearpoint and Button Hook in an Overall Scheme

Contemporary Russian maneuver forces deploy three types of lead elements—reconnaissance, forward detachment, and enveloping detachment. While the first has traditionally tried to avoid combat, the others are fully prepared to fight. Yet, they will only do so on a selective basis. In a meeting engagement, they will wait for the main force to fix the adversary in place before becoming one arm of a double-envelopment.[13] Normally, they will only assault a prepared enemy position to facilitate their parent unit's movement forward.

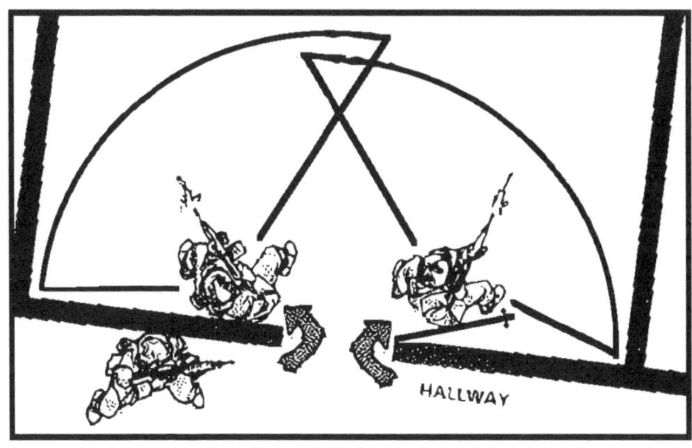

Figure 22.1: Button-Hook Room Entry
(Source: TC 90-1 [1986], p. E-4.)

Operating independently at the front of a Russian column, the forward detachment contributes to its command and control by performing "reconnaissance-pull" through the enemy's forward defense zone. To help in this regard, its commander has an extensive portfolio of deceptive measures.[14]

When the forward detachment encounters the enemy's main line of resistance, it looks for gaps and again waits for the parent unit. At the head of the main body is a battalion with reinforced platoons (and squads) that have been specially trained as assault groups.[15] While the main force attacks an encapsulated enemy concentration from the front, at least part of the forward detachment or follow-on "enveloping detachment" may try to sneak around behind it. The main-force assault will be on a narrow frontage and then sometimes followed by a "double button hook" to widen the breakthrough.[16] It then goes on to exploit the enemy's other newly exposed flanks and rear.

The button-hook maneuver was quite frequently employed by the Communist Chinese at the Chosin Reservoir in November of 1950.

> Ultimately, the Reds broke through . . . where the two units were joined. They poured troops into the gap, and as they attempted to roll back the newly exposed [frontline] flanks, they overran part of Fox Company.[17]
>
> – *U.S. Marine Operations in Korea*
> History Branch, HQMC

23 Inside-Out Attacks After Sneaking to the Middle

- Would arriving by surprise at target center help the
- Why is attacking outward easier than inward?

Key buildings can sometimes be entered through a sewer.

(Source: FM 90-10-1 [1982], p. E-11.)

The Most Famous Inside-Out Attacks Were Large Scale

Throughout history, attackers have snuck to the center of a city and then attacked back outwards. This, after all, is the essence of the North Vietnamese Blooming Lotus maneuver. It may have gotten its inspiration from the expansion portion of the ancient Chinese Cloud Battle Array.[1] (See Figure 23.1.) A period tactician once remarked, "if attacked from four sides, form a circle and fight from all sides."[2] This implies everyone moving outboard. Once the center of an enemy's camp had been reached through infiltration, even Sun Tzu would advise expanding the bridgehead.

Figure 23.1: Expansion Portion of the Cloud Battle Array
(Source: "Phantom Soldier," by Poole, p. 37.)

> You can be sure of succeeding in your attacks if you only attack places which are undefended.[3]
>
> — Sun Tzu

> Attack him where he is unprepared, appear where you are not expected.[4]
>
> — Sun Tzu

If what is less well defended has symbolic significance to one's adversary, then its capture could lead to defeatism among his troops.

> The general who is skilled in defense hides in the most secret recesses of the earth; he who is skilled in attack flashes forth from the topmost heights of heaven.[5]
>
> — Sun Tzu

> A whole army may be robbed of its spirit; a commander-in-chief may be robbed of his presence of mind.[6]
>
> — Sun Tzu

Suddenly finding oneself completely surrounded by opposition troops would generate quite a bit of interest in breaking the encirclement.

> Do not linger in dangerously isolated positions. In hemmed-in situations, you must resort to stratagem. In desperate position, you must fight.[7]
>
> — Sun Tzu

The Hue City Example

Much of the battle for Hue City during the Vietnam war was from the inside out. At the very center of this capital of Vietnam from 1802 to 1945 was an ancient fort called the Citadel. Within the Citadel was another walled enclave—the Imperial Palace compound. It and the nearby Citadel flagpole may have been the initial focus of main effort for the 31 January 1968 attack by NVA forces. Both had symbolic significance to the city's ARVN defenders.[8] The best previous example of the Blooming Lotus at Phat Diem in 1952 had consisted of infantry columns striking quickly at command-and-control facilities at the center of town. Those columns then headed back out to systematically destroy the now leaderless units manning the city's peripheral defenses.[9] But, the Hue City attack was different.

At Hue City some 16 years later, a major infiltration preceded all conventional drives into the urban center. In fact, 30 days of supplies may have been smuggled into the city before the battle even started. The Perfume River, Phu Cam Canal, and most roads had been clogged with traffic throughout the month of January. This elevated level of activity had provided ample opportunity for smuggling.

> Hundreds of infantry weapons — including .51 caliber heavy machineguns and perhaps hundreds of tons of ammunition, demolitions, and supplies—had been smuggled into Hue disguised as civilian goods.[10]
>
> — *Fire in the Streets,* by Hammel

Not surprisingly, the Hue City VC had not only been helping to pre-stage supplies, but also to insert NVA operatives and com-

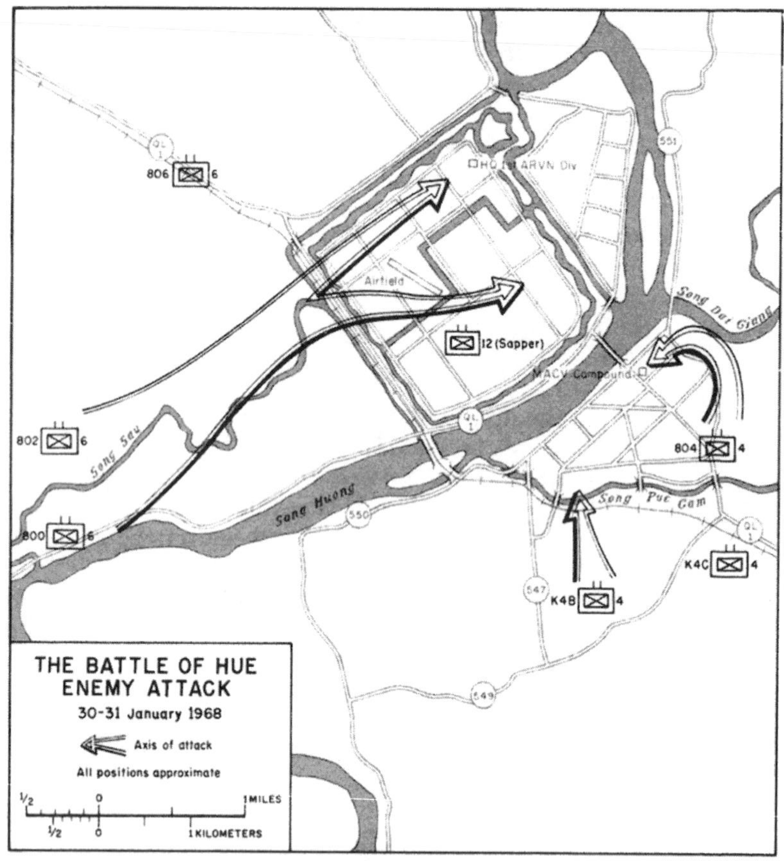

Map 23.1: Map of the Attack on Hue City
(Source: "Map_Battle_of_Hue-Army_MHC.gif," U.S. Army Ctr. for Mil. Hist, retrieved at url: http://www.tom.pilsch.com/AirOps/hue-battle.html.)

mandos. Map 23.1 shows the 12th NVA Sapper Battalion already inside the Citadel when two NVA infantry regiments hit the city from the outside on the night of 31 January. From in or around the Imperial Palace, those sappers may have had a twofold job: (1) secure it and the nearby flagpole as a symbol of NVA domination; and (2) reconnoiter military headquarters in other parts of the fort. If necessary, they could have even helped with the Citadel gates. But, a day before the main attack from nearby mountains, commandoes attached to each approaching NVA regiment had entered Hue to do those kinds of things. Disguised as pilgrims and ARVN soldiers on holiday leave, their mission was to control all important bridges, road junctions, and Citadel gates.[11] (See Map 23.2.)

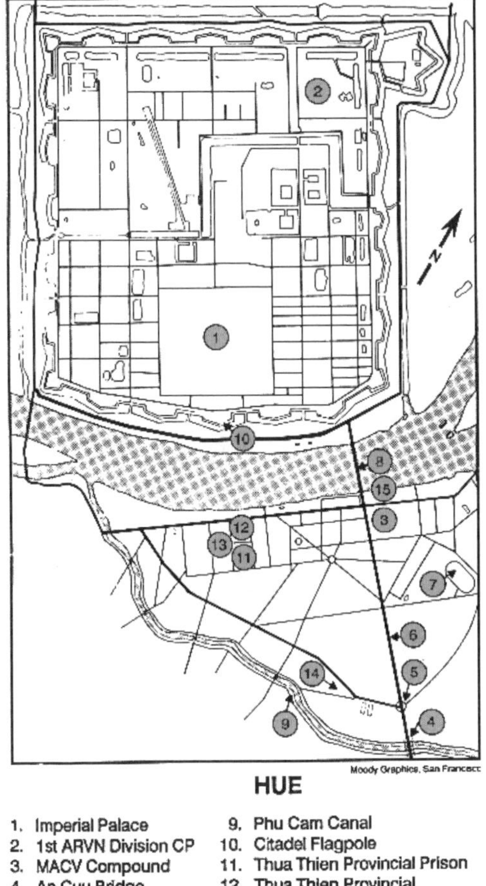

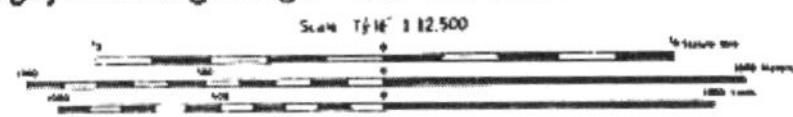

Map 23.2: Hue's Targets of Strategic Significance

(Source: Courtesy of Pacifica Military History, from "Fire in the Streets: The Battle for Hue, Tet 1968," © 1991 by Eric Hammel.)

> On 30 January, some of the enemy shock troops and sappers entered the city disguised as simple peasants. With their uniforms and weapons hidden in baggage, boxes and under their street clothes, the Viet Cong and NVA mingled with the Tet holiday crowds (Col. John F. Barr, Comments on draft, dtd 24Nov94). Many donned ARVN uniforms and then took up predesignated positions that night to await the attack signal (FMFPac, MarOpsV, Jan68, pp. 18-20, and Feb68, pp. 8-10).[12]
>
> —*U.S.Marines in Vietnam:The Defining Year,1968*
> History and Museums Division, HQMC

Then, when the two main NVA thrusts came in, their lead elements had enough local assistance to easily penetrate the old fortress.

> The North Vietnamese unit, augmented by area Vietcong *[sic]* troops, infiltrated through the [ARVN] Reconnaissance Company screen toward the Citadel's southwestern wall, where they waited for the signal to storm the city. When the signal came, they were aided by confederates inside the Citadel who dispatched any ARVN guards and opened the gates for them. . . .
>
> Meanwhile the enemy positioned a third battalion, the 806th, outside the northwestern wall to form a blocking position astride Route 1 to prevent any reinforcements from reaching the city. The battalion's best company . . . had the mission of attacking the 1st Division Headquarters in the Citadel just over the wall. The invading force was bolstered by the [already positioned] NVA 12th Sapper Battalion.[13]
>
> — *The Siege of Hue,* by Smith

Inside-Out Attacks Require No Grandiose Setting

Within the Orient have also been countless inside-out attacks on a much smaller scale. Some of the Chinese soldiers, who got through while probing Marine lines in Korea, then went after U.S. mortar pits and command bunkers.[14] Others waited to interfere with the perimeter machineguns during the main attack.

While beating back what seemed to be a Chinese human-wave assault, frontline Marine defenders more than once received concussion grenades and "burpgun" fire from the rear.[15] Such activity would have greatly facilitated the entry of one of the stormtrooper-like squad columns that had actually approached the U.S. position side by side.

> As the left platoon braced to take the brunt of the assault, a lone Chinese burpgunner infiltrated to the Marine rear and squeezed off telling bursts as he scrambled from position to position to escape detection.[16]
>
> – *Chosin,* by Hammel

Meanwhile, the members of other Chinese squads were alternating grenade tosses and small-arms fire to grind their way through their assigned sector.[17] Any who succeeded could have simply turned around to grenade,[18] or shoot,[19] frontline defenders from the back.

What's To Be Gained from an Interior Bridgehead

SWAT teams have long dreamed of inserting a master *ninja* into a hostage situation during the night before their planned assault. Such personnel are so skilled at fortress entry that they could find where the hostages were held, hide nearby, and then neutralize hostage guards during the final assault. To someone highly trained in *ninjutsu,* such a mission would seem quite doable. But, there is no known example of it ever being tried in modern police work. Even in the state-of-the art rescue of hostages at the Japanese ambassador's house in Peru on 22 April 1997, the closest facsimile was an initial tunnel entry to the floor below where the hostages were being kept.[20]

Still, something just as helpful is possible in rural terrain. Experienced sappers had no trouble entering U.S. positions in Vietnam after dark. (See Figure 23.2.) One morning just outside the big Marine base at Dong Ha in late 1966, a U.S. Marine lieutenant saw something so unbelievable he believed it to be ARVN training and never reported it. From about 25 yards away, a totally blackened and gearless figure had run behind a tiny-bush-covered hillock and disappeared. For a full half hour, the young officer had no luck

Figure 23.2: An Objective of Any Size Can Be Infiltrated
(Sources: FMFM1-3B [1981], p. 4-9; FM 5-103 [1985], p. 4-4.)

locating the hole, while systematically tromping through (and pulling on every bush in) a 10-meter-square search area. On his second tour in 1968, he was told by a fellow officer that a similar figure had just been encountered in the darkened billeting area of 27th Marines' headquarters.[21] Such sightings may help to explain some of the damage to expensive American equipment that was later attributed to either accidental mishap or lucky mortar hit throughout the war zone.

One of the best documented examples of such activity was the attack by infiltrators on the U.S. 81mm mortar crew a full hour before the main ground assault on Con Thien in May 1967.[22] Because the long-range 175mm guns at Gio Linh had no illumination rounds, it was the job of those Marine mortars to provide all high-altitude flares during the initial stages of any attack on the base. Being able to clearly see enemy soldiers coming through the wire makes them much easier to stop.

Vietnam Was Not the First Example of This Type of Thing

Command-and-control facilities have previously been targeted by enemy personnel who somehow penetrate a U.S. perimeter. During the initial fight for Bloody Ridge on Guadalcanal in mid-September 1942, portions of up to three Japanese companies were able to skirt the frontline Marine defenses. From there, they headed inland as far as a secondary runway of Henderson Field.[23] While Marine Raiders, Paratroopers, and grunt reinforcements were making their famous "stand" on Bloody Ridge, a small group of enemy sappers was being evicted from the 1st Marine Division Headquarters—almost a mile behind the perimeter fight.[24] (See Map 23.3.)

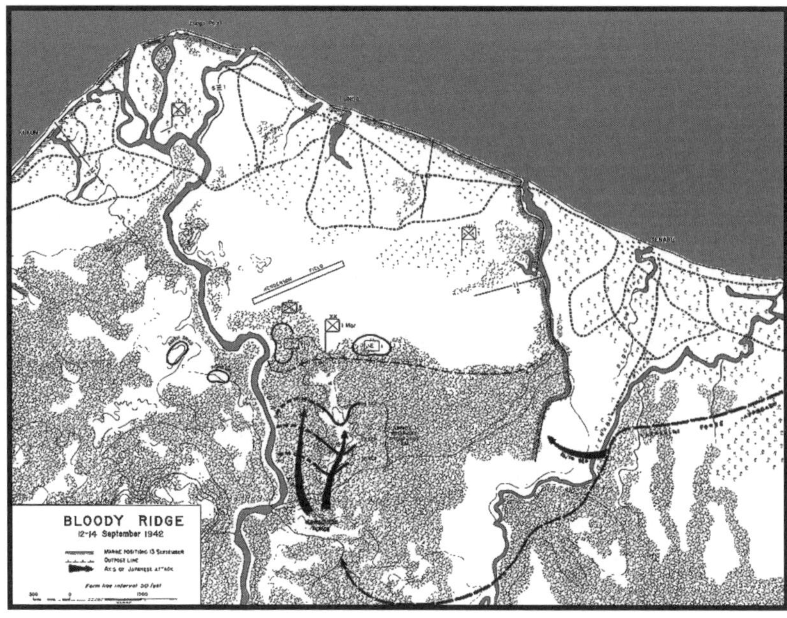

Map 23.3: Infiltrators Hit 1stMarDiv CP After Bloody Ridge
(Source: U.S. Army Center of Military History, The Green Books, "Guadalcanal: The First Offensive," illustration designator "lmap-vi.jpg.")

There are vital areas within the center of any protective formation, however small. To mortar pits and command/communication centers, one can add ammunition dumps, first aid stations, food/water supplies, and bomb shelters. Without such assets, the unit under attack becomes devoid of intelligence, direction, supporting arms, illumination, hydration, food, bullets, medical attention, medevac, and overhead cover. That's why the Chinese have since made short-range infiltration of the most promising rearward enclave of an enemy outpost their main attack. (Look back at Figure 1.3.) After the complete seizure of this "defense area" would come attacks across the undefended boundaries of sister areas.

New Dimension in the Consolidation of a Foe Position

Just as a U.S. target can be hard to carry in a single assault, the average Chinese target requires a series of composite battles. While the model PLA attack does not head for the objective's center, so it is not quite like a Blooming Lotus. It only seizes a rearward part, so that the other parts will be easier to take. Their eventual reduction could be through any number of other maneuvers depending on the terrain. They may include encirclement, probing, spearpoint, button-hook, dissection, sniping, or just an old-fashioned on-line assault. However, all would most probably be accomplished through crawling.

If the foe happened to be Eastern in a heavily fortified area, each of those interior enclaves would have its own barrier system, perimeter foxholes, and central machinegun. As such, its entry through burrowing or short-range infiltration would be out of the question.

Those who haven't worked much with U.S. squads may fail to realize their potential. If Russian, German, Japanese, and Asian Communist soldiers can safely conduct squad maneuvers this complicated, then so can Americans. Even if they are never allowed to, they will still need to know of their enemy counterpart's capabilities to have the best chance of survival.

24 Subterranean Tactics

- What are subterranean maneuvers?
- Why have U.S. forces been hesitant to use them?

Other armies evade enemy firepower through tunneling.

(Source: "North Korean Handbook," PC-2600-6421-94 [Washington, D.C.: U.S. Defense Intelligence Agency, 1994], p. 3-125.)

The Oriental Way of Doing Things

Asian armies and their affiliates are more likely to perform subterranean warfare than those from the West. One of the oldest tricks of the *ninja* is, after all, to predict where an opposing force will bivouac and then hide there below ground.[1] If that force is well enough endowed, he will soon have free access to whatever he wants or needs.

The first move is always the same—wait below ground for the enemy to either pass by or camp overhead. Then reemerge at night to conduct his mischief.

The Chinese Just Prior to WWII

In a secluded alcove at the rear of Beijing's military museum sits a glass case containing a miniature mock-up of a complete below-ground Chinese village during the Japanese occupation.[2] From such hidden villages, Chinese guerrillas would frequently embark on foraging expeditions.

The Japanese in WWII

Near the end of WWII in the Pacific, the beleaguered island defenders could most easily raid their tormentors through subterranean passageways. They could also best launch defensive spoiling attacks from bypassed caves. The Japanese had set the stage for the purely offensive "tunnel" attack of the VC. The underground position was, after all, a foolproof way to bypass every barrier and defender.

On Iwo Jima, there had been an underground thoroughfare that, among other things, linked the three main defense belts.[3] How else could a Kuribayashi-led force of 300 have mounted a surprise attack on Airfield Number One two weeks after the official end to hostilities.[4] His supposed last stand had been some 4000 meters to the north of there.[5]

A few months later on Okinawa, the Japanese would often allow themselves to be overrun and then attack from below. This was standard operating procedure for Japanese antitank troops.[6] They would wait in a spider hole (or tunnel opening) for the forward echelon of U.S. ground pounders to pass, pop a smoke, and then run forward to affix a satchel charge to an American tank. To escape U.S. supporting-arms fire, whole Nipponese units may have also waited below ground to attack American forces passing overhead. This was particularly true of the Sugar Loaf Complex at the north end of the infamous Shuri Line.

> We received many reports of valorous fighting [for the Shuri Line], such as "Our soldiers jumped out of their caves as soon as the enemy tanks passed, crawled forward, and engaged in hand-to-hand combat with enemy soldiers."[7]
>
> — Col. Yahara, Japanese veteran of Okinawa

The Germans at Berlin

While the Germans had been advisors to the Japanese Army since 1885,[8] it's not quite clear if they had learned about subterranean warfare from them. The outgunned defenders of Berlin would often change location through the subways and then emerge unexpectedly to defend some strongpoint. But, this was not the same as secretly attacking a Russian staging area through the hole knocked in some basement wall from a sewer line.

Further Refinements to the Subterranean Foray in Korea

To prevent further U.S. incursions beyond the 38th parallel in Korea, the Chinese dug 1250 kilometers of tunnels toward the end of the Korean War.[9] These tunnels provided ample chance for offensive action. So did the natural and man-made below ground openings.

> Whether we can defend our positions is a question that was resolved last year. The solution was to hide in [collocated] grottos *[sic]*.[10]
>
> — *Mao's Generals Remember Korea*

> The Chinese liked to construct tunnels and caves at launching-attack points.[11]

More Refinement to the Subterranean Attack in Vietnam

Hundreds of miles to the south and 15 years later, the Viet Cong would continue the tradition of suddenly appearing from out of nowhere.

> At least once during the Vietnam War, an American army base was inadvertently built over a Vietcong *[sic]* tunnel complex. Whether this occurred because of coincidence or the Vietcong's anticipating the Americans' intent to build the camp on the site and then simply extending their vast system of tunnels to the site, the result was the same: en-

> emy sappers appeared and disappeared at will within the perimeter of the base.[12]
>
> — *Knights of Darkness,* by Lung

Underground feeder passageways to the famous Cu Chi tunnel complex northwest of Saigon may have extended almost to Cambodia. This underground network was so long and broad that U.S. units operating in the area couldn't help but bivouac above one of the hidden entrances. So doing would have automatically compromised their security.

Western soldiers have occasionally burrowed to emplace obstacle-breaching charges. Eastern soldiers keep going. In Vietnam, the VC and North Vietnamese often used tunnels to enter their objectives.

> During the American occupation [of Vietnam], tunnels were dug near, into, and completely around American bases. In places, these access tunnels allowed sappers to come and go from American installations at will.[13]
>
> — *Knights of Darkness,* by Lung

As mentioned in Chapter 14, the defenders of the Dong Ba Gate to the Hue City Citadel repeatedly counterattacked from its subsurface passageways.

Same Thing Possible from Above Ground Locations

During the Vietnam War, attacks were regularly launched on the Marble Mountain Helicopter Base from tunnels and caverns later discovered inside the same hill mass. Few now doubt that at least one passageway led to the top and thus someplace inside the Marine Corps perimeter.

In the city, surprise attacks can also be launched from supposedly secure above-ground spaces. The Jews in the Warsaw Ghetto may have counterattacked that way.

> Trenches and ditches were dug under pavements [in the Warsaw Ghetto], behind walls and through sewers. Attics also became vital passageways. . . . [H]oles were cut in

walls, making it possible for people to move from house to house and street to street.[14]

— *The Holocaust,* by Levin

Underground Conduits Play a Big Role in Urban Combat

As noted in Chapters 13 and 14, considerable urban combat takes place below ground. In fact, an entire city could be captured or held this way. (See Figures 24.1 and 24.2.)

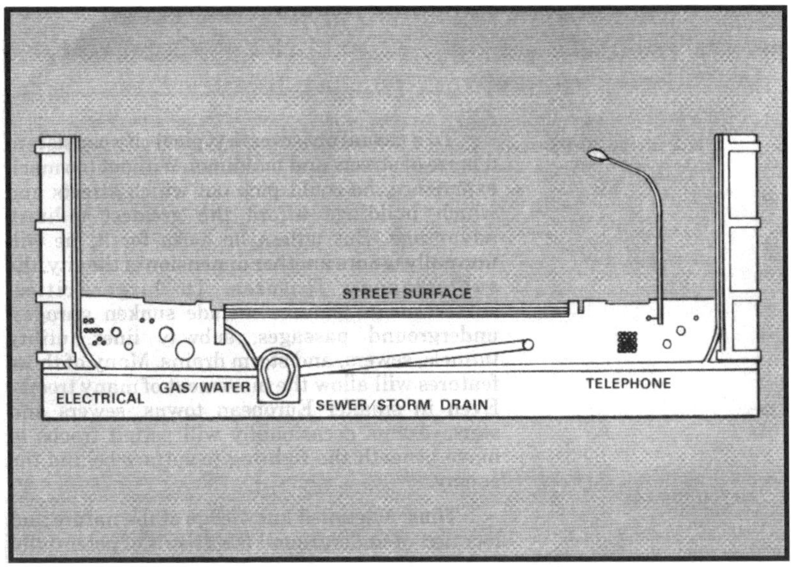

Figure 24.1: Underground Conduits

(Source: FM 90-10-1 [1982], p. J-2.)

Figure 24.2: Even Old Cities Have Drainage Systems
(Source: MCRP 3-02H [1999], p. IX-1.)

25 *Motti* Attacks

- What are *Motti* maneuvers?
- Were the Finns the only ones to use them?

Semi-autonomous fireteams can isolate a foe position.

(Source: Unknown artist, used after asking permission of pinterest.com, from image designator "b0a98fccc5628b9163cedb39ff43e0cc.jpg," poss. © Pinterest.)

Historical Backdrop for *Motti* Warfare

The Finns were to use "*Motti* Warfare" to stymie a huge and fully supported Russian invasion of their country in 1939. To do so, their tiny detachments needed only a limited supply of small-arms ammunition, demolitions, and antitank mines.

"*Motti*" is Finnish military slang for a totally encircled enemy unit, or center of resistance.[1] The reference to *mottis* then came to mean the formation of "bite-sized" enemy units.[2]

Associated with this new type of warfare was a multi-faceted maneuver for destroying a more powerful enemy piecemeal. Used extensively by the Finns in their Winter (Russo-Finnish) War of 1939-40, it was especially effective against a motorized enemy force moving up a forest road. Once committed to such a confining avenue of advance, all column participants could eventually be trapped. Where water features or heavy woods precluded any interference from opposition tanks, a good-sized Finnish light-infantry unit would intercept the convoy to stop and isolate it. Then, through a combination of mines, ambush, and trees across the road, the Finns would sever the stalled procession of vehicles at several susceptible places. Light-infantry detachments moved through those cuts to double-envelop and harass all resulting segments. As those segments or *mottis* became sufficiently weakened, a special assault unit from the Finnish reserve would be brought to bear against them, one at a time. If any *motti* proved too strong to be fully attacked, it was simply left to run out of food, fuel, and ammunition.

The Finns did not have enough wartime materiel to defeat the Russian bear. Their only hope was to steal some of his, while delaying the invasion long enough to secure a favorable peace accord. *Motti* tactics made such an acquisition of supplies and equipment possible.

Motti Strategy Was Landscape and Weather Related

The beleaguered Finns had learned that an invading force of any size—in constrictive terrain—would eventually follow a route that made it possible to immobilize and then subdivide. At this point, the weather and lack of resupply would help to weaken each segment.

> The basic tactical doctrine assumes that the enemy will follow avenues of approach which will make him vulnerable to encirclement, after which his forces are to be destroyed piecemeal. This is accomplished by forcing the enemy to follow routes outlined by either natural or artificial obstacles until he reaches the terrain selected for his annihilation.[3]
>
> — *Tactical and Technical Trends,* August 1942

But *Motti* tactics did not strictly require cold weather. In the late summer of 1944 at the Battle of Ilomansti (in the Continuation

War), the Finns again used them against two much-bigger and better-armed Red Army contingents.[4] That battlefield was also heavily forested and crisscrossed by connecting rows of rivers, lakes, and swamps. As a result, few roads ran through it.

The Strategic Genius Was in the Details

First, the approaching procession of Soviet vehicles was reconnoitered by small Finnish patrols. Then, at an appropriate place where the road-bound invader would not want to be ambushed (like while crossing a water feature), he was. After the front of the column was pinned down, the remainder was cut off at its very rear from outside support. Other road-crossing attacks simultaneously divided the force into sections.[5] The double-envelopment of each section created a *motti*. And that *motti* could be systematically weakened by tiny Finnish teams.

Most Westernized armies heavily rely on their "command and control" networks. As such, both create centers of gravity—key targets for 3GW. Besides campfires and field kitchens, the harassing Finnish teams also targeted headquarters elements and communication lines.[6]

Those Finns Knew of Evolutionary German Doctrine

Most Finnish troops had German training manuals in their possession. They were thus fully "familiar with the ideology of the post-WWI German soldier."[7] Encirclement had always been a German specialty.[8] One of the advantages of a soft defense-in-depth had been the chance to close in the breach behind an attacking enemy force, and thereby entrap it. So, a German strongpoint belt of semi-autonomous squads could—in this way—be turned into an engulfing swarm.

The same thing held true for a Japanese defense matrix. And that's how Cushman's Pocket was formed on Iwo Jima. In fact, the Marines on that island regularly found themselves taking fire from every direction after passing the tunnel-connected fallback positions of a forward-facing string of contested bunkers. Such a thing often resulted in a kind of standoff swarm by fire alone.

The *Motti* Attack Involved Swarming

A "quarry-hugging" harassment mission is most logically the job of a squad-sized element. Only something that small can sneak through the protective screen of opposition outposts. After finding a soft spot in the enemy's main body, it then conducts a limited, pinpoint attack of some sort. This attack can range anywhere from a lethal spray of automatic weapons fire to a well-placed thermite grenade or molotov cocktail. Because no ground-gaining assault had actually taken place, the attackers easily withdraw to do damage elsewhere.

> In military usage, *motti* refers to an enemy group surrounded by Finnish patrols each of from eight to twelve men armed with automatic arms.[9]
>
> — *Combat Forces Journal,* January 1950

Slightly larger elements may have be used to divide an enemy target into a sufficient number of segments to individually annihilate.

> The strength of patrols varies from a squad to a platoon. Their missions demand speed and surprise; consequently, they are lightly equipped and travel on skis. . . . They are armed with light automatic weapons and hand grenades, and carry light demolitions. . . .
>
> Following the initial reconnaissance, they attack the enemy from all directions. This creates the illusion that the attacking force is everywhere, and the enemy never knows where to expect the next attack. . . . Enemy security posts are avoided. Patrols hold fire until within close combat range of the main enemy force. . . . Favorable objectives are marching troops, bivouacked units, motor columns, and supply dumps. Guerrilla patrols . . . [sometimes] plant mines . . . in the rear of the enemy. . . . Each patrol carries out more than one mission; after attacking at one point, it moves rapidly by ski and attacks a different part of the column.[10]
>
> — *Combat Forces Journal,* January 1950

Only when the target had been sufficiently softened up and demoralized, would an all-out assault ensue.

Motti Attacks by the Russian Shock Groups at Stalingrad

Soviet Gen. Vasily Chuikov had fought in the Russo-Finnish War. From it, he must have learned about *motti* tactics, because he went on to use something very similar at Stalingrad, and then expand upon the same idea.

Many German assault columns were channelized into preplanned kill zones as they neared the Volga. Like the Finns had done to road-bound convoys, the visible end of each German column was then severed from everything behind it. Next came a series of attacks from every direction by tiny Russian shock groups. As in the below excerpt, they first tried to segment the column, because so doing was Soviet doctrine for urban warfare in WWII.

> Two basic types of attack are employed: the systematic attack against continuous defensive lines in depth, and the accelerated attack against weak sectors such as . . . open spaces. Seizure of the latter divides the defending forces into smaller pockets.[11]
>
> – *Handbook for U.S.S.R. Forces,* November 1945
> U.S. War Dept., TM 30-340

Then came the annihilation of each pocket. Closely approximating *Motti* tactics (but without the preliminary harassment), it may have entailed an assault by a single shock group or many groups at once. Because the state of the art for tank killing was fire from every direction, the latter maneuver was more probable. The entire effort would have then looked like all tracked vehicles being individually swarmed.

Motti Tactics by the Chinese at Chosin

Within the journal on the Chosin Reservoir campaign of the Korean War, there appeared an article in 2002 claiming the Chinese had used *Motti* tactics. The encirclement of Marine units came as no surprise, because Mao had done likewise in his war against the Nationalists.[12] But the article suggests the application of Finnish maneuvers against the ensuing pockets of American resistance *(mottis)*. This should have included standoff harassment attacks of the smaller pockets before an annihilation attempt by specially trained assault force. However, no standoff harassment attacks occurred (not even sniping), only the squad-sized probes leading up to a well-placed main attack. So, the similarity of the Communist effort to *Motti* tactics may have ended with the confining nature of the location in which both occurred. This time it had been mountainous terrain traversed by few roads. (See Map 25.1.)

First apparent from the article was the intentional segmenting of the U.S. force—which Figures 1.2 and 12.2 have already shown to be an inherent part of Chinese tactics.

> At Chosin, the Chinese did an excellent job of using information gained by reconnaissance to develop their plan to cut the roads and chop up American units into what they thought would be manageable mottis. However, they soon learned that all mottis are not the same when two marine regiments appeared at Yudam-ni, rather than one as expected, and one small regiment east of the reservoir. When they executed phase one of their overall plan, they created a grand motti at Yudam-ni, two small mottis between Yudam-ni and Hagaru-ri, multiple mottis east of the reservoir, and one motti at Hagaru-ri at the base of the reservoir. From Koto-ri south the road remained open until the final cut at the gatehouse bridge in the Funchilin Pass. East of Chosin they initially separated the Americans with a cut between the two lead battalions and a serious separation at Hill 1221.[13]
>
> — *Changjin Journal,* August 2002

Then, because of the barren landscape and eventual arrival of U.S. planes, the Chinese did not have the time to fully isolate and harass the existing *mottis.* Nor did they make any attempt to annihilate the little ones. Instead, they further tried to dissect the big ones.

> The CCF were not flexible enough to take advantage of favorable situations by quickly massing and destroying small mottis, such as those in the Toktong Pass area. In the case of the grand motti the Chinese continued to dissipate their forces by throwing weakness against strength rather than continuing the strategy of striking deep and separating smaller enemy elements.[14]
>
> — *Changjin Journal,* August 2002

The dissection effort itself may have been half-hearted in at least one location. Instead of remaining inside the U.S. perimeter to exploit the new boundary, some the Chinese forces just kept going.

> While the roadblock [in the valley] was being hit, the Chinese came back against How Company, beginning with the usual shower of concussion grenades. . . .
>
> The Chinese were all over the dwindling perimeter, too close and too intermingled to be dealt with in any way but hand-to-hand. *The [Asian] attackers were more intent upon breaking through How / 7 than in destroying it*, and [several] surprised Marines emerged from losing scuffles as their adversaries scrambled over the crest and descended toward the valley below [italics added].[15]
>
> — *Chosin,* by Hammel

Of major concern to the Chinese was the effect American airpower would have on the battle once the weather had cleared a little.

> The Americans had firepower and airpower when weather permitted. The Chinese had troops in large numbers with firepower based on the numbers of rifles and machine guns supported by a very long supply line operated during hours of darkness by coolies and pack animals. The Americans had almost unlimited supplies dropped from the air when weather was favorable during daylight. As the days went on the Chinese continued to throw their dwindling numbers against the mottis, while the American strength continued to grow through the accurate use of firepower when and where possible.[16]
>
> — *Changjin Journal,* August 2002

Then, the fear of U.S. air cover, must have caused the Chinese to ignore the protection that hugging U.S. units would have provided. The Chinese supply lines were also overextended.

> Although the grand motti at Yudam-ni continued to suffer casualties, they were far less than those suffered by the Chinese who continued to have less to throw back at the

Americans, and finally reaching the point when lack of ammunition forced the commander to commit units because his supply line was running dry.[17]

— *Changjin Journal,* August 2002

However, there was one apparent success to the Chinese maneuvers. One encircled Marine unit got hurt when it attempted to withdraw.

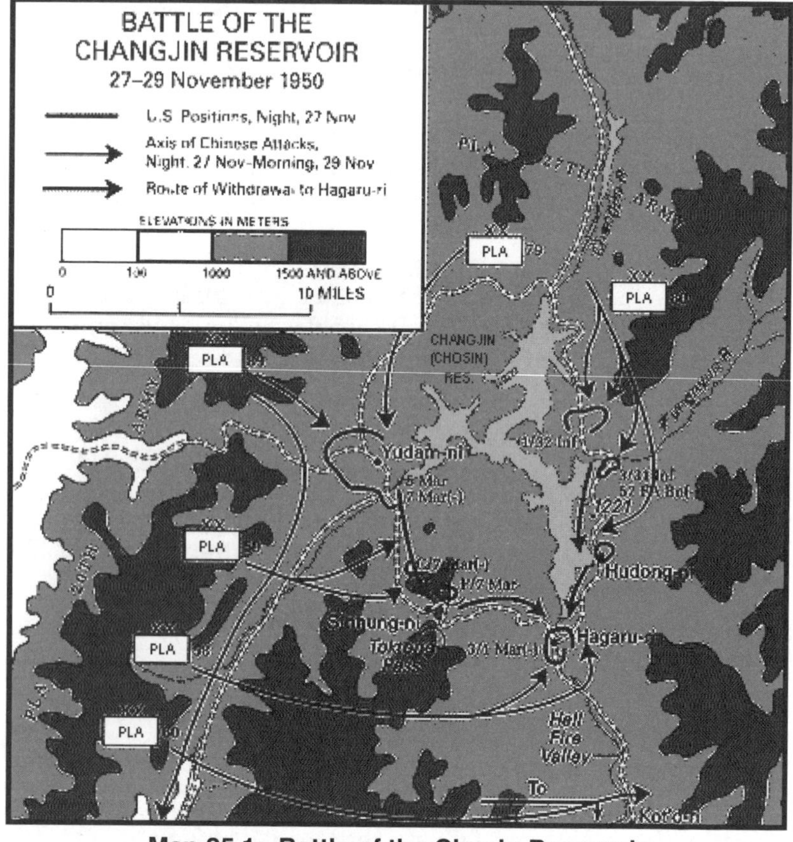

Map 25.1: Battle of the Chosin Reservoir

(Source: "Map of the Battle of the Changjin (Chosin) Reservoir," U.S. Army Ctr. of Mil. Hist, from this url: http://www.history.army.mil/brochures/kw-chinter/chinter.htm.)

> East of Chosin, the Chinese had committed two full divisions against one RCT [Regimental Combat Team] consisting of only two infantry battalions and one artillery battalion, reinforced with heavy mortars and a battery of AAA [Anti-Aircraft Artillery] AW [automatic weapons] tracks. Although the Chinese suffered heavy casualties in their attacks against the firepower of a tight perimeter, they did whittle down the defenders who were at the unfavorable end of inaccurate air drops that also benefitted the enemy. In the end this motti began its breakout attempt against impossible odds, with a result similar to the Soviet breakout from the Lemetti Motti.[18]
>
> — *Changjin Journal,* August 2002

In Finland, roadblocks had been used to segment enemy columns. At the Chosin, they were apparently used to complete the encirclement. Whereas the cold had been the Finns' ally in Europe, it badly affected the Chinese at Chosin.

> The Chosin battle became a matter of undoing motti roadblocks by the use of dominating firepower, much coming from air strikes directed from the ground by forward air controllers. As the breakout battle continued from Yudam-ni through its phases of Hagaru-ri and Koto-ri to Chinghung-ni, there was less and less Chinese resistance. The Chinese motti tactic was no longer effective because of a reduction in firepower and the impact of the weather on manpower. The Chinese soldier who happened to have a few bullets for his rifle soon realized they were useless in his frozen hands.[19]
>
> — *Changjin Journal,* August 2002

> "[T}he Kiinalainen Motti of Chosin" [article] concludes that the Chinese commander with his mass of manpower not only wasted his soldiers through ineffective attacks, but also did not look far enough ahead to take advantage of critical terrain. He did not encircle Yudam-ni in sufficient depth nor capture key terrain in the Toktong Pass. He did not perform a similar deep envelopment east of Chosin and take East Hill at Hagaru-ri, thus wasting his resources on a smaller motti and losing time which ultimately abetted the American breakout from Yudam-ni. From then on he

> miscalculated the effectiveness of his dwindling resources as the game reached closure at the most critical terrain objective of the Chosin campaign, the Funchilin Pass [south of Koto-ri].[20]
>
> — *Changjin Journal*, August 2002

On both battlefields, the up-close harassment of enemy enclaves made its perpetrators immune to outside supporting-arms fire. In this way, it closely resembles the "hugging tactics" for which Asian Communist armies have since become famous.

Earlier Facsimiles of the Original *Motti* Tactics

The gradual reduction of perimeter defense through periodic sniping goes back into history—far beyond discouraging warming, cooking, meetings, or signalling. The American Indians often encircled a settler camp and then gradually picked off anyone who showed themselves.

Motti Tactics by the NVA in Vietnam

America's less-well-equipped foe during the Vietnam War also demonstrated knowledge of the *motti* decimation procedure. For example, the NVA appear to have used it on a largely road-bound contingent of U.S. Marines approaching the DMZ on "Operation Buffalo" in 1967. At least, that's what the civilian chronicle of this operation indicates.[21] Not only was that column segmented and then attacked piecemeal, but the Finnish trick of dragging a mine across the path of an armored vehicle may have also been applied to the relief force.

Motti Tactics by Muslim Rebels in South Asia

What happened in Korea would also apply to the mountainous terrain of Afghanistan. The key to the isolation of each pocket had mostly to do with the scarcity of roads in that tiny nation. It was therefore easy to limit an invading unit's resupply.

> In the 1980's, the Soviet Union experienced similar difficulties in the mountains of Afghanistan. In both instances, the road and trail-bound nature of their forces and their basic tactics left them vulnerable to motti tactics in mountainous terrain.[22]
>
> – U.S. Army, *Mountain Warfare,* FM 3-97.6

What *Motti* Tactics Subsequently Grew Into

It's no coincidence that after applying *motti*-creating ambushes at Stalingrad, Soviet Gen. Vasily Chuikov then went on to develop "hugging tactics." The Asian Communists would subsequently become renown for the maneuver. Its use in Korea should not surprise anyone because in the North Korean tactics in 1950 were largely influenced by Soviet doctrine. Then, the maneuver came into most famous play at Dien Bien Phu and Khe Sanh.

> In an attempt to reduce Viet Minh casualties, General Vo Nguyen Giap . . . ordered his troops to secretly dig more than 50 miles of trenches. The Viet Minh did exactly what Chuikov had told his Soviet troops 12 years earlier. They got close to the enemy's positions, . . . moved on all fours, made use of craters and ruins, dug their trenches by night, camouflaged them by day.[23]
>
> – *Quora*, May 2016

The hugging maneuver at Khe Sanh was quite different.[24] As Chapter 20 has pointed out, the gradually closer entrenching had been replaced by invisible tunneling.

26 Swarm Tactics

- What exactly is a "swarm"?
- Why does looser control over its participants still work?

Foe armor most easily killed through a swarm in the city.

(Source: FM 5-103 [1985], p. D-9.)

Tactical Swarms Never Considered by the U.S. Military

The generally accepted definition of swarming has comes from the federally contracted Rand Corporation: "Engaging an adversary from all directions simultaneously, either with fire or in force."[1] Yet, its original source admits to swarms normally consisting of ground attacks. They come in from so many different sides that the defenders are not able to counter them all.[2] Thus, the Chinese encirclement of a U.S. position at the Chosin Reservoir in Chapter 4 (where Red squads took turns assaulting) involved a swarming variant.[3]

It was during the Chinese Communist attack on Fox Company, 5th Marines, during the night of 27 November 1950 in Korea that this version of swarming was first noticed.

> There was a lull in the fighting, but there was no telling how long it might last, nor where the Chinese would strike next.[4]
>
> – *Chosin,* by Hammel

For Easy Company on the adjoining hilltop, the same thing was happening. Right at 10:00 P.M. began two distinct rounds of probing.[5] Squads containing both grenadiers and burpgunners would hit the Marine lines and then recoil. About midnight, the Chinese sent what appeared to be four human waves against the position.[6] Then began a period of consecutive assaults at different locations along the line.[7] The Chinese were conducting a series of widely separated and seemingly random squad rushes.

> Resorting to grinding tactics, the Chinese repeatedly assaulted [at different places along the perimeter of] Company E's position from midnight until 0200 . . . [with] charging squads of infantry.[8]
>
> – *U.S. Marine Operations in Korea 1950-1953*
> History Branch, HQMC

Latest American Connotation of the Term

The most recent Pentagon interest in swarming has involved drones. During the various Persian Gulf episodes, it was with IRGC (Iranian Revolutionary Guard Corps) speed boats.[9] Next, it will be on what armed robots might accomplish in tandem. Wherever the overriding government agency cares mostly about equipment, that's where the swarming focus is likely to be.

But trying to spot swarming at too large a scale in ground operations can also cause a distortion of the concept. U.S. military organizations are top-down in structure and therefore regularly in pursuit of overall "big-picture" solutions. Traditional swarming has more to do with what many "little pictures" might accomplish together. That's why only bottom-up Eastern cultures tend to try it through tiny contingents of soldiers.

Whether Swarming Occurred Depends on Encounter Size

The so-called Stalingrad "pocket" was full of 330,000 German troops and created when the Red Army encircled the city in 1942. The multiple Soviet thrusts into this pocket did not constitute "swarm tactics" in the true sense of the term—despite Rand's conclusion to the opposite.[10] But, the joint attacks by reinforced-squad-sized Russian "shock groups" on German thrusts into Russian enclaves at the city's center in 1941 did. Those enclaves were in tiny rubbled areas along the Volga River (where some resupply was possible). Precisely how those shock groups cooperated is evident from a single historical reference. A preplanned kill zone may have been the target of each swarm, with every swarm participant already acquainted with the approach route.

> [The Russians] had perfected the use of "shock groups," small bodies of mixed arms . . . who gave one another support in lightning counterattacks; and they had developed the creation of "killing zones," houses and squares heavily mined to which the defenders knew all the approach routes, where the German advance could be canalized. . . . By the end of October the Russian positions at Stalingrad had been reduced to a few pockets of stone, seldom more than three hundred yards deep, bordering on the right bank of the Volga. . . . But these last islets of resistance, hardened in the furnace of repeated attacks, were irreducible.[11]
>
> — A.J.P. Taylor

When under attack from several sides at once, most infantry members of any German penetration would have taken cover in the nearby buildings and courtyards. If those locations had been mined, the overall damage to the column would have been greatly magnified.

First Battle for Grozny Definitely Involved Swarm Tactics

On 31 December 1994, a few thousand lightly armed and loosely controlled Muslim rebels were able to defeat a mechanized Russian assault on Grozny. The Russians had the Chechens outnumbered, outgunned, and surrounded,[12] but they had apparently forgotten how downtown Stalingrad had been defended in 1941. Purportedly to avoid casualties, they had become too dependent on technology and firepower. Against a quick-witted opponent in built-up terrain, such weapons are largely useless.[13]

> [T]he 6,000 Russians troops ran headlong into approximately 15,000 urban guerrillas. . . . The Chechens waited until the armored columns were deep into the confines of the urban sprawl before initiating their ambush with a hail of hit-and-run rocket-propelled-grenade (RPG) attacks. Within 72 hours, nearly 80 percent of the Maikop Brigade were casualties, while 20 of their 26 tanks and 102 of their 120 armored vehicles were destroyed.[14]
>
> — *Marine Corps Gazette,* October 2001

Grozny would be defended in much the same way as the Volga enclaves had been at Stalingrad. The main avenue of approach to the center of Grozny would be subdivided into tiny sectors. Each sector would then be defended by several, loosely controlled maneuver elements.

> The Chechen standard hunter-killer team consisted of an RPG gunner, machinegunner, and sniper. Three to five hunter-killer teams would work together in a sector.[15]
>
> — *Marine Corps Gazette,* April 2000

The standard method of engagement would be ambush. The Chechen hunter-killer teams would surprise their quarry from every direction at once (while staying in their assigned sector). Under random fire from sewer opening, ground level, and rooftop, the victim would have trouble acquiring a target and thus become quickly disoriented. In other words, armor was handled in almost the same way it had been at Hue City in 1968—with a barrage of RPG rounds from all sides at once. Opportunism took the place of established procedure and detailed orders. And, the ambushers could decide when to break off the attempt. They always had a preplanned escape route.[16]

> RPGs were shot at everything that moved. They were [sometimes] fired at high angle over low buildings. . . .

> Multiple RPG rounds flying from different heights and directions limit a [Russian] vehicle commander's ability to respond. . . .
>
> Chechens chose firing positions high enough or low enough to stay out of the field of fire of tank and BMP weapons. . . . The Chechens used mobile tactics and "let the situation do the organizing," while the Russians relied more on brute strength.[17]
>
> — *Marine Corps Gazette,* April 2000

Why Small-Unit Swarms Are So Unpopular in Washington

Swarming worked during the first battle for Grozny because the Chechen rebels had little, if any, organization. As their military activities became more and more structured, they could no longer keep the Russians out of the city. The idea that additional command and control may have proved counterproductive flies squarely in the face of Western bureaucracy. Yet, before being summarily disbanded, Carlson's Raiders had successfully conducted swarming attacks during their Long Patrol on Guadalcanal.[18] And objective military studies still say such attacks work. According to a West Point think-tank, "The U.S. military can use rules-based decision making and . . . environmental cues (as signals). . . to generate self-organizing swarms that function without electronic communications [direct headquarters control]."[19] The separate detachments could still coordinate by cell phone, as long as headquarters didn't try to intercede after issuing its initial guidance on things like individual sectors, when to strike, how to break contact, etc.

> Using simple rules-based paradigms, small units can quickly swarm the ground and carry out specific missions without significant risk of detection.[20]
>
> — West Point, Modern War Institute, April 2018

Truly caring military leaders are again starting to warm up to the idea of many tiny units operating separately to better protect their personnel from modern enemy ordnance.

> Just to survive, our formations, whatever the wire diagram looks like, will likely have to be small. They will have to

> move constantly. They will have to aggregate and disaggregate rapidly.[21]
>
> – General Mark A. Milley,
> Army Chief of Staff

After all, didn't the American Minutemen repeatedly snipe at the British column on its way back to Boston from Concord in 1775 in a type of swarm? [22]

All Eastern Soldiers May Be Capable of Swarming

All armies that pursue the encirclement of small enemy objectives may have a swarming variant available. Of the major Eastern armies, only the Germans may not have followed their WWII encirclements with swarming. The Russians not only did it in tiny enclaves along the Volga in Stalingrad, but also in compliance with their encirclement doctrine.

> [The attack's] . . . mission is to encircle . . . enemy groupings and destroy them by simultaneous attacks from all directions. This scheme of maneuver is fundamental . . . for units of every size from the platoon [up].[23]
>
> – *Handbook on U.S.S.R. Military Forces*
> U.S. War Dept., TM 30-340

During the second night of the Battle of Edson's Ridge on Guadalcanal, the Japanese attack force can be said to have been swarming.

> The next night's attacks were as fierce as any man had seen. The Japanese were everywhere, fighting hand-to-hand in the Marines' foxholes and gun pits and filtering past forward positions to attack from the rear.[24]
>
> – *First Offensive,* by Shaw

Red Chinese soldiers had swarmed during their attacks at the Chosin Reservoir. Those who got through the perimeter defenses assisted others by grenading,[25] or shooting,[26] frontline defenders from the back.

> The Chinese were all over the dwindling [U.S. Marine] perimeter, too close and too intermingled to be dealt with in any way but hand-to-hand.[27]
>
> — *Chosin,* by Hammel

Guerrilla Warfare Inherently Entails Swarming

Every modern-day Chinese soldier is required to know GW.[28] Carlson's Raiders had been following Maoist tactics during their Long Patrol. That's why their swarming can be said to be an inherent part of PLA GW. Like hounds nipping at a fox's heels, they would creep up on the Japanese, strike swiftly, and then quickly retire guerrilla fashion.[29] Such tactics were purely Maoist in origin.

> Enemy advances, we retreat.
> Enemy halts, we harass.
> Enemy tires, we attack.
> Enemy retreats, we pursue.[30]
>
> — Mao's guerrilla guidance

Eastern Grunts Fight a Tank in a Type of Swarm

During the Korean War, Chinese PVA also liked to attack American armor while still in column moving up to or away from the combat zone. They would approach that column from both sides on a narrow mountain road, damage the lead tank's tracks, and then swarm in on the others. Every PVA fireteam knew how to finish off an immobilized tracked vehicle. A single soldier normally jumped up on each vehicle while his comrades watched for ground opposition. He probably had at his disposal a small shaped charge or thermite grenade.[31] The column commander came to believe he had been attacked every place at once.

Swarming also occurred around well separated armored vehicles at Grozny and Hue City. Thus, modern warfare has become necessarily more decentralized. And those loosely controlled small units will have a better chance in tandem. That such activity doesn't mesh well with the orderly way in which U.S. forces like to operate is unfortunate, but fully consistent with 3GW.

27 The Squad's Role in "Hugging" Tactics

- Which of the world's armies are best known for hugging?
- Does Stormtrooper technique play any part in this?

How near were the Germans at Normandy hedgerows?

(Source: "From Cornrow to Hedgerow," by Keith Rocco, National Guard Image Gallery, Historical Paintings, Heritage Series, ©.)

Which Armies Have Been Hugging U.S. Forces?

Combatants of the major Eastern armies have been closely engaging better-supported adversaries—those with more standoff firepower. That's how the one most adept at short-range combat is able to regularly evade the other's artillery and air strikes.

Chapter 25 has already demonstrated hugging by the Russians and Asian Communists. Even a limited knowledge of WWII suggests the same ability from Japanese and Germans. Both would stay in contact for as long as it took to achieve their goals. So, one wonders what the various steps to this maneuver might be, and to what extent individual squads contributed. The most detailed examples of hugging come from the Japanese on Guadalcanal in WWII and the Chinese at the Chosin Reservoir during the Korean War.

The WWII Nipponese Embrace of Extended U.S. Lines

During Chesty Puller's famous defense of Henderson Field at Guadalcanal on the night of 24-25 October 1942, the Japanese attackers did four things: (1) hug American lines; (2) probe U.S. wire for a weak spot; (3) breach that wire with a bangalore; and (4) then try to fit several squads—one after another—through the tiny gap. The jungle vegetation had made it easy for literally thousands of those attackers to get up next to that barrier without being taken under fire. (See Figure 27.1.) If the Marines had possessed all the barbed wire they wanted, that barrier and the defender positions behind it would have looked something like Figure 27.2.

> At dusk, as usual, the [Marine] artillerymen registered their guns, and shells exploded in the thick growth a few yards beyond Puller's lines. . . . First Battalion, Seventh Marines was ready for its night of trial. . . . At 9:30 the phone rang in the Battalion. . . "Colonel, there's about three thousand Japs between you and me, [reported an LP occupant]." . . . The front erupted with blazing weapons, and over their heads the artillery shells soughed through the rainstorm. Explosions farther back in the jungle halted Japanese columns . . . but the vanguard pressed against the wire along a narrow front. . . .Puller had almost doubled the normal strength of machinegun companies. . . . Sergeant Manila John Basilone's nest of guns was about the center of C Company. . . . Captured documents [later] revealed that his [Puller's] half-battalion had beaten off the suicidal attack of . . . the equivalent of a Japanese division.[1]
>
> — *Marine,* by Davis

From the *Handbook on Japanese Military Forces,* the possibility of squad columns approaching their mutual objective side by side is already evident.[2] The Davis biography of Chesty Puller confirms Stormtrooper-like Japanese actions on the night in question: (1) sneaking up to the protective wire, (2) bangaloring that wire during

Figure 27.1: Guadalcanal Defense Took Cutting MG Fire Lanes
(Source: Sketch by Capt. Donald L. Dickson, "A Concise History of the Unites States Marine Corps 1775-1969," by Capt. William D. Parker, Hist. Div., HQMC,1970, p. 62.)

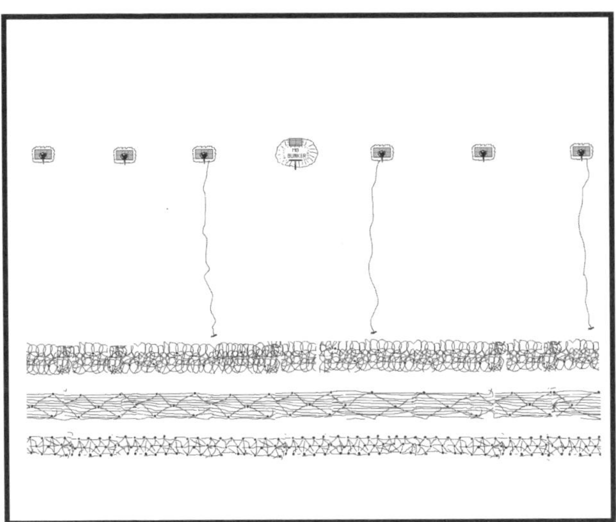

Figure 27.2: Section of U.S. Lines with MG and Claymores

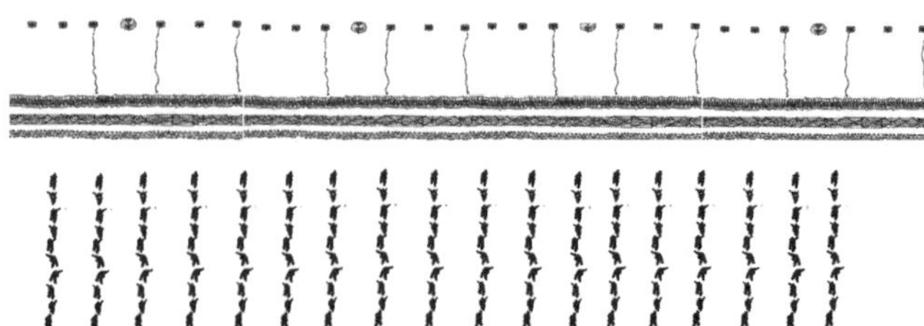

Figure 27.3: Japan's Troops Just Outside Extended U.S. Lines

an artillery barrage, and then (3) transiting the breach with bayonets and grenades only.[3] (See Figures 27.3 through 27.6.) There is also hard evidence of some Japanese troops already sneaking through 1/7's lines that night. A few may have then tried—from the back—to silence the Marine machineguns during the main assault. (See Figure 27.7.)

> While the enemy was hammering at the Marines' defensive positions, Sgt. Basilone, in charge of 2 sections of heavy machine guns, fought valiantly to check the savage and determined assault. In a fierce frontal attack with the Japanese blasting his guns with grenades and mortar fire, one of Sgt. Basilone's sections, with its gun crews, was put out of action, leaving only 2 men able to carry on. Moving an extra gun into position, he placed it in action, then, under

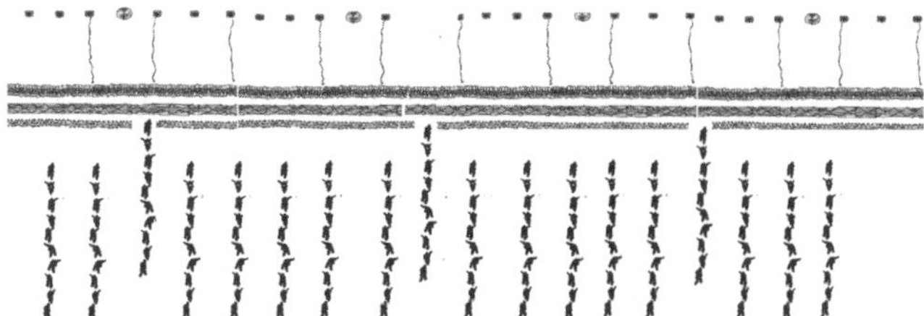

Figure 27.4: Sector of Lines Silently Probed in Several Places

Figure 27.5: Weak-Spot Probe Can Result in Unobserved Entry
(Source: FM 7-11B1/2 [1978].)

Figure 27.6: Rigging with Bangalore of Promising Assault Site

continual fire, repaired another and personally manned it, gallantly holding his line until replacements arrived. A little later, with ammunition critically low and the supply lines cut off, Sgt. Basilone, at great risk of his life and in the face of continued enemy attack, battled his way through hostile lines [enemy pockets] with urgently needed shells for his gunners, thereby contributing in large measure to the virtual annihilation of a Japanese regiment.[4]

— MoH citation for John Basilone

In addition to Furimiya's enclave [a 60-man breakthrough of Chesty Puller's lines just before dawn], a few dozen other Japanese soldiers had infiltrated in ones and twos.[5]

— *History Net,* "Battle of Henderson Field"

Next, the Japanese horde made its main attack through however many holes in the wire it had created with bangalores. John Basilone could not have killed as many opposition soldiers with

Figure 27.7: Intruder Intent on Attacking U.S. MG from Back
(Source: Army/Marine Clipart, Air University, retrieved from www.au.af.mil/au/awc/awcgate/cliparmy.htm.)

his machinegun that night if each enemy squad had made its own breach. So, sister squads must have followed the initial squads through. (See Figure 27.8.)

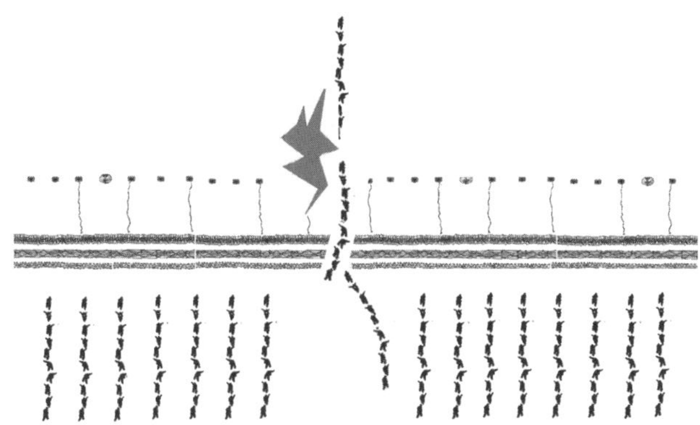

Figure 27.8: Bangalore Blown, MG Hit, Adjacent Squads Enter

The Korean War Hugging

The Red Chinese hugging attacks of U.S. perimeters at the Chosin Reservoir were largely comprised of other advanced maneuvers by separate squads: (1) swarming; (2) inside-out efforts after short-range infiltration; (3) spearpoint and "button-hook" evolutions; (4) probing and dissection; plus (5) encirclement. A stratagem completely new to the literature also appeared. The official battle chronicles called it "grinding," as part of a holding attack.

Chinese Doctrine for a Fully Enclosed Target

Figure 1.3 has depicted the PLA's basic model for attacking an insular objective. Below is a detailed (though somewhat hypothetical) version of its application in Korea. That version has been derived from the same government pamphlet and various accounts of the attacks on U.S. bastions during the nights of 27 and 28 November 1950 at the Chosin Reservoir. (See Map 27.1.) There was little barbed wire on those ridgelines above Yudam-ni, and all Marine positions were of the oval variety. So, the foe was free to envelop them. Nor was there much vegetation in this cold and mountainous region of North Korea. So, the most secretive Red activity occurred before any moon had risen. (See Figure 27.9.)

Most of the following focus will be on the Communist push down Northwest Ridge on the first night. (See Map 27.2.) The approaching Chinese division did not send successive lines of assault personnel against those American outposts as is commonly believed. Those many Red soldiers came in as a row of extended squad columns. When well enough organized, side-by-side files of soldiers can be made to look like human waves. Such a deception would serve a very useful purpose. It encouraged the American units to stick with their outmoded "continuous-line" formation, instead of trying the squad strongpoint belt that had become the state of the defensive art in 1918.

Upon reaching the Marines' barbed wire, those so-called waves then quickly closed in upon themselves. What remained was a "brace" of Stormtrooper-like squad columns—each fully prepared to conduct its own assault against the Marine sector to its immediate front.

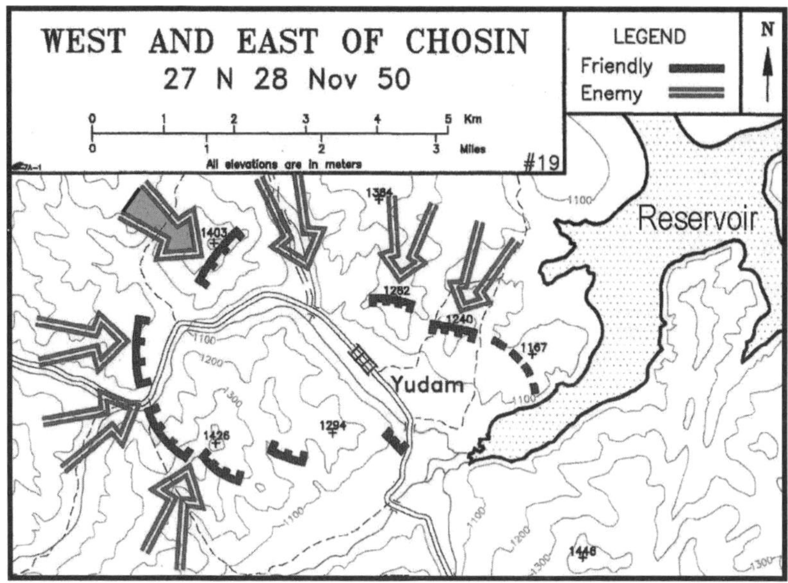

Map 27.1: All Attacks West of Reservoir in Late November 1950
(Source: Map by Melville J. Coolbaugh, from "The Chosin Chronology", © George A. Rasula, 2007, "Changjin Journal," 01/20/08, Chapt. 70.)

Figure 27.9: Only Dark-Night Hugs Possible at Barren Chosin
(Source: FM 7-11B1/2 [1978], pp. 2-11-A-4.2 , 3-11-A-4.2; OPNAV P34-03 [1960], p. 40.)

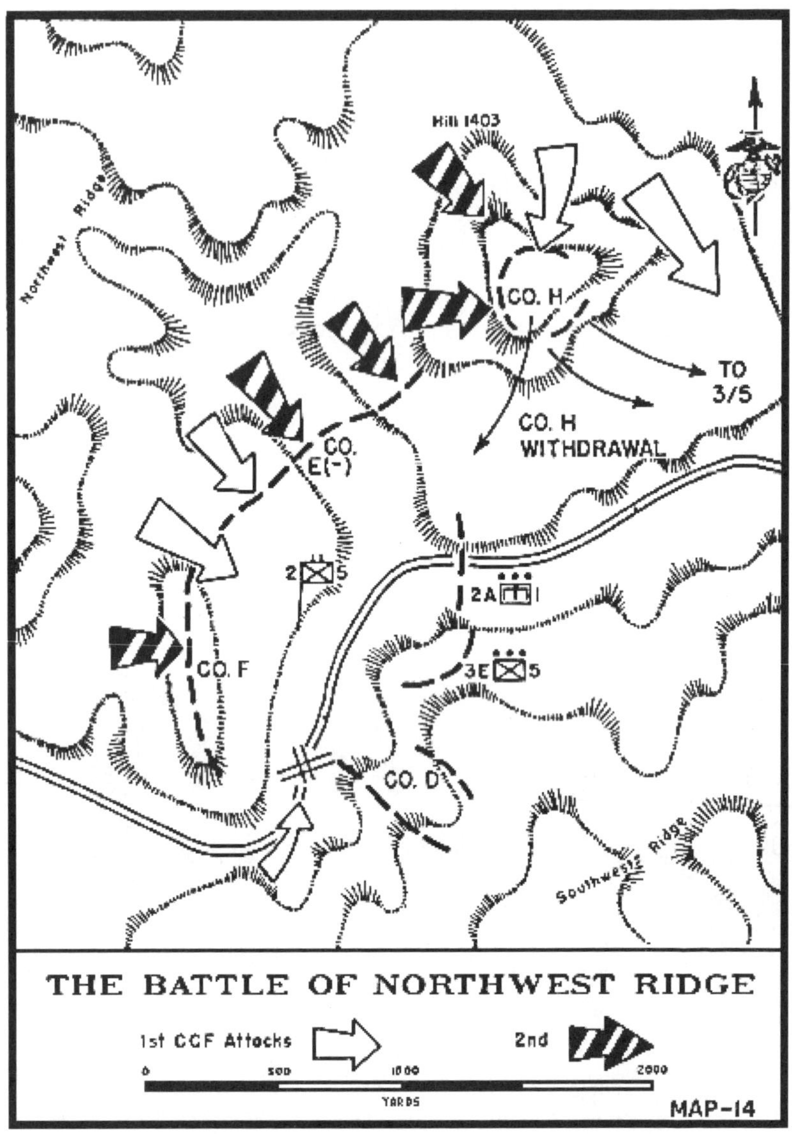

Map 27.2: The Chinese Attack Down Northwest Ridge

(Source: "The Chosin Reservoir Campaign," by L. Montross and N. Canzona, vol. III, U.S. Marine Operations in Korea: 1950—1953, Hist. & Museums Div., HQMC, p. 162.)

Already in single file, squads at either end of this Red "horde" then moved around back of the target in a controlled swarm. At the same time, sister squads started separately to probe and "grind" away at the objective from the front as a type of holding attack. Each grinding attempt consisted of concussion-grenades followed by burpgun fire, in probable combination with manual wire cutting. Decidedly deliberate to permit repeated attempts with some degree of safety, it likely involved no fully upright rushes, but only a gradual crawl forward through all available irregularities in the microterrain.

At some point, those Chinese squads now behind the objective would perform their more secretive aspects of the mission. In accordance with Figure 1.3, one blocked reinforcement from the back, two or more took turns "demonstrating" on one side, and the last made the main attack from the other side via short-range infiltration.

First Stage of the Attack at the Front of the Objective

On the barren slopes of Northwest Ridge, the arriving Chinese units could not have dispersed into several successive lines of troops without creating noticeable sound and motion signatures. So instead, company columns dispersed into platoon columns and finally into squad columns as they neared the U.S. lines.[6] To a firepower-oriented Westerner, waves of trigger pullers might seem more powerful. But Stormtrooper-like files can more easily penetrate a prepared enemy position at night. That's because all members have only to follow the man to their front.

The forward portion of a U.S. company-sized outpost in Korea wasn't very wide. Nor did it have much barbed wire. But its parts still resembled Figure 27.2, and its challenges were the same as those of the Japanese on Guadalcanal. Once the arriving Chinese squads had closed up the interval between members, the first job of some would be to probe for weak spots in the Marines' lines. (See Figures 27.10 and 27.11.) That could be done in two ways: (1) through noisy partial assault; or (2) via silent inspection of the defensive array. The former sometimes resulted in undetected Red soldiers entering American lines. From the inside, some would later support other assaults.

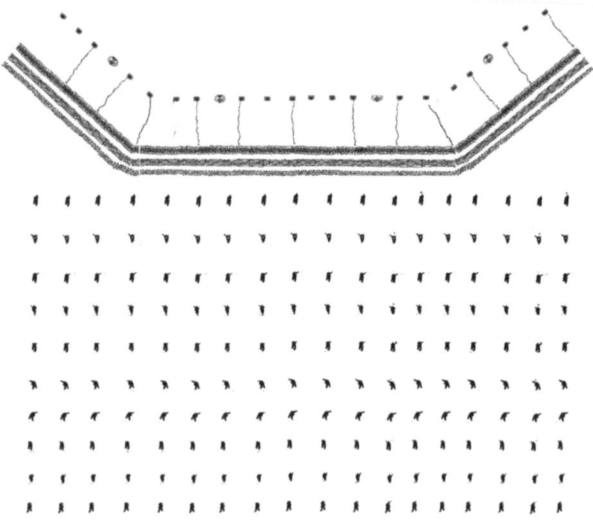

Figure 27.10: Chinese "Human Waves" Approach Perimeter

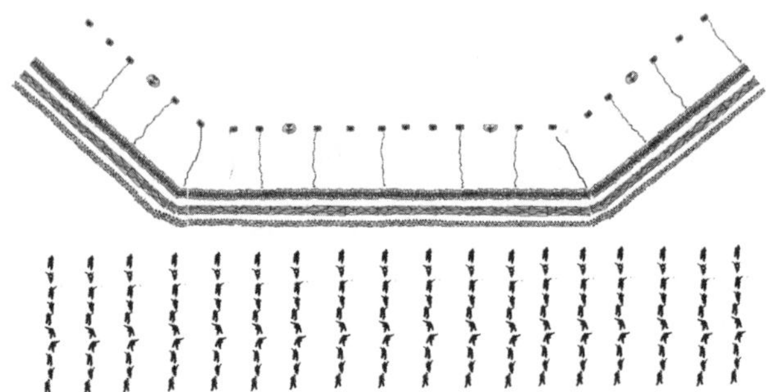

Figure 27.11: When the Spacing Between Waves Closes

Meanwhile, Chinese Communist squads at the ends of the formation had begun to encircle the target. (See Figures 27.12 and 27.13.)

Main Attack Would Eventually Come from a Back Corner

While creating a diversion at one side of the rearward portion of the objective, the bypassing contingent then conducted the main attack through short-range infiltration of the opposite side. A single squad of Red infantry quietly cut any wire and crawled in probably looking for the foe's command post (CP). (See Figures 27.14 and 27.15.) Nearby would have been any mortar tubes and stores of ammunition, food, or water. Without leadership, communications, illumination, and resupply, the parent American unit would become far easier for its frontal squads to overrun.

At Northwest Ridge, there is ample evidence of infiltrators entering the F/5 position from the rear. They were after U.S. mortars to curtail illumination, and U.S. leaders to diminish control.[7]

> A Chinese infiltrator shot at Sergeant Johnson as he stood in the momentary flash caused as a round left the [81mm mortar] tube he was steadying.[8]
>
> — *Chosin,* by Hammel

> [A bazooka] rocket sergeant [had earlier been] . . . shot by an infiltrator hiding on the rear slope of the ridge.[9]
>
> — *Chosin,* by Hammel

Later that night, the enemy troops also occupied the company headquarters of How/7 (while apparently attached to 2/5). Atop Hill 1403—the highest ground in the area—the Reds may have thought a battalion headquarters to exist. (Look back at Map 27.2.)

> While the roadblock [in the valley] was being hit, the Chinese came back against How Company, beginning with the usual shower of concussion grenades. . . .
>
> The Chinese were all over the dwindling perimeter, too close and too intermingled to be dealt with in any way but hand-to-hand.[10]
>
> — *Chosin,* by Hammel

Figure 27.12: A Column More Easily Changes Location

(Source: Courtesy of Sorman Information and Media, from "Soldf: Soldaten i falt," @2001 by Forsvarsmakten and Wolfgang Bartsch, Stockholm, p. 225.)

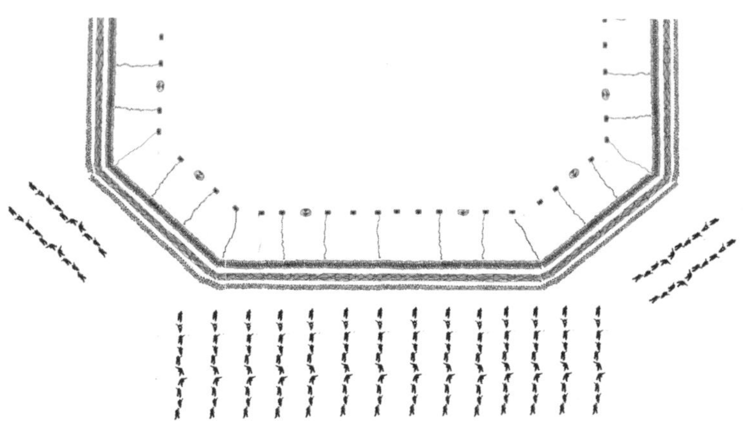

Figure 27.13: Two Red Squads Go Around Each End

Meanwhile on Hill 1240 a little to the east of 1403, Dog/7 had been getting similar treatment. (Look back at Map 27.1.) Shortly after 10:00 P.M. on the night of 27 November, it experienced an extended period of light probing. Before long, infiltrators were tossing grenades at Marine mortarmen.

> [At] 2345 [11:45 P.M.], Company D of 2/7 reported enemy infiltration on Hill 1240.[11]
> – *U.S. Marine Operations in Korea*
> History Branch, HQMC

Holding Attack Was to Reinforce the Rearward Infiltration

Meanwhile, the Chinese squads along the front of 2/5's multi-sided formation had been probing and grinding as part of their holding attack. (See Figures 27.16 and 27.17.) So doing had more than one purpose. Not only was it to draw attention away from any activity at the back of the objective, but also to put more frontal squads into a position to quickly enter the front. The infiltration squad could then receive timely support.

On more than one occasion at the Chosin Reservoir, some of those holding-attack elements were partially to break through the Marine cordon. That left a few of their members with an alternate mission.

> [A] lone Chinese burpgunner infiltrated to the Marine rear [of H/7 on Hill 1403] and squeezed off telling bursts as he scrambled from position to position to escape detection.[12]
> – *Chosin,* by Hammel

Details of the Probing

Communist Chinese probes at the Chosin were supposedly of two kinds that played off each other (one serving as a diversion for its partners). There was not as much barbed wire as at Guadalcanal, so their mutual focus may have been on other things. The more demonstrative (noisy) kind of probing may have been to discover the location of Marine machineguns, whereas the silent kind was

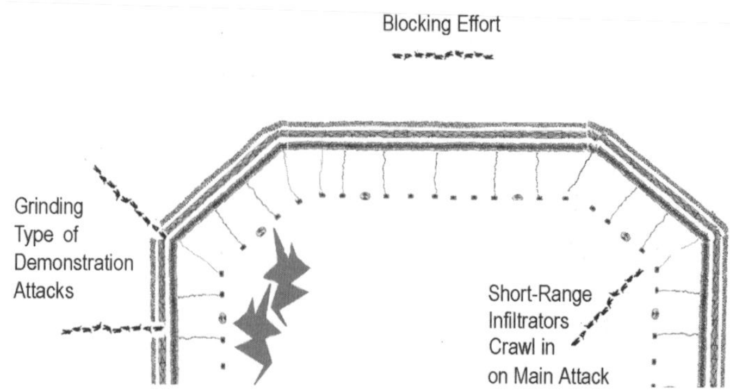

Figure 27.14: Rear Diversions and Opposite-Flank Infiltration

Figure 27.15: Main Attack Via Silent Barrier Breach at Back
(Sources: FMFM 0-1 [1979], p. 7-7; FM 21-75 [1967], p. 67.)

short-range infiltration to silence them. Of course, given the opportunity, those same infiltrators would have gone after other targets (like those associated with command and control.)

> [L]ight probes were launched by very small Chinese groups along the Fox/5 line. The Chinese recoiled wherever they met resistance, but by drawing fire they exposed the locations of . . . Marine automatic weapons.
>
> While attention was drawn to the light probes [elsewhere], infiltrators intent upon breaching the Marine line crawled to within a few feet of the junction of Fox and Easy Companies [possibly to discover a break in the interlocking machinegun fire].[13]
>
> —*Chosin,* by Hammel

How the Probing and Grinding Worked Together

Once an under-defended part the U.S. perimeter had been spotted through probing, all Red squads nearby may have had the power to penetrate any barrier through Stormtrooper banagalore method. But, there was now an ongoing mortar barrage.[14] The longer it lasted, the greater was the chance that some defender would stick his head up out of the foxhole and notice the penetration. Nor were those well-positioned Chinese squads supposed to break all the way through Marine lines until the infiltration at the back of the objective had been completed.

So, the Chinese squads (however far from the weak spot) opted for a slower and safer method of entry. The probes would have already generated some defender shooting, so there was no longer any need for any Communist squad member to withhold his small-arms fire. What the first squads had done through probing,[15] the others would now attempt through "reconnaissance pull" (exploiting local openings) during a full-fledged (albeit careful) attack with limited objectives.[16]

All movements forward would be through crawling and supported by a combination of concussion grenades and burpgun fire. In this way, even the less-well positioned squads were able to exploit gaps, unit boundaries, and breaks in the machinegun fire to move gradually forward. Squads containing both grenadiers and burp-

Figure 27.16: Red Soldiers Mixed Grenades with Burpgun Fire
(Source: Search.usa.gov public-domain image from this url: http://kynghistory.ky.gov/NR/rdonlyres/7BD9F986-EEF2-45C5-BC77-A641F0A6CFAC/0/shadowingbygallon.jpg)

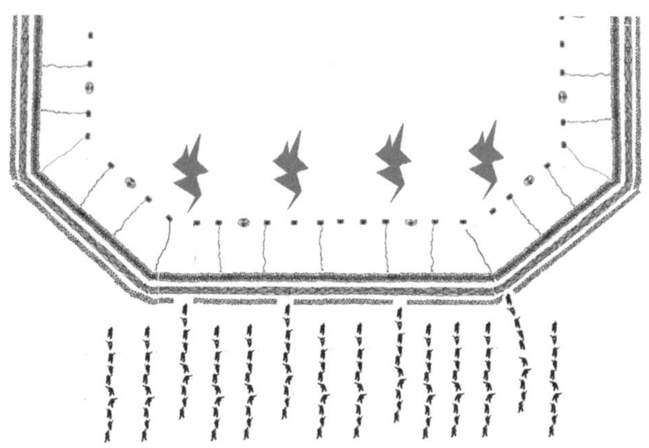

Figure 27.17: Frontal Squads Grind As Part of Holding Attack

gunners had attacked the lines for E/7 on Hill 1282 [a little east of 1403 and on North Ridge.] Of particular note, they then quickly recoiled.[17]

> Resorting to grinding tactics, the Chinese repeatedly assaulted Company E's position from midnight until 0200 [2:00 A.M.] . . . [with] charging squads of infantry.[18]
>
> – *U.S. Marine Operations in Korea*
> History Branch, HQMC

As this holding attack had all the earmarks of a main attack, the annals of history have generally reported it as such and any infiltration as a second thought. Yet, those Chinese "hordes" had only allowed one squad at a time to participate in the grinding evolution. That must have been to create a diversion while keeping most squads unnoticeably ready to reinforce the rearward infiltration. There was ample whistle and bugle blowing during one of these Chinese attacks at the Chosin to accommodate such a sequence of events. When the word came down for the final frontal assault, several squads would have probably attacked at the same time. (See Figure 27.18.) Once through the Marines' front lines, they may have headed off in different directions to more completely segment the whole. (See Figure 27.19.)

Only while intentionally grinding, might any PVA squad have briefly spread out to maximize its firepower—probably into two short rows. Once through Marine lines, it would have returned to column formation to more easily move forward. A well-researched movie about the Vietnam War actually shows Asian Communist squads assaulting in column formation, often with an RPG gunner in the lead.[19]

The Final Assault on a U.S. Position

This complicated a seizure of an insular objective may seem overly fanciful to a Western military thinker, but it continues to obey the doctrinal pattern in Figure 1.3. And another factor makes such a roundabout method viable. While the main attack may come through sapper-like actions at the objective rear, the frontal holding attack is fully capable of carrying the objective. Its most-concerted pushes would come through the weak points uncovered by the probes. That's probably what happened after a rearward infiltration at Fox and Echo 2/5.

> Ultimately, the Reds broke through . . . where the two units were joined [F/5 and E/5]. They poured troops into the gap, and as they attempted to roll back the newly exposed flanks [a type of "button-hook]," they overran part of Fox Company.[20]
>
> – *U.S. Marine Operations in Korea*
> History Branch, HQMC

Once inside the original objective in enough force, the Reds would have treated what was left as their new objective—this time without obstacles. They could not have easily swept an irregularly shaped expanse *en masse,* so they likely continued on with the doctrinal creation in Figure 12.2 of more manageable pieces. Then, only the smallest pockets would be instantly overwhelmed.

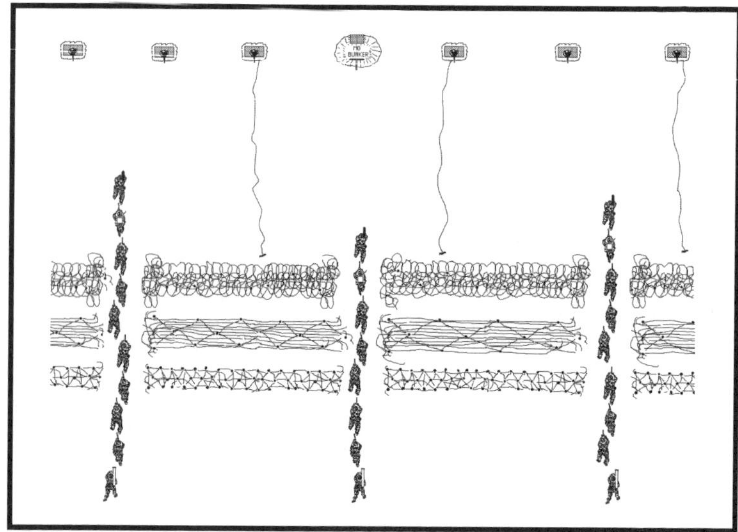

Figure 27.18: Diversionary Elements Then Enter Objective

The Probable Scenario

If the squad-sized attack on a weak spot created too tenuous a bridgehead for reinforcement, it may have been directed sideways against an enemy machinegun. That way, other squads could more safely enter. Only upon word of the rearward infiltration, would all squads advance to subdivide the objective along just a few dissection routes. Three from the front and one from the back would have gotten the job done. (Look again at Figure 27.19.)

> *Strategic penetration* is defined as a massive frontal attack against an enemy in a fixed defense line, the flanks of which are secure. The operation is designed to breach the defense at selected locations, create flanks, and permit passage of mobile forces deep into the enemy rear, to envelop and destroy him.[21]
>
> — *Handbook of the Chinese Communist Army*
> U.S. Army, DA Pamphlet 30-51, December 1960

That all dissections are in different directions need not be a problem. With an RPG gunner in the lead and all small-arms fire aimed downward and to the side, the various dissection columns could safely cross each other's path.

By pumping enough squads up each route for their members to finally stretch single file across the entire objective, one could automatically encircle all composite segments. If all members were then to get down, they could crawl on line into the various enemy pockets to annihilate them. By using mostly concussion grenades, they would have avoided fratricide. Along level ground, any upwards shooting would have also been safe.

Against 2/7 on Hill 1282, the Reds demonstrated a slightly different way to handle an individual segment. It too would "divide and destroy" its occupiers through an expanding wedge.

> The Reds finally drove a wedge between the Marine defenders on the summit [of Hill 1282 and probably protecting the CP] and the platoons . . . on the [mountain] spur. . . .
>
> By 0500, CCF infantrymen . . . occupied the summit of Hill 1282. . . . The remnants of the [Marine] platoons . . . had been driven to the reverse slope in the west. . . . Easy

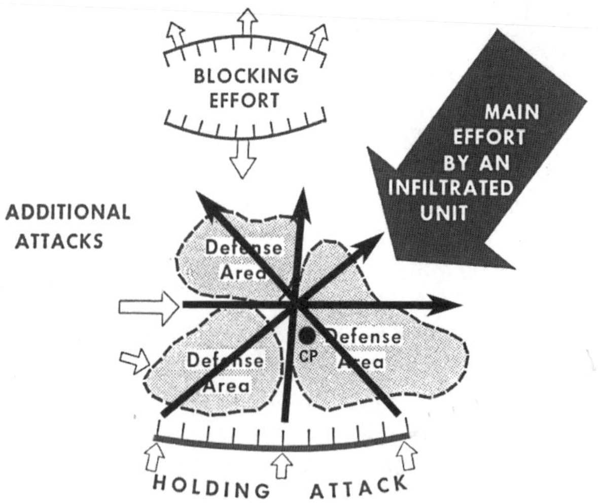

Figure 27.19: Objective Segmented After Sappers Attack CP
(Source: "Handbook on the Chinese Communist Army," DA Pamphlet 30-51 [1960], p. 24.)

Company [7th Marines] had been reduced to the effective strength of a rifle platoon (split in two).[22]
– *U.S. Marine Operations in Korea*
History Branch, HQMC

For how this wedge may have been formed, look back at Figure 5.2. Maneuvers like this would seem perfectly legitimate to a bottom-up Eastern thinker. His military planning has long entertained annihilation, while Western officials have been in no hurry to acknowledge the prerequisite squad tactics.

28 COUNTERATTACKING AFTER A TACTICAL WITHDRAWAL

- What form does such a counterattack usually take?
- Is it generally preceded by an ambush?

Regain forfeited ground after foe's push runs out of steam.

(Sources: FM 22-100 [1983], p. 185; FM 90-10-1 [1982], pp. B-3, B-4.)

What Form Can a Counterattack Take?

As noted in Chapter 14, the Japanese, North Koreans, Germans, and Russians all counterattacked with a special assault group after exhausting an urban attacker with "retreat combat." Only for the Russians did that renewed offensive sometimes take the form of a "swarm" by squad-sized elements. At other times, the lead enemy tank was simply hit by anti-armor rounds from every direction, accompanying infantrymen shot, and a determined ground assault launched.

At Stalingrad, Seoul, the Vietnam Marketplace, and Grozny, this swarm-like response to an enemy probe first looked like a *Haichi Shiki* ambush. The opposition column was stopped, cut off from any rearward aid, subdivided, and then reduced piecemeal. That reduction took place through various kinds of attrition. (Look back at Figures 12.1 and 12.2.)

But, however the intruding column was stopped, the whole reason for "retreat combat" was a better chance of evicting it. A full fledged counterattack was the next logical step, because along with the stoppage of armor had come the removal of protective infantrymen.[1]

This Eastern Counterattack Can Take Many Forms

After a soft strongpoint array had been partially dented, the Germans would sometimes close the enemy salient from either side to encircle its occupants. At the Sugar Loaf Complex on Okinawa's Shuri Line, Japanese defenders moved through tunnels to behind U.S. lines.[2] In Korea, Communists sometimes emerged from the subterranean depths of a hill they had just lost.[3] And, particularly in the Orient, a counterattack can be launched at any time through short-range infiltration. Those are just four of the most common formats for this maneuver.

Of note, this rapid a switch from defense to offense would not occur head on. It almost always came from a flank. That's why German urban assault columns carefully guarded the sidestreets,[4] and their Japanese counterparts erected barricades at the big ones.[5] For the same reason, Russian assault units were constantly on guard against encirclement.[6]

Counterattacks in a Rural Setting

On Okinawa, the first major Japanese counterattack involved short-range infiltration. On 12 April 1945, tiny elements from four separate battalions successfully sneaked between American holes, concealed themselves for a while in caves and tombs, and then attacked those lines from the rear. The least successful of these four battalions still managed to penetrate 500 yards into the U.S. backfield.[7]

In Korea, the Chinese and North Koreans frequently excavated hidden rooms beneath their defensive strongpoints. Soon after the strongpoint was taken by the Americans, they would reemerge to take it back. In this way, they regularly resupplied themselves with much-needed materiel.

> We dug out a two-level fortification. . . . Once the enemy entered the surface positions, we started counterattacks and inflicted heavy casualties on them [from below]. By this crude means we were able to seize and take away the equipment left by the enemy.[8]
>
> — *Mao's Generals Remember Korea*

Counterattacks in the City

Chapter 14 has shown the state of the art for defeating an urban attack to be repeatedly moving backwards through minefield, ambush, barricade, and strongpoint matrix. The ambush is sprung at the back of the attack column after its front has been halted at the machinegun-covered barricade. Its purpose is to remove any towed artillery or chance of reinforcement from the rear. After the enemy infantrymen have been stripped away from their armor at the front of the column, a counterattack is sometimes launched from one or more side streets. As in the *Haichi Shiki* ambush, its aim is to further segment the column. Before moving back along the enemy's avenue of advance, the counterattacking force must first destroy/capture all parts of the besieged column. That takes encircling each foe pocket, and an appropriate assault regimen for each (as in Figure 1.3).

Russian Method of Counterattacking a Built-Up Area

Of the major Eastern armies, the Russians have arguably the most experience in attacking (or counterattacking) through an urban landscape. According the TM 30-340, "The strength of Red Army defensive tactics lies in . . . decisive counterattacks."[9] A large mobile reserve is maintained precisely for this purpose. If mechanized, it is concealed well to the rear of the defensive sequence and has a route already reconnoitered to hit a flank of the attacking force.[10]

In fact, aiming at that flank under such circumstances is actually part of Russian doctrine.[11] The targeted area is often near the back of the opposition's assault formation.[12]

The Soviet defense can be either centralized or decentralized. In the former, the foe is channelized until he can assailed by armor and massed artillery.

> A favorite Soviet maneuver is to allow the enemy to penetrate deeply into the lines and trap him in a firesack. The counterattack takes the form of a large-scale ambush on the deep flank, [with] the counterattacking units being supported by massed, registered artillery.[13]
>
> — *Handbook on U.S.S.R. Military Forces*
> U.S. War Dept., TM 30-340, November 1945

If the Soviet defense is decentralized, numerous responses to the enemy assault are launched through the initiative of local commanders.[14] But, an indirect-fire kill zone can still exist. Such was probably the case near the Volga in Stalingrad, where Russian shock groups from several sectors all converged on the same noisy kill zone to swarm the tail end of the German column just interrupted by it.

The North Korean Counterattacks in Seoul

North Korean tactical doctrine was still largely Russian when the Americans tried to retake Seoul in September 1950. The first counterattack as they approached that city's outskirts was by a small detachment of armor followed by troops.[15] Notice the point of attack.

> The 87th NKPA Regiment launched two predawn spoiling attacks against both [U.S.] flanks. The southern attack, led by five T-34 tanks, posed the greatest threat.[16]
>
> — *Battle of the Barricades,* by Alexander

Then came more of these so-called "spoiling attacks" wherever U.N. forces seemed to be overextended. Many involved loosely coordinated tank/infantry assaults. Others were by non-supported grunts at night or sappers.

> Far from fleeing the city, the enemy—at least this particular battalion of the 25th NKPA Brigade—was charging due south down Ma Po Boulevard with six to 12 tanks and self-propelled guns, accompanied by infantry [on the night of 25 September]. . . .
>
> The North Koreans executed a third major spoiling attack [in a different sector] at 0500.[17]
>
> — *Battle of the Barricades,* by Alexander

But the opposition in Seoul also recognized the power of individual effort. As such, some of the counterattacks took on the quality of a swarm by lone antitank personnel. Once again, they came from a flank. Only Western forces demand the "integrity" of a straight-up frontal response.

> In downtown Seoul on 26 September, . . . [a] nimble-footed North Korean darted out from the rubble, caught 2d Battalion, 1st Marines' riflemen by surprise, and flung a satchel charge atop a passing flame tank, then vanished in the blast and smoke. The crew escaped unscathed, but the tank was destroyed. Angered and embarrassed by this bad luck, 2d Battalion's NCOs forcibly reminded their men to watch the adjacent alleys and rubble piles, not the tanks. This paid off. The NKPA launched a dozen more sapper attacks against Marine tanks operating in the center of the boulevard; Lieutenant Colonel Sutter's troops cut each one of them down.[18]
>
> — *Battle of the Barricades,* by Alexander

29 Final Requirement for Top Squad Performance

- What additional preparation would super-squad still need?
- Shouldn't it have special moves for recurring situations?

Squad techniques must be continually practiced/refined.

(Source: Courtesy of Sorman Information and Media, illustration by Wolfgang Bartsch, from "SoldF: Soldaten i falt," © 2001 Forsvarsmakten, Stockholm, pp. 22, 23.)

Fully Utilizing a Rifle Squad Is Like Football

Due to the 10-15 man size, an infantry squad can be run in combat like a football team—repeatedly on autopilot while using pre-practiced procedure. Any preliminary guidelines would be like the "rule-based paradigms" that the Modern War Institute at West Point says make squad swarms possible.[1]

Only when a "tactical play" meets too much enemy resistance or runs afoul a guideline, must another play be called by the squad leader. Thus operating gives his tiny unit a much better chance of momentum than when it is under constant scrutiny from its chain-of-command. But, only if the squad's parent organization values such a capability, will it be possible. Where "the squad is regarded as merely a subset of the platoon, [and] seldom trained for independent action [as in present-day America],"[2] it will seldom make such an important contribution to the war effort.

This book has demonstrated what a properly prepared squad can make possible for its parent unit. For American squads ever again to attain this level of proficiency, they will have to be trained and utilized more like those from an Eastern "bottom-up" society. At least, this was the U.S. Marine Raiders' secret to success in WWII.[3]

No amount of study into structure and armament can produce U.S. squads like those that—through cohesion and impromptu procedure—did the impossible at Iwo Jima and Hamburger Hill. The members of those squads will be remembered, and then hopefully emulated.

A Justifiably Proud Defense Establishment

Since WWI, U.S. service men and women have been fighting and dying around the world to keep the people of other nations free. For every act of extreme bravery formally recorded by the U.S. military, there have been thousands of others that only a young GI or his closest buddies even knew about. As a result, most U.S. military personnel are exceedingly proud of not only their organizational heritage, but also of their personal contributions. While a few headquarters "oversights" may have occurred along the way, nothing of any consequence has been admitted.

Even if there had been organizational "miscues," they would in no way lessen the magnificent performance—on the field of honor—by the vast majority of U.S. troops.

Yet, throughout this dutiful service by the rank and file, there has been an ongoing effort to improve the battlefield proficiency of all ground units. Of late, the Pentagon's fascination with firepower and technology has been generally credited with the shortfall. But, even the most vocal critic has been unwilling to call for tactical reform. He or she worries about wasteful spending and collateral damage, but is unwilling to show as much loyalty down the chain as up it.

What if too much focus on new equipment has had a more serious effect than anyone thought possible? Wouldn't the squad stratagems from other nations now be of more interest after this great nation has failed to decisively win any big ground conflict since WWII? From a religious standpoint, too much pride can have negative consequences. The correct order of every U.S. service member's allegiance is first to God, next to his country, and only then to his branch of the service.[4] Those who must fight the next war deserve to know every advance in squad maneuver. Cover-ups, however well-intended, can't help but lead to chronic deficiencies. As the Appendix will show, this particular deficiency is so simple to correct that no commander would regret doing so.

What This Study Has Demonstrated So Far

Super-Squad has mostly focused on the proper composition and weaponry for the U.S. infantry squad of the future. By concurrently showing what more maneuver-oriented armies have collectively learned about all-out conflict, it has also identified the state-of-the-nonelectronic-art for all categories of ground combat. In almost every instance, no amount of subsequent enemy gadgetry will invalidate this time-tested procedure. And simple modifications would adequately alleviate any modern concern (like staying in "hull defilade" or bushes to avoid thermal imaging). Nowhere else does such a comprehensive list exist. These various maneuvers are a much better point of departure for advanced technique than the "pre-machinegun" methods in the U.S. manuals. This makes this study quite useful to American leaders not wanting to lose another war.

Most U.S. voters already know that all Eastern armies have been fighting differently than U.S. counterparts at the small-unit level. What they have failed to realize is the astounding consistency with which those Eastern armies have waged this alternative style of warfare. Those other armies were not operating this way out of any shortage of ordnance or technology, but because it was more efficient than the American way.

For U.S. troops continuously to hear they are the best in the world has only exacerbated this long-term shortfall in their preparation. The unpleasant reality is that the American way of war involves little, if any, maneuvering at the small-unit level. Every attack and defense has been done essentially on line to achieve maximum firepower. In other words, the U.S. infantry has become tactically challenged by design.

Just as most Americans have come to believe they need a new car every three years, the average military member thinks the latest paraphernalia gives him a better chance in combat. Under ideal circumstances, it may be of some help. But, it is still hard to master, susceptible to moisture and gunshot, heavy, and often distracting. Because Eastern foes continually study how to counter U.S. gadgetry, the new gear will not greatly alter the nature of most GI missions.[5] Only if the U.S. squad leader wants it, should his people be required to carry it. Otherwise, any chance at momentum will be automatically forfeited through too heavy an individual load.

The Ultimate Source of America's Wartime Problems

"Top-down" military organizations tend to do what best facilitates the whole. That's why their tactical doctrine allows so little small-unit maneuver and their manuals push elementary procedure. No wonder Western armies tend be least proficient at their lowest echelons. Junior ranks get too little practice at initiative, decision making, and technique development. Then, their parent units under-perform at short range in both conventional or unconventional combat. Both U.S. infantry services have long sought a way to correct this deficiency—to somehow harness their NCOs collective experience to come up with more advanced technique. That way has recently been found—through a combination of collective opinion and field experimentation. It has so far been adopted (during a single Commanding Officer's tenure) by three Marine infantry battalions. By now making it mandatory throughout the American infantry establishment, the Pentagon could effectively compensate for this unfortunate by-product of its "top-down" way of handling every problem. (See Figure 29.1.)

Designed for supplementary use at the company level, this method accomplishes several things at once: (1) better tactical technique (through experimentation); (2) less predictability (no two companies alike); (3) better learning dynamic (competition between units); and (4) better morale, initiative, and tactical-decision making at the lowest echelons (every NCO a trainer).

When every company's squad and fireteam leaders train this way, they collectively develop three (or more) "numbered" maneuvers for each of the most probable combat scenarios (e.g., ambushing). They then practice those maneuvers daily with their squads (during boots-and-rifles physical training [PT]). When the unit gets sent overseas and an enemy shows up, the squad leader has only to ask his deployed fireteam leaders (by radio or hand-and-arm signal) which number to run. By simply considering their advice, he makes possible a "deliberate attack" (one already reconnoitered and rehearsed). As most professional tacticians can attest, trying to carry a "prepared enemy position" with anything less will result in too many casualties. That the squad leader can launch a deliberate attack so quickly makes possible the Holy Grail of short-range combat—momentum. This was the German Stormtroopers' secret to success during the Spring Offensives of 1918.

Within the Appendix exists a way to make other methods of this same caliber possible. When told what Eastern armies do for urban defense, a former MARSOC (Marine Special Operations Command) member claimed he and his buddies had come up with the same rearward sequence.[6] That's too big a coincidence to ignore. It means the state of the tactical art for any wartime situation can be determined through either the Appendix or a comparison of Eastern armies. This latter option should be of interest to all students of history.

Commanders Prefer Non-Disruptive Solutions

Western-style bureaucracies are too tall to readily accept any change, however useful. So, field commanders routinely operate through established tactical procedures. Yet, to meet expeditionary needs, most are still authorized to add a few of their own. Therein lies the easiest way to correct any perceived shortfall in small-unit tactics. For example, if a U.S. unit was about to go against a strongpoint array, it might want to practice a technique developed through use of the Appendix—that in Figure 29.2.[7] (Figure 3.2 has shown that such an array often has a straight row of Western-looking barbed wire to its direct front.) With this new way of entering the array, its commander would be spared the carnage of a hasty attack.

Modern-day infantry outfits are quite busy. They often work 12 hours a day, six days a week. But upon closer examination, one easily sees that only their leadership cadres are totally employed. The majority of their troops still spend a lot of time waiting around for the accomplishment of command-level milestones. So, if a little supplementary squad training could be inserted into their schedule without much top-echelon involvement, the overall unit would be none the worse for wear. In fact, the increase in small-unit proficiency might even lower the number of top-echelon problems. That's what the well-tested method in the Appendix can provide.

Big Victories Necessarily Consist of Many Tiny Wins

Until all the little (tactical) pictures for the U.S. military improve, its big (operational or strategic) collages will remain mostly illusions. (Look again at Figure 28.1.) This book has provided the

Figure 29.1: Wars Are Also Won Through the Little Picture
(Source: FM 90-5 [1982], p. 5-4.)

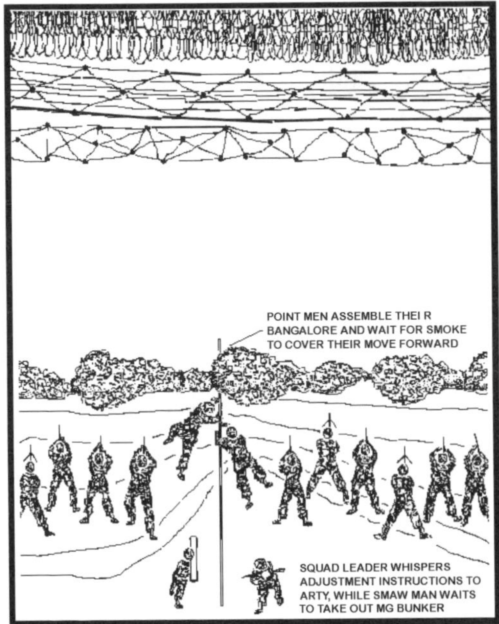

Figure 29.2: Modern U.S. Version of Stormtrooper Attack
(Sources: FM 5-103 [1985], p. 4-6; TC 90-1 [1986], cover; FM 7-11B1/2, p. 2-III-E-8.2; FM 7-11B3 [1976], p. 2-VII-C-4.4.)

nonelectronic state of the tactical art for each category of small-unit encounter. More-technology-compliant methods would be possible through the "bottom-up" training method in the Appendix. Until more experimentation with tactical technique is allowed at the rifle company level, the Pentagon won't be able to evolve tactically at the squad level. Such is the cost of the "big-picture" mindset that so dominates Western society.

More Proficient Squads Also Take Fewer Casualties

Ordnance-spewing U.S. sweeps will continue to produce hasty attacks against prepared enemy positions. Wouldn't a maneuver like that in Figure 28.2 be more appropriate than the standard "bum rush." Like the German Stormtrooper assault of WWI, it combines "recon pull" with prior rehearsal. This makes it a "quick deliberate attack."

This guided tour through squad history has concluded. Until the Pentagon realizes the disastrous effect its preoccupation with firepower has had on small-unit U.S. maneuvers, its forces will have considerable trouble with all Eastern opponents—militias included.

Epilogue

The Importance of This Research

This study was not done by a modern-day mechanized infantry expert struggling to make sense of the evolution of "straight-leg" tactics worldwide. It is the culmination of over 50 years of research into the subject by a career grunt. The current source of advanced small-unit method may be shocking, but nonetheless accurate. Any GI now wishing to do well at dismounted infantry combat has only to copy the tiny element maneuver of a major Eastern army during the latter part of the 20th Century. All he (or she) must slightly alter is how the surprise is generated. Herein lie the most effective squad techniques for almost every aspect of ground combat.

The Chronic Nature of the Problem

America hasn't won an extended ground conflict since WWII. This study has exposed the underlying reason in enough detail to reach even those who have unknowingly traded victory for total control over all wartime activity and a thriving arms industry. No country doing its own fighting will win an armed conflict from which it makes money. The balance between economy-enhancing firepower and *gratis* maneuver would become too badly skewed. That's why two-time Medal of Honor winning U.S. Gen. Smedley Darlington Butler risked his good name in 1935 to write the book, "War Is a Racket."

The all-powerful military-industrial complex need not go away, but simply allow for the cost-free "in-unit development" of more surprise-oriented small-unit tactics. That cannot be done by college kids fresh out of Quantico or Fort Benning. It will take every U.S. infantry company harnessing the collective experience of its NCOs. (See Figure E.1.) Only then will American commanders attempt the core small-unit maneuvers of 3GW in actual combat. Nor will this country stop sending teenagers knowing little more than how to follow orders and shoot their weapons up against light-infantry experts.

There's an old Marine Corps adage that the road to hell is paved with good intentions. For almost 25 years, Posterity Press has been trying to help this nation's armed forces catch up with the ongoing evolution of small-unit tactics in the Eastern World. It has now concluded that the U.S. infantry's continuing use of elementary, surprise-free (pre-machinegun) tactics has automatically derived from the Pentagon's focus on firepower.

U.S. military reformers have long complained about too much bombardment. Among its most often noted pitfalls have been collateral damage and "short rounds." In fact, the most highly decorated veteran of the Vietnam era revealed an official accounting of how many friendly casualties had been caused by errant U.S. bombs and shells.

> As our [U.S. Army] study shook out, the fact became inescapable that a staggering 15 to 20 percent of all U.S. casualties in Vietnam were caused by friendly fire.[1]
>
> — *About Face,* by Col. Hackworth

The Pentagon has since tried to rectify this problem. It has added precision targeting to many of its munitions and demanded more firing discipline for others. Yet, depending on the quality of the intelligence, the smartest-round can still kill somebody's mother by accident. And too many weapon safety rules have consequences in a fast-moving environment. In fact, the latter of those two Pentagon initiatives has provided the most striking revelation of this current study.

With overwhelming firepower as one's principal wartime strategy, a number of unproductive things will happen in pursuit of safety: (1) mostly linear (outmoded) formations with little small-unit activity to their front; (2) the full compliance of every weapon toter with all instructions; and (3) no frontline initiative.[2] In other words, there will be few advanced small-unit tactics (to include the infiltration and multiple ambush that have come to define the UW part of 3GW).

This is the only way the U.S. military could have become so

tactically stagnant under the supervision of as many dedicated leaders. For the sake of safety, they have unintentionally denied themselves enough squad skill to practice the more advanced forms of combat. They also have made it harder for their lowest-ranking ground troops to survive.

Other well-respected studies have shown that the huge technological advantage U.S. units enjoyed in Vietnam made little, if

Figure E.1: The Most Logical Squad Training Facilitator
(Source: FM 12-75Z3/4 [1979], cover.)

any, difference to the war's outcome. In fact, before those units were forced by Congress to depart, their opponent had needed little artillery, only a few amphibious tanks, and no airpower south of the DMZ.

Yet, throughout these various disclosures, the military brass and their civilian overlords in Washington have remained resolute in their belief that America's military is the best in the world at all things. While there had been rumors of Eastern small-unit tactics being superior, most had risen through the ranks too quickly to know the difference. So, a few careerist captains were easily able—through the so-called "professional" journals—to dispel such a pride-threatening generalization.

Unfortunately, that's precisely what the current research has now indisputably proven. It has also shown all major Eastern armies to be using almost identical tactical techniques since WWII. Because many of those tiny-element procedures had been designed to counter a foe with superior firepower, they now help to define the current state-of-the-art for all 3GW maneuvers.

Meanwhile, the U.S. Army, and to a somewhat lesser extent, the USMC have doggedly stuck with their old 2GW ways of doing things in actual combat. Those ways are still valid, of course, just not as productive under all circumstances. Only the Chinese government has figured out how to eliminate the resistance to change. Since the days of Mao, its ground combat units (of whatever size) have been required to know, and then rapidly alternate between, 2GW and 3GW methods.[3]

There are those who would say the Eastern similarities make it even more important that the U.S. military fight in a different manner. But, the universal thread throughout Eastern tactics (which their Western counterpart lacks) is the element of surprise. The Asians will even wait for a diversion in the natural flow of events (like for the moon to go behind a cloud). U.S. tactics are more time-oriented and impetuous. They involve infantry units being instantly required to force their way into contested areas without any regard for their own visibility or the target's unique characteristics. There's a price to be paid for this latter way of fighting. It involves more danger for the participating foot soldier. And the Eastern commander is more likely to alter his standard operating procedure (what amounts to state-of-the-art maneuver) to compensate for changing circumstances.

How Such a Major Military Shortfall Has Been Perpetuated

Attempting safely to use too much firepower has—over time—created the problem. Wanting to handle all unit deficiencies "in house" keeps it from reaching those in overall charge. While in search of new equipment and sufficient funds, those higher-ups continue to profess training progress. The official manuals still discuss (in generalities) a few advanced maneuvers—like short-range infiltration. And the military journals go on talking about every new issue, as if all previous combat lessons had been fully assimilated by the bureaucracy.

Sensing no major change to conventional wisdom, U.S. expeditionary force commanders then operate in much the way as they always have. It's high diddle diddle up the middle with all of their more advanced weapons firing. Only their commandos ever try a deliberate attack. Their regular infantry forays are much like the tortoise shell arrays of Operations Killer and Ripper in Korea or multi-unit sweeps of Gen. Westmoreland in Vietnam. Those ordnance spewing formations are good at going wherever they want, just not very good at limiting collateral damage, short rounds, or bypassed opposition. In actuality, they are little more than a high-tech display of 2GW momentum, that will occasionally change course to mimic a large-scale 3GW maneuver.

The challenge then becomes convincing those who have been regularly rewarded for supporting headquarters' policies, that their overriding allegiance is to God and the nation. The Marines' most beloved general—Lewis B. "Chesty" Puller—was never given an MoH after earning five Navy Crosses and one Army Distinguished Service Cross. That's because, he too often argued with headquarters on the troops' behalf. America's current military leaders now need to follow his selfless example. Otherwise, they run more risk of a tarnished reputation than any military reformer. The now 19 publications from Posterity Press should provide any infantry outfit with enough operational and training specifics to internally eliminate most tactical deficiencies.

The Key to Problem Solution

It has been often said that forgiveness is easier to obtain than permission in the U.S. military. This holds particularly true within any of the "top-down" bureaucracies that now make up America's Armed Forces. But one's parent-unit headquarters is always in search of good news, and will not normally question a subordinate-unit's accomplishment. So, why couldn't a problem that has been perpetuated through "keeping it in-house," finally be resolved in-house?

On an issue as controversial as battlefield maneuver, it may be more prudent to apprise superiors of the improvement to wargaming and morale, than the responsible training initiative. For all infantry outfits, the supplementary training package in the Appendix has already been tested/refined throughout the Fleet. But, any shift from firepower to surprise in the unit's combat SOP would help. That's where the unit commander still has enough leeway to try something new.

What must now be avoided at all cost is failing to take any corrective action whatsoever. The *status quo* in squad capabilities can only lead to two things: (1) more ground conflicts lost; and (2) the eventual discrediting of a magnificent infantry heritage. All contested land must eventually be consolidated through dependable small-unit outposting. Local militia are often too easy to corrupt to perform such a mission alone. Thus, no more "U.S. boots on the ground" will automatically forfeit any chance of America *decisively* winning another overseas conflict.

Appendix: Prerequisite Squad Training

1. In 3rd Generation (Maneuver) Warfare, grunts are often outnumbered.

2. For enough skill to operate alone and in small units, they will need "bottom-up" training that is supplementary to their normal regimen.

   a. There can be no true "Maneuver Warfare" capability without some decentralization of control and more initiative at bottom-echelons.

   b. Each company must learn to operate as nine semi-independent maneuver squads.

      (1) Squads can fight like football teams.

         (a) If they've practiced and numbered several "plays" for each category of enemy contact.
         (b) If the squad leader asks his fireteam leaders (by hand-and-arm signal) which play to run before picking.
         (c) If that play need not be run exactly as rehearsed (so individuals can react to unforeseen circumstances).

      (2) Each squad leader will have adequate control if all plays practiced in varied terrain before attempted in war.

      (3) Training for squad combat is like football too.

         (a) Individual, buddy team, fireteam, and squad drills are followed by force-on-force scrimmage.
         (b) Instead of daily physical training (PT), squads do battledrills on cross-country runs with boots and rifles.

   c. Training must give every squad member initiative, tactical-decision-making practice, and non-predictability.

      (1) Best way is to let the junior NCOs of each company collectively identify and fix their own tactical deficiencies.

(2) Companies no longer need identical squad maneuvers.

(3) Only through local experimentation can the lowest echelons of a "top-down" organization gain "world class" tactical proficiency.

d. Officers must control "bottom-up" training indirectly.

(1) By providing options from history.

(2) By choosing situations to be solved.

(3) By monitoring improvement in surprise generated and simulated-casualties suffered.

3. Planning Phase.

a. CO and plt. leaders publish "mission-type" training order to Gy.Sgt.—short list of squad combat situations to be solved.

(1) E.g., security patrol, counterambush, ambush, chance contact, day attack, night attack, short-range infiltration, urban attack, urban defense, sapper-oriented defense.

(2) Best are those involving large numbers of enemy soldiers, because they will require total surprise.

b. Gy.Sgt. will function as facilitator of group knowledge (as opposed to enforcer of organizational procedure).

c. Gy.Sgt. convenes NCO conference to record on the blackboard what will be needed to comply with officers' goals.

(1) Group arrives at prerequisite skills for each situation—what squads, fireteams, buddy teams, and individuals must do.

(2) Elementary "basics" will no longer be enough.

(a) All must be able to covertly shoot, move, and communicate.
(b) All must have microterrain appreciation, harnessing of senses, night skills, deception, decision practice as well.

d. Gy.Sgt. then schedules supplementary instruction for progressively larger elements (individuals first).

(1) Any weapons training will have one of two formats.

(a) Explain, demonstrate, imitate, practice, test.
(b) Create situation for students to solve (more retention and applicable to enemy weapons).

(2) Established tactical maneuvers taught through battledrills.

(a) Attention gainer and lecture.
(b) Demonstration and practical application.
1 Outdoors.
2 Blackboard or overhead projector.
3 Sand table with miniatures.
(c) Practical application testing (e.g., count U.S. losses).

(3) New tactical maneuvers taught thru "situation stations" (with participants allowed to arrive at own solutions).

(4) NCO assigned to each period of instruction.

(a) Leaders of next-higher echelon will do the teaching.
(b) Situation station "experiments" given to NCOs with "by-the-book" mentalities.

(5) Instructors told to refer to *The Last Hundred Yards* and *The Tiger's Way* for guidance on what to teach.

(a) Fully tested maneuver warfare methods.
(b) No squad-level maneuver in conflict with U.S. doctrine.

(6) All instruction will takes place near unit's headquarters or barracks with rubber rifles and makeshift training aids.

4. Execution Phase.

a. Training is conducted for whole company at once.

(1) Either sequentially or in "round-robin" format.

(2) Normally in 20-minute sessions for 12-man "sticks."

(3) Assigned instructor can ask any number of peers to help.

(4) Most training consists of movement technique rehearsal.

(a) Success measured through surprise generated (speed, stealth, deception) or simulated-casualties suffered.
(b) Individuals and subunits are asked to compete with each other or improve themselves on successive tries.
(c) "Super squad" determined for each training period.

(5) Instructors statistically track how well the techniques they are teaching work, and keep notes on how to improve them.

b. Next comes the "Tactical Demonstration."

(1) Officers arrange training support and recreate situations.

(2) Squads run through situations under simulated fire.

(a) Machinegun and artillery simulators add realism.
(b) Surprise indicators and friendly casualties measured.

(3) Only recourse for dissatisfied officers is to change situations or pick another group facilitator (SNCO).

c. Then comes "Free Play" — a force-on-force exercise in which the side with the fewest simulated casualties wins.

(1) Sides required to solve—twice—certain situations for which technique was taught (e.g., two assaults on foe's camp).

(a) One side reverses its shirts.
(b) Sides assigned command posts (CPs) not too far apart.
(c) One third of each force defends own CP with no outposts.
(d) Two thirds of each force must assault enemy CP.
(e) Each man records any 3-second sight picture of upright foe or flour grenade hit within 10 feet of himself.
(f) Casualties reenter problem via own CP after short delay.
(g) Secretly seizing the enemy's flag nets bonus points (flag must be unattached and at ground level in CP).
(h) Umpires assess demerits for any bodily contact or not doing required events.

(2) At end of the event, sides are moved beyond earshot of each other while all counts are made and winner determined.

d. Finally, "Lessons-Learned Field Day" is held.

(1) All junior enlisted personnel are assembled in bleachers.

(2) Privates given chance to demonstrate better ways.
(3) Gy.Sgt. gauges worth of each way through show of hands.
(4) No promises made as to training changes.
(5) Troops reminded of existing "NCO-Conference" techniques
(6) New PT method demonstrated.

5. All squads are expected to practice existing NCO Conference movement techniques during daily PT.

 a. First some combat warm-ups.

 (1) Crawling races (with squad leader participating).
 (2) Duck walking as if as under a wall aperture.
 (3) Practice in window entry over any horizontal obstruction.

 b. Then each squad takes its own combat run with boots and rifles.

 (1) Move in "Indian" file (column) through all types of terrain.
 (2) Periodically slow to practice one of the squad techniques.
 (3) Make mental note of terrain limitations to each maneuver.

6. Gy.Sgt. convenes all NCOs quarterly to modify the company's portfolio of squad, fireteam, buddy team and individual techniques, and to plan the next training evolution.

 a. Shortfalls in last training session identified.

 (1) If fewer mock casualties possible than with existing techniques.
 (2) Whether all instructor modifications considered.
 (3) Whether officers' and privates' expectations met.
 (4) Whether overall organizational doctrine still followed.

 b. All techniques modified as necessary.

7. Gy.Sgt. develops next training schedule.

8. This "bottom-up" cycle becomes a recurring and supplementary part of each company's training program (whether in garrison or deployed).

9. Only now is each battalion fully capable of employing its new tactical doctrine—3rd Generation (Maneuver) Warfare.

10. Only now can the theater commander employ the state of the small unit art—by starting an attack with a squad-sized penetration or building a defensive matrix from squad-sized strongpoints.

Notes

SOURCE NOTES

Illustrations:

The cover image is from page 3 of "Fortitudine," volume 37, number 4, of 2013. A bulletin of the Historical Division, HEADQUARTERS U.S. MARINE COPRS. "Fortitudine" is a government periodical, all contents of which are supposedly in the public domain. Portraying 1st Raider Battalion's fight for Edson's (Bloody) Ridge at Henderson Field in 1942, this painting was probably done on active-duty by a veteran of the Guadalcanal Campaign—Col. Donald L. Dickson. Unfortunately, he can no longer be contacted. So, as an educational nonprofit, Posterity Press considers the reprinting of this low resolution version of his work to be fair usage. It was retrieved in October 2018 from the following website address: https://www.marines.mil/Portals/59/Publications/Fortitudine%20Vol%2037%20No%204.pdf. Others must be more mindful of a possible copyright. All rights reserved. Copyright © n.d.

The picture on page vi is from "First Offensive: The Marine Campaign for Guadalcanal, by Hentry I. Shaw, Jr. Drawn by Donald L. Dickson, it comes from page 25 of this Marines in WWII Commenorative Series pamphlet by HEADQUARTERS U.S. MARINE CORPS in 1992. It was retrieved in October 2018 from the following website address: https://www.marines.mil/Portals/59/Publications/First%20Offensive-The%20Marine%20Campaign%20for%20Guadalcanal%20%20PCN%2019000311700_3.PDF. All contents of a government publication are theoretically in the public domain. So, as an educational nonprofit, Posterity Press considers the reprinting of this low resolution black and white version of the original artwork to be fair usage.

Picture on page xxii is from U.S. GOVERNMENT. It's a drawing by C.H. Waterhouse, in "Closing In: Marines in the Seizure of Iwo Jima," by J.H. Alexander, *Marines in WWII Commemorative Series,* Headquarters Marine Corps, 1994. Its reprinting is deemed minimally fair usage. Possible ©.

Picture on page 3 is from "Army/Marine Clipart," U.S. AIR UNIVERSITY (www.au.af.mil/au/awc/awcgate/cliparmy.htm). It has image designator "1-07a.tif."

Images on pages 5, 7, 14, 31, 35, 47, 53, 62, 64, 236, and 279 are from "Artphoto Archives" of the U.S. ARMY'S CENTER OF MILITARY HISTORY (http://www.history.army.mil/html/artphoto/artwork.html). Their respective file designators are: (1) "w_1_9_68.jpg"; (2) "jungle.jpg"; (3) "1-38-49.jpg"; (4) "1-15-49.jpg"; (5) "6_5_77.jpg"; (5) "9-28-90.jpg"; (7) "1-15-49.jpg"; (8) "0507-3.jpg"; (9) "1951.jpg"; (10) "61_30_45-s.jpg"; and (11) "19b.jpg." See picture captions for title, artist, and exact url. Only for an educational nonprofit does their reproduction constitute fair usage. Others must be more mindful of possible copyright. Copyright © n.d. All rights reserved.

Picture on page 17 reprinted after written assurance from GLOBAL SECURITY that it does not own its copyright or know if it has one. This image appears at globalsecurity.org under "PLA History," and has file designator "C14053PictPowPpleArmy53.jpg." The same picture appears at Wikipedia.org, s.v. "People's Liberation Army," with file designator "peoples_army.jpg" and would be covered by the provisions of GNU Free Documentation License. It's not for sale as part of the 1ISH Collection at ChinesePosters.net. Repro@iisgl.nl writes that China may have trouble claiming copyrights retroactively to any image created prior to the mid-1980's. As an educational nonprofit, Posterity Press considers its reproduction to be fair usage, but others must be more mindful of its possible copyright. Copyright © n.d. All rights reserved.

Pictures on pages 21, 90, 107, 177, 274, and 318 are in the public domain from WIKIMEDIA COMMONS (https://commons.wikimedia.org). The art is named "Rock of the Marne"; "The American Soldier, 1966"; "Bild eines Sturm-Pioniers vom Sturm-Bataillon 5 Rohr"; "Indiana Rangers"; "Zulu Warrior"; "Map of the Battle of the Changjin (Chosin) Reservoir."

Images on pages 28 and 272 from WIKIMEDIA.ORG. They are in the public domain at *Wikipedia Encyclopedia,* s.v. "Battle of Belleau Wood" and "Battle of Rorke's Drift." They have the following image designators: "Scott Belleau Wood.jpg" and "Rorke's.Drift.Post.jpg." See picture caption for title, artist, and exact url.

Images on pages 59, 193, and 335 reprinted from NATIONAL GUARD IMAGE GALLERY (https://www.nationalguard.mil/Resources/Image-Gallery/Historical-Paintings/Heritage-Series) from file designators: "sunshinedivision.jpg"; "arramadi.jpg"; "fromcornrowtohedgerow.jpg." Only for an educational nonprofit is this fair usage. Copyright © n.d.

Images on pages 146 and 166 are U.S. GOVERNMENT drawn or commissioned, and thus either public domain or fair usage, from this url: http://search.usa.gov. See each caption for exact url.

Pictures on page 100 reproduced with permission of Dr. Anatol Taras, Minsk, Belarus, from *PODGOTOVKA RAZVEGCHIKA: SISTEMA SPETSNAZA GRU,* by A.E. Taras and F.D. Zaruz. The illustrations are from pp. 278/279. Copyright © 1998 by A.E. Taras and F.D. Zaruz. All rights reserved.

Pictures on page 105, 275, and 350 reprinted with permission of SORMAN INFORMATION AND MEDIA and SWEDISH ARMED FORCES, from *Soldf: Soldaten i Falt,* by Forsvarsmakten, with illustrations by Wolfgang Bartsch. These illustrations are from pages 370, 23, and 225 of the Swedish publication, respectively. Copyright © 2001 by Forsvarsmakten, Stockholm. All rights reserved.

Picture on page 120 reproduced after asking permission of NIPPON TV. It is a still-frame photo from "A Tribute to WWII Combat Cameramen of Japan." Videocassette, n.d. Copyright © Nippon TV.

Image on page 145 is part of STEFAN R. LANDSBERGER COLLECTION at Leiden University in the Netherlands under the care of International Institute of Social History (IISH). Its website, Chinaposters.net explains reprint rights. Designers/artists of these posters were employees of art academies, museums, or publishers. During the high tide of socialism, it was seen as counterrevolutionary to make any claims as to personal ownership. Therefore, it would be safe to consider the academies, etc., as copyright holders. In the experience of the IISH, these institutions have not exercised their copyrights for materials published in the period 1949 to the mid-1980's. Until then, China was not a signatory of any International Copyright Convention. Thus, IISH thinks China will find it hard to claim copyrights retroactively and sees no problem with Posterity Press reprinting these images for educational purposes.

Pictures on page 156 and 241 reprinted from "Posters" of the U.S. ARMY'S CENTER OF MILITARY HISTORY. They have the following illustration designators: "p_3_4_67.jpg" and "1-36-49.jpg." Having been drawn/painted by active-duty personnel, they are deemed to be in the public domain.

Picture on page 169 is reproduced after asking the permission of OSPREY. It is from "Armies of the Vietnam War 1962-75," *Men-at-Arms Series.* Plate C, Number 2. Copyright © 1980 by Osprey.

Picture on page 195 reprinted after written assurance from ORION BOOKS, London, that the copyright holders for *World Army Uniforms Since 1939,* text by Andrew Mollo and Digby Smith, color plates by Malcolm McGregor and Michael Chappell, can no longer be contacted. This illustration is from Part II, Plate 193, of the Orion publication. Copyright © 1975, 1980, 1981, 1983 by Blandford Books Ltd. All rights reserved.

Map on page 208 is from WIKIMEDIA COMMONS. Entitled "Political Map of Metro Manila, Philippines," it is the work of Adkranz and authorized for reproduction under Creative Commons Attribution-Share Alike 4.0 International license. Copyright © 2014.

Map on page 211 is from the U.S. GOVERNMENT in "Battle of the Barricades: U.S. Marines in the Recapture of Seoul," by Col. Joseph H. Alexander USMC (Ret.). As part of the *Marines in the Korean War Commemorative Series* by Headquarters Marine Corps, its reprinting for educational purposes is deemed to be minimally fair usage.

Map on page 216 used after permission from RESEARCHGATE.NET and IWA PUBLISHING (London) was requested via e-mail. It comes from "Characterization of Water Pollution in Drainage Networks . . . ," by Y. Nagano, et al, from*Water Science & Technology,* August 2014, at this url: https://www.researchgate.net/publication/264793281_Characterization_of_water_pollution_in_drainage_networks_using_continuous_monitoring_data_in_the_Citadel_area_of_Hue_City_Vietnam.

Illustration on page 249 reprinted from the U.S. GOVERNMENT in "First Offensive: The Marine Campaign for Guadalcanal," by Henry I. Shaw. As part of the *Marines in WWII Commemorative Series,* by Headquarters Marine Corps in 1992, it's reprinting is considered to be minimally fair usage.

Illustration on page 268 is from the U.S. GOVERNMENT in "From Makin to Bouganville: Marines Raiders in the Pacific War," by Maj. Jon T. Hoffman. As part of the *Marines in WWII Commemorative Series,* by Headquarters Marine Corps in 1995, its use for educational purposes is deemed to be minimally fair usage.

Maps on pages 269 and 309 are from the U.S. ARMY CENTER OF MILITARY HISTORY in the following books: (1) "Okinawa: The Last Battle," by Roy Appleman, James Burns, Russell Gugeler, and John Stevens, map 38, from the *U.S. Army in World War II Series,* in 2000; (2) "Guadalcanal: The First Offensive," from the *Green Books.* As part of publications from the Center of Military History, U.S. Army, their reproduction for educational purposes is deemed to be at least fair usage.

Picture on page 283 reproduced after being unable to contact NHA XUAT BAN VAN HOA DAN TOC PUBLISHERS, Hanoi It is from "The War 1858-1975 in Vietnam," by Nguyen Khac Can, Phan Viet Thuc, and Nguyen Ngoc Diep, figure 540. Its use for educational purposes is deemed fair usage.

Map on page 305 reproduced with permission of PACIFICA MILITARY HISTORY, Pacifica, CA, from *Fire in the Streets: The Battle for Hue, Tet 1968,* by Eric Hammel, pages xv-xvii (artwork by Moody Graphics of San Francisco).

Picture on page 311 reprinted after asking permission by e-mail of PINTEREST.COM. This drawing was made in 1940 and has image designator "b0a98fccc5628b9163cedb39ff43e0cc.jpg." As an educational nonprofit, Posterity Press considers the use of something of this age and low resolution to be fair usage, but others must be more mindful of its possible copyright.

Picture on page 345 reprinted after asking permission by e-mail of "CHANGJIN JOURNAL." It is from the 01/20/08 issue of that publication, chapter 70. The map is by Melville J. Coolbaugh, from "The Chosin Chronology," © George A. Rasula, 2007. As an educational nonprofit, Posterity Press considers the use of a small portion of this map to be fair usage, but others must be more mindful of its copyright.

Image on page 354 is U.S. GOVERNMENT drawn or commissioned from http://search.usa.gov. See caption for exact url.

ENDNOTES

Preface

1. Memorandum for the record by H.J. Poole, when in charge of the Marine Super-Squad Competition Finals on Okinawa in 1992.
2. CWO-4 Charles "Tag" Guthrie USMC (Ret.) [former member of A/1/4, A/1/4 historian, and "super-squad" participant], in various conversations and e-mails with author over the years.
3. 2nd Marine Division squad leader, in conversation with author in the Spring of 2018.
4. *AZ Quotes,* s.v. "Chester W. Nimitz," as retrieved in October 2018 from the following url: https://www.azquotes.com/author/10830-Chester_W_Nimitz.
5. "Sands of Iwo Jima," Republic Pictures, 1988, videocassette, 109 min.
6. Gy.Sgt. Rodney Walker USMC (Ret.) [career infantryman and former super-squad member], in various telephone conversations with author from 2013 to 2019.
7. M.Gy.Sgt. Bob O'Bday USMC (Ret.) [Marine machinegunner at Khe Sanh and CAP platoon veteran], in conversations with author in November 2018.
8. William S. Lind, in Foreword of *One More Bridge to Cross,* by H. John Poole (Emerald Isle, NC: Posterity Press, 1998).
9. Xiaobing Li, *China's Battle for Korea: The 1951 Spring Offensive* (Bloomington, IN: Indiana Univ. Press, 2014), pp. xxv-xxvi.
10. *AZ Quotes,* s.v. "George S. Patton," as retrieved in October 2018 from the following url: https://www.azquotes.com/quote/226589.
11. Gen. Vo Nguyen Giap, "Once Again We Will Win," in *The Military Art of People's War,* ed. Russel Stetler (New York: Monthly Review Press, 1970), pp. 264, 265.

Chapter 1: *Recent Abandonment of Functional Heritage*

1. Gy.Sgt. Rodney Walker, in conversations with author.
2. "One General's Bet on Reshaping the Marines," by Sam Walker, *Wall Street Journal,* 1 July 2018, p. B5.
3. Shawn Snow, "It Soon May Be a 15 Marine Rifle Squad—Most Likely for MEU Deployments," *Marine Corps Times* on line, 10 October 2018.

4. "12-Man Rifle Squads, Including a Squad Systems Operator, Commandant Says," by Todd South, *Marine Corps Times* on line, 3 May 2018; "USMC Issues M320 Grenade Launcher to Bolster Squads," by Mon Berenguer, *Gun World,* 21 May 2018.

5. *Warfare History Network* website, s.v. "Carlson's Long Patrol: Marine Raiders at Guadalcanal."

6. "The Marine Rifle Squad: The Beginnings of the Modern Fireteam," *Leatherneck Magazine* on line forum, n.d., with information taken from www.ww2gyrene.org, the "GI Intelligence Department" [www.hardscrabblefarm.com/ww2], and Osprey's *Battle Orders 1: U.S. Marine Corps Pacific Theater of Operations 1941-1943.*

7. "From Makin to Bougainville: Marine Raiders in the Pacific War," by Maj. Jon T. Hoffman, *Marines in WWII Commemorative Series* (Washington, D.C.: Marine Corps Historical Ctr., 1995), p. 5; Joseph H. Alexander, *Edson's Raiders: 1st Marine Raider Battalion in World War II* (Annapolis, MD: Naval Inst. Press, 2001), p. 242.

8. Ed Gilbert, *U.S. Marine Corps Raider 1942-43* (London: Osprey Publishing, 2006), caption to toggle drawing.

9. "From Makin to Bougainville," by Hoffman, pp. 5, 24.

10. Gilbert, *U.S. Marine Corps Raider 1942-43,* pp. 1-25.

11. "The Marine Rifle Squad: The Beginnings of the Modern Fireteam," *Leatherneck Magazine* on line forum, n.d.

12. Joseph H. Alexander. *Edson's Raiders: 1st Marine Raider Battalion in World War II* (Annapolis, MD: Naval Inst. Press, 2001), pp. 242, 243.

13. "Marines in the Central Solomons," by Maj. John N. Rentz, *USMC Historical Monograph,* chapt. 4—From Rice to Bairoko (Washington, D.C.: Hist. Branch, HQMC, 1952).

14. Assoc. of U.S. Marine Raiders website, s.v. "Chronology."

15. "Okinawa: The Last Battle," by Roy E. Appleman, James M. Burns, Russell A. Gugeler, and John Stevens, *United States Army in World War II Series* (Washington, D.C.: U.S. Army's Ctr. of Mil. Hist., 2000), pp. 322, 323.

16. *Gung Ho: The Corp's Most Progressive Tradition,* by H. John Poole (Emerald Isle, NC: Posterity Press, 2012), chapt. 10.

17. *Handbook of the Chinese People's Liberation Army,* DDB-2680-32-84 (Washington, D.C.: DIA, November 1984), p. 33.

18. Ibid., p. 16.

19. Ibid., appendix E, p. A-5.

20. "WWII Squads," as retrieved in November 2018 from this url: www.scribd.com/document/54115611/WWII-Squads; *German Squad Tactics in WWII,* by Matthew Gajkowski (West Chester, OH: Nafziger, 1995), reprint of *The German Squad in Combat*, trans. and ed. U.S. Mil. Intel. Service (N.p., 1943), p. 15; *Soviet Infantry Tactics in World War II: Red Army Infantry Tactics from Squad to Rifle Company from the Combat Regulations,* with trans., intro., and notes by Charles C. Sharp (West Chester, OH: Nafziger, 1998), reprint of *Soviet Combat Regulations of November 1942* (Moscow: Stalin, n.d.), pp. 20, 84.

21. Gy.Sgt. Rodney Walker in conversations with author; Memorandum for the record by H.J. Poole, after a 28-year career in the U.S. Marine Corps.

22. *Marine Rifle Company / Platoon* FMFM 6-4 (Quantico, VA: Marine Corps Develop. and Educ. Cmd., 1978), p. 5.

23. Timothy L. Lupfer, "The Dynamics of Doctrine: The Changes in German Tactical Doctrine during the First World War," *Leavenworth Papers No. 4* (Ft. Leavenworth, KS: Combat Studies Inst., U.S. Army Cmd. & Gen. Staff College, 1981), p. 53; Bruce I. Gudmundsson, *Stormtroop Tactics—Innovation in the German Army 1914-1918* (New York: Praeger, 1989), pp. 92-94, 167-168.

24. Martin Samuels, *Command or Control,* pp. 93-94, and Bruce Gudmundsson, *Stormtroop Tactics,* in "Development of the Squad: Historical Analysis," by Ahmed Hashim with contributions from Lt.Gen. Paul Van Riper USMC (Ret.), (Alexandria, VA: Ctr. for Naval Analyses, 2000), p. 18.

25. Bruce I. Gudmundsson, *Stormtroop Tactics—Innovation in the* German Army 1914-1918 (New York: Praeger, 1989), pp. 162-178; *The Tiger's Way: A U.S. Private's Best Chance for Survival*, by H. John Poole (Emerald Isle, NC: Posterity Press, August 2003), pp. 280-283.

26. Maj. Norman L. Cooling, "Russia's 1994-96 Campaign for Chechnya: A Failure in Shaping the Battlespace," *Marine Corps Gazette,* October 2001, pp. 61, 62.

27. *Warfighting,* MCDP 1 (Washington, D.C.: HQMC, 1997), pp. 42, 43.

Chapter 2: *The Evolutionary Changes to Squad Combat in WWI*

1. *U.S. Army Heritage and Information Center* website, s.v. "Yorktown Redoubt #10," as retrieved in January 2017 from the following url: http://www.carlisle.army.mil/ahec/trail/Redoubt10/.

2. *Texas Military Forces Museum* website, s.v. "San Jacinto," as retrieved in December 2016 from the following url: http://www.texasmilitaryforcesmuseum.org/tnghist5.htm.

3. Gregory Jaynes and the eds., *The Civil War: The Killing Ground—Wilderness to Cold Harbor* (Alexandria, VA: Time-Life Books, 1986), p. 33.

4. *War History* on line, s.v. "Second Battle of Champagne WWI–High Hopes and Lessons Learned," as retrieved in November 2018 from the following url: https://www.warhistoryonline.com/world-war-i/second-battle-of-champagne-wwi.html.

5. *World Atlas* on line, s.v. "Major Battles of WWI," as retrieved in November 2018 from the following url: https://www.worldatlas.com/articles/major-battles-of-world-war-i-ww1.html.

6. Gudmundsson, *Stormtroop Tactics,* pp. 20-21, 165-166; *Wikipedia Encyclopedia,* s.v. "Imperial Japanese Army" and "Boer Foreign Volunteers."

7. Ibid., pp. 50-51, 85-86, chapt. 6.

8. President John F. Kennedy, quote from his 1962 West Point graduation speech, in "Unconventional Warfare Fundamentals," at *The Irregular Warrior* website.

9. Gudmundsson, *Stormtroop Tactics,* p. 172.

10. Graeme C. Wyne, *If Germany Attacks* (N.p., n.d.; reprint Westport, CT, 1976), p. 295, from Lupfer, "The Dynamics of Doctrine," *Leavenworth Papers No. 4,* p. 27.

11. Lupfer, "The Dynamics of Doctrine," *Leavenworth Papers No. 4,* p. 15.

12. Ibid., p. 15.

13. Ibid.

14. Gudmundsson, *Stormtroop Tactics,* p. 94.

15. Lupfer, "The Dynamics of Doctrine," *Leavenworth Papers No. 4,* p. 13.

16. Ibid., p. 12.

17. Gudmundsson, *Stormtroop Tactics,* p. 94.

18. Graeme C. Wyne, *If Germany Attacks* (N.p., n.d.; reprint Westport, CT, 1976), p. 295, from Lupfer, "The Dynamics of Doctrine," *Leavenworth Papers No. 4,* p. 27; Corum, *The Roots of Blitzkrieg* (N.p.: 1992), p. 9, in *1914-1918 Online: International Encyclopedia of the First World War,* s.v. "Military Developments of WWI," as retrieved in November 2018 from the following url: https://encyclopedia.1914-1918-online.net/article/military_developments_of_world_war_i.

19. *Wikipedia Encyclopedia,* s.v. "MG 08."

20. "German WW1 MG 08/15 Machine Gun—How Does It Work," videocassette, as retrieved in November 2018 from the following url: https://www.youtube.com/watch?v=uwgGok9cYcw.

21. *1914-1918 Online: International Encyclopedia of the First World War,* s.v. "Military Developments of WWI."

22. Gudmundsson, *Stormtroop Tactics,* p. 87, chapt. 10.

23. "Organization of an Infantry Company," *151 Regiment d'Infanterie de Ligne,* n.d., as retrieved in November 2018 from the following url: http://www.151ril.com/content/history/french-army/9.

24. *The Miniatures Page,* s.v. "French Platoon/Squad Organization During 1914-1935," as retrieved November 2018 from the following url: http://theminiaturespage.com/boards/msg.mv?id=307363; Gy.Sgt. Rodney Walker in conversations with author.

25. *Wikipedia Encyclopedia,* s.v. "Chatellerault M24/29" and "*Fusil-mitrailleur Modele 1915 CSRG.*"

26. Ibid., s.v. "Section (military unit)."

27. "Evolution of the British Infantry Section—1916-1945," by Michael Dorosh, *Axis History Forum,* 18 January 2007, as retrieved in November 2018 from the following url: https://forum.axishistory.com/viewtopic.php?t=114564.

28. "Organization and Equipment of the Infantry Rifle Squad," by Virgil Ney, *Memorandum CORG-M-194m,* Hdqts. U.S. Army Development Cmd., January 1965.

29. "The Infantry Squad Part 1: How Did We Get Here," by Chris Raynor, *NCO Journal,* 19 March 2018.

30. *Infantry: Part I—Regular Army,* by John K. Mahon and Romana Danysh (Washington, D.C.: Chief of Staff of Mil. Hist., U.S. Army, 1972), p. 38.

31. Ibid., p. 48.

32. *Wikipedia Encyclopedia,* s.v. "M1918 Browning Automatic Rifle" and "Hotchkiss M1909 Benét–Mercié Machine Gun."

33. "U.S. Defensive Grenades in World War I," by Glen Hyatt, *WorldWar1.com,* n.d.

34. "U.S. Marine Squad in World War I, 1918: You Take Command," by John Antal, *Warfare History Network*, n.d.; *Wikipedia Encyclopedia,* s.v. "M1918 Browning Automatic Rifle"; "The Marine Rifle Squad: The Beginnings of the Modern Fireteam," *Leatherneck Magazine,* on line forum.

35. *1914-1918: International Encyclopedia of the First World War,* s.v. "Hand Grenade," as retrieved in December 2018 from the following url: https://encyclopedia.1914-1918-online.net/article/hand_grenade.

36. *Wikipedia Encyclopedia,* s.v. "Stielhandgranate."

37. *1914-1918: International Encyclopedia of the First World War,* s.v. "Hand Grenade"; *Ej's Ordnance Show & Tell Pages*, s.v. "American Hand Grenades of WWI," as retrieved in December 2018 from the following url: http://www.inert-ord.net/usa03a/usa1/index.html.

38. *Wikipedia Encyclopedia,* s.v. "Stielhandgranate."

39. "The Marine Rifle Squad: The Beginnings of the Modern Fireteam," *Leatherneck Magazine* on line forum, n.d.; Gy.Sgt. Rodney Walker, in conversations with author.

40. "U.S. Marine Squad in World War I, 1918: You Take Command," by Antal.

41. *Gung Ho,* by Poole, chapt. 5.

42. William S. Lind, *The Maneuver Warfare Handbook* (Boulder, CO: Westview Press, 1985); *Warfighting,* FMFM 1 (Washington, D.C.: HQMC, 1989); *Tactics,* FMFM 1-3 (Washington, D.C.: HQMC, 1991).

43. President John F. Kennedy, quote from his 1962 West Point graduation speech.

44. *Warfighting,* MCDP 1, pp. 42, 43.

Chapter 3: *How Squads of the World Then Operated in WWII*

1. John Shaw and the editors of Time-Life Books, *Red Army Resurgent* (Chicago: Time-Life Books, 1979), p. 165.

2. *German Squad Tactics in WWII,* by Matthew Gajkowski (West Chester,OH: Nafziger, 1995), reprint of *The German Squad in Combat,* trans. and ed. by the U.S. Mil. Intel. Service (N.p., 1943), pp. 26, 27.

3. *Handbook on German Military Forces,* TM-E 30-451 (Washington, D.C.: U.S. War Dept., 1945; reprint Baton Rouge, LA: LSU Press, 1990), p. 231.

4. Ibid.

5. *Handbook on Japanese Military Forces,* TM 30-480 (Washington, D.C.: U.S. War Dept., 1944), pp. 145-150.

6. *Soviet Tactical Doctrine in WWII,* with foreword by Shawn Caza (West Chester, OH: Nafziger, 1997), reprint of chapt. V, *Handbook on U.S.S.R. Military Forces,* TM 30-340 (Washington, D.C.: U.S. War Dept., 1945), p. V-47.

7. *Soviet Infantry Tactics in World War II: Red Army Infantry Tactics from Squad to Rifle Company from the Combat Regulations,* with trans., intro., and notes by Charles C. Sharp (West Chester, OH: Nafziger, 1998), reprint of *Soviet Combat Regulations of November 1942* (Moscow: Stalin, n.d.), p. 75.

8. Ibid., p. 23.

9. "Condor Legion: The Wehrmacht's Training Ground," by Ian Westwell (N.p.: Ian Allan Publishers, 2004), Google Books synopsis.

10. *Handbook on German Military Forces*, p. 209.

11. *German Squad Tactics in WWII,* by Gajkowski, p. 1.

12. Ibid.

13. "German Squad Tactics in World War 2," *Military History Visualized,* partial translation by the U.S. Mil. Intel. Service in January 1943 of a German field manual entitled "German Squad in Combat," as retrieved in December 2018 from the following url: https://www.youtube.com/watch?v=-rKRt5zVZgw; *Handbook on German Military Forces*, p. 114; *German Squad Tactics in WWII,* by Gajkowski, pp. 2-6.

14. "German Squad Tactics in World War 2," *Military History Visualized.*

15. *The Tiger's Way: A U.S. Private's Best Chance for Survival,* by H. John Poole (Emerald Isle, NC: Posterity Press, August 2003), pp. 280-283; Gudmundsson, *Stormtroop Tactics*, pp. 162-178.

16. *German Squad Tactics in WWII,* by Gajkowski, p. 5.

17. "How a German Squad Attacks a Position (WWII)," *Footage Archive,* from a training film entitled "The German Infantry Squad in Action: A Demonstration of Minor Field Tactics," as retrieved in December 2018 from this url: www.youtube,comwatch?v= GDZMJXaADQI.

18. Ibid.; *German Squad Tactics in WWII,* by Gajkowski p. 20.

19. "How a German Squad Attacks a Position (WWII)," *Footage Archive.*

20. *German Squad Tactics in WWII,* by Gajkowski, pp. 3, 8.

21. Ibid., p. 4.

22. *Soviet Infantry Tactics in World War II,* with trans., intro., and notes by Sharp, p. 13.

23. *German Squad Tactics in WWII,* by Gajkowski, pp. 42, 43.

24. "German Infantry Anti-Tank Tactics 1941/1942: Eastern Front Edition," *Military History Visualized,* as retrieved in December 2018 from this url: https://www.youtube.com/watch?v=FxJZJflMEiw.

25. *German Squad Tactics in WWII,* by Gajkowski, pp. 3, 23.

26. Ibid., p. 23.

27. "How a German Squad Attacks a Position (WWII)," *Footage Archive.*

28. *German Squad Tactics in WWII,* by Gajkowski, p. 14.

29. Ibid., p. 15.

30. Ibid., pp. 14, 21.

31. Ibid., p. 23.

32. *Wikipedia Encyclopedia,* s.v. "Stielhandgranate," "Splitterring," and "Model 24 Grenade."

33. *Encyclopedia Britannica,* s.v. "Second Sino-Japanese War."

34. *Wikipedia Encyclopedia,* s.v. "Battles of Khalkhin Gol."

35. *Handbook on Japanese Military Forces,* pp. 114, 115.

36. Ibid., p. 86.

37. Ibid., pp. 114, 115.

38. Ibid., p. 117.

39. "German Infantry Anti-Tank Tactics 1941/1942: Eastern Front Edition," *Military History Visualized.*

40. *Handbook on Japanese Military Forces,* p. 34.

41. "Japanese Organisation in WWII," as retrieved in November 2018 from this url: http://www-solar.mcs.st-and.ac.uk/~aaron/WW2ORG/jap.html; "WWII Squads."

42. *Handbook on Japanese Military Forces*, p. 85.

43. Ibid., p. 91.

44. Ibid., p. 98.

45. Ibid.

46. Ibid.

47. Ibid., p. 87.

48. Burke Davis, *Marine* (New York: Bantam, 1964), p. 140; *Fighting on Guadalcanal,* FMFRP 12-110 (Washington, D.C.: U.S.A. War Office, 1942), pp. 2, 22.

49. *Handbook on Japanese Military Forces*, pp. 208-214.

50. Gudmundsson, *Stormtroop Tactics,* pp. 20-21, 165-166; *Wikipedia Encyclopedia,* s.v. "Imperial Japanese Army"; "How a German Squad Attacks a Position (WWII)," *Footage Archive.*

51. "Photos of Japanese WWII Replica Stick Grenade," *Stewarts Military Antiques;* "Discover Ideas About Ww2 Weapons," *Printerest,* as retrieved in December 2018 from the following url: https://www.pinterest.com/pin/708261478872881928/.

52. *Wikipedia Encyclopedia,* s.v." Stielhandgranate."

53. Ibid., "Battles of Khalkhin Gol."

54. Ibid., "Winter War."

55. *Soviet Infantry Tactics in World War II,* with trans., intro., and notes by Sharp, p. 20.

56. Ibid., p. 21.

57. Ibid., pp. 117, 118.

58. Ibid., p. 13.

59. Ibid., p. 19.

60. Ibid., pp. 18, 21.

61. Ibid., p. 19.

62. Ibid. p. 20.

63. Ibid., p. 22.

64. Ibid., p. 21.

65. *Wikipedia Encyclopedia,* s.v. "Model 1914 Grenade."

66. Ibid., s.v. "National Revolutionary Army" and "88th Division (National Revolutionary Army)."

67. "WW2 German Trained Chinese National Revolutionary Army (p1)," *Kobetang,* as retrieved in December 2018 from the following url: https://www.youtube.com/watch?v=P6UBRMQFEzM.

68. "WWII Factions: The Chinese Armies," *Simple History,* as retrieved in December 2018 from the following url: https://www.youtube.com/watch?v=Ei_oMWw2DwM; *Handbook of the Chinese People's Liberation Army,* DDB-2680-32-84, p. 2.

69. *Wikipedia Encyclopedia,*, s.v. "88th Division (National Revolutionary Army)."

70. Ibid., s.v. "National Revolutionary Army."

71. *Handbook on the Chinese People's Liberation Army,* DDB-2680-32-84, pp. 16, A-5, A-15.

72. Ibid.

73. "The Experimental Chinese Mech Infantry," *Strategy Page,* September 2012; *Wikipedia Encyclopedia,* s.v. "Peoples Liberation Army Ground Force"; *Handbook of the Chinese People's Liberation Army,* DDB-2680-32-84, p. A-5.

74. *Wikipedia Encyclopedia,* s.v. "National Revolutionary Army."

75. *The People's Army,* by Israel Epstein (N.p.: Gollancz, 1939), p. 172.

76. "German Infantry Anti-Tank Tactics 1941/1942: Eastern Front Edition," *Military History Visualized.*

77. *Wikipedia Encyclopedia* (2016), s.v. "The M24 Grenade," as retrieved in December 2018 from the following url: https://ipfs.io/ipfs/QmXoypizjW3WknFiJnKLwHCnL72vedxjQkDDP1mXWo6uco/wiki/Model_24_grenade.html.

78. *Handbook of the Chinese People's Liberation Army,* DDB-2680-32-84, p. 33.

79. *North Korea's Hidden Assets,* by H. John Poole (Emerald Isle, NC: Posterity Press, 2018), chapt. 15.

80. *Wikipedia Encyclopedia,* s.v. "Treaty of Brest-Litovsk."

81. *North Korea's Hidden Assets,* by Poole, chapt. 15.

82. *Wikipedia Encyclopedia,* "List of Revolutions and Rebellions."

83. "Evolution of the British Infantry Section—1916-1945."

84. Ibid.

85. Place, *Military Training in the British Army, 1940-1944: From Dunkirk to D-Day,* p. 69, in "Evolution of the British Infantry Section—1916-1945."

86. "Evolution of the British Infantry Section—1916-1945."

87. Ibid.

88. *Wikipedia Encyclopedia,* s.v. "No. 69 Grenade"; *Ej's Ordnance Show and Tell Pages,* s.v. "British Hand Grenade No. 69 Mk I," as retrieved in January 2019 from the following url: http://www.inert-ord.net/brit/no69/index.html.

89. "Organization of the WWII U.S. Army Infantry Rifle Squad," *GI History Handbook,* videotape, 25 May 2017, as retrieved in November 2018 from the following url: https://www.youtube.com/watch?v=hUOz13oJnCQ.

90. "Development of the Squad: Historical Analysis," by Ahmed Hashim with contributions from Lt.Gen. Paul Van Riper USMC (Ret.) (Alexandria, VA: Ctr. for Naval Analyses, 2000), p. 20.

91. "Organization of the WWII U.S. Army Infantry Rifle Squad," *GI History Handbook.*

92. "Development of the Squad: Historical Analysis," by Hashim, p. 21; "The Evolution of the U.S. Army Infantry Squad: Where Do We Go from Here: Determining the Optimum Infantry Squad Organization for the Future," by Maj. S.E. Hughes, *monograph* (Ft Leavenworth, KS: School of Advanced Mil. Studies, U.S. Army Cmd. and Gen. Staff College, 1994), pp. 5, 6.

93. *Ej's Ordnance Show & Tell Pages*, s.v. "American Hand Grenades of W.W.I," as retrieved in December 2018 from the following url: http://www.inert-ord.net/usa03a/usa1/index.html.

94. *Wikipedia Encyclopedia,* s.v. "MK3 Grenade."

95. *Ej's Ordnance Show & Tell Pages*, s.v. "Mk.3A2 Blast Grenade," as retrieved in January 2019 from the following url: http://www.inert-ord.net/usa03a/usa3/mk3a2/index.html.

96. "Development of the Squad: Historical Analysis," by Hashim, p. 25.

97. Ibid.

98. Alexander, *Edson's Raiders,* pp. 242, 243.

99. "Development of the Squad: Historical Analysis," by Hashim, p. 25.

100. "French Infantry Company 1940," *Quartermaster Section,* https://www.quartermastersection.com/french/companies/1781/FRENCHINFANTRYCOMPANY1940.

101. "Châtellerault Model 1924 M29 LMG," by Jean Huon, *Small Arms Review,* as retrieved in January 2019 from the following url: http://www.smallarmsreview.com/display.article.cfm?idarticles=1408.

102. "Free French Infantry Squad Attack, 1945," *History Net,* as retrieved in January 2019 from the following url: http://www.historynet.com/free-french-infantry-squad-attack-1945.htm.

103. *Wikipedia Encyclopedia,* s.v. "F1 Grenade (France)."

104. *The German Squad Tactics in WWII,* by Gajkowski, p. 15.

105. *Handbook on German Military Forces*, p. 113.

106. Ibid., pp. 117, 119.

107. "The Japanese Nambu Type 96 6.5mm Light Machinegun," by Edwin F. Libby, *Small Arms Review,* n.d. "Japanese Type 11 LMG," videotape, as retrieved in November 2018 from the following url: https://www.youtube.com/watch?v=iwi-3pSFKGc.

108. *Handbook on Japanese Military Forces,* TM 30-480 (1942 ed.), p. 32.

109. Ibid., p. 34.

110. George, John B. (LTC), *Shots Fired in Anger* (NRA Press (1981), p. 343, in *Wikipedia Encyclopedia,* s.v. "Rifle Grenades."

111. *Wikipedia Encyclopedia,* s.v. "Rifle Grenades."

112. *Soviet Infantry Tactics in World War II,* with trans., intro., and notes by Sharp, p. 118.

113. *Handbook on U.S.S.R. Military Forces,* TM 30-340 (Washington, D.C.: U.S. War Dept., 1945), chapt. III, pp. III-11 and III-12.

114. "Indigenous Machine Guns of China," *Small Arms Defense Journal* on line, 20 March 2014.

115. Philip Jowett, "China's Wars: Rousing the Dragon 1894-1949," p. 130, in *Wikipedia Encyclopedia,* s.v. "List of Chinese Military Equipment in World War II"; *Wikipedia Encyclopedia,* s.v. "M2 Mortar."

116. *Handbook of the Chinese People's Liberation Army,* DDB-2680-32-84, p. A-5.

117. *Fighting on Guadalcanal,* FMFRP 12-110 (Washington, D.C.: U.S.A. War Office, 1942), pp. 2, 22; "Photos of Japanese WWII Replica Stick Grenade," *Stewarts Military Antiques;* "Discover Ideas About Ww2 Weapons," *Printerest,* as retrieved in December 2018 from the following url: https://www.pinterest.com/pin/708261478872881928/.

118. Burke Davis, *Marine*, p. 140.

119. "Sands of Iwo Jima," Republic Pictures, Tarawa portion.

120. S.Sgt. Chris Ronin USMC (Ret.) [former Marine scout/sniper and special operator], in various conversations with author from 2017 to 2019.

121. *German Squad Tactics in WWII,* by Gajkowski, p. 14.

122. Gudmundsson, *Stormtroop Tactics,* pp. xi, xii.

123. David M. Glantz, "August Storm: Soviet Tactical and Operational Combat in Manchuria, 1945," *Leavenworth Papers No. 8* (Ft. Leavenworth, KS: Combat Studies Inst., U.S. Army Cmd. & Gen. Staff College, 1983), p. 176.

124. *Historical Study—Night Combat,* DA Pamphlet 20-236 (Washington, D.C.: Hdqts. Dept. of the Army, 1953), pp. 19-21.

125. Bill D. Ross, *Iwo Jima—Legacy of Valor* (New York: Vintage Books, 1986), p. 333; Col. Joseph H Alexander, "Closing In: Marines in the Seizure of Iwo Jima," *Marines in World War II Commemorative Series* (Washington, D.C.: Hist. & Museums Div., HQMC, 1994), p. 46.

126. Col. Hiromichi Yahara, *The Battle for Okinawa,* trans. Roger Pineau and Masatoshi Uehara (New York: John Wiley & Sons, 1995), pp. 36, 213.

127. Ibid., p. 59.

128. Montross and Canzona, "The Chosin Reservoir Campaign," *U.S. Marine Operations in Korea, 1950-1953,* vol. III, p. 92, in "A Historical Perspective on Light Infantry," by Maj. Scott R. McMichael, chapt. 2—The Chinese Communist Forces in Korea, *Research Survey No. 6* (Ft. Leavenworth, KS: Combat Studies Inst., U.S. Army Cmd. & Gen. Staff College, 1987), p. 60.

129. *Handbook on the Chinese Communist Army,* DA Pamphlet 30-51 (Washington, D.C.: Hdqts Dept. of the Army, 7 December 1960), p. 29.

130. Col. G.C. Thomas USMC, Maj.Gen. Vandegriff's Chief of Staff, as quoted in *Fighting on Guadalcanal,* FMFRP 12-110, p. 65.

131. "First Offensive: The Marine Campaign for Guadalcanal," by Henry I Shaw, Jr., *Marines in World War II Commemorative Series* (Washington, D.C.: Hist. & Museums Div., HQMC, 1992), p. 25.

132. *Jungle Warfare,* FMFRP 12-9 (Quantico, VA: Marine Corps Combat Develop. Cmd., 1989), p. 41.

133. Unidentified NCOs to Chesty Puller, as quoted in *Fighting on Guadalcanal,* FMFRP 12-110, pp. 35-37.

134. Eric M. Hammel, *Guadalcanal: Starvation Island* (New York: Crown Publishers, 1987), p. 315.

135. Richard Tregaskis, *Guadalcanal Diary* (New York: Landmark Books, an imprint of Random House, 1955), p. 167.

136. Hammel, *Guadalcanal: Starvation Island,* pp. 318-320.

137. William J. Owens, *Green Hell: The Battle for Guadalcanal* (Central Point, OR: Hellgate Press, a Div. of PSI Research, 1999), p. 145.

138. *Wikipedia Encyclopedia,* s.v. "Two-Inch Mortar," "M2 Mortar."

Chapter 4: *Squad Activity During the Korean War*

1. *This Kind of War,* by T.R. Fehrenbach (Washington, D.C.: Brassey's, 1994), orig. pub. in New York by MacMillan in 1963, p. 4; "The Koreas," ed. Mary E. Connor, *Asia in Focus Series* (Santa Barbara, CA: ABC-CLIO, 2009), p. 45; "Korean War." *History Channel* on line, n.d.; "North Korea, a Country Study," DA Pamphlet 550-81, 5th ed., ed. Robert L. Worden, *Area Handbook Series* (Washington, D.C.: Fed. Research Div., Library of Congress, 2008), p. 238.

2. *This Kind of War,* by Fehrenbach, p. 352.

3. Jian Chen, *China's Road to the Korean War: The Making of the Sino-American Confrontation* (New York: Columbia Univ. Press, 1996), in *Wikipedia Encyclopedia,* s.v. "Peoples Volunteer Army Order of Battle."

4. *This Kind of War,* by Fehrenbach, p. 352.

5. "How Did the Chinese Army Defeat the U.S. Tanks and Helicopters During the Korean War," *Quora,* n.d.

6. Eric M. Hammel, *Chosin: Heroic Ordeal of the Korean War* (Novato, CA: Presidio Press, 1981), p. 87.

7. Lynn Montross and Capt. Nicholas A. Canzona, "The Chosin Reservoir Campaign," *U.S. Marine Operations in Korea 1950-1953,* vol. III (Washington, D.C.: Hist. Branch, HQMC, 1957), p. 168.

8. Hammel, *Chosin,* p. 55.

9. Ibid., p. 87.

10. *East of Chosin: Entrapment and Breakout in Korea, 1950,* by Roy Edgar Appleman (College Station, TX: Texas A&M Univ. Press, 1990), p. 125.

11. Hammel, *Chosin,* pp. 56-59.

12. Montross and Canzona, "The Chosin Reservoir Campaign," p. 163.

13. Hammel, *Chosin,* pp. 56-59.

14. Ibid., pp. 64, 65.

15. *Wikipedia Encyclopedia,* s.v. "Peoples Volunteer Army."

16. "A Description of Combat Rifle Squads on the Korean MLR During the Winter of 1952-53," by Rodney A. Clark and Martha B. Myers, Human Resources Research Office, George Washington Univ., while under contract to the U.S. Army, June 1954. p. 58.

17. *Wikipedia Encyclopedia,* s.v. "Bangolore Torpedo."

18. "1/4 After-Action Report for May 1967."

19. Kevin Mahoney, *Formidable Enemies: The North Korean and Chinese Soldier in the Korean War* (N.p.: Presidio Press, 2001), p. 36, in *Wikipedia Encyclopedia,* s.v. "Peoples Volunteer Army."

20. *Wikipedia Encyclopedia,* s.v. "Peoples Volunteer Army."

21. Ibid., s.v. "PPSh-41."

22. "The Marine Rifle Squad: The Beginnings of the Modern Fireteam," *Leatherneck Magazine* on line forum, n.d.

23. "The Infantry Squad Part 2: How Did We Get Here," by Chris Raynor. *NCO Journal,* 23 March 2018.

24. Ibid.

25. *Commentary on Infantry Operations and Weapons Usage in Korea: Winter 1950-1951,* by Brig.Gen. S.L.A. Marshall, ed. Nafziger (Chevy Chase, MD: The Johns Hopkins Univ. Press, 1951), pp. 53, 54.

26. "Development of the Squad: Historical Analysis," by Hashim, p. 26.

27. Ibid., pp. 26, 27.

28. J.C. Fry, "Battle Drill," *Combat Forces Journal,* April 1953, pp. 18-22, and May 1953, pp. 37-39, in "Development of the Squad: Historical Analysis," by Hashim, p. 27.

29. Ibid.

30. Ibid.

31. Maj.Gen. Carl Ernest, "The Infantry Squad: How Much Is Enough," *Infantry Magazine,* January-February 1997, pp. 1, 2, in "Development of the Squad: Historical Analysis," by Hashim, p. 42.

32. Ibid. p. 41.

33. "The Infantry Squad Part 1," by Raynor; *Wikipedia Encyclopedia,* s.v. "Squad."

34. "The Infantry Squad Part 1," by Raynor.

Chapter 5: *The Various Squads in Vietnam*

1. *NVA-VC Small Unit Tactics & Techniques Study, Part I,* USARV, ed. Thomas Pike (Washington, D.C.: Archival Publishing, 1997), p. VI-5.

2. Memorandum for the record by H.J. Poole, after serving two infantry tours in Vietnam.

3. Ibid.

4. Gudmundsson, *Stormtroop Tactics,* pp. 147-149; *The Tiger's Way,* by Poole, chapt. 19.

5. "1/4 After-Action Report for May 1967," as retrieved from the 1/4 Assoc. website.

6. Gudmundsson, *Stormtroop Tactics,* pp. 147-149; *The Tiger's Way,* by Poole, chapt. 19.

7. Ibid.

8. "Lost Battles of the Vietnam War," *G2mil.com,* n.d.

9. "Attacks on MAG-16, Hill 22, and the Attempted Attack on the Da Nang Airfield, *3rd Marines in Vietnam* website, n.d.

10. Memorandum for the record by H.J. Poole, after personally seeing the article in *Stars and Stripes.*

11. *Guardian Joe: How Less Force Helps the Warrior,* by H. John Poole (Emerald Isle, NC: Posterity Press, 2018), chapt. 23.

12. "Lost Battles of the Vietnam War."

13. "Biên Hòa Air Base Ammo Dump Explosion Sapper Attack," by Arnold John Houchin, originally written on 12 January 1972, then published by the Assoc. for USAF Vietnam War Veterans of Air/Security Police, through *Vietnam War Stories,* in 2005.

14. "1/4 Command Chronology," as quoted in CWO-4 Guthrie e-mail to author of 8 May 2017.

15. U.S. *Marines in Vietnam: An Expanding War—1966,* by Jack Shulimson (Washington, D.C.: Hist. & Museums Div., HQMC, 1982), pp. 186, 187.

16. Ibid.

17. Peter Mancuso (A/1/4 member), as quoted in CWO-4 Guthrie e-mail to author of 8 May 2017.

18. Larry Schorr (A/1/4 member), as quoted in CWO-4 Guthrie e-mail to author of 8 May 2017.

19. *U.S. Marines in Vietnam: Fighting the North Vietnamese 1967,* Maj. Gary Tefler, Lt.Col. Lane Rogers, and V. Keith Fleming, Jr. (Washington, D.C.: Hist. and Museums Div., HQMC, 1984), pp. 19-21.

20. *U.S. Marines in Vietnam: Fighting the North Vietnamese 1967,* by Tefler, Rogers, and Fleming, pp. 33-35.

21. CWO-4 Guthrie, in e-mail to author in December 2011.

22. *U.S. Marines in Vietnam: Fighting the North Vietnamese 1967,* by Tefler, Rogers, and Fleming, pp. 33-35.

23. CWO-4 Guthrie, in e-mail to author of December 2011.

24. *U.S. Marines in Vietnam: Fighting the North Vietnamese 1967,* by Tefler, Rogers, and Fleming, pp. 33-35.

25. "1/4 After-Action Report for May 1967."

26. "1/4 Intelligence Summary for 7-8 May 1967," as retrieved from the 1/4 Assoc. website.

27. CWO-4 Guthrie, in e-mail to author of December 2011.

28. "1/4 After-Action Report for May 1967."

29. Capt. Patrick J. McDonnell, 4th Platoon Amtrac leader, in written recollection "Hill of Angels—My 1967," at official 1st Amtrac Battalion website (Amtrac.org), s.v. "1st Amtrac Battalion History" and "Bravo Company Arrives First."

30. Cpl. Aldo Betta, the lead Amtrac commander, in interview with CWO-4 Guthrie, as relayed by e-mail to author in December 2011.

31. "1/4 After-Action Report for May 1967."

32. McDonnell, 4th Platoon Amtrac leader, in written recollection "Hill of Angels—My 1967."

33. "1/4 Intelligence Summary for 7-8 May 1967."

34. CWO-4 Guthrie, in e-mail to author of 26 March 2012; *U.S. Marines in Vietnam: Fighting the North Vietnamese 1967,* by Tefler, Rogers, and Fleming, pp. 33-35.

35. "1/4 After-Action Report for May 1967."

36. McDonnell, 4th Platoon Amtrac leader, in written recollection "Hill of Angels—My 1967"; Betta, the lead Amtrac commander, in interview with CWO-4 Guthrie.

37. "1/4 After-Action Report for May 1967."

38. *Handbook on the Chinese Communist Army,* DA Pamphlet 30-51, pp. 23, 24.

39. Dennis Mansuour (A/1/4 member), as quoted in CWO-4 Guthrie e-mail of 15 My 2017.

40. CWO-4 Guthrie, in e-mail to author of 26 March 2012; Steve Hohenstein (A/1/4 ambush squad member), in written recollections, from CWO-4 Guthrie e-mail to author of 2011; "1/4 After-Action Report for May 1967."

41. CWO-4 Guthrie, in e-mail to author on 9 June 2012.

42. Terrence Maitland and Peter McInerney, *Vietnam Experience: A Contagion of War* (Boston, MA: Boston Publishing, 1968), p. 94.

43. Keith William Nolan, *Operation Buffalo: USMC Fight for the DMZ* (New York: Dell Publishing, 1991), p. 77.

44. "Sapper Attack: The Elite North Vietnamese Units," by Arnold Blumberg, *History Net,* 1 February 2017.

45. *Wikipedia Encyclopedia,* s.v. "RPD Machine Gun."

46. Ibid.

47. *2-12 INF Warriors,* s.v. "NVA Army" as retrieved in February 2019 from the following url: http://www.212warriors.com/NVA_army.html.

48. *Wikipedia Encyclopedia* (2016), s.v. "The M24 Grenade."

49. Gen. Van Tien Dung, *Our Great Spring Victory: An Account of the Liberation of South Vietnam,* trans. John Spragens, Jr. (Hanoi: The Gioi Publishers, 2001), p. 113.

50. Nguyen Van Mo, as quoted in *Portrait of the Enemy,* by David Chanoff and Doan Van Toai (New York: Random House, 1986), p. 162.

51. James F. Dunnigan and Albert A. Nofi, *Dirty Little Secrets of the Vietnam War* (New York: Thomas Dunne Books, 1999), pp. 279, 280.

52. Nguyen Van Mo, as quoted in *Portrait of the Enemy,* by Chanoff and Doan Van Toai.

53. "Sapper Attack," by Blumberg.

54. Ibid.

55. Nolan, *Operation Buffalo,* p. 298.

56. *Wikipedia Encyclopedia*, s.v. "M79 Grenade Launcher."

57. Memorandum for the record by H.J. Poole, after serving two infantry tours in Vietnam.

58. "The Evolution of the U.S. Army Infantry Squad: Where Do We Go from Here: Determining the Optimum Infantry Squad Organization for the Future," by Maj. S.E. Hughes, *monograph* (Ft. Leavenworth, KS: School of Advanced Mil. Studies, U.S. Army Cmd. and Gen. Staff College, 1994), pp. 7-9.

59. Ibid.; *Wikisource,* s.v. "Infantry, Part I: Regular Army /ROAD and Flexible Response," as retrieved in February 2019 from the following url: https://en.wikisource.org/wiki/Infantry,_Part_I:_Regular_Army_/ROAD_and_Flexible_Response.

60. B. Cranfield, B. (2016, April 28), "The M14 Rifle: John Garand's Final Legacy," in "The Infantry Squad Part 2," by Raynor.

61. M.S. Morgan, (2017, September 20), "M16: A Half-Century of America's Combat Rifle," in "The Infantry Squad Part 2," by Raynor.

62. "Development of the Squad: Historical Analysis," by Hashim, p. 36.

63. "Rethinking the U.S. Army Infantry Rifle Squad," by Maj. Hassan Kamara, *Military Review,* March-April 2018.

64. "Development of the Squad: Historical Analysis," by Hashim, p. 40.

65. "The Evolution of the U.S. Army Infantry Squad," by Hughes, p. 17.

Chapter 6: *Deliberate Attack*

1. *FM 5-71-2,* "Engineer Combat Operations," chapt. 3, as retrieved in February 2019 from the following url: https://www.globalsecurity.org/military/library/policy/army/fm/5-71-2/chap3.htm.

2. *Tactical Fundamentals.* MCI 7401. 1st course in Warfighting Skills Program (Washington, D.C.: Marine Corps Inst, 1989), pp. 37, 38.

3. *The Infantry Platoon and Squad,* FM 3-21.8 (precedes FM 7-8), chapt. 7 (Washington, D.C.: Hdqts. Dept. of the Army, March 2007), pp. 7-14 to 7-17, as retrieved in February 2019 from these two urls: http://www.infantrydrills.com/fm-3-21-8-chapter-7-section-iv-platoon-attacks/ and https://www.mtu.edu/arotc/cadet-portal/docs/fm3-21 infantryrifle-sqpl.pdf.

4. Memorandum for the record by H.J. Poole, after personally disarming a foe-controlled U.S. claymore during firefight in Vietnam.

5. Vic Taylor, "Hotel Company-Day Three," *Marine Corps Gazette,* April 2004.

6. "1/4's Intelligence Summary for 7-8 May 1967."

7. *FAS Military Analysis Network,* s.v. "Squad Automatic Weapon (SAW), M249 Light Machine Gun," as retrieved in February 2019 from the following url: https://fas.org/man/dod-101/sys/land/m249.htm.

8. "A Survey of the Effects of Load-Carrying and Equipment Design upon Tasks Performed by the Combat Infantryman," by Morris Kolnicker and Martin A. Tolcott (N.p.: Human Factors Research Div., Army Research Office, 15 November 1962), pp. 5, 6.

9. "Soldier's Load and the Mobility of a Nation," by S.L.A. Marshall (Quantico, VA: Marine Corps Assoc., 1980), pp. 69, 70.

10. Memorandum for the record by H.J. Poole, after two infantry tours in Vietnam.

11. Gudmundsson, *Stormtroop Tactics,* pp. 46-78; *Wikipedia Encyclopedia,* s.v. "Stormtrooper" and "MP18."

Chapter 7: *Enemy Bunker Seizure*

1. "Sands of Iwo Jima," Republic Pictures, Tarawa portion.
2. *Wikipedia Encyclopedia,* s.v. "William D. Hawkins."
3. Ross, *Iwo Jima,* pp. 70, 71.
4. *Strategic Rifleman: Key to More Moral Warfare,* by H. John Poole (Emerald Isle, NC: Posterity Press, 2014), chapt. 17; "The Coolest Weapon in CoD History: The Stinger LMG," *Reddit*, n.d.
5. *Wikipedia Encyclopedia,* s.v. "Tony Stein."
6. Ross, *Iwo Jima,* pp. 70, 71.
7. "The Coolest Weapon in CoD History: The Stinger LMG," *Reddit*, n.d.
8. *Gung Ho,* by Poole, chapts. 9 and 10.
9. Ibid., chapts. 11 and 13.
10. Taylor, "Hotel Company-Day Three."
11. Gordon L . Rottman, *U.S. Airborne Units in the Pacific Theater 1942–45* (N.p.: Osprey, 2007), p. 43; and Peter Harclerode, *Wings of War–Airborne Warfare 1918–1945* (N.p.: Weidenfeld & Nicolson, 2005), pp. 332–333; in *Wikipedia Encyclopedia,* s.v. "Bazooka."
12. *Wikipedia Encyclopedia,* s.v. "Douglas T. Jacobson."
13. Ibid.
14. Gudmundsson, *Stormtroop Tactics,* pp. xi, xii.
15. "How a German Squad Attacks a Position (WWII)," *Footage Archive.*
16. M.Gy.Sgt. O'Bday, in conversation with author in August 2019.

Chapter 8: *Deliberate Defense*

1. *Soviet Infantry Tactics in World War II,* with trans., intro., and notes by Sharp, p. 23.
2. Ibid., p. 52.
3. Ibid., p. 23.
4. William P. Baxter, *Soviet Airland Battle Tactics* (Novato, CA: Presidio Press, 1986), p. 138.
5. Ibid.; *The Bear Went over the Mountain: Soviet Combat Tactics in Afghanistan,* trans. and ed. Lester W. Grau, Foreign Mil. Studies Office, U.S. Dept. of Defense (Originally from the Soviet Union: Frunze Mil. Academy, n.d.; reprint Washington, D.C.: Nat. Defense Univ. Press, 1996), p. 102.
6. *Soviet Tactical Doctrine in WWII,* with foreword by Caza, p. V-145.
7. Col. Joseph H Alexander, "Closing In: Marines in the Seizure of Iwo Jima," *Marines in World War II Commemorative Series* (Washington, D.C.: Hist. & Museums Div., HQMC, 1994), illustration, p. 8.

8. Yahara, *The Battle for Okinawa,* p. 228.
9. *Phantom Soldier: The Enemy's Answer to U.S. Firepower,* by H. John Poole (Emerald Isle, NC: Posterity Press, August 2001), p. 202.
10. Maj. Scott R. McMichael, "A Historical Perspective on Light Infantry," chapt. 2—The Chinese Communist Forces in Korea, *Research Survey No. 6* (Ft. Leavenworth, KS: Combat Studies Inst., U.S. Army Cmd. & Gen. Staff College, 1987), p. 71.
11. Ibid.
12. Ibid.
13. Douglas Pike, *PAVN: People's Army of Vietnam* (Novato, CA: Presidio Press, 1986), p. 268.
14. *The Tiger's Way,* by Poole, pp. 168-172.
15. M.Gy.Sgt. O'Bday, in conversation with author on 30 August 2019.
16. *Gung Ho,* by Poole, chapt. 10.
17. *German Squad Tactics in WWII,* by Gajkowski, p. 42.
18. *Night Movements*, trans. and preface by C. Burnett (Tokyo: Imperial Japanese Army, 1913; reprint Port Townsend, WA: Loompanics Unlimited, n.d.), p. 66.
19. Ibid., pp. 67, 68.
20. Edward J. Drea, "Nomonhan: Japanese—Soviet Tactical Combat, 1939," *Leavenworth Papers No. 2* (Ft. Leavenworth, KS: Combat Studies Inst., U.S. Army Cmd. & Gen. Staff College, 1981), p. 62.
21. *Night Movements*, trans. and preface by Burnett, pp. 70, 71.
22. Ibid., pp. 72, 73.
23. Ibid., p. 73.
24. *The Bear Went over the Mountain: Soviet Combat Tactics in Afghanistan,* trans. and ed. Lester W. Grau, Foreign Mil. Studies Office, U.S. Dept. of Defense (Originally from the Soviet Union: Frunze Mil. Academy, n.d.; reprint Washington, D.C.: Nat. Defense Univ. Press, 1996), p. 129.
25. S.Sgt. Lee Bergee and PFC Fred Davidson, as quoted in *The Korean War: Pusan to Chosin, An Oral History,* by Donald Knox (San Diego: Harcourt Brace Jovanovich, 1985), pp. 289-291; *The Tiger's Way,* by Poole, p. 291.
26. *Handbook on Japanese Military Forces,* p. 34.

Chapter 9: *Anti-Armor Capabilities*

1. "Finnish Tactics—Small Units," a U.S. Intelligence Report on Finnish Tactics in WWII, *Tactical and Technical Trends,* no. 6, 27 August 1942.

2. *Handbook on Japanese Military Forces*, p. 117.

3. Memorandum for the record by H.J. Poole, while a member of A/1/4.

4. "German Infantry Anti-Tank Tactics 1941/1942: Eastern Front Edition," *Military History Visualized*.

5. *Wikipedia Encyclopedia,* s.v. "Anti-Tank Grenade" and "Panzerwurfmine."

6. *Wikipedia Encyclopedia,* s.v. "Anti-Tank Grenade."

7. "WW2 Men Against Tanks - Training Film 1943 for German Soldiers - Tank Hunters - Männer gegen Panzer," by *Petr Warry,* as retrieved in March 2019 from the following url: https://www.youtube.com/watch?v=eDbFdngVOJk.

8. *Handbook on Japanese Military Forces*, p. 117.

9. Ibid.

10. *Wikipedia Encyclopedia,* s.v. "Anti-Tank Grenade."

11. "Sands of Iwo Jima," Republic Pictures.

12. *Wikipedia Encyclopedia,* s.v. "Anti-Tank Grenade."

13. *Soviet Infantry Tactics in World War II,* with trans., intro., and notes by Sharp, p. 13.

14. *Wikipedia Encyclopedia,* s.v. "Anti-Tank Warfare."

15. "How Did the Chinese Army Defeat the U.S. Tanks and Helicopters During the Korean War," *Quora,* n.d.

16. "Xinhui Presents: Chinese Tank Forces and Battles Before 1949," *Wayback Machine.*

17. Memorandum for the record by H.J. Poole, after two infantry tours in Vietnam.

18. Cooling, "Russia's 1994-96 Campaign for Chechnya."

19. Ibid., p. 62.

20. Gen. Mikhail Surkov, as quoted in "The World Turned Upside Down: Military Lessons of the Chechen War," by Anatol Lieven, *Armed Forces Journal International,* August 1998, pp. 40, 41.

21. "The World Turned Upside Down: Military Lessons of the Chechen War," by Anatol Lieven, *Armed Forces Journal International,* August 1998, p. 61.

22. "N. Korea Claims Test of Laser-Guided Anti-Tank Missile," *Russia Today (RT) News* on line, 2 Mar 2016; "New North Korean Rocket Turns Enemy Tanks into 'Boiled Pumpkin'," *Agence France-Presse,* 27 February 2016.

23. "Don't Mess with Israel," *Israeligal1000,* 9 April 20111, as retrieved in March 2019 from the following url: https://www.youtube.com/watch?v=E5cg57z9100.

24. Maj.Gen. Robert H. Scales, U.S. Army (Ret.), "Infantry and National Priorities," *Armed Forces Journal,* December 2007, pp. 14-17.

Chapter 10: *Roving Ambushes and Fighting Outposts*

1. Memorandum for the record by H.J. Poole, while CO of G/2/5.
2. Ibid., while a member of A/1/4.
3. "Pearl Harbor to Guadalcanal," FMFRP 12-34-I, by Lt.Col. Frank O. Hough, Maj. Verle E. Ludwig, and Henry I. Shaw, Jr., vol. I, *History of the U.S. Marine Corps Operations in World War II Series* (Washington, D.C.: Hist. Branch, HQMC, n.d.; reprint Quantico, VA: Marine Corps Combat Develop. Cmd., 1989), p. 334.
4. *Fighting on Guadalcanal,* FMFRP 12-110, p. 25.
5. Irving Werstein, *Guadalcanal* (New York: Thomas Y. Crowell Co., 1963), p. 150.
6. William H. Bartsch, "Crucial Battle Ignored," *Marine Corps Gazette,* September 1997, pp. 82-84.
7. Maj. Claude R. Sasso, "Soviet Night Operations in World War II," *Leavenworth Papers No. 6* (Ft. Leavenworth, KS: Combat Studies Inst., U.S. Army Cmd. & Gen. Staff College, 1982), p. 35.
8. Memorandum for the record by H.J. Poole, while CO of G/2/5.
9. Ibid., while CO of Hdqts. Company, 27th Marines.
10. *Gung Ho,* by Poole, chapt. 12.
11. Lt.Col. Timothy L. Thomas and Lester W. Grau, "Russian Lessons Learned from the Battles for Grozny," *Marine Corps Gazette,* April 2000, p. 45.
12. *Phantom Soldier,* by Poole, chapt. 12.
13. Thomas and Grau, "Russian Lessons Learned from the Battles for Grozny," p. 46.
14. *Gung Ho,* by Poole, chapt. 14.
15. "The Battle That Helped Change the Course of the 'Israeli' Occupation," *Daily Star* (Lebanon), 6 September 2000.
16. Naomi Segal, Jewish Telegraphic Agency, "IDF Absolved of Blame in Deaths of Naval Commandos in Lebanon," *San Francisco Jewish Community Publication,* 31 October 1997.
17. *The Last Hundred Yards: The NCO's Contribution to Warfare,* by H.J. Poole (Emerald Isle, NC: Posterity Press, 1997), chapt. 16.
18. Shaw et al, *Red Army Resurgent,* p. 167.
19. Memorandum for the record by H.J. Poole, while CO of Hdqts. Company, 27th Marines.

Chapter 11: *Security Patrolling*

1. *German Squad Tactics in WWII,* by Gajkowski, p. 5; *Soviet Infantry Tactics in World War II,* with trans., intro., and notes by Sharp, p. 19.

2. Memorandum for the record by H.J. Poole, after two infantry tours in Vietnam.

3. "The Experimental Chinese Mech Infantry"; *Wikipedia Encyclopedia,* s.v. "Peoples Liberation Army Ground Force"; *Handbook of the Chinese People's Liberation Army,* DDB-2680-32-84, p. A-5.

4. Gordon L. Rottman, *The Rocket Propelled Grenade: Weapon 2* (N.p.: Osprey Publishing, 2010), p. 19, in *Wikipedia Encyclopedia,* s.v. "RPG-2" and "RPG-7."

5. Memorandum for the record by H.J. Poole, after two infantry tours in Vietnam.

6. Edwin P. Hoyt, *The Marine Raiders* (New York: Pocket Books, 1989), p. 129.

7. *German Squad Tactics in WWII,* by Gajkowski, pp. 15, 22.

8. Ibid., p. 15.

9. Ibid.

10. Ibid., p. 9.

11. *Soviet Infantry Tactics in World War II,* with trans., intro., and notes by Sharp, p. 26.

12. Memorandum for the record by H.J. Poole, after visiting Moscow's Armed Forces Museum.

13. *Handbook on German Military Forces*, pp. 109, 113; *Handbook on Japanese Military Forces,* TM 30-480 (1942 ed.), p. 32.

14. *Soviet Infantry Tactics in World War II,* with trans., intro., and notes by Sharp, p. 118.

15. *Handbook of the Chinese People's Liberation Army,* DDB-2680-32-84, p. A-5.

16. Japanese Organisation in WWII"; "WWII Squads."

17. *Handbook on Japanese Military Forces,* TM 30-480 (1942 ed.), p. 34.

18. Michael O'Brien, *Conscripts and Regulars: With the Seventh Battalion in Vietnam* (St. Leonards, Australia: Allen & Unwin, 1995), p. 239.

19. Memorandum for the record by H.J. Poole, while CO of G/2/5.

20. Ibid.

21. *German Squad Tactics in WWII,* by Gajkowski, p. 29.

22. Ibid., p. 20.

23. *Soviet Infantry Tactics in World War II,* with trans., intro., and notes by Sharp, pp. 22, 29.

24. M.Sgt. Lester J. Ford, Jr., USMC (Ret.) [Vietnam-era platoon sergeant], in conversations with author on 7 April 2002, 27 November 2002, and 17 January 2003.

25. 2nd Lt. Karl Metcalf, as quoted in *Conscripts and Regulars,* by O'Brien, p. 199.

26. A.E. Taras and F.D. Zaruz, *Podgotovka Razvegchika: Sistema Spetsnaza GRU* (Minsk, Belarus: AST Publishing, 2002), p. 533.
27. *Wikipedia Encyclopedia,* s.v. "RPG-7.
28. Ibid., "Type 89 Grenade Discharger."
29. Memorandum for the record by H.J. Poole, while CO of G/2/5.
30. Ibid., while a member of A/1/4.
31. *Guardian Joe,* by Poole, chapt. 23.
32. Memorandum for the record by H.J. Poole, while CO of G/2/5.
33. *Strategic Rifleman,* by Poole, pp. 138-147.

Chapter 12: *The Hasty Attack Options*

1. *The Last Hundred Yards,* by Poole, p. 153.
2. Davis, *Marine*, pp. 29. 112.
3. *Soviet Infantry Tactics in World War II,* with trans., intro., and notes by Sharp, p. 26.
4. *Handbook on German Military Forces,* p. 214.
5. *Handbook on Japanese Military Forces,* p. 86.
6. Maj. John L. Zimmerman, *The Guadalcanal Campaign* (Washington, D.C.: Hist. Div., HQMC, 1949), p. 145.
7. Joseph C. Goulden, *Korea: The Untold Story of the War* (New York: Times Books, 1982), p. 295.
8. Nolan, *Operation Buffalo*, pp. 72, 73.
9. *Guardian Joe,* by Poole, chapt. 9.
10. "How a German Squad Attacks a Position (WWII)," *Footage Archive.*
11. Ibid.; *German Squad Tactics in WWII,* by Gajkowski, pp. 14, 20.
12. "How a German Squad Attacks a Position (WWII)," *Footage Archive.*
13. *Handbook on Japanese Military Forces*, p. 91.
14. *Soviet Infantry Tactics in World War II,* with trans., intro., and notes by Sharp, p. 26.
15. Memo for the record by H.J. Poole, after visiting Moscow's Armed Forces Museum.
16. *Soviet Infantry Tactics in World War II,* with trans., intro., and notes by Sharp, pp. 18, 21.
17. Ibid., p. 19.
18. Ibid., p. 20.
19. Memo for the record from H.J. Poole, while CO of G/2/5.
20. McMichael, "A Historical Perspective on Light Infantry," chapt. 2—The Chinese Communist Forces in Korea, *Research Survey No. 6,* p. 59.
21. Truong Chinh, *Primer for Revolt,* intro. Bernard B. Fall (New York: Praeger, 1963), pp. 114-117.

22. *Handbook of the Chinese People's Liberation Army,* DDB-2680-32-84, p. 26.

23. Ibid., p. 27.

24. Nolan, *Operation Buffalo*, pp. 72, 73.

25. Keith William Nolan, *The Magnificent Bastards: The Joint Army-Marine Defense of Dong Ha, 1968* (New York: Ballantine, 2007), p. 137.

26. Hammel, *Chosin,* pp. 55-59; *Phantom Soldier,* by Poole, p. 86.

27. Keith William Nolan, "The Battle of Dai Do," *Leatherneck,* August 1994; Weise, "Memories of Dai Do [a Sequel]," *Marine Corps Gazette,* April 2004.

28. James E. Livingston, Colin D. Heaton, and Anne-Marie Lewis, *Noble Warrior* (Minneapolis: Zenith Press, 2010), p. 93.

29. Gudmundsson, *Stormtroop Tactics,* p. 21.

30. Weise, "Memories of Dai Do [a Sequel]," *Marine Corps Gazette,* April 2004.

31. Ibid.

32. "Pearl Harbor to Guadalcanal," p. 334.

33. Hammel, *Chosin,* p. 71.

34. *Night Movements*, trans. and preface by Burnett, pp. 37-59.

35. Ibid., p. 40.

36. *Soviet Infantry Tactics in World War II,* with trans., intro., and notes by Sharp, p. 16.

37. *German Squad Tactics in WWII,* by Gajkowski, p. 42; *Night Movements*, trans. and preface by Burnett, pp. 72, 73.

Chapter 13: *Urban Offense*

1. *Handbook on German Military Forces*, p. 253; *Wikipedia Encyclopedia,* s.v. "Urban Warfare"; Photo #4—Japanese soldiers involved in street fighting in Shanghai, China in 1937, "World War II: Before the War," by Alan Taylor, *The Atlantic* on line, 19 June 2011.

2. Nora Levin, *The Holocaust* (New York: Thomas Y. Crowell Co., 1968), pp. 343-352.

3. A.J.P. Taylor, *The Second World War – An Illustrated History* (New York: G.P. Putnam's Sons, 1975), p. 146; *The Tiger's Way,* by Poole, chapt. 23; *Guardian Joe,* by Poole, chapt. 24.

4. *Handbook on German Military Forces*, p. 253.

5. Ibid.

6. Ibid.

7. "Japanese infantry use a roadblock as cover during street fighting in Shanghai, China, 1937," *WWII Pictures,* n.d.

8. *Wikipedia Encyclopedia,* s.v. "Battle of Shanghai."

9. Ibid., s.v. "Battle of Singapore."

10. *The Tiger's Way,* by Poole, table 2.2.

11. Thomas M. Huber, "The Battle of Manila" (Ft. Leavenworth, KS: Combat Studies Inst., U.S. Army Cmd. & Gen. Staff College, n.d.), in CSI Home Publications Research MHIST database on line; updated 30 September 2002; cited 1 January 2003]), pp. 11, 12.

12. Lieven, "The World Turned Upside Down," p. 40.

13. *Soviet Tactical Doctrine in WWII,* with foreword by Caza, p. V-121.

14. Ibid.

15. *Soviet Tactical Doctrine in WWII,* with foreword by Caza, pp. V-121, V-122.

16. Ibid., p. V-122.

17. Bogusław Perzyk, *Niemieckie granatniki przeciwpancerne Panzerfaust w Wojsku Polskim 1944-1955,* cz.I (N.p.: Poligon, 2/2011), pp. 56-62, in *Wikipedia Encyclopedia,* s.v. "Panzerfaust."

18. Anthony Beevor, *Berlin: The Downfall 1945* (London and New York: Viking-Penguin Books, 2002), pp. 316-319, in *Wikipedia Encyclopedia,* s.v. "Urban Warfare."

19. Ibid.

20. Shaw et al, *Red Army Resurgent,* p. 161.

21. *Soviet Tactical Doctrine in WWII,* with foreword by Caza, p. V-121.

22. *Wikipedia Encyclopedia,* s.v. "Battle of Shanghai."

23. Nayan Chanda, *Brother Enemy: The War after the War* (New York: Collier Books, 1986), pp. 356, 357.

24. Stephen K. Hayes, *The Ninja and Their Secret Fighting Art* (Rutland, VT: Charles E. Tuttle Company, 1981), p. 18; Dr. HaHa Lung, *Knights of Darkness: Secrets of the World's Deadliest Night Fighters* (Boulder, CO: Paladin Press, 1998), pp. 8, 9.

25. Dung, *Our Great Spring Victory,* p. 51.

26. Lt.Col. Robert W. Lamont, "'Urban Warrior' — A View from North Vietnam," *Marine Corps Gazette,* April 1999, p. 33.

27. Ho Khang, *The Tet Mau Than 1968 Event in South Vietnam* (Hanoi: The Gioi Publishers, 2001), p. 66.

28. Gen. Hoang Van Thai, *How South Vietnam Was Liberated* (Hanoi: The Gioi Publishers, 1996), p. 119.

29. Ibid., p. 235.

30. Ibid., p. 254.

31. Ibid., pp. 237, 238.

32. *Handbook on German Military Forces*, pp. 94, 111.

33. *Handbook on U.S.S.R. Military Forces*, pp. III-11 and III-12.

34. *Soviet Tactical Doctrine in WWII,* with foreword by Caza, p. V-122.

35. Shaw et al, *Red Army Resurgent,* p. 161.

36. Hammel, *Chosin,* pp. 56-59.
37. Lieven, "The World Turned Upside Down," p. 40.

Chapter 14: *Urban Defense*

1. Huber, "The Battle of Manila," p. 15.
2. Ibid.
3. Robert R. Smith, "Triumph in the Philippines," *The War in the Pacific* (Washington, D.C.: U.S. Army Ctr. of Mil. Hist., 1963), p. 308, and Richard Connaughton, John Pimlott, and Duncan Anderson, "The Battle for Manila" (Novato, CA: Presidio Press, 1995), pp. 189-191, and U.S. Army, "37th Div. Report after Action" (Okinawa: Hdqts., 37th Infantry Div., 1945), p. 51, from Huber, "The Battle of Manila," p. 4.
4. Huber, "The Battle of Manila," p. 8.
5. Ibid.
6. Smith, "Triumph in the Philippines," pp. 287-290, from Huber, "The Battle of Manila," p. 10.
7. Huber, "The Battle of Manila," p. 8.
8. U.S. Army, "37th Div. Report after Action" (Okinawa: Hdqts., 37th Infantry Div., 1945), pp. 276-280, and Smith, "Triumph in the Philippines," pp. 280-283, from Huber, "The Battle of Manila," p. 9.
9. Smith, "Triumph in the Philippines," pp. 287-290, from Huber, "The Battle of Manila," p. 10.
10. Richard Connaughton, John Pimlott, and Duncan Anderson, "The Battle for Manila" (Novato, CA: Presidio Press, 1995), pp. 189-191, and U.S. Army, "37th Div. Report after Action," p. 51, and Smith, "Triumph in the Philippines," p. 308, from Huber, "The Battle of Manila," p. 4.
11. Stanley L. Frankel, "The 37th Infantry Div. in World War II (Washington, D.C.: *Infantry Journal Press,* 1948), pp. 276-280, and Smith, "Triumph in the Philippines," pp. 280-283, from Huber, "The Battle of Manila," p. 9.
12. Ibid.
13. Huber, "The Battle of Manila," p. 12.
14. U.S. Army, "37th Div. Report after Action," p. 51, from Huber, "The Battle of Manila," p. 8.
15. Ibid.
16. Frankel, "The 37th Infantry Div. in World War II," pp. 273, 275, and "37th Div. Report after Action," p. 49, from Huber, "The Battle of Manila," p. 8.
17. Huber, "The Battle of Manila," p. 7.
18. Ibid., p. 12.
19. Smith, "Triumph in the Philippines," p. 253, from Huber, "The Battle of Manila," p. 6.

20. Smith, "Triumph in the Philippines," pp. 259-260, and Connaughton et al, "The Battle for Manila," p. 109, and "37th Div. Report after Action," p. 45, and Frankel, "The 37th Infantry Division in World War II," p. 272, from Huber, "The Battle of Manila," p. 7.

21. "Final Attack on Shanghai (1937)," *British Pathe Gazette,* 1937, as retrieved in April 2019 from the following url: https://www.youtube.com/watch?v=02xprjZ2sh4.

22. Lieven, "The World Turned Upside Down," p. 40; *Wikipedia Encyclopedia,* s.v. "Operation Ripper."

23. "The Koreas," ed. Mary E. Connor, *Asia in Focus Series* (Santa Barbara, CA: ABC-CLIO, 2009), p. 45.

24. "Battle of the Barricades: U.S. Marines in the Recapture of Seoul," by Col. Joseph H. Alexander USMC (Ret.), *Marines in the Korean War Commemorative Series* (N.p., n.d.), p. 4.

25. *The Korean War: History and Tactics,* ed. David Rees (New York: Crescent Books, 1984), p. 45.

26. Max Hastings, *The Korean War* (New York: Simon and Schuster, 1987), p. 112.

27. Philip Warner, "Japanese Army of World War II," vol. 20, *Men-at-Arms Series* (London: Osprey Publications Ltd., 1972), pp. 23-25.

28. *The Korean War: History and Tactics,* ed. Reese, p. 45.

29. Ibid.

30. "Battle of the Barricades," by Alexander, p. 13.

31. Ibid., p. 8.

32. Ibid., pp. 10-12.

33. Ibid., p. 28.

34. Ibid., p. 37.

35. U.S. Army, "37th Div. Report after Action," p. 51, from Huber, "The Battle of Manila," p. 8.

36. "Battle of the Barricades," by Alexander, p. 28.

37. Ibid.

38. Ibid., p. 29.

39. Ibid., pp. 32, 33.

40. Ibid., p. 41.

41. Ibid., p. 1.

42. Ibid., p. 25.

43. Unidentified NCOs to Chesty Puller, as quoted in *Fighting on Guadalcanal,* FMFRP 12-110, pp. 35-37.

44. S.Sgt. Lee Bergee, as quoted in *The Korean War: Pusan to Chosin,* by Knox, p. 289.

45. PFC Win Scott, as quoted in *The Korean War: Pusan to Chosin, An Oral History,* by Donald Knox (San Diego: Harcourt Brace Jovanovich, 1985), p. 291.

46. PFC Jack Wright, quoted in *The Korean War: Pusan to Chosin, An Oral History,* by Donald Knox (San Diego: Harcourt Brace Jovanovich, 1985), pp. 292, 293.

47. Ross, *Iwo Jima,* p. 149.

48. PFC Win Scott, as quoted in *The Korean War,* by Knox, p. 293.

49. "Battle of the Barricades," by Alexander. p. 28.

50. Ibid., pp. 22, 27.

51. Eric Hammel, *Fire in the Streets: The Battle for Hue, Tet 1968* (Pacifica, CA: Pacifica Press, 1991), p. 296.

52. George W. Smith, *The Siege at Hue* (New York: Ballantine Publishing, 1999), p. 203.

53. Nicholas Warr, *Phase Line Green: The Battle for Hue, 1968* (Annapolis, MD: Naval Inst. Press, 1997), pp. 155-160.

54. *Phantom Soldier,* by Poole, p. 178.

55. Ibid., p. 194.

56. Anthony Read and David Fisher, *The Fall of Berlin* (New York: Da Capo Press, 1995), p. 385.

57. Editor's footnote, in *From Moscow to Berlin: Marshal Zhukov's Greatest Battles,* by Marshal Georgi K. Zhukov, ed. and intro. by Harrison E. Salisbury, trans. Theodore Shabad, War and Warrior Series (Costa Mesa, CA: The Noontide Press, 1991), pp. 288, 289.

58. Read and Fisher, *The Fall of Berlin,* pp. 387, 388.

59. *The Doomed City of Berlin,* Cities at War Series (Simon & Schuster Video, 1986), 65 min., videocassette #62159-9.

60. Ibid.

61. Ibid.

62. Read and Fisher, *The Fall of Berlin,* p. 385.

63. Field Marshal Georgi K. Zhukov, *From Moscow to Berlin: Marshal Zhukov's Greatest Battles,* ed. and intro. by Harrison E. Salisbury, trans. Theodore Shabad, War and Warrior Series (Costa Mesa, CA: The Noontide Press, 1991), pp. 279, 286.

64. Read and Fisher, *The Fall of Berlin,* p. 411.

65. Ibid., p. 391.

66. Ibid., p. 387.

67. Ibid., pp. 387, 388.

68. *The Last Hundred Yards,* by Poole, p. 272.

69. Read and Fisher, *The Fall of Berlin,* p. 386.

70. *The Doomed City of Berlin,* videocassette #62159-9.

71. Zhukov, *From Moscow to Berlin,* p. 284.

72. *The Doomed City of Berlin,* videocassette #62159-9.

73. Read and Fisher, *The Fall of Berlin,* p. 387.

74. Ibid., p. 396.

75. Ibid., p. 387.

76. Ibid., p. 407.

77. Ibid., p. 393.
78. Ibid., p. 406.
79. Ibid., pp. 393-395.
80. Ibid., p. 415.
81. Ibid., p. 389.
82. Ibid., p. 422.
83. Ibid., pp. 423, 424.
84. Ibid., pp. 449, 450.
85. *The Doomed City of Berlin,* videocassette #62159-9.
86. Zhukov, *From Moscow to Berlin,* p. 288.
87. *The Doomed City of Berlin,* videocassette #62159-9.
88. A.J.P. Taylor, as quoted in *Stormtroop Tactics,* by Gudmundsson, p. 143.
89. Shaw et al, *Red Army Resurgent,* pp. 163-165.
90. Ibid.
91. Ibid., p. 158.
92. William Craig, *Enemy at the Gates* (New York: Penguin Books, 1973), pp. 90, 91, and Antony Beevor, *Stalingrad.* (New York: Viking, 1998), pp. 128, 129, in *Wikipedia Encyclopedia,* s.v. "Vasily Chuikov."
93. Duc Quyen, "Is the Soviet tactic of hugging still relevant in the today's battles," *Quora,* 5 May 2016.
94. Shaw et al, *Red Army Resurgent,* p. 167.
95. Ibid., p. 161.
96. *Global Warrior: Averting WWIII,* by H. John Poole (Emerald Isle, NC: Posterity Press, 2011), appendix A; *Strategic Rifleman,* by Poole, parts four and five.

Chapter 15: *Context in Which to Assess These Findings*

1. *Handbook on Japanese Military Forces,* p. 34.
2. *North Korea's Hidden Assets,* by Poole, chapt. 19.
3. Col. Wesley L. Fox, *Marine Rifleman: Forty-Three Years in the Corps* (Dulles, VA: Brassey's, 2002), pp. 237, 238.

Chapter 16: *Contributions of Other Ordnance / Equipment*

1. A.J.P. Taylor, as quoted in *Stormtroop Tactics,* by Gudmundsson, p. 143.
2. "From Makin to Bougainville," by Hoffman, pp. 5, 19-22.
3. "Organization of the WWII U.S. Army Infantry Rifle Squad," *GI History Handbook.*
4. *Wikipedia Encyclopedia,* s.v. "Volksgrenadier."

5. *Handbook on German Military Forces*, pp. 117, 119.
6. *The Doomed City of Berlin,* videocassette #62159-9.
7. *Handbook on U.S.S.R. Military Forces,* chapt. III, pp. III-11 and III-12.
8. *German Squad Tactics in WWII,* by Gajkowski, pp. 3, 8.
9. Ibid., p. 5.
10. *Wikipedia Encyclopedia,* s.v. "Peoples Volunteer Army."
11. Hammel, *Chosin,* pp. 56-59
12. "Battle of the Barricades." by Alexander, p. 40.
13. "Soldier's Load and the Mobility of a Nation," by S.L.A. Marshall, pp. 69, 70.
14. Memorandum for the record by H.J. Poole, while CO of G/2/5.
15. "From Makin to Bougainville: Marine Raiders in the Pacific War," by Hoffman, p. 18.
16. *The Last Hundred Yards,* by Poole, p. 123.

Chapter 17: *Complying with Infantry Conference Conclusions*

1. James M. Gibson, "Rifled Squads Tailored for Teamwork," *Army Magazine,* May 1956, pp. 33-34, in "The Evolution of the U.S. Army Infantry Squad," by Hughes, p. 6.
2. V. Ney, "Evolution of the U.S. Army Infantry Battalion: 1939-1968" (Washington, D.C.: U.S. Army, 1968), in "The Infantry Squad Part 1," by Raynor.
3. "The Infantry Conference, Report of Committee "B" on Tactics and Techniques (Ft. Benning, GA: The U.S. Army Infantry School, 1946), pp. 5-6, in "The Evolution of the U.S. Army Infantry Squad," by Hughes, p. 6.
4. Robert Dupree and Horace Homesly, Jr., " History of United States Army Squads and Platoons: 1935-1967" (Ft. Benning, GA: Combat Developments Cmd. Infantry Agency, 1967), p. 37, in "The Evolution of the U.S. Army Infantry Squad," by Hughes, p. 7.
5. "The Evolution of the U.S. Army Infantry Squad," by Hughes, in "The Infantry Squad Part 2," by Raynor.
6. "Development of the Squad: Historical Analysis," by Hashim, pp. 26, 27.
7. Ibid., p. 36.
8. "The Evolution of the U.S. Army Infantry Squad," by Hughes, p. 39.
9. Ibid., p. 36.
10. Alexander, *Edson's Raiders,* pp. 242, 243.
11. T.X. Hamme, "Rethinking the Rifle Squad," *Marine Corps Gazette,* July 1984.

12. "Development of the Squad: Historical Analysis," by Hashim, pp. 25, 26.
13. Ferdinand Otto Miksche, *Attack: A Study of Blitzkrieg Tactics* (New York: Random House, 1942), p. 148.
14. Ibid.
15. Ibid.
16. "Development of the Squad: Historical Analysis," by Hashim, p. 36.
17. Truong Chinh, *Primer for Revolt*, pp. 114-117.

Chapter 18: *Reducing Foe Firepower Through Maneuver*

1. "How a German Squad Attacks a Position (WWII)," *Footage Archive"; Soviet Infantry Tactics in World War II,* with trans., intro., and notes by Sharp, pp. 18, 21.
2. Yahara, *The Battle for Okinawa,* p. 228.
3. "How a German Squad Attacks a Position (WWII)," *Footage Archive"; German Squad Tactics in WWII,* by Gajkowski, p. 20.
4. *Soviet Infantry Tactics in World War II,* with trans., intro., and notes by Sharp, p. 20.
5. *German Squad Tactics in WWII,* by Gajkowski, pp. 3, 8.
6. *Handbook on Japanese Military Forces*, p. 91.
7. *Soviet Infantry Tactics in World War II,* with trans., intro., and notes by Sharp, p. 26.
8. "German Infantry Anti-Tank Tactics 1941/1942: Eastern Front Edition," *Military History Visualized.*
9. *Soviet Infantry Tactics in World War II,* with trans., intro., and notes by Sharp, p. 13.
10. *Handbook on Japanese Military Forces,* p. 86.
11. *Wikipedia Encyclopedia,* s.v. "National Revolutionary Army."
12. Xiaobing Li, *China's Battle for Korea*, pp. xxv-xxvi.
13. "Secret Manual Gives Glimpse of North Korean Military Tactics," by Steve Herman, *Voice of America* on line, 18 September 2010.
14. *Gung Ho,* by Poole, chapt. 5.
15. Anthony Beevor, *Berlin: The Downfall 1945* (London and New York: Viking-Penguin Books, 2002), pp. 316-319, in *Wikipedia Encyclopedia,* s.v. "Urban Warfare."
16. *Handbook on German Military Forces*, p. 253.
17. Smith, "Triumph in the Philippines," pp. 287-290, from Huber, "The Battle of Manila," p. 10.
18. Lieven, "The World Turned Upside Down," p. 40.

Chapter 19: *Double-Envelopment of a Small Target*

1. "Isolation of Rabaul," by Henry I. Shaw and Maj. Douglas T. Kane, *History of U.S. Marine Corps Operations in World War II Series*, vol. II. Washington, D.C.: Historical Branch, HQMC, 1963, chapt. 2—Elkton Underway, p. 76.
2. Ibid., part II, chapt. 4—The Dragon's Peninsula Campaign, pp. 130-145.
3. "Okinawa: Victory in the Pacific," by Maj. Chas. S. Nichols, Jr. USMC, and Henry I. Shaw, Jr., *USMC Historical Monograph* (Washington, D.C.: Historical Branch, HQMC, 1955. p. 183; *Gung Ho,* Poole, p. 139.
4. *Gung Ho,* by Poole, pp. 110-114, 141-145.
5. "Okinawa: Victory in the Pacific," by Nichols and Shaw, p. 255.
6. "Battle of the Barricades," by Alexander, p. 39.
7. *Handbook on Japanese Military Forces,* p. 86.
8. *Handbook on German Military Forces,* p. 214.
9. *The Bear Went over the Mountain,* trans. and ed. by Grau, p. 132; Glantz, *The Soviet Conduct of Tactical Maneuver,* p. 54.
10. Erich Ludendorff, *The General Staff and Its Problems,* two vols., trans. F.A. Holt (New York: Dutton, 1934), 1.324, in Lupfer, "The Dynamics of Doctrine," *Leavenworth Papers No. 4,* p. 44.
11. "Zulu and Zulu Wars," in *Reader's Companion to Military History* (Boston, MA: Houghton Mifflin, College Division, n.d.).
12. *Wikipedia Encyclopedia,* s.v. "Battle of Isandlwana."
13. *Terrorist Trail: Backtracking the Foreign Fighter,* by H. John Poole (Emerald Isle, NC: Posterity Press, 2006), chapt. 7.
14. "Zulu," Platinum Disc Corp., 2000, 139 min., videocassette.
15. "Battle Stack: The Battle of Rorke's Drift Tactics," as retrieved in June 2019 from the following url: https://www.youtube.com/watch?v=7B9dRpWMp80.
16. *Terrorist Trail,* by Poole, chapt. 7.
17. "Battle Stack: The Battle of Rorke's Drift Tactics."
18. Ibid.
19. *Terrorist Trail,* by Poole,, p. 109.
20. *Wikipedia Encyclopedia,* s.v. "Smokeless Powder."
21. "Zulu and Zulu Wars," in *Reader's Companion to Military History.*
22. *Soviet Infantry Tactics in World War II,* with trans., intro., and notes by Sharp, p. 20.
23. "Zulu," videocassette #02863.
24. "Scouting in South Africa, 1884-1890," as extracted from *Scouting with Baden-Powell,* by Russell Freedman (New York: Holiday House, 1967).
25. *Wikipedia Encyclopedia,* s.v. "Battle of Chochiwon."

26. Ibid.
27. Nolan, *Operation Buffalo.*

Chapter 20: *Tactical Encirclements*

1. *100 Strategies of War,* trans. Yeo Ai Hoon, p. 17.
2. Michael Lee Lanning and Dan Cragg, *Inside the VC and the NVA: The Real Story of North Vietnam's Armed Forces* (New York: Ivy Books, 1992), pp. 206-208.
3. *Handbook on Japanese Military Forces,* p. 86.
4. Drea, "Nomonhan: Japanese—Soviet Tactical Combat, 1939," p. 19.
5. *Handbook on Japanese Military Forces,* p. 86.
6. *Soviet Tactical Doctrine in WWII,* with foreword by Caza, p. V-19.
7. George Robert Elford, *Devil's Guard* (New York: Dell Publishing, 1971), p. 101.
8. Gens. Vo Nguyen Giap and Van Tien Dung, *How We Won the War* (Philadelphia, PA: Recon Publications, 1976), pp. 52-54.
9. *Gung Ho,* by Poole, p. 140.
10. McMichael, "A Historical Perspective on Light Infantry," chapt. 2—The Chinese Communist Forces in Korea, *Research Survey No. 6,* p. 71.
11. Gen. Vo Nguyen Giap, *Dien Bien Phu,* 6th ed. supplemented (Hanoi: The Gioi Publishers, 1999), p. 121.
12. *The Battle of Dien Bien Phu,* Visions of War Series, vol. 10 (New Star Video, 1988), 50 min., videocassette #4010.
13. Ibid.
14. M.Gy.Sgt. O'Bday, in conversations with author in November 2018.
15. *The Battle of Dien Bien Phu,* videocassette #4010.
16. M.Gy.Sgt. O'Bday, in conversations with author in November 2018.
17. Soviet Infantry Tactics in World War II, with trans., intro., and notes by Sharp, p. 26.
18. *Handbook on German Military Forces,* p. 214.
19. *Phantom Soldier,* by Poole, chapt. 9.
20. Ibid.
21. Nolan, *Operation Buffalo,* p. 77.
22. *Phantom Soldier,* by Poole, chapt. 9.
23. Alvin D. Coox, *Nomonhan: Japan against Russia, 1939* (Stanford, CA: Stanford Univ. Press, 1985), p. 999; Sasso, "Soviet Night Operations in World War II," pp. 14, 15; *Soviet Tactical Doctrine in WWII,* with foreword by Caza, p. V-2; *The Bear Went over the Mountain,* trans. and ed. by Grau, p. 18.

24. Glantz, "August Storm," *Leavenworth Papers No. 8,* pp. 60-70.

25. *The Bear Went over the Mountain,* trans. and ed. by Grau, pp. 45, 46.

26. Maj.Gen. Hoang Min Thao, *The Victorious Tay Nguyen Campaign* (Hanoi: Foreign Languages Publishing House, 1979), p. 132.

Chapter 21: *Probing and Dissection Attacks*

1. *Soviet Tactical Doctrine in WWII,* with foreword by Caza, p. V-19.

2. Ibid., V-39, V-43.

3. *British Official History 1918,* vol 1. (N.p., n.d.), p. 166, in Lupfer, "The Dynamics of Doctrine," *Leavenworth Papers No. 4,* p. 50.

4. Ludendorff, *The General Staff and Its Problems*, 1.324, in Lupfer, "The Dynamics of Doctrine," *Leavenworth Papers No. 4,* p. 44.

5. *World War II History Info., s.v.* "The Marines on Guadalcanal," as retrieved in June 2019 from the following url: http://www.worldwar2history.info/Guadalcanal/Marines.html.

6. "The Defense of Henderson Field, Guadalcanal," by Brian A. Filler, *thesis,* Marine Corps Cmd. and Staff College, n.d.

7. "Pacific Odyssey: Guadalcanal and Bloody Ridge, Solomon Islands," by Matthew Stevenson, *Counterpunch.org.*

8. *Fighting on Guadalcanal,* FMFRP 12-110, p. 18.

9. Ibid., p. 22.

10. "Frozen Chosin: U.S. Marines at the Changjin Reservoir," by B.Gen. Edwin H. Simmons USMC (Ret.), *official document,* PCN 19000410000_3.pdf (N.p., November 2002).

11. Hammel, *Chosin,* p. 87.

12. Montross and Canzona, "The Chosin Reservoir Campaign," pp. 87, 88.

13. Ibid.

14. Maj. Don H. Campbell USMC (Ret.) [platoon sergeant during Korean hill battles of 1952-53], in conversation with author on 26 March 2001.

15. Hammel, *Chosin,* p. 71.

16. Montross and Canzona, "The Chosin Reservoir Campaign," pp. 87-89.

17. Hammel, *Chosin,* pp. 89, 90.

18. Ibid., p. 68.

19. Weise, "Memories of Dai Do [a Sequel]."

20. Kelley Navy Cross citation, as retrieved from the Assoc. of 3rd Battalion, 4th Marines website.

21. Erich Ludendorff, *The General Staff and Its Problems,* 1.324 in "The Dynamics of Doctrine," by Lupfer, *Leavenworth Papers No. 4,* p. 44.

22. *Soviet Tactical Doctrine in WWII,* with foreword by Caza, p. V-19.

23. *Handbook on German Military Forces*, p. 253.

24. *Handbook on the Chinese Communist Army,* DA Pamphlet 30-51, pp. 23, 24.

25. Giap and Dung, *How We Won the War*, pp. 52-54.

Chapter 22: *Spearpoint and "Button-Hook" Attacks*

1. *1914-1918 Online,* s.v. "Stormtrooper," as retrieved in May 2019 from the following url: https://encyclopedia.1914-1918-online.net/article/stormtrooper.

2. Gudmundsson, *Stormtroop Tactics,* p. 88.

3. *The Infantry Rifle Platoon and Squad,* FM 3-21.8 (Washington, D.C.: Hdqts. Dept. of the Army), section IX, chapt. 7, "Attacking Fortified Positions," par. 7-233, as retrieved in May 2019 from this url: http://www.infantrydrills.com/fm-3-21-8-chapter-7-section-ix-attacking-fortified-positions/.

4. Col. G.C. Thomas USMC, Maj.Gen. Vandegriff's Chief of Staff, as quoted in *Fighting on Guadalcanal,* FMFRP 12-110, p. 64.

5. *North Korea's Hidden Assets,* by Poole, chapt. 15.

6. "1/4 After-Action Report for May 1967"; CWO-4 Guthrie, e-mail to author on 26 March 2012.

7. "1/4 Intelligence Summary for 7-8 May 1967," as retrieved from the 1/4 Assoc. website.

8. *Wikipedia Encyclopedia,* s.v. "Stormtrooper."

9. Steve Hohenstein, an ambush squad member, in written recollections for CWO-4 Guthrie, as relayed by e-mail to the author in the Fall of 2011.

10. *U.S. Marines in Vietnam: Fighting the North Vietnamese 1967,* by Tefler, Rogers, and Fleming, pp. 33-35.

11. Capt. Patrick J. McDonnell, 4th Platoon Amtrac leader, in written recollection "Hill of Angels—My 1967," at official 1st Amtrac Battalion website (Amtrac.org), s.v. "1st Amtrac Battalion History" and "Bravo Company Arrives First."

12. *Gung Ho,* by Poole, pp. 222, 223.

13. David M. Glantz, *The Soviet Conduct of Tactical Maneuver: Spearhead of the Offensive* (London: Frank Cass, 1991), p. 54.

14. Ibid., p. 17.

15. Glantz, "August Storm," *Leavenworth Papers No. 8,* p. 170.

16. Glantz, *The Soviet Conduct of Tactical Maneuver,* p. 25.
17. Montross and Canzona, "The Chosin Reservoir Campaign," p. 163.

Chapter 23: *Inside-Out Attacks After Sneaking to the Middle*

1. *Phantom Soldier,* by Poole, p. 37.
2. *100 Strategies of War,* trans. Yeo Ai Hoon, p. 17.
3. *The Art of War,* by Sun Tzu, trans. Lionel Giles (N.p., n.d.).
4. Ibid.
5. Ibid.
6. Ibid.
7. Ibid.
8. *Phantom Soldier,* by Poole, p. 150.
9. Lamont, "'Urban Warrior' – A View from North Vietnam," p. 33.
10. Hammel, *Fire in the Streets,* p. 29.
11. Smith, *The Siege at Hue,* p. 171.
12. *U.S. Marines in Vietnam: The Defining Year, 1968,* by Lt.Col. Jack Shulimson et al (Washington, D.C. Hist. and Museums Div., HQMC, 1997), pp. 164-167.
13. Smith, *The Siege at Hue,* p. 31.
14. Hammel, *Chosin,* pp. 89, 90.
15. Ibid., p. 68.
16. Ibid.
17. Ibid., pp. 55-59.
18. Ibid., pp. 56-59.
19. Ibid., p. 100.
20. *Phantom Soldier,* by Poole, pp. 145-149.
21. Memorandum for the record by H.J. Poole, after two infantry tours in Vietnam.
22. CWO-4 Guthrie, in e-mail to the author during December 2011.
23. Michael S. Smith, *Bloody Ridge: The Battle That Saved Guadalcanal* (Novato, CA: Presidio Press, 2000), pp. 175–176; *Wikipedia Encyclopedia,* s.v. "Battle of Edson's Ridge."
24. "First Offensive: The Marine Campaign for Guadalcanal," by Shaw, p. 25; *Jungle Warfare,* FMFRP 12-9, p. 41.

Chapter 24: *Subterranean Tactics*

1. Dr. HaHa Lung, *Knights of Darkness: Secrets of the World's Deadliest Night Fighters* (Boulder, CO: Paladin Press, 1998), p. 112.

2. Memorandum for the record by H.J. Poole, while on a trip to China around 2002.

3. Still frame from *A Tribute to WWII Combat Cameramen of Japan* (Tokyo: Nippon TV, 1995), 85 min., videocassette, in *Phantom Soldier,* by Poole, p. 79.

4. *Phantom Soldier,* by Poole, pp. 81, 82.

5. Ibid., p. 82.

6. *Handbook on Japanese Military Forces,* p. 117.

7. Yahara, The Battle for Okinawa, p. 60.

8. *Wikipedia Encyclopedia,* s.v. "Germany-Japan Relations."

9. *Mao's Generals Remember Korea,* trans. and ed. by Xiaobing Li, Allan R. Millett, and Bin Yu (Lawrence, KS: Univ. Press of Kansas, 2001), p. 154.

10. Ibid.

11. Ibid., p. 168.

12. Lung, *Knights of Darkness,* p. 112.

13. Ibid., p. 27.

14. Levin, *The Holocaust,* p. 346.

Chapter 25: *Motti Attacks*

1. "Finnish Tactics—Small Units," a U.S. Intelligence Report on Finnish Tactics in WWII, *Tactical and Technical Trends,* no. 6, 27 August 1942.

2. *Warfare in the Far North,* DA Pamphlet 20-292 (Washington, D.C.: Hdqts. Dept. of the Army, n.d.), pp. 18, 19; *Wikipedia Encyclopedia,* s.v. "Salients, e-entrants and pockets."

3. "Finnish Tactics—Small Units."

4. *Warfare in the Far North,* DA Pamphlet 20-292, p. 65.

5. Jenkki Soturi [U.S. Marine veteran of Vietnam and student of Finnish tactics], in a letter to author of 7 November 2001.

6. "Finnish Tactics—Small Units."

7. *Warfare in the Far North,* DA Pamphlet 20-292, pp. 18, 19.

8. "Motti Tactics," *Combat Forces Journal,* January 1950, pp. 10, 11.

9. Ibid., pp. 12, 13.

10. "Finnish Tactics—Small Units."

11. *Soviet Tactical Doctrine in WWII,* with foreword by Caza, p. V-121.

12. "Kiinalainen [Chosin] Motti: The Chinese Encirclement," *Changjin Journal,* 1 August 2002.

13. Ibid.

14. Ibid.

15. Hammel, *Chosin,* pp. 71, 72.

16. "Kiinalainen [Chosin] Motti: The Chinese Encirclement."
17. Ibid.
18. Ibid.
19. Ibid.
20. Ibid.
21. Nolan, *Operation Buffalo.*
22. *Mountain Warfare,* FM 3-97.6 (Washington, D.C.: Hdqts. Dept. of the Army, November 2000), p. 4-23.
23. Duc Quyen, "Is the Soviet tactic of hugging still relevant in the today's battles."
24. Ibid.

Chapter 26: *Swarm Attacks*

1. "Swarming and the Future of Warfare," by Sean J. A. Edwards, dissertation, The Pardee RAND Graduate School, 2005, in "Soldier Swarm: New Ground Tactics for the Era of Multi-Domain Battle," by Justin Lynch and Lauren Fish, Modern War Inst. at West Point, 5 April 2018.
2. "Soldier Swarm: New Ground Tactics for the Era of Multi-Domain Battle," by Justin Lynch and Lauren Fish, Modern War Inst. at West Point, 5 April 2018.
3. *Wikipedia Encyclopedia,* s.v, "Swarming (military)."
4. Hammel, *Chosin,* pp. 64, 65.
5. Montross and Canzona, "The Chosin Reservoir Campaign," pp. 87, 88.
6. Ibid., p. 89.
7. Ibid., p. 168.
8. Ibid.
9. *Wikipedia Encyclopedia,* s.v, "Swarming (military)."
10. "Swarming and the Future of Warfare," by Edwards.
11. A.J.P. Taylor, as quoted in *Stormtroop Tactics,* by Gudmundsson, p. 143.
12. Cooling, "Russia's 1994-96 Campaign for Chechnya," p. 60.
13. Lieven, "The World Turned Upside Down," p. 42.
14. Cooling, "Russia's 1994-96 Campaign for Chechnya," p. 62.
15. Thomas and Grau, "Russian Lessons Learned from the Battles for Grozny," p. 45.
16. Ibid., p. 46.
17. Ibid., pp. 45, 46.
18. *Gung Ho,* by Poole, pp. 17-19.
19. "Soldier Swarm: New Ground Tactics for the Era of Multi-Domain Battle," by Lynch and Fish.

20. Ibid.
21. General Mark A. Milley, as quoted in "Soldier Swarm: New Ground Tactics for the Era of Multi-Domain Battle," by Lynch and Fish.
22. *Wikipedia Encyclopedia,* s.v. "Minutemen."
23. *Soviet Tactical Doctrine in WWII,* with foreword by Caza, p. V-19.
24. "First Offensive: The Marine Campaign for Guadalcanal," by Shaw.
25. Hammel, *Chosin,* p. 100.
26. Ibid., p. 64.
27. Ibid., pp. 68-72.
28. Truong Chinh, *Primer for Revolt,* pp. 114-117.
29. John Wukovits, *American Commando* (New York: New American Library, 2009), p. 213.
30. Geoffrey Perret, "Warrior Mao," *MHQ: The Quarterly Journal of Military History,* issue 19, no. 3, Spring 2007, p. 6, in *American Commando,* by Wukovits, pp. 10, 11,
31. "Xinhui Presents: Chinese Tank Forces and Battles Before 1949," *Wayback Machine.*

Chapter 27: The *Squad's Role in "Hugging" Tactics*

1. Davis, *Marine,* pp. 159-162.
2. *Handbook on Japanese Military Forces,* p. 98.
3. Davis, *Marine*, p. 140; *Fighting on Guadalcanal,* FMFRP 12-110, p. 2.
4. MoH citation for John Basilone, in *Wikipedia Encyclopedia,* s.v. "John Basilone."
5. "Battle for Henderson Field," *History Net,* n.d.
6. *Phantom Soldier,* by Poole, p. 93.
7. Hammel, *Chosin*, p. 99.
8. Ibid., pp. 64, 65.
9. Ibid., pp. 56-59.
10. Ibid., pp. 71, 72.
11. Montross and Canzona, "The Chosin Reservoir Campaign," p. 168.
12. Hammel, *Chosin,* p. 88.
13. Ibid., pp. 56-59.
14. Goulden, *Korea: The Untold Story of the War,* p. 358.
15. Hammel, *Chosin,* p. 88.
16. Ibid., pp. 99, 100.
17. Ibid., p. 88.

18. Montross and Canzona, "The Chosin Reservoir Campaign," p. 168.

19. "Platoon," MGM, 1986, videocassette, 119 min.

20. Montross and Canzone, "The Chosin Reservoir Campaign," p. 163.

21. *Handbook on the Chinese Communist Army,* DA Pamphlet 30-51, pp. 23, 24.

22. Montross and Canzone, "The Chosin Reservoir Campaign," p. 174.

Chapter 28: The *Counterattacking After a Tactical Withdrawal*

1. *Soviet Infantry Tactics in World War II,* with trans., intro., and notes by Sharp, p. 77.
2. *Gung Ho,* by Poole, p. 133.
3. *Mao's Generals Remember Korea,* p. 154.
4. *Handbook on German Military Forces*, p. 253.
5. "Japanese infantry use a roadblock as cover during street fighting in Shanghai, China, 1937," *WWII Pictures,* n.d.
6. *Soviet Tactical Doctrine in WWII,* with foreword by Caza, p. V-27.
7. Yahara, *The Battle for Okinawa,* pp. 36, 213.
8. *Mao's Generals Remember Korea,* p. 154.
9. *Soviet Tactical Doctrine in WWII,* with foreword by Caza, p. V-25.
10. Ibid.
11. *Soviet Infantry Tactics in World War II,* with trans., intro., and notes by Sharp, p. 77.
12. *Soviet Tactical Doctrine in WWII,* with foreword by Caza, p. V-26.
13. Ibid.
14. Ibid.
15. "Battle of the Barricades," by Alexander, pp. 210, 211.
16. Ibid.
17. Ibid., pp. 32, 33.
18. Ibid., p. 41.

Chapter 29: *The Final Requirement for Top Squad Performance*

1. "Soldier Swarm: New Ground Tactics for the Era of Multi-Domain Battle," by Lynch and Fish.
2. William S. Lind, in Foreword of *One More Bridge to Cross,* by H. John Poole (Emerald Isle, NC: Posterity Press, 1998).

3. *Gung Ho,* by Poole, parts one and two.

4. "Command Philosophy," by Capt. James A. Letexier, Medical Service Corps, USN, 1st Medical Bn, 1st Marine Logistics Group, n.d.

5. S.Sgt. Chris Ronin, in conversation with author of 16 July 2019.

6. Ibid.

7. *The Last Hundred Yards*, by Poole, pp. 183-200.

Epilogue

1. Col. David H. Hackworth U.S. Army (Ret.) and Julie Sherman, *About Face* (New York: Simon & Schuster, 1989), p. 594.

2. *The Encyclopedia of the Korean War,* s.v. "Meatgrinder (maneuver)."

3. *Mao Tse-tung: An Anthology of His Writings,* ed. Anne Fremantle (New York: Mentor, 1962), pp. 132, 133; Truong Chinh, *Primer for Revolt,* intro. Fall, pp. 114-117.

Glossary

AAA	Anti-Aircraft Artillery	Guns to shoot down planes.
AEF	Allied Expeditionary Forces	Anti-Axis forces in WWI.
AK47	Soviet Weapon Designator	Communist bloc assault rifle.
AN/M2	U.S. Weapon Designator	Aircraft-mounted machinegun
ARVN	Army of the Republic of Vietnam	South Vietnamese ground forces during Vietnam War.
AT-4	U.S. Weapon Designator	Shoulder-fired antitank wpn.
AW	Automatic Weapons	Rapid-firing small arms.
B-40	Soviet Weapon Designator	RPG.
BAR	Browning Automatic Rifle	Heavy repeating rifle used mostly in WWII.
BMP	Soviet Vehicle Designator	Amphibious tracked infantry fighting vehicle.
BOF	Base of Fire	Support element that provides covering fire during an infantry assault.
C-4	U.S. Explosive Designator	Plastic detonative matter.
C-47	U.S. Aircraft Designator	"Skytrain/Dakota" developed from a Douglas DC-3 transport plane and then reconfigured to drop illumination flares as "Puff the Magic Dragon."

CCF	Chinese Communist Forces	Same as PVA in Korea.
CP	Command Post	Location of unit commander.
CWO-4	Chief Warrant Officer Fourth Class	Intermediate rank between officer and enlisted.
DA	Department of the Army	Pentagon agency for extended ground combat.
DIA	Defense Intelligence Agency	U.S. information bureau on alien foes.
DMZ	Demilitarized Zone	No-mans land between countries.
DoD	Department of Defense	Headquarters for all U.S. military services.
E&E	Escape and Evasion	Art of dodging a pursuer.
F1	French Weapon Designator	WWI fragmentation grenade.
FAS	Federation of American Scientists	Association of professional U.S. researchers.
FDC	Fire Direction Center	Where indirect-fire missions are processed.
1/4	1st Battalion, 4th Marines	Marine infantry outfit.
1/7	1st Battalion, 7th Marines	Marine infantry outfit.
1/9	1st Battalion, 9th Marines	Marine infantry outfit.
FM	Field Manual	U.S. Army publication.
4GW	4th Generation Warfare	War waged in four arenas at once—martial, religious/psychological, economic, and political.
GI	Government Issue	Colloquial term for low-ranking member of U.S. Armed Forces.

GPS	Global Positioning System	Device that resects satellite signals to determine location.
GW	Guerrilla Warfare	UW carried out by tiny contingents of insurgents.
H	Hours	Measure of time.
H&I	Harassing and Interdiction	Type of indirect-fire barrage of limited duration.
HQMC	Headquarters Marine Corps	Highest echelon of USMC.
IA	Immediate Action	Type of small-unit tactical drill.
IED	Improvised explosive device	Remotely detonated land mine.
IJA	Imperial Japanese Army	Nipponese ground forces in WWII.
IRGC	Iranian Revolutionary Guard Corps	Iranian commandos.
LMG	Light Machinegun	Limited-weight machinegun.
KMT	Kuomintang	Nationalist Party of China.
LP	Listening Post	Nighttime observation post.
LPO	Soviet Weapon Designator	Flame thrower used by foe in the Vietnam War.
LVT	Landing Vehicle Tracked	Amphibious transport.
LVTH	Landing Vehicle Tracked (with) Howitzer	Amphibious platform carrying indirect-fire gun.
M1	U.S. Weapon Designator	Garand rifle and semi-automatic carbine of WWII.
M2	U.S. Weapon Designator	Identifier assigned to many WWII-era weapons, to include a 60mm mortar.

M7	U.S. Weapon Designator	Grenade launcher for M1 rifle
M14	U.S. Weapon Designator	Semi-automatic rifle of Vietnam-era.
M15	German Weapon Designator	Concussion grenade in WWI (*stielhandgranate)*.
M16A1	U.S. Weapon Designator	Assault rifle known for jamming when dirty.
M1903	U.S. Weapon Designator	Springfield rifle of WWI.
M1918A2	U.S. Weapon Designator	Identifier assigned to many WWII-era weapons, to include a BAR.
M1919A4	U.S. Weapon Designator	Identifier assigned to many WWII-era weapons, to include a rifle sight.
M27	U.S. Weapon Designator	Infantry automatic rifle
M32	U.S. Weapon Designator	Hand-held multiple grenade launcher.
M38	U.S. Weapon Designator	Marksman rifle.
M-42	U.S. Weapon Designator	Army self-propelled 40mm anti-aircraft gun.
M60	U.S. Weapon Designator	Light machinegun.
M79	U.S. Weapon Designator	Grenade launcher in Vietnam
M249	U.S. Weapon Designator	SAW.
M320	U.S. Weapon Designator	Single-shot grenade launcher.
MAAWS	Multi-Role Anti-Armor Anti-Personnel Weapons System	New bunker buster capable of anti-armor and limited anti-aircraft missions
MANPADS	Man-portable air-defense systems	Shoulder-fired antiaircraft missile for low-flying targets.

MARSOC	Marine Special Operations	USMC commando hdqts.
MCI	Marine Corps Institute	USMC educational materials.
MG	Machinegun	Fully automatic small arm.
MG08/15	German Weapon Designator	Light machinegun of WWI.
MG34	German Weapon Designator	Light machinegun of WWII.
MK1	U.S. Weapon Designator	WWI fragmentation grenade.
MK2	U.S. Weapon Designator	WWI fragmentation grenade.
MK3A2	U.S. Weapon Designator	Concussion grenade in WWII.
MKIII	U.S. Weapon Designator	Improvised cardboard concussion grenade of WWI.
MLR	Main Line of Resistance	Linear formation of defensive positions.
MM	Millimeter	Measure of width.
MoH	Medal of Honor	Highest U.S. award for valor.
MP18	German Weapon Designator	Berman submachinegun used in WWI.
MW	Maneuver Warfare	Way of fighting where tactical surprise replaces firepower.
NATO	North Atlantic Treaty Organization	Western military alliance.
NCO	Non-Commissioned Officer	Lower-echelon enlisted leader
NKPA	North Korean Peoples Army	Pyongyang-directed ground forces.
NVA	North Vietnamese Army	Hanoi-directed ground forces.
ONTOS	U.S. Weapon Designator	Six 106mm recoilless rifles mounted on a tracked vehicle.

PAVN	Peoples Army of Vietnam	Communist ground forces after the Vietnam War.
PFC	Private First Class	Lower echelon enlisted rank.
PLA	Peoples Liberation Army	Ground forces of Communist China.
POW	Prisoner of War	Captured combatant.
PPSh-41	Soviet Weapons Designator	Submachinegun carried by PVA soldiers in the Korean War.
PRC	Peoples Republic of China	Communist China.
PT	Physical Training	Bodily exercise.
PVA	Peoples Volunteer Army	Same as CCF in Korea.
RCT	Regimental Combat Team	Reinforced infantry regiment.
ROAD	Reorganization Objective Army Divisions	U.S. Army restructuring initiative.
RPD	Soviet Weapon Designator	Light machinegun with bipod used by foe in Vietnam War.
RPG	Rocket Propelled Grenade	Personal antitank weapon.
S/A	Small Arms	Small-caliber weaponry.
SA-7	Soviet Weapon Designator	Anti-aircraft missile.
SAW	Squad Automatic Weapon	Rapid-firing machine rifle.
2/4	2nd Battalion, 4th Marines	Marine infantry outfit.
2/5	2nd Battalion, 5th Marines	Marine infantry outfit.
2/7	2nd Battalion, 7th Marines	Marine infantry outfit.
2GW	2nd Generation Warfare	Focus is on killing enemy personnel, same as traditional U.S. style (attrition warfare).

SKS	Soviet Weapons Designator	Single-shot rifle used by Communists in Vietnam War.
SMAW	Shoulder-Launched Multipurpose Assault Weapon	Bunker buster.
SNCO	Staff Non-Commissioned Officer	Higher-echelon enlisted leader.
SOCOM	Special Operations Command	America's overall commando headquarters.
T-34	Soviet Weapon Designator	WWII-era tank.
TAOR	Tactical Area of Responsibility	Assigned area over which a military unit is supposed to maintain control.
T&E	Traversing and Elevating	Steadying and aiming mechanism for either a machinegun or mortar.
3/4	3rd Battalion, 4th Marines	Marine infantry outfit.
3/5	3rd Battalion, 5th Marines	Marine infantry outfit.
3GW	3rd Generation Warfare	Focuses on bypassing foe's strongpoints to more easily attack his strategically vital assets.
TNT	Trinitrotoluene	Explosive used for satchel charges in Vietnam.
TOE	Table of Organization and Equipment	Assigned staffing and gear for military units.
U.N.	United Nations	Worldwide alliance of countries.
U.S.	United States	America.
USMC	U.S. Marine Corps	America's amphibious landing force in readiness.

USSR	Union of Soviet Socialist Republics	Communist bloc of countries until 1991.
UW	Unconventional Warfare	Attack by infiltration and defense by ambush; consists mainly of GW, sabotage, intel. gathering, evading pursuit.
VC	Viet Cong	NVA-advised guerrilla enemy during the Vietnam Conflict.
WERM	Width = Range x Mils	Distance estimation formula.
YD	Yard	Codified indicator of location along the McNamara Line in Vietnam
WWI	World War I	First global conflict.
WWII	World War II	Second global conflict.

Bibliography

U.S. Government Publications and News Releases

"Battle of the Barricades: U.S. Marines in the Recapture of Seoul." By Col. Joseph H. Alexander USMC (Ret.). *Marines in the Korean War Commemorative Series.* N.p: n.d. As retrieved in April 2019 from the following url: http://www.koreanwar2.org/kwp2/usmckorea/PDF_Monographs/KoreanWar.Battle-Barricades.pdf.

The Bear Went over the Mountain: Soviet Combat Tactics in Afghanistan. Translated and edited by Lester W. Grau. Foreign Military Studies Office. U.S. Department of Defense. Originally from the Soviet Union: Frunze Military Academy, n.d. Reprint Washington, D.C.: National Defense University Press, 1996.

"Command Philosophy." By Capt. James A. Letexier, Medical Service Corps, USN. 1st Medical Battalion, 1st Marine Logistics Group, n.d. As retrieved in June 2019 from the following url: https://www.1stmlg.marines.mil/Portals/123/Docs/Medical%20Bn/COMMAND%20PHILOSOPHY[1].pdf.

"The Defense of Henderson Field, Guadalcanal." By Brian A. Filler. *Thesis.* Marine Corps Command and Staff College, n.d. As retrieved in June 2019 from the following url: https://apps.dtic.mil/dtic/tr/fulltext/u2/a600662.pdf.

"A Description of Combat Rifle Squads on the Korean MLR During the Winter of 1952-53." By Rodney A. Clark and Martha B. Myers. Human Resources Research Office. George Washington University, while under contract to the U.S. Army, June 1954. As retrieved in January 2019 from the following url: https://apps.dtic.mil/dtic/tr/fulltext/u2/a068260.pdf.

"Development of the Squad: Historical Analysis." By Ahmed Hashim. With contributions from Lt.Gen. Paul Van Riper USMC (Ret.). Alexandria, VA: Center for Naval Analyses, 2000. As retrieved in January 2019 from the following url: www.dtic.mil/dtic/tr/fulltext/u2/1014512.pdf.

Drea, Edward J. "Nomonhan: Japanese—Soviet Tactical Combat, 1939." *Leavenworth Papers No. 2*. Fort.Leavenworth, KS: Combat Studies Institute, U.S. Army Command and General Staff College, 1981.

"The Evolution of the U.S. Army Infantry Squad: Where Do We Go from Here: Determining the Optimum Infantry Squad Organization for the Future." By Maj. S.E. Hughes. *Monograph*. Fort Leavenworth, KS: School of Advanced Military Studies, U.S. Army Command and General Staff College, 1994. As retrieved in May 2019 from the following url: http://citeseerx.ist.psu.edu/viewdoc/download?doi=10.1.1.914.6649&rep=rep1&type=pdf.

Fighting on Guadalcanal. FMFRP 12-110. Washington, D.C.: United States of America War Office, 1942. As retrieved in June 2019 from the following url: https://www.globalsecurity.org/military/library/policy/usmc/fmfrp/12-110/fmfrp12-110.pdf.

"First Offensive: The Marine Campaign for Guadalcanal." By Henry I. Shaw, Jr. *Marines in World War II Commemorative Series*. Washington, D.C.: History and Museums Division, Headquarters Marine Corps, 1992. As retrieved in June 2019 from the following url: https://www.nps.gov/parkhistory/online_books/npswapa/extcontent/usmc/pcn-190-003117-00/sec3a.htm.

"From Makin to Bougainville: Marine Raiders in the Pacific War." By Maj. Jon T. Hoffman. *Marines in WWII Commemorative Series*. Washington, D.C.: Marine Corps Historical Center, 1995.

"Frozen Chosin: U.S. Marines at the Changjin Reservoir." By B.Gen. Edwin H. Simmons USMC (Ret). *Official document,* PCN 19000410000_3.pdf. N.p., November 2002. As retrieved in June 2019 from the following url: (https://www.marines.mil/Portals/59/Publications/Frozen%20Chosin%20US%20Marines%20at%20the%20Changjin%20Reservoir%20%20PCN%2019000410000_3.pdf.

German Squad Tactics in WWII. By Matthew Gajkowski. West Chester, OH: Nafziger, 1995. Reprint of *The German Squad in Combat*. Translated and edited by the U.S. Military Intelligence Service from a German manual. N.p., 1943.

Glantz, David M. "August Storm: Soviet Tactical and Operational Combat in Manchuria, 1945." *Leavenworth Papers No. 8*. Fort Leavenworth, KS: Combat Studies Institute, U.S. Army Command and General Staff College, 1983.

Handbook of the Chinese People's Liberation Army. DDB-2680-32-84. Washington, D.C.: Defense Intelligence Agency, November 1984. As retrieved in December 2018 from the following url: https://archive.org/stream/pdfy-WidHRLGeFX0jiTJF/Handbook+Of+The+Chinese+People%27s+Liberation+Army_djvu.txt.

Handbook on German Military Forces. TM-E 30-451. Washington, D.C.: U.S. War Department, 1945. Reprint Baton Rouge, LA: LSU Press, 1990.

Handbook on Japanese Military Forces. TM-E 30-480. Washington, D.C.: U.S. War Department, 1944. Reprint, Baton Rouge, LA: LSU Press, 1991. As retrieved in November 2018 from this url: https://archive.org/stream/1942TM30480/1942TM30-480_djvu.txt.

Handbook on the Chinese Communist Army. DA Pamphlet 30-51. Washington, D.C.: Headquarters Department of the Army, 7 December 1960.

Handbook on U.S.S.R. Military Forces. TM 30-340. Washington, D.C.: U.S. War Department, 1945. Various chapters—including Field Organization, Chapter III—retrieved in December 2018 from the following url: http://digitalcommons.unl.edu/dodmilintel/23/.

Historical Study—Night Combat. DA Pamphlet 20-236. Washington, D.C.: Headquarters Department of the Army, 1953.

Huber, Thomas M. "The Battle of Manila." Fort Leavenworth, KS: Combat Studies Institute, U.S. Army Command and General Staff College, n.d. In CSI Home Publications Research MHIST database on line; updated 30 September 2002; cited 1 January 2003. Available from the CSI website at www-cgsc.army.mil/csi/research/mout/mouthuber.asp.

"The Infantry Squad Part 1: How Did We Get Here?" By Chris Raynor. *NCO Journal,* 19 March 2018. As retrieved in January 2018 from the following url: https://www.armyupress.army.mil/Journals/NCO-Journal/Archives/2018/March/Infantry-Squad-Part-1/.

"The Infantry Squad Part 2: How Did We Get Here?" By Chris Raynor. *NCO Journal,* 23 March 2018. As retrieved in January 2018 from the following url: https://www.armyupress.army.mil/Journals/NCO-Journal/Archives/2018/March/Infantry-Squad-Part-2/.

The Infantry Platoon and Squad. FM 3-21.8. Washington, D.C.: Headquarters Department of the Army, March 2007.

"Isolation of Rabaul." By Henry I. Shaw and Maj. Douglas T. Kane. *History of U.S. Marine Corps Operations in World War II Series.* Volume II. Washington, D.C.: Historical Branch, Headquarters Marine Corps, 1963. As retrieved from the following url: www.ibiblio.org/hyperwar/USMC/II/index.html#contents.

Jungle Warfare. FMFRP 12-9. Quantico, VA: Marine Corps Combat Development Command, 1989.

Kennedy, President John F. Quote from his 1962 West Point graduation speech. In "Unconventional Warfare Fundamentals." At *The Irregular Warrior* website. As retrieved in April 2018 from this url: http://irregularwarrior.com/unconventional-warfare.

Lupfer, Timothy L. "The Dynamics of Doctrine: The Changes in German Tactical Doctrine during the First World War." *Leavenworth Papers Number 4.* Fort Leavenworth, KS: Combat Studies Institute, U.S. Army Command and General Staff College, 1981.

Marine Rifle Company / Platoon. FMFM 6-4. Quantico, VA: Marine Corps Development and Education Command, 1978.

"Marines in the Central Solomons." By Maj. John N. Rentz. *USMC Historical Monograph.* Chaper 4—From Rice to Bairoko. Washington, D.C.: History Branch, Headquarters Marine Corps, 1952.

McMichael, Maj. Scott R. "A Historical Perspective on Light Infantry." Chapter 2—The Chinese Communist Forces in Korea. *Research Survey No. 6.* Fort Leavenworth, KS: Combat Studies Institute, U.S. Army Command and General Staff College, 1987. As retrieved in November 2019 from the following url: https://www.armyupress.army.mil/Portals/7/combat-studies-institute/csi-books/Historical-Perspective-Light-Infantry.pdf

Montross, Lynn and Capt. Nicholas A. Canzona, "The Chosin Reservoir Campaign." *U.S. Marine Operations in Korea 1950-1953.* Volume III. Washington, D.C.: History Branch, Headquarters Marine Corps, 1957.

Mountain Warfare. FM 3-97.6. Washington, D.C.: Headquarters Department of the Army, November 2000. As retrieved in June 2019 from the following url: https://fas.org/irp/doddir/army/fm3-97-6.pdf.

"North Korea, a Country Study." DA Pamphlet 550-81. 5th edition. Edited by Robert L. Worden. *Area Handbook Series.* Washington, D.C.: Federal Research Division, Library of Congress, 2008.

NVA-VC Small Unit Tactics & Techniques Study, Part I. U.S.A.R.V. Edited by Thomas Pike. Washington, D.C.: Archival Publishing, 1997.

"Okinawa: The Last Battle." By Roy E. Appleman, James M. Burns, Russell A. Gugeler, and John Stevens. *United States Army in World War II Series.* Washington, D.C.: U.S. Army's Center of Military History, 2000.

"Okinawa: Victory in the Pacific." By Maj. Chas. S. Nichols, Jr. USMC, and Henry I. Shaw, Jr. *USMC Historical Monograph.* Washington, D.C.: Historical Branch, Headquarters Marine Corps, 1955. As retrieved from the following url: www.ibiblio.org/hyperwar/USMC/USMC-M-Okinawa/index.html#index.

"1/4 After-Action Report for May 1967." As retrieved in June 2012 through the 1/4 Association website, from the following url: http://jones-thompson.com/onefour/AFTACTREP/1967/MAY67/aftactrep2-may67.htm.

"1/4 Intelligence Summary for 7-8 May 1967." As retrieved from the 1/4 Assoc. website at the following url: http://jones-thompson.com/onefour/AFTACTREP/1967/MAY67/intelsum2-may67.htm.

"Organization and Equipment of the Infantry Rifle Squad." *Memorandum CORG-M-194m.* By Virgil Ney. Headquarters U.S. Army Development Command, January 1965. As retrieved in January 2019 from the following url: www.dtic.mil/dtic/tr/fulltext/u2/461439.pdf.

"Pearl Harbor to Guadalcanal." FMFRP 12-34-I. By Lt.Col. Frank O. Hough, Maj. Verle E. Ludwig, and Henry I. Shaw, Jr. Volume I. *History of the U.S. Marine Corps Operations in World War II Series.* Washington, D.C.: History Branch, Headquarters Marine Corps, n.d. Reprint Quantico, VA: Marine Corps Combat Development Command, 1989.

"Rethinking the U.S. Army Infantry Rifle Squad." By Maj. Hassan Kamara. *Military Review.* March-April 2018. As retrieved in September 2019 from the following url: https://www.armyupress.army.mil/Journals/Military-Review/English-Edition-Archives/March-April-2018/Kamara-Infantry-Rifle-Squad/.

Sasso, Maj. Claude R. "Soviet Night Operations in World War II." *Leavenworth Papers No. 6.* Fort Leavenworth, KS: Combat Studies Institute. U.S. Army Command and General Staff College, 1982.

Shaw, John and the editors of Time-Life Books. *Red Army Resurgent.* Chicago: Time-Life Books, 1979.

"Soldier Swarm: New Ground Tactics for the Era of Multi-Domain Battle." By Justin Lynch and Lauren Fish. Modern War Institute at West Point, 5 April 2018. As retrieved in June 2019 from the following url: https://mwi.usma.edu/soldier-swarm-new-ground-combat-tactics-era-multi-domain-battle/.

Soviet Tactical Doctrine in WWII. With foreword by Shawn Caza. West Chester, OH: Nafziger, 1997. Reprint of Chapter V, *Handbook on U.S.S.R. Military Forces,* TM 30-340. Washington, D.C.: U.S. War Department, 1945.

"A Survey of the Effects of Load-Carrying and Equipment Design upon Tasks Performed by the Combat Infantryman." By Morris Kolnicker and Martin A. Tolcott. N.p.: Human Factors Research Division, Army Research Office [Contract No. DA 44-188-ARO-5 /], 15 November 1962.

Tactical Fundamentals. MCI 7401. 1st course in Warfighting Skills Program. Washington, D.C.: Marine Corps Institute, 1989.

Tactics. FMFM 1-3. Washington, D.C.: Headquarters Marine Corps, 1991.

U.S. Army Heritage and Information Center. From its website, http://www.carlisle.army.mil/.
U.S. *Marines in Vietnam: An Expanding War—1966*. By Jack Shulimson. Washington, D.C.: History and Museums Division, Headquarters Marine Corps, 1982.
U.S. Marines in Vietnam: Fighting the North Vietnamese 1967. By Maj. Gary Tefler, Lt.Col Lane Rogers, and V. Keith Fleming, Jr. Washington, D.C.: History and Museums Division, Headquarters Marine Corps, 1984.
U.S. Marines in Vietnam: The Defining Year, 1968. By Lt.Col. Jack Shulimson, Lt.Col. Leonard A. Blasiol, Charles R. Smith, and Capt. David A. Dawson. Washington, D.C. History and Museums Division, Headquarters Marine Corps, 1997.
Warfare in the Far North. DA Pamphlet 20-292. Washington, D.C.: Headquarters Department of the Army, n.d.
Warfighting. FMFM 1. Washington, D.C.: Headquarters Marine Corps, 1989.
Warfighting. MCDP 1. Washington, D.C.: Headquarters Marine Corps, 1997.
Zimmerman, Maj. John L. *The Guadalcanal Campaign*. Washington, D.C.: Historical Division, Headquarters Marine Corps, 1949.

Civilian Publications

Analytical Studies

Alexander, Joseph H. *Edson's Raiders: 1st Marine Raider Battalion in World War II*. Annapolis, MD: Naval Institute Press, 2001.
The Art of War. By Sun Tzu. Translated by Lionel Giles. N.p., n.d. As retrieved in July 2019 from the following url: http://classics.mit.edu/Tzu/artwar.html.
Association of 1st Battalion, 4th Marines. From its website, http://1stbn4thmarines.com/.
Association of 3rd Battalion, 4th Marines. From its website, http://thundering-third.org.
Association of U.S. Marine Raiders. From its website, http://www.usmarineraiders.org/.
AZ Quotes. From its website, https://www.azquotes.com.
Baxter, William P. *Soviet Airland Battle Tactics*. Novato, CA: Presidio Press, 1986.

Chanda, Nayan. *Brother Enemy: The War after the War.* New York: Collier Books, 1986.

Commentary on Infantry Operations and Weapons Usage in Korea: Winter 1950-1951. By Brig.Gen. S.L.A. Marshall. Edited by George F. Nafziger. Chevy Chase, MD: The Johns Hopkins University Press, 1951.

"Condor Legion: The Wehrmacht's Training Ground." By Ian Westwell. N.p.: Ian Allan Publishers, 2004. Google Books synopsis. As retrieved in December 2018 from this url: https://books.google.com/books/about/Condor_Legion.html?id=aoFmPgAACAAJ.

Coox, Alvin D. *Nomonhan: Japan against Russia, 1939.* Stanford, CA: Stanford University Press, 1985.

Davis, Burke. *Marine.* New York: Bantam, 1964.

Dung, Gen. Van Tien. *Our Great Spring Victory: An Account of the Liberation of South Vietnam.* Translation by John Spragens, Jr. Hanoi: The Gioi Publishers, 2001.

Dunnigan, James F. and Albert A. Nofi. *Dirty Little Secrets of the Vietnam War.* New York: Thomas Dunne Books, 1999.

East of Chosin: Entrapment and Breakout in Korea, 1950. By Roy Edgar Appleman. College Station, TX: Texas A&M University Press, 1990. As retrieved in September 2019 from the following url: https://books.google.com/books?id=E9Dd7-ht9pEC&pg=PA125&lpg=PA125&dq=bangalore+at+chosin&source=bl&ots=I35w5fj-q9&sig=ACfU3U0A5E9FFnyMzLpJqsGMSI4c8YaR3A&hl=en&sa=X&ved=2ahUKEwiV_4Gq9cbkAhWFpFkKHR_zCR4Q6AEwC3oECAkQAQ#v=onepage&q=bangalore&f=false.

Ej's Ordnance Show & Tell Pages. From its website, http://www.inert-ord.net/.

Elford, George Robert. *Devil's Guard.* New York: Dell Publishing, 1971.

Encyclopedia Britannica. From its website. https://www.britannica.com.

The Encyclopedia of the Korean War: A Political, Social, and Military History. Edited by Spencer C. Tucker and Paul G. Pierpaoli, Jr. Three Volume Set, 2nd Edition. N.p., ABC-CLIO, 9 April 2010.

The Fall of Berlin. By David Fisher and Anthony Read. New York: Da Capo Press, 1995.

Federation of American Scientists Military Analysis Network. From its website, https://fas.org.

"Finnish Tactics—Small Units." A U.S. Intelligence Report on Finnish Tactics in WWII. *Tactical and Technical Trends.* Number 6, 27 August 1942.

Fox, Col. Wesley L. *Marine Rifleman: Forty-Three Years in the Corps.* Dulles, VA: Brassey's, 2002.

Giap, Gen. Vo Nguyen. *Dien Bien Phu.* 6th edition supplemented. Hanoi: The Gioi Publishers, 1999.

Giap, Gen. Vo Nguyen and Gen. Van Tien Dung. *How We Won the War* Philadelphia, PA: Recon Publications, 1976.

Giap, Gen. Vo Nguyen. "Once Again We Will Win." In *The Military Art of People's War*. Edited by Russel Stetler. New York: Monthly Review Press, 1970.

Gilbert, Ed. *U.S. Marine Corps Raider 1942-43*. London: Osprey Publishing, 2006.

Glantz, David M. *The Soviet Conduct of Tactical Maneuver: Spearhead of the Offensive*. London: Frank Cass, 1991.

Global Warrior: Averting WWIII. By H. John Poole. Emerald Isle, NC: Posterity Press, 2011.

Goulden, Joseph C. *Korea: The Untold Story of the War*. New York: Times Books, 1982.

Guardian Joe: How Less Force Helps the Warrior. By H. John Poole. Emerald Isle, NC: Posterity Press, 2018.

Gudmundsson, Bruce I. *Stormtroop Tactics—Innovation in the German Army 1914-1918*. New York: Praeger, 1989.

Gung Ho: The Corp's Most Progressive Tradition. By H. John Poole. Emerald Isle, NC: Posterity Press, 2012.

Hackworth, Col. David H. U.S. Army (Ret.) and Julie Sherman. *About Face*. New York: Simon & Schuster, 1989.

Hammel, Eric M. *Chosin: Heroic Ordeal of the Korean War*. Novato, CA: Presidio Press, 1981.

Hammel, Eric. M. *Fire in the Streets: The Battle for Hue, Tet 1968*. Pacifica, CA: Pacifica Press, 1991.

Hammel, Eric. M. *Guadalcanal: Starvation Island*. New York: Crown Publishers, 1987.

Hastings, Max. *The Korean War*. New York: Simon and Schuster, 1987.

Hayes, Stephen K. *The Ninja and Their Secret Fighting Art*. Rutland, VT: Charles E. Tuttle Company, 1981.

Hoyt, Edwin P. *The Marine Raiders*. New York: Pocket Books, 1989.

Infantry: Part I—Regular Army. By John K. Mahon and Romana Danysh. Washington, D.C.: Chief of Staff of Military History, U.S. Army, 1972.

Jaynes, Gregory and the editors of Time Life-Books. *The Civil War: The Killing Ground—Wilderness to Cold Harbor*. Alexandria, VA: Time-Life Books, 1986.

Khang, Ho. *The Tet Mau Than 1968 Event in South Vietnam*. Hanoi: The Gioi Publishers, 2001.

This Kind of War. By T.R. Fehrenbach. Washington, D.C.: Brassey's, 1994. Originally published in New York by MacMillan in 1963.

The Korean War: History and Tactics. Edited by David Rees. New York: Crescent Books, 1984.

The Korean War: Pusan to Chosin, An Oral History. By Donald Knox. San Diego: Harcourt Brace Jovanovich, 1985.

"The Koreas." Edited by Mary E. Connor. *Asia in Focus Series*. Santa Barbara, CA: ABC-CLIO, 2009.

Lanning, Michael Lee and Dan Cragg. *Inside the VC and the NVA: The Real Story of North Vietnam's Armed Forces*. New York: Ivy Books, 1992.

The Last Hundred Yards: The NCO's Contribution to Warfare. By H.J. Poole. Emerald Isle, NC: Posterity Press, 1997.

Levin, Nora. *The Holocaust*. New York: Thomas Y. Crowell Co., 1968.

Lind, William S. *The Maneuver Warfare Handbook*. Boulder, CO: Westview Press, 1985.

Livingston, James E., Colin D. Heaton, and Anne-Marie Lewis. *Noble Warrior*. Minneapolis: Zenith Press, 2010.

Lung, Dr. HaHa. *Knights of Darkness: Secrets of the World's Deadliest Night Fighters*. Boulder, CO: Paladin Press, 1998.

Mao's Generals Remember Korea. Translated and edited by Xiaobing Li, Allan R. Millett, and Bin Yu. Lawrence, KS: University Press of Kansas, 2001.

Maitland, Terrence and Peter McInerney. *Vietnam Experience: A Contagion of War*. Boston, MA: Boston Publishing, 1968.

Mao Tse-tung: An Anthology of His Writings. Edited by Anne Fremantle. New York: Mentor, 1962.

Miksche, Ferdinand Otto. *Attack: A Study of Blitzkrieg Tactics*. New York: Random House. 1942. As partially retrieved in May 2019 from the following url: https://books.google.com/books/about/Attack.html?id=awggAAAAMAAJ.

The Miniatures Page. From its website, http://theminiaturespage.com.

Night Movements. Translated and preface by C. Burnett. Tokyo: Imperial Japanese Army, 1913. Reprint Port Townsend, WA: Loompanics Unlimited, n.d.

1914-1918 Online: International Encyclopedia or the First World War. From its website, https://encyclopedia.1914-1918-online.net.

Nolan, Keith William. *Operation Buffalo: USMC Fight for the DMZ*. New York: Dell Publishing, 1991.

Nolan, Keith William. *The Magnificent Bastards: The Joint Army-Marine Defense of Dong Ha, 1968*. New York: Ballantine, 2007.

North Korea's Hidden Assets. By H. John Poole. Emerald Isle, NC: Posterity Press, 2018.

O'Brien, Michael. *Conscripts and Regulars: With the Seventh Battalion in Vietnam*. St. Leonards, Australia: Allen & Unwin, 1995.

Official 1st Amtrac Battalion website, at www.amtrac.org.

100 Strategies of War: Brilliant Tactics in Action. Translated by Yeo Ai Hoon. Singapore: Asiapac Books, 1993.

One More Bridge to Cross. By H. John Poole. Emerald Isle, NC: Posterity Press, 1998.

Owens, William J. *Green Hell: The Battle for Guadalcanal*. Central Point, OR: Hellgate Press, a Division of PSI Research, 1999.

The People's Army. By Israel Epstein. N.p.: V. Gollancz, 1939. As retrieved in December 2018 from this url: https://books.google.com/books?id=TevqAAAAIAAJ&q=The+men+in+the+trenches+waited+till+the+tanks+came+close,+then+jumped+out+and+threw+bundles+of+hand-+grenades+under+their+wheels+and+into+their+ports.+Four+tanks+were+destroyed,+neatly+pierced+by+anti-tank+shells,+and+nine+others+were&dq=The+men+in+the+trenches+waited+till+the+tanks+came+close,+then+jumped+out+and+threw+bundles+of+hand-+grenades+under+their+wheels+and+into+their+ports.+Four+tanks+were+destroyed,+neatly+pierced+by+anti-tank+shells,+and+nine+others+were&hl=en&sa=X&ei=9HDbU9iuMq3esATmw4L4Dw&ved=0CBwQ6AEwAA.

Phantom Soldier: The Enemy's Answer to U.S. Firepower. By H. John Poole. Emerald Isle, NC: Posterity Press, August 2001.

Pike, Douglas. *PAVN: People's Army of Vietnam*. Novato, CA: Presidio Press, 1986.

Portrait of the Enemy. By David Chanoff and Doan Van Toai. New York: Random House, 1986.

Ross, Bill D. *Iwo Jima—Legacy of Valor*. New York: Vintage Books, 1986.

"Scouting in South Africa, 1884-1890." As extracted from *Scouting with Baden-Powell*. By Russell Freedman. New York: Holiday House, 1967. As retrieved in 2006 from the following url: www.pinetreeweb.com.

"Secret Manual Gives Glimpse of North Korean Military Tactics." By Steve Herman. *Voice of America* on line, 18 September 2010. As retrieved in May 2018 from the following url: https://www.voanews.com/a/secret-manual-gives-glimpse-of-north-korean-military-tactics-103253534/126266.html.

Shaw, John and the editors of Time-Life Books. *Red Army Resurgent*. Chicago: Time-Life Books, 1979.

Smith, George W. *The Siege at Hue*. New York: Ballantine Publishing, 1999.

Smith, Michael S. *Bloody Ridge: The Battle That Saved Guadalcanal*. Novato, CA: Presidio Press, 2000.

"Soldier's Load and the Mobility of a Nation." By S.L.A. Marshall. Quantico, VA: Marine Corps Association, 1980.

Soviet Infantry Tactics in World War II: Red Army Infantry Tactics from Squad to Rifle Company from the Combat Regulations. With translation, introduction, and notes by Charles C. Sharp. West Chester, OH: George Nafziger, 1998. Reprint of *Soviet Combat Regulations of November 1942*. Moscow: Stalin, n.d.

Strategic Rifleman: Key to More Moral Warfare. By H. John Poole. Emerald Isle, NC: Posterity Press, 2014.

Taras, A.E. and F.D. Zaruz. *Podgotovka Razvegchika: Sistema Spetsnaza GRU.* Minsk, Belarus: AST Publishing, 2002.

Taylor, *A.J.P. The Second World War—An Illustrated History.* New York: G.P. Putnam's Sons, 1975.

Terrorist Trail: Backtracking the Foreign Fighter. By H. John Poole. Emerald Isle, NC: Posterity Press, 2006.

Texas Military Forces Museum. From its website, http://www.texasmilitaryforcesmuseum.org.

Thai, Gen. Hoang Van. *How South Vietnam Was Liberated.* Hanoi: The Gioi Publishers, 1996.

Thao, Maj.Gen. Hoang Min. *The Victorious Tay Nguyen Campaign.* Hanoi: Foreign Languages Publishing House, 1979.

The Tiger's Way: A U.S. Private's Best Chance for Survival. By H. John Poole. Emerald Isle, NC: Posterity Press, 2003.

Tregaskis, Richard. *Guadalcanal Diary.* New York: Landmark Books, an imprint of Random House, 1955.

Truong Chinh. *Primer for Revolt.* Introduction by Bernard B. Fall. New York: Praeger, 1963.

2-12 INF Warriors. From its website, http://www.212warriors.com.

Van Tien Dung, Gen. *Our Great Spring Victory: An Account of the Liberation of South Vietnam.* Translated by John Spragens, Jr. Hanoi: The Gioi Publishers, 2001.

Vietnam War Stories. From its website, https://www.americanveteranscenter.org/category/home-of-the-brave/vietnam-war-stories/.

Warfare History Network. From its website, warfarehistorynetwork.com.

War History Online. From its website, www.warhistoryonline.com.

Warner, Philip. "Japanese Army of World War II." Volume 20. *Men-at-Arms Series.* London: Osprey Publications Ltd., 1972.

Warr, Nicholas. *Phase Line Green: The Battle for Hue, 1968.* Annapolis, MD: Naval Institute Press, 1997.

Wikipedia Encyclopedia. From its website, https://www.wikipedia.org.

Wikisource. From its website, https://en.wikisource.org/wiki/Main_Page.

World Atlas on line. From its website, www.worldatlas.com.

World War II History Info. From its website, http://www.worldwar2history.info.

Wukovits, John. *American Commando.* New York: New American Library, 2009.

Xiaobing Li. *China's Battle for Korea: The 1951 Spring Offensive.* Bloomington, IN: Indiana University Press, 2014.

Yahara, Col. Hiromichi. *The Battle for Okinawa.* Translated by Roger Pineau and Masatoshi Uehara. New York: John Wiley & Sons, 1995.

"Zulu and Zulu Wars." In *Reader's Companion to Military History.* Boston, MA: Houghton Mifflin, College Division, n.d.

Photographs, Videotapes, Movies, TV Programs, and Slide Shows

The Battle of Dien Bien Phu. Visions of War Series. Volume 10. New Star Video, 1988. 50 minutes. Videocassette #4010.

"Battle Stack: The Battle of Rorke's Drift Tactics." As retrieved in June 2019 from the following url: https://www.youtube.com/watch?v=7B9dRpWMp80.

"Don't Mess with Israel." *Israeligal1000,* 9 April 2011. As retrieved in March 2019 from the following url: https://www.youtube.com/watch?v=E5cg57z9100.

"Final Attack on Shanghai (1937)." British Pathe Gazette. As retrieved in April 2019 from the following url: https://www.youtube.com/watch?v=02xprjZ2sh4.

"German Infantry Anti-Tank Tactics 1941/1942: Eastern Front Edition." *Military History Visualized.* As retrieved in December 2018, from this url: https://www.youtube.com/watch?v=FxJZJflMEiw.

"German Squad Tactics in World War 2." *Military History Visualized.* Partial translation by the Military Intelligence Service in January 1943 of a German field manual entitled "German Squad in Combat." As retrieved in December 2018 from the following url: https://www.youtube.com/watch?v=-rKRt5zVZgw.

"German WW1 MG 08/15 Machine Gun—How Does It Work." Videotape. As retrieved in November 2018 from the following url: https://www.youtube.com/watch?v=uwgGok9cYcw.

"How a German Squad Attacks a Position (WWII)." *Footage Archive.* From a training film entitled "The German Infantry Squad in Action: A Demonstration of Minor Field Tactics." As retrieved in December 2018 from this url: www,youtube,com/watch?v=GDZMJXaADQI.

"Japanese infantry use a roadblock as cover during street fighting in Shanghai, China, 1937." *WWII Pictures,* n.d. As retrieved in October 2019 from the following url: https://twitter.com/WWIIpix/status/989408968907816960.

"Korean War." *History Channel* on line, n.d. As retrieved in August 2018 from the following url: https://www.history.com/topics/korean-war.

"Organization of the WWII U.S. Army Infantry Rifle Squad." *GI History Handbook*. Videotape, 25 May 2017. As retrieved in November 2018 from the following url: https://www.youtube.com/watch?v=hUOz13oJnCQ.

Photo #4—Japanese soldiers involved in street fighting in Shanghai, China in 1937. "World War II: Before the War." By Alan Taylor. *The Atlantic* on line, 19 June 2011. As retrieved in October 2019 from the following url: https://www.theatlantic.com/photo/2011/06/world-war-ii-before-the-war/100089/.

"Photos of Japanese WWII Replica Stick Grenade." *Stewarts Military Antiques*. As retrieved in December 2018 from the following url: https://www.google.com/search?q=Japanese+concussion+stick+grenade+of+wwii&tbm=isch&source=iu&ictx=1&fir=jx62KjqtPFE-yM%253A%252CjUQzaKN6U3JPJM%252C_&usg=AI4_-kQY73cDHhZm6EcnJ-c1qn_t722eyA&sa=X&ved=2ahUKEwjWlPXa3rPfAhUv0FkKHRKIAiYQ9QEwBXoECAQQDg&cshid=1545492291926000#imgrc=jx62KjqtPFE-yM:.

"Platoon." MGM.1986, Videocassette. 119 minutes.

"Sands of Iwo Jima." Republic Pictures, 1988. Videocassette. 109 minutes.

"WWII Factions: The Chinese Armies." *Simple History*. As retrieved in December 2018 from the following url: https://www.youtube.com/watch?v=Ei_oMWw2DwM.

"WW2 German Trained Chinese National Revolutionary Army (p1)." *Kobetang*. As retrieved in December 2018 from the following url: https://www.youtube.com/watch?v=P6UBRMQFEzM.

"WW2 Men Against Tanks - Training Film 1943 for German Soldiers - Tank Hunters - Männer gegen Panzer." By *Petr Warry*. As retrieved in March 2019 from the following url: https://www.youtube.com/watch?v=eDbFdngVOJk.

"Zulu." Platinum Disc Corp., 2000. 139 minutes. Videocassette #02863.

Letters, E-Mail, and Verbal Conversations

Campbell, Maj. Donald H. USMC (Ret.) [platoon sergeant during Korean hill battles of 1952-53]. In conversation with author on 26 March 2001.

Ford, M.Sgt. Lester J., Jr., USMC (Ret.) [Vietnam-era platoon sergeant]. In conversations with author on 7 April 2002, 27 November 2002, and 17 January 2003.

Guthrie, CWO-4 Charles "Tag" USMC (Ret.) [former member of A/1/4, A/1/4 historian, and "super-squad" participant]. In various telephone and e-mail conversations with author over the years.

O'Bday, M.Gy.Sgt. Bob USMC (Ret.) [Marine machinegunner at Khe Sanh and CAP platoon member]. In conversations with author from 2014 to 2019.

Ronin, S.Sgt. Chris USMC (Ret.) [former Marine scout/sniper and special operator]. In conversations with author from 2017 to 2019.

2nd Marine Division squad leader. In conversation with author in the Spring of 2018.

Soturi, Jenkki [U.S. Marine veteran of Vietnam and student of Finnish tactics]. In a letter to author on 7 November 2001.

Walker, Gy.Sgt. Rodney USMC (Ret.) [career infantryman and former super-squad member]. In various telephone and face-to-face conversations with author between 2013 and 2018.

Newspaper, Magazine, and Website Articles

"Attacks on MAG-16, Hill 22, and the Attempted Attack on the Da Nang Airfield." *3rd Marines in Vietnam* website, n.d.

Bartsch, William H. "Crucial Battle Ignored." *Marine Corps Gazette,* September 1997.

"Battle for Henderson Field." *History Net,* n.d. As retrieved in August 2019 from the following url: https://www.historynet.com/battle-for-henderson-field-lieutenant-colonel-lewis-b-puller-commanded-the-1st-battalion-7th-marines.htm.

"The Battle That Helped Change the Course of the 'Israeli' Occupation." *Daily Star* (Lebanon), 6 September 2000.

"Biên Hòa Air Base Ammo Dump Explosion Sapper Attack." By Arnold John Houchin. Originally written on 12 January 1972, then published by the Association for U.S. Air Force Vietnam War Veterans of Air/Security Police, through *Vietnam War Stories,* in 2005.

"Châtellerault Model 1924 M29 LMG." By Jean Huon. *Small Arms Review.* As retrieved in January 2019 from the following url: http://www.smallarmsreview.com/display.article.cfm?idarticles=1408.

"The Coolest Weapon in CoD History: The Stinger LMG." *Reddit,* n.d. As retrieved in February 2019 from the following url: https://www.reddit.com/r/WWII/comments/8n1co9/the_coolest_weapon_in_cod_history_the_stinger_lmg/.

Cooling, Maj. Norman L. "Russia's 1994-96 Campaign for Chechnya: A Failure in Shaping the Battlespace." *Marine Corps Gazette,* October 2001.

Duc Quyen, "Is the Soviet Tactic of Hugging Still Relevant in the Today's Battles." *Quora,* 5 May 2016. As retrieved in August 2019 from the following url: https://www.quora.com/Is-the-Soviet-tactic-of-hugging-still-relevant-in-the-todays-battles-What-terrain-favors-this-tactic-and-is-hugging-usually-associated-with-low-tech-armies-and-larger-manpower-resources-When-was-this-tactic-last-used.

"Evolution of the British Infantry Section—1916-1945." By Michael Dorosh. *Axis History Forum,* 18 January 2007. As retrieved in November 2018 from the following url: https://forum.axishistory.com/viewtopic.php?t=114564.

"The Experimental Chinese Mech Infantry." *Strategy Page,* September 2012. As retrieved in December 2018 from the following url: https://strategypage.com/htmw/htinf/articles/20120901.aspx.

"Finnish Tactics—Small Units." A U.S. Intelligence Report on Finnish Tactics in WWII. *Tactical and Technical Trends.* Number 6, 27 August 1942.

"Free French Infantry Squad Attack, 1945." *Warfare History Network.* As retrieved in January 2019 from the following url: http://www.historynet.com/free-french-infantry-squad-attack-1945.htm.

Hamme, T.X. "Rethinking the Rifle Squad." *Marine Corps Gazette,* July 1984.

"How Did the Chinese Army Defeat the U.S. Tanks and Helicopters During the Korean War." *Quora,* n.d. As retrieved in March 2019 from the following url: https://www.quora.com/How-did-the-Chinese-army-defeat-the-US-tanks-and-helicopters-during-the-Korean-War.

"Indigenous Machine Guns of China." *Small Arms Defense Journal* on line, 20 March 2014. As retrieved in November 2018 from the following url: http://www.sadefensejournal.com/wp/?p=2406.

"The Japanese Nambu Type 96 6.5mm Light Machinegun." By Edwin F. Libby. *Small Arms Review,* n.d. As retrieved in November 2018 from the following url: http://www.smallarmsreview.com/display.article.cfm?idarticles=2790.

"Kiinalainen [Chosin] Motti: The Chinese Encirclement." *Changjin Journal,* 1 August 2002. As retrieved in June 2019 from the following url: http://bobrowen.com/nymas/Changjinjournal020801.html.

Lamont, Lt.Col. Robert W. "'Urban Warrior'—A View from North Vietnam." *Marine Corps Gazette,* April 1999.

Lieven, Anatol. "The World Turned Upside Down: Military Lessons of the Chechen War." *Armed Forces Journal International,* August 1998.

"Lost Battles of the Vietnam War." *G2mil.com.* As retrieved in April 2017 from the following url: http://www.g2mil.com/lost_vietnam.htm.

"The Marine Rifle Squad: The Beginnings of the Modern Fireteam." *Leatherneck Magazine* on line forum, n.d. With information from several sources: (1) www.ww2gyrene.org; (2) the "GI Intelligence Department" [www.hardscrabblefarm.com/ww2]; and (3) Osprey's *Battle Orders 1: U.S. Marine Corps Pacific Theater of Operations 1941-1943.* As retrieved in October 2018 from the following url: http://www.leatherneck.com/forums/showthread.php?87120-The-Marine-Rifle-Squad-The-begginings-of-the-modern-fireteam.

"Motti Tactics." *Combat Forces Journal,* January 1950.

"New Hollow-Charge Antitank Grenade for Close Combat." *Lone Sentry.* As retrieved in March 2019 from the following url: http://www.lonesentry.com/articles/ttt_faustpatrone/.

"New North Korean Rocket Turns Enemy Tanks into 'Boiled Pumpkin'." *Agence France-Presse,* 27 February 2016. As retrieved in June 2008 from this url: http://newsinfo.inquirer.net/769105/new-n-korean-rocket-turns-enemy-tanks-into-boiled-pumpkin.

Nolan, Keith William. "The Battle of Dai Do." *Leatherneck,* August 1994.

"N. Korea Claims Test of Laser-Guided Anti-Tank Missile. *Russia Today (RT) News* on line, 2 Mar, 2016. As retrieved in June 2018 from the following url: https://www.rt.com/news/334282-north-korea-laser-missile/.

"One General's Bet on Reshaping the Marines. By Sam Walker. *Wall Street Journal,* 1 July 2018.

"Organization of an Infantry Company." *151 Regiment d'Infanterie de Ligne,* n.d. As retrieved in November 2018 from the following url: http://www.151ril.com/content/history/french-army/9.

"Pacific Odyssey: Guadalcanal and Bloody Ridge, Solomon Islands." By Matthew Stevenson. *Counterpunch.org.* As retrieved in June 2019 from the following url: https://www.counterpunch.org/2019/04/19/pacific-odyssey-guadalcanal-and-bloody-ridge-solomon-islands/.

"Sapper Attack: The Elite North Vietnamese Units." By Arnold Blumberg. *History Net,* 1 February 2017. As retrieved in February 2019 from the following url: https://www.historynet.com/sapper-attack-the-elite-north-vietnamese-units.htm.

Scales, Maj.Gen. Robert H. U.S. Army (Ret.). "Infantry and National Priorities." *Armed Forces Journal,* December 2007.

Segal, Naomi. Jewish Telegraphic Agency. "IDF Absolved of Blame in Deaths of Naval Commandos in Lebanon." *San Francisco Jewish Community Publication,* 31 October 1997.

Snow, Shawn. "It Soon May Be a 15 Marine Rifle Squad—Most Likely for MEU Deployments." *Marine Corps Times* on line, 10 October 2018. As retrieved in October 2018 from the following url: https://www.marinecorpstimes.com/news/your-marine-corps/2018/10/10/a-15-marine-rifle-squad-may-be-the-reality-for-MEU-deployments/.

Snow, Shawn. "Shrinking the Infantry Squad: Why the Corps Wants to Fight with Fewer Marines." *Marine Corps Times* on line, 10 October 2018. As retrieved in October 2018 from the following url: https://www.marinecorpstimes.com/newsletters/daily-news-roundup/2018/05/21/shrinking-the-infantry-squad-why-the-corps-wants-to-fight-with-fewer-marines/.

"Swarming and the Future of Warfare." By Sean J. A. Edwards. Dissertation, The Pardee RAND Graduate School, 2005. As retrieved in June 2019 from the following url: https://apps.dtic.mil/dtic/tr/fulltext/u2/a434577.pdf.

Taylor, Vic. "Hotel Company-Day Three." *Marine Corps Gazette,* April 2004.

Thomas, Lt.Col. Timothy L. and Lester W. Grau. "Russian Lessons Learned from the Battles for Grozny." *Marine Corps Gazette,* April 2000

"12-Man Rifle Squads, Including a Squad Systems Operator, Commandant Says." By Todd South. *Marine Corps Times* on line, 3 May 2018. As retrieved in October 2018 from the following url: https://www.marinecorpstimes.com/news/your-marine-corps/2018/05/04/12-man-rifle-squads-including-a-squad-systems-operator-commandant-says/.

"U.S. Defensive Grenades in World War I." By Glen Hyatt. *WorldWar1.com,* n.d. As retrieved in January 2019 from the following url: http://www.worldwar1.com/sfusdg.htm.

"U.S. Marine Squad in World War I, 1918: You Take Command." *Warfare History Network.* By John Antal, n.d. As retrieved in January 2019 from the following url: https://www.historynet.com/u-s-marine-squad-world-war-1918-take-command.htm.

"USMC Issues M320 Grenade Launcher to Bolster Squads." By Mon Berenguer. *Gun World* on line, 21 May 2018. As retrieved in November 2018 from the following url: https://www.gunworld.com/news/usmc-issues-m320-grenade-launcher-to-bolster-squads/.

Weise, William. "Memories of Dai Do [a Sequel]." *Marine Corps Gazette,* April 2004.

"The World Turned Upside Down: Military Lessons of the Chechen War." By Anatol Lieven. *Armed Forces Journal International.* August 1998.

"WWII Squads." As retrieved in November 2018 from this url: www.scribd.com/document/54115611/WWII-Squads.

"Xinhui Presents: Chinese Tank Forces and Battles before 1949." *Wayback Machine.* As retrieved in March 2019 from the following url: https://web.archive.org/web/20140808050643/http://mailer.fsu.edu/~akirk/tanks/Stories/Newsletter1-8-2/xinhui.htm.

About the Author

After 28 years of commissioned and noncommissioned infantry service, John Poole retired from the United States Marine Corps in April 1993. While on active duty, he studied small-unit tactics for nine years: (1) six months at the Basic School in Quantico (1966); (2) seven months as a rifle platoon commander in Vietnam (1966-67); (3) three months as a rifle company commander at Camp Pendleton (1967); (4) five months as a regimental headquarters company (and camp) commander in Vietnam (1968); (5) eight months as a rifle company commander in Vietnam (1968-69); (6) five and a half years as an instructor with the Advanced Infantry Training Company (AITC) at Camp Lejeune (1986-92); and (7) one year as the Staff Noncommissioned Officer in Charge (SNCOIC) of the 3rd Marine Division Combat Squad Leaders Course (CSLC) on Okinawa (1992-93).

While at AITC, he developed, taught, and refined courses on maneuver warfare, land navigation, fire support coordination, call for fire, adjust fire, close air support, M203 grenade launcher, movement to contact, daylight attack, night attack, infiltration, defense, offensive Military Operations in Urban Terrain (MOUT), defensive MOUT, Nuclear/Biological/Chemical (NBC) defense, and leadership. While at CSLC, he further refined the same periods of instruction and developed others on patrolling.

He has completed all of the correspondence school requirements for the Marine Corps Command and Staff College, Naval War College (1,000-hour curriculum), and Marine Corps Warfighting Skills Program. He is a graduate of the Camp Lejeune Instructional Management Course, the 2nd Marine Division Skill Leaders in Advanced Marksmanship (SLAM) Course, and the East-Coast School of Infantry Platoon Sergeants' Course.

In the 25 years since retirement, Poole has researched the small-unit tactics of other nations and written 18 other books: (1) *The Last Hundred Yards,* a squad combat study based on the consensus opinions of 1,200 formal school NCOs and casualty statistics of AITC and CSLC field trials; (2) *One More Bridge to Cross,* a treatise on enemy proficiency at short range and how to match it; (3) *Phantom Soldier,* an in-depth look at the highly deceptive Asian style of war; (4) *The Tiger's Way,* the fighting styles of Eastern fireteams and soldiers; (5) *Tactics of the Crescent Moon,* insurgent procedures in Palestine, Chechnya, Afghanistan, and Iraq; (6) *Militant Tricks,* how Muslim insurgents fight in an urban environment; (7) *Terrorist Trail,* tracing the jihadists in Iraq back to their home countries; (8) *Dragon Days,* an unconventional warfare technique manual; (9) *Tequila Junction,* how to fight narco-guerrillas; (10) *Homeland Siege,* countering the 4GW assault on America by a foreign power's organized-crime proxies; (11) *Expeditionary Eagles,* how to outmaneuver the Taliban; (12) *Global Warrior,* forestalling WWIII through tiny-contingent activity; (13) *Gung Ho,* how supporting arms are not needed to take strongpoint matrices; (14) *Strategic Rifleman,* how to produce tiny semi-autonomous combat elements; (15) *Afrique,* with Africa as a model how U.S. intelligence is being gathered incorrectly for certain adversaries; (16) *Sinoland,* how the U.S. has been under 4GW attack from China since 9/11; (17) *Guardian Joe,* how—through more skilled infantry squads—the Pentagon can use less force to more easily win a modern war; and (18) *North Korea's Hidden Assets,* 13 little-known wartime capabilities of what has been erroneously called the Hermit Kingdom.

Since retirement, Poole has traveled extensively in both Communist and Islamist worlds to study the infantry tactics of America's enemies. He has done research in Mainland China (twice), North Korea, Vietnam, Cambodia, Pakistan (twice), Bangladesh, Malaysia, Iran, Lebanon, Turkey, the Emirates, Egypt, Sudan, Tanzania, Zambia, South Africa, Morocco, and Venezuela. Over the course of his lifetime, he has visited scores of other nations on all five continents.

As of April 2014, John Poole had conducted multi-day training sessions (on advanced squad tactics) at 41 (mostly Marine) battalions, nine Marine schools, and seven special-operations units from all four U.S. service branches.

Between early tours in the Marine Corps (from 1969 to 1971), he served as a criminal investigator with the Illinois Bureau of Investigation (IBI). After attending the State Police Academy for several months in Springfield, he was assigned to the IBI's Chicago office. There, he worked mostly on general criminal and drug cases.

Several periods in Poole's life have qualified him to accurately mirror the viewpoints of America's true fighters— its junior enlisted infantrymen. In 1965, his first official orders were for "Private Poole." From 1992 to 1993, he served as SNCOIC of a divisional squad leaders school. Then, almost all of the 1100 students who attended his "post-retirement" training sessions were E-5's and below.

Poole is one of the very few Americans with an extensive enough background to know how to fix the ongoing tactical shortfall within the U.S. military. After some 60 multi-day training sessions at different active-duty units, he has developed, tested, and refined its solution (through a "bottom-up" training supplement). He has also become adept at the now virtually lost art of field training light infantrymen (those who are able do well on their own in the absence of orders).

Name Index

H

I

No entries.

J

K

L

M

N

O

P